D0886723

WILLA CATHER

The Writer and Her World

WILLA CATHER

The Writer and Her World

JANIS P. STOUT

UNIVERSITY PRESS OF VIRGINIA

CHARLOTTESVILLE AND LONDON

The University Press of Virginia
© 2000 by the Rector and Visitors of the University of Virginia
All rights reserved
Printed in the United States of America
First published in 2000

Frontispiece: Willa Cather in Denver, while writing *Death Comes for the Archbishop.*
Photo by W. W. Wilson (Nebraska State Historical Society)

♾ The paper used in this publication meets the minimum requirements of
the American National Standard for Information Sciences—Permanence of Paper
for Printed Library Materials, ANSI Z39.48-1984.

Library of Congress Cataloging-in-Publication Data

Stout, Janis P.
　Willa Cather : the writer and her world / Janis P. Stout.
　　p. cm.
　Includes bibliographical references and index.
　ISBN 0-8139-1996-7 (alk. paper)
　　1. Cather, Willa, 1873–1947. 2. Novelists, American—20th century—Biography. 3.
Women and literature—United States—History—20th century. I. Title.

PS3505.A87 Z863 2000
813'.52—dc21
[B]

00-034975

to *Loren Daniel Lutes,*
Nebraskan

Contents

Illustrations

PREFACE

IN THE past two decades, Cather studies have assumed the proportions of a small industry. Despite the abundance of the scholarship, however, and despite the fact that much of that work has been of a very high order, we still lack, I believe, an adequate conception of the mind of this esteemed but nevertheless underestimated writer and thinker. That is, we lack an adequate understanding of the complexity of her sense of the world and her historic and cultural moment and a fully satisfying exposition of how that sense is manifest in her fiction and critical writing. It is that lack that I propose to address in the present study—though not without a sense of what a daunting task it is.

Willa Cather has all too often been seen as a writer of certitude and calm who made clear, confident distinctions between the moral and the immoral, the cultured and the vulgar, the savage and the civilized. Her popular audience—still a considerable one—seems to have valued her chiefly as a voice of reassurance, a writer who holds up in affirmation a sturdier, more wholesome America than our own. That kind of view of her is advanced, for example, in a recent newsletter of the Nebraska Alumni Association (the spring 1999 *GoodNUz*), which proclaims that "most" of her novels are about "hardy immigrant women on the prairies." No serious scholar would so blatantly take the part for the whole. Yet much of even the most important and substantive work on Cather has tended to place her inside one or another conceptual box, with label firmly affixed.

I see Cather, instead, as a deeply conflicted writer who fits comfortably into no box, a person of profound ambivalence about many, if not most, of the important questions she faced, who *therefore* structured her writing in such ways as to control her uncertainty and project a serenity she did not, in fact, feel. A view of Willa Cather emphasizing conflict, evasion, and unresolved ambiguities governs everything that follows and shapes my conception of Cather's place in the great aesthetic and intellectual sea change that we call modernism.

Certainly I am not the first to argue that Cather is best seen as a modernist. Most arguments of her modernism, however, have been insistently formalist in nature. They have, in a sense, taken as a positive the negative critique brought by influential 1930s Marxists who accused her of aesthetic escapism, of turning aside from the social issues of her day. (She responded defiantly that all art was escapist.) In the wake of such critiques, which became for some years the standard view, Cather has at times been viewed as a figure preoccupied with the past, whose literary project had little to do with the intellectual currents of her own time. On the contrary, she was fully a participant in the uncertainties and conflicts of twentieth-century modernity. It was in recoil from their distresses that she turned to overt celebrations of the past and home pieties and constructed a retiring, crotchety persona. She can well be thought of as a modernist conservative much like T. S. Eliot. But for all her evasion and indirectness, she was, I believe, more fully responsive to her time than Eliot, as well as far less assured in her pronouncements.

In exploring Cather's sense of her world, I emphasize three main issues or clusters of issues: her sometimes puzzled performance of gender, including her relation to the emergence of the New Woman; her participation in, but also resistance to, pervasive cultural assumptions regarding ethnicity and American pluralism, including issues of social class; and her participation in both the ideology and (through her family's westering) the actual historic pursuit of Manifest Destiny. We see this participation especially clearly in her treatment of Native Americans (or its absence) and her relation to the phenomenon of romanticized popular interest in the Southwest, but we see it, too, in her lifelong sense of displacement from Virginia. Associated with that displacement was a conflict between impulses toward Europe and toward a kind of heartland Americanism—or to borrow her own words in *Death Comes for the Archbishop*, a "desire to go and . . . necessity to stay." In relation to all of these issues, the view of Cather that I seek to develop emphasizes fracture, doubt, and multiplicity of both visions and options. Merrill Skaggs and Hermione Lee, in particular, have observed Cather's intellectual and emotional dualities. Yet I believe that her dividedness of mind and the consequent indeterminacy of meaning in her work are more deeply pervasive than even these scholars have argued.[1] To borrow a phrase from Leo Bersani in a discussion of the painter Caravaggio, her work is "intractably enigmatic" (13).

With respect to the question of sexuality, my purpose here is not to offer a "normalized" Willa Cather. I agree with Elizabeth Ammons that there has already been quite enough effort to defend a traditional and sanitized (usually meaning nonlesbian) conception of her ("New Canon" 264), and I have no wish to participate in such a project of traditionalist veneration. If I at times question some of the interpretations related to readings of Cather as lesbian, it is because I believe that position, too, has now tended to harden into an absolute and to become itself a kind of orthodoxy, not always reflecting the complexity or even uncertainty of her experience and her thinking about the world.

A word about organization. I have taken an approach that attempts to combine the chronological with the thematic. Moving through the unfolding of Cather's career and the sequence of her books, I emphasize in each chapter what I discern as the particular emphases that emerge most clearly in that particular period or that particular book. Discussion of these emerging emphases, however, entails moving forward and backward in time. For example, the fourth chapter, centering on *O Pioneers!*, is concerned primarily with Cather's turn from the externally derived standards of appropriate novelistic material to the writing of what she knew best, the material that she sensed as being authentically her own. That discussion opens into a consideration of the autobiographical method in Cather's works generally—a topic that might be examined at any point in the study but is taken up here because it is at this point in Cather's career that the autobiographical method most clearly emerged and came to dominate her approach to fiction. Chapter 5, centering on *The Song of the Lark*, is concerned primarily with that book's exploration of issues of female departure from the domestic world to the world of public careers, a topic that entails recapitulation of much of the previous discussion of Cather's own early years and comparison with similar aspects of her later work. And so forth.

This book is not, in the strictest sense, a biography. Rather, it is a biographically based critical study that establishes, in as full a way as possible, a sense of the author's mind and personhood, of who she was and who she believed she was, of what she thought about major issues, how she saw and responded to her culture, and always how she realized, or failed to realize, all of this in her art. It might be called an intellectual biography, broadly defined, or, perhaps better, a cultural biography.

The methods of cultural studies have only recently been brought to bear on the study of Willa Cather, mainly with the publication of Mike Fischer's challenging article "Pastoralism and Its Discontents: Willa Cather and the Burden of Imperialism" (1990), Joseph Urgo's *Willa Cather and the Myth of American Migration* (1995), and Guy Reynolds's *Willa Cather in Context: Progress, Race, Empire* (1996). I am indebted to these scholars both for their demonstration of the value and importance of reading Cather from a cultural studies perspective and for their specific insights and discoveries. I am also particularly indebted to the work of Susan J. Rosowski and Ann Romines, both of whom I greatly esteem. But it is a mistake to begin to enumerate one's intellectual debts in this way, because the list is so extensive and the likelihood of omitting a name of absolutely crucial importance is so great.

Let me, then, simply thank the following persons, who have contributed in particular and personal ways to this project: Pat Phillips and Sue Fintel at the Willa Cather Pioneer Memorial in Red Cloud, Nebraska, who smoothed the way for my research into the Cather letters there (as did librarians and photo archivists at many other institutions, especially Chad Wall at the Nebraska State Historical Society) and who also answered questions, extended to me their friendship, and in every way exceeded the demands of obligation; Ann Romines and Susan Rosowski, who said things I needed at the times I needed them; Susan Rosowski, again, and another reader for the University Press of Virginia, who read the entire manuscript and offered many valuable suggestions; Deborah Williams, who through our e-mail conversations kept enlightening me about Cather's connections with other modernists and many other matters; Robert K. Miller, who shared his insights, particularly into *A Lost Lady* and *The Professor's House*; Bob Thacker, who shared his work on S. S. McClure; Patricia Lee Yongue, who invited me into her home to use her collection of materials relating to Stephen Tennant; Marian Eide and Kate Kelly for sharing their time by reading and making suggestions on various parts of the work as it came along; David McWhirter, Mary Ann O'Farrell, and other members of the Interdisciplinary Group for Humanities Studies at Texas A&M University, who helped me with their encouragement and their astute questioning (and David suggested the phrase "modernist conservative"); my graduate students, especially Tomas Pollard, Jean Griffith, and Robin Cohen; and the Interdisciplinary Group, the College of Liberal Arts, and the Office of the Vice President for Research, Texas A&M University, for grants that assisted with the research and writing.

Acknowledgments

Brief passages in chapters 6 and 8 appeared in different form in *Through the Window, Out the Door: Women's Narratives of Departure, from Austin and Cather to Tyler, Morrison, and Didion*, by Janis P. Stout, copyright 1998 by The University of Alabama Press and are used by permission.

Portions of chapters 3, 4, and 6 are reprinted from "Willa Cather's Early Journalism: Gender, Performance, and the 'Manly Battle Yarn,'" *Arizona Quarterly* 55.3 (1999) by permission of the Regents of the University of Arizona.

Letter from Sinclair Lewis to Willa Cather, November 21, 1930, is quoted by permission of the Pierpont Morgan Library, New York (MA 3229).

Letters from Ferris Greenslet to Willa Cather (shelf mark bMS Am 1925 341) are quoted by permission of the Houghton Library, Harvard University, and Houghton Mifflin.

Letter from Katherine Anne Porter to Donald Elder, January 30, 1941, from the Papers of Katherine Anne Porter, Special Collections, University of Maryland Libraries, is quoted by permission of the Libraries and of Barbara Thompson Davis, literary trustee for the estate of Katherine Anne Porter.

Letter of Dorothy Canfield Fisher to Willa Cather, January 1, 1905, is quoted by permission of the Bailey/Howe Library, The University of Vermont.

Unless otherwise noted, photographs are reprinted by permission of the Nebraska State Historical Society. Full reproduction information not accompanying text captions for material used by permission of other archives is as follows:

Figure 15. Edward Steichen. *Willa Cather* (1926). Gelatin-silver print, 16 ¾ x 13 ⅜" (42.5 x 34 cm). The Museum of Modern Art, New York. Gift of the photographer. Photograph ©1999 The Museum of Modern Art, New York.

Figure 20. John Singer Sargent, *Nonchaloir (Repose)*, 1911. Gift of Curt H. Reisinger. Photograph © 1999 Board of Trustees, National Gallery of Art, Washington, D.C.

Figure 21. Jules Breton, French, 1827–1906. *The Song of the Lark*, oil on canvas, 1884, 110.6 x 85.8 cm. Henry Field Memorial Collection, 1894.1033. Photograph courtesy of The Art Institute of Chicago.

Figure 25. Willa Cather in New Mexico. Courtesy of the University of Nebraska.

Abbreviations

The following abbreviations are used without first-reference notes:

AB	*Alexander's Bridge*
ALL	*A Lost Lady*
CSF	*Willa Cather's Collected Short Fiction, 1892–1912*
DCA	*Death Comes for the Archbishop*
KA	*The Kingdom of Art*, ed. Bernice Slote
LG	*Lucy Gayheart*
MA	*My Ántonia*
MME	*My Mortal Enemy*
OD	*Obscure Destinies*
OO	*One of Ours*
OP	*O Pioneers!*
OW	*Willa Cather on Writing*
PH	*The Professor's House*
SL	*The Song of the Lark*
SPO	*Stories, Poems, and Other Writings* (Library of America, 1992)
SR	*Shadows on the Rock*
SSG	*Sapphira and the Slave Girl*
TG	*The Troll Garden*
W&P	*The World and the Parish: Articles and Reviews, 1893–1902*, ed. William M. Curtin
WCIP	*Willa Cather in Person: Interviews, Speeches, and Letters*, ed. L. Brent Bohlke
WCPM	The Willa Cather Pioneer Memorial, located in Red Cloud, Nebraska
YBM	*Youth and the Bright Medusa*

After first reference, the names of libraries will be given in easily recognizable short forms, e.g., Beinecke for the Beinecke Library, Yale University; Yale for holdings at Yale University other than the collections of the

Beinecke; Huntington for the Huntington Library; Virginia for Alderman Library, University of Virginia; HRC for Harry Ransom Humanities Research Center, University of Texas; TWU for Texas Woman's University; etc.

In annotations of letters, WC means, of course, Willa Cather.

East / West, Home's Best
Heritage and Disruption

Stricken, she left familiar earth behind her

—"Macon Prairie (Nebraska)"

A sudden sickness for the hills of home

—"Prairie Dawn"

WILLA CATHER has often been regarded as a writer of serenity and certainty who celebrated the pioneers, praised a symbol of fertility called Ántonia ("a rich mine of life," "a founder of early races"), and turned back to America's past in nostalgic escape. According to this traditional view, her books are easy to read, her values are wholesome, and we can all be glad that she knew who she was, a member not of any lost generation but of the hearty midwestern stock that by 1900 had come to represent bedrock national values, blessedly removed from an industrialized East and a retrograde South.

Behind the appearance of affirmation, however, stands a writer of conflict and ambivalence, doubtful of even the possibility of knowing truth, whose apparent nostalgia for a simpler pioneering time disguises a complex engagement with the present. Her celebration of the agricultural frontier was couched in a language that signaled her demurral, in many ways, from conventions of frontier heroics, and she could not entirely ignore the impoverishment of life that fertility and constricted opportunities meant for her frontier heroine Ántonia, as well as the ease with which her male narrator brushes those minor drawbacks aside. Cather's books are easy to read only if we are content to take the smooth surface for the whole. If we read alertly, unlulled by a prose style of calculated limpidness, we realize that even the surface is not so smooth after all. Affirming as they are in many ways, her books are also sown with doubt and discouragement, terror and violence, and she often did not at all know who she was or what she thought. In that respect, as much as any other, she was a woman of her time, in literary terms a modernist, in sociohistorical terms a New Woman, in almost every way a member of the disillusioned post–World War I generation that would be reduced from disheartenment to despair by the realization that war not only could but did come again, within their own lifetimes.

The key, the initial source of Cather's complex and often conflicted sense of the world, is to be found in the fact that she was born where she was, when she was: in the hills of far northern Virginia, near the West Virginia line, less than a decade after the Civil War. West Virginia had come into existence as a state only ten years before her birth, as a result of the great division of opinion between the people of the eastern and central sections of Virginia and those to the west of the Blue Ridge. Culminating a long agitation for separation from the state's center of political power to the east, western Virginians voted in the summer of 1861 to remain with the Union and to set up a separate state government. Back Creek, the rural community just west of Winchester where both the house of Cather's birth (her maternal grandmother's) and the one nearby that was her childhood home (her paternal grandfather's, Willow Shade) still stand, is scarcely five miles from the state line. During the Great Conflict the area was torn by divided loyalties that not only set neighbor against neighbor but family member against family member, including the Cathers and the Boaks, her mother's family. Dividedness was her birthright.

The Cathers were for the most part Unionists, although great-grandfather James supported the Confederacy despite believing slavery wrong. William and Caroline Cather, Willa's grandparents, sent their two military-age sons, George and Charles, over into the newly created state of West Virginia to avoid conscription into the Confederate army.[1] The Boaks were mostly Confederates. Rachel Seibert Boak, Cather's maternal grandmother, had three sons who fought for the South. One of them, William Seibert Boak, died from wounds suffered at Manassas. It was in memory of this uncle, dead before her birth, that Cather would later adopt the middle name Sibert, which she used during her earlier professional years. Why she considered the name to have come from him rather than from her grandmother is not clear.[2] Grandmother Boak herself so hated slavery that before the war she helped one of her mother's slaves escape to Canada. That story of daughterly insurrection must have been a very powerful one in the incipient writer's awareness. She returned to it late in life in *Sapphira and the Slave Girl*.

It strikes one as surprising that Rachel Boak could so easily make her peace with a family who supported the North as to agree to the marriage of her daughter Mary Virginia to Charles Fectigue Cather in 1872. Perhaps the idea of quality marrying quality, old blood marrying old blood, mattered more than the fact of enmities that had been uncertain enough anyway. Or perhaps she was reconciled by the thought that Mary Virginia would be securing a haven in a family that, unlike most others thereabouts, had not lost financially by the war but actually gained. As a result of his loyalty to the Union, William Cather was appointed sheriff of Frederick County and his sons made deputies.[3] At any rate, Rachel Boak, a remarkable woman in other ways as well, not only acceded to the marriage but moved west with the young couple in 1883 to join her son-in-law's Unionist father and brother and their families. Until her death in 1893, Mrs. Boak made her home in her daughter's household. Her gifted granddaughter, named Wilella for an aunt who died in childhood but long since called Willa (dropping the awkward middle syllable), would celebrate Mrs. Boak's conciliatory and wise presence when she reached her own later years in what is perhaps her greatest single work, "Old Mrs. Harris," and again in the portrait of the independent-minded abolitionist Rachel Blake in *Sapphira*. The circle was closed.

What all this means is that in her origins Willa Cather was a southerner, born of parents and grandparents and great-grandparents who were southern through and through, however their views of the "peculiar institution" might differ from those that predominated in the Confederacy and however they resolved the issue of "national" loyalty at the time of secession. She lived her formative years in the close-knit structure of an extended southern family, and she carried an awareness of her southern roots wherever she went for as long as she lived. Yet she spent her late-childhood and adolescent years not in the South but on midwestern prairie land as recently wrested from Native people when she moved there as West Virginia had been from the seceding South at the time of her birth. As an adult she lived mostly in the Northeast, first in Pittsburgh and then, from the age of thirty-three until her death at seventy-four, in New York—traveling continually all the while.

Cather can certainly be regarded (and generally *has* been regarded) as a Great Plains writer, a writer of the midwestern frontier. The Great Plains were her milieu and her subject in most of the early work that has been taken to define her. She can also be appropriately thought of as a writer of the rugged Southwest, which elated her and in 1912 reshaped her life when she had gone stale in her work. She wrote about the Southwest in *The Professor's House* and *Death Comes for the Archbishop* as well as in an important section of *The Song of the Lark*. She can well be located, too, though she seldom is, in the burgeoning business of letters anchored in New York in the early years of the century, a business only recently (as William Dean Howells shows in *The Rise of Silas Lapham* and as Cather knew quite well from personal experience) transferred there from Boston. She can be characterized geographically in all these ways. But the fact remains that she was southern first—and in a very real way, last.

Cather, a person of powerful homing instinct though continually on the move, in her last completed novel turned back to Virginia, the mother state of her family and the state bearing the name of her mother, Mary Virginia. Like virtually everything else in Cather's thinking and creativity, however, this was an ambiguous turn, made not only in love and reconciliation but also in aversion and judgment. That same ambivalence characterizes her pronouncements on the South in fiction and in personal communications throughout her adult life. When she referred to her father's boyishness and his southernness, in a grieving letter informing her writer-friend Dorothy Canfield Fisher of his death, the terms carry overtones of affectionate pride. In 1932 she referred to southerners in the first person plural, "we." Writing to her old friend and former editor Ferris Greenslet following the publication of *Sapphira*, she could say that thinking about the customs and manners of Virginia during the writing of the book had been comforting.[4] Yet when her favorite niece moved to Tennessee in 1942, she fretted that "going south" had "a slight connotation of going backward,"[5] and Edith Lewis noted that when the two of them went to Virginia in 1938, Cather "spoke of the limp, drooping acacia trees in bloom along all the roadsides" as having "the shiftless look that characterized so many Southern things" (182). The South remained a problem for her.

The Cather family's life in Back Creek during the 1870s seems to have been in some ways idyllic. Not wealthy but well off especially in comparison to most of their neighbors, they maintained a comfortable and dignified manner of living in their three-story brick house, not so much a beautiful house as an impressive one. (With windows set in the end wall of the back porch, it was designed to look, from the road, more impressive than it was; see figure 1.) But the semblance of idyl conceals darker facts, such as resentment left from the Civil War and its aftermath. It may have been resentment of collaborators with the Reconstruction government that flared up—literally—in a fire that destroyed the Willow Shade barn in 1882. Disease was another dark fact: tuberculosis stalked the family.[6] Sexual peril, too, is glimpsed in the unexplained

Fig. 1. Willow Shade, Cather's childhood home.
(Nebraska State Historical Society)

marriage of one of William Cather's daughters (thus Willa's aunt) to a hired man who quickly deserted her. The hired man's name was Webb Clutter; a close version appears in *My Ántonia* as the name of one of Cather's most despicable and sexually threatening characters, Wick Cutter.

Another dark fact was the heritage of slavery. The fact of racism and racial fear is evident in Edith Lewis's story of how, in the middle of a sedate visit in the Willow Shade parlor, the young Willa burst out, to her mother's chagrin, "I'se a dang'ous nigger, I is!" (13). This outburst does not necessarily mean she had picked up a notion that all "niggers" were dangerous; perhaps she only wished to shock her mother by claiming to be not only one of the black people (all of whom were referred to as "niggers") but a bad one at that. Either way, she had imbibed, at what seems to have been a very early age, an awareness of racial otherness and of its being at least potentially a threat.

Charles Cather had read law, but he made his livelihood by raising sheep. He was good enough at it to maintain the family's habitual position of patronage among nearby plainer folk, who served as occasional employees, even after his more aggressive brother migrated to Nebraska in 1873, followed soon afterward by their father. Not that this position of patronage necessarily meant popularity. Community resentment of the Cathers' Unionist position may have contributed to George's and then William's move west, even before the sheep barn burned. Charles Cather was an unaggressive, gentle man, tenderhearted enough to bother making leather boots for his sheepdogs to protect their paws in rocky terrain, and a man who wrote an elegant hand—as demonstrated in a letter he wrote to his brother and sister-in-law on January 22, 1874, bragging about the baby girl affectionately called Willie who was "just as good as she is pretty."[7] It was the discovery of this letter that enabled E. K. Brown, who wrote the first scholarly biography of Cather (completed after his death by Leon Edel), to establish her correct birth date. She had claimed December 7, 1876—shaving three years off her age, probably in chagrin at her slow start as a writer.

It is well to remember, when Charles Cather is judged to have been too amiable or simply too weak to get ahead in life on the prairie, that he had possessed enough initiative and physical stamina to drive flocks of sheep all the way to Baltimore to get the higher price paid at the city market. If the barn had not burned, he might have continued in the pastoral way of life he had established among the verdant Virginia hills and maintained his family's fortunes there despite the collapsed southern economy.

The very fact of Virginia's lovely greenness, however, contributed to driving Charles Cather away to a life for which he was never quite so well fitted, where the qualities he needed to exert were those of entrepreneur and competitor rather than caretaker and preserver. A part of the great Shenandoah and Potomac River drainage basins, the Back Creek region is so well watered that its climate is oppressively humid. That is the reason for its verdant beauty but also for the prevailing dampness that the Cathers believed made it an unhealthy climate. Willow Shade, situated astride a creek that flowed through the front yard, was especially damp. A cool spring was enclosed in the basement, making a convenient food-storage space behind the kitchen. (It looks today very much like a shallow indoor well, and the entire lower level of the house is indeed quite damp.) Whatever the role of lingering partisan resentments, a drop in wool prices, and the ruin of the South's economy generally, it was in part for the sake of health that George Cather, the older brother, took his wife Frances (Cather's Aunt Franc, a major personage in her life) to southern Nebraska, a recently opened frontier area where land prices were still low and the humidity lower, in the early 1870s—the move that accounts for the new father's having to brag about his baby daughter by mail, rather than in person. When the barn burned, William Cather declined to rebuild. He instructed his son to sell out, bring his family to Nebraska, and take over the homestead that was proving to be more land than he could work himself, at his age.[8]

Cather's mother, Mary Virginia Boak Cather, was generally called by a familiar version of her middle name, Jennie. Pictures of her show a woman of beauty and grace, painstakingly groomed, seemingly proud or even haughty, a woman inclined to stand on ceremony, who expected to be—and was—valued and deferred to by her family (see figure 2). Her new mother-in-law, Caroline Cather, remarked in 1873, in a letter she expected to be burned, that Jennie Cather was "easily insulted," and Edith Lewis, Cather's companion for almost half her life, characterized her as being "imperious, with a strong will and a strong nature . . . always the dominating figure in the family" (6). How this daughter of Virginia, named by its name, felt about uprooting her family (which by that time included three more little ones besides nine-year-old Wilella)

and moving west to join her in-laws is not recorded. She must have realized it would be an arduous life, since she managed to take along not
only her mother but a maid of all work, Margie or Marjorie Anderson,
the slightly retarded daughter of nearby mountain folk who had numerous other children and may have been glad enough to see one of them
go into someone else's care. After the publication of *Sapphira and the
Slave Girl*, Cather wrote to a niece of Marjorie's, still living in Virginia,
that her aunt had remained with the family until her death in 1928 and
had been much loved.[9]

If Jennie Cather's views about migrating to Nebraska are not recorded, her discontent after the family reached Webster County is. Isolated
and living in far more primitive conditions than she had been accustomed to in their long-settled community in Virginia, where she could
call on poorer women in the neighborhood such as Marjorie's mother
when she needed extra help or a few days at the nearby Capon Springs
resort, she was discontented enough to propel a second move, eighteen
months later, into the muddy-streeted frontier town of Red Cloud.
Somewhat bigger then than it is today, this town that would prove so
important in Willa Cather's writing had been founded only eleven years
before the family's arrival. It was named, with an irony that was surely
unconscious, for the Sioux chief whose people had been displaced from
land guaranteed them under treaty with the U.S. government, in order
to make way for white Americans such as the Cathers, who poured in
along with various white Europeans. In Red Cloud, Virginia Cather's
children could go to school, and she herself could again enjoy the company of other women, as Victoria Templeton does in "Old Mrs. Harris."

THE MOVE from Virginia to the Nebraska Divide (the relatively high-
lying expanse of open prairie lying between the Republican River and
the Little Blue) was a great trauma for the not-yet-ten-year-old child.[10]
Her portrayal of Jim Burden's initial impressions of the West in *My
Ántonia* essentially reproduces her own. She arrived with her family by
train (the Burlington, from which her uncle George had bought part of
his land) after crossing the "never-ending miles" of the continent's great
midsection. In 1913, before she had learned caution in giving out interviews, she told a reporter for the *Philadelphia Record* that her first impression was of "a country as bare as sheet iron," and after she got down
from the train and began to ride across the roadless bare prairie in her

Fig. 2. Jennie Cather as a young woman in Nebraska.
(Nebraska State Historical Society)

grandfather's wagon she felt that her "one purpose in life just then was not to cry." She recalled her initial impressions more expansively in a 1905 letter to fellow *McClure's* editor Witter Bynner in explanation of the grim quality of descriptions of the West in some of her short stories, saying that he could not possibly "imagine anything so bleak and desolate" as a Nebraska ranch of the time and that having left a beautiful valley for a place like this, she came close to "dying of homesickness." Her descriptions convey a landscape lacking gentleness. In one of her early short stories she called it "a country as flat and gray and as naked as the sea" and observed laconically that "insanity and suicide [were] very common things on the Divide."[11] Suicide would be a recurrent motif in her early fiction set in Nebraska.

In particular, Cather's response to the abrupt shift of place—specifically, of topography—was characterized by a sense of exposure. She told Elizabeth Shepley Sergeant (59) many years later that there was "no place to hide in Nebraska." It was as if, in the exacerbated sensitivity to landscape evoked by the move, she began to sense a protectiveness of personhood itself in the folds and hollows and tree canopy she had experienced in Virginia, but in Nebraska a liability to being blotted out, becoming indistinguishable from any other human creature, just as the prairie landscape itself lacked landmarks (see figure 3). In the 1913 interview she described the anxiety it caused her as "a kind of erasure of personality" (*WCIP* 10).

The configuration of Cather's sense of being at home in the world would always to a great extent reflect this sense of liability to exposure and erasure and her preference for the kind of shelter by a folded and foliaged earth that she had experienced in her earliest years, a need for an enclosure suggestive of the maternal body. O'Brien describes the topographical forms of Virginia as a "maternal embrace" (*Emerging* 63). Cather's most instinctual sense of the well-being she desired implies a world that is gendered female. Ellen Moers's insight in reading the Panther Canyon passage of *The Song of the Lark* as a feminized, sexualized landscape (258–59) has proven compelling, but such a sense of what Cather wished the nature of the world around her to be was pervasive in Cather's mind and in her writing. It sprang from her childhood awareness of her place of origins, and that awareness, used as an instinctual measure by which to assess all other places, was never eradicated, even after she came to love Nebraska. We see it in her persistent preference for sheltered places *within* the outdoors, with large openings affording a visual sense of expansiveness—caves and attic rooms with cozy, cave-like sloping ceilings or her pup tent in the meadow at Jaffrey, New Hampshire, another shelter with an attic-like sloping top but open at the end to afford a sense of being outdoors and free, even while being within, at once inside and outside, boundless and enclosed.

The family reached Webster County in April, which in Nebraska is still early spring, though days can be sun-filled and warm. It seems to have been several months before she felt reconciled to her new surroundings. But by the fall of that year (1883), if we can take the 1913

Fig. 3. Landscape, Webster County, Nebraska.
(Nebraska State Historical Society)

interview statements at face value, she had begun to feel "gripped" by the "shaggy grass country" with a "passion" that she was "never . . . able to shake." The 1905 letter to Witter Bynner implies a somewhat longer adjustment period. Her exclamation that she would never forget her first Christmas in the West seems to indicate that it epitomized what was still a bad time; she recalls (in implied contrast to evergreens remembered from earlier Christmases) the "naked little box-elder . . . wrapped in green tissue paper cut in fringes" that had to serve as a Christmas tree.[12]

Whether the change came in the fall of 1883 or the spring of 1884, a native resilience and curiosity about the world took over, and Cather came to relish the freedom of her life on the ranch, all the more precious because for a while she apparently suffered some kind of paralytic illness that required her to use a crutch (Bennett 40). This may have been the origin of her later insistence, speaking of her mother's stroke, that paralysis is the worst thing that can happen to a person.[13] Like Jim Burden in *Ántonia*, she rode her pony to a postal distribution point a few miles away and circled back by way of neighbors' houses, delivering their mail and stopping to visit, watch, and listen (*WCIP* 127). These neighbors were mostly, as she summarized them in her 1913 interview, "Swedes and Danes, Norwegians and Bohemians," with a sprinkling of French, Swiss, and Russians. But although she did not mention them in the interview and scarcely acknowledged their presence in any of her prairie novels except *One of Ours*, Germans were actually the most numerous group. It was a richly varied human spectacle for a child of her alertness and powers of observation—varied, that is, within an all-white Eurocentric spectrum. By the time the family decided to move into town in the winter of 1884–85, Cather was not only reconciled to being on the prairie but was taking considerable pleasure in her life there. It is scarcely surprising, then, that she found this second move also disruptive and life in their rented house "cramped" (Woodress, *Literary* 47) after her freedom on the ranch and the more spacious scale of domestic life in Virginia.

The move to Red Cloud meant that by the age of eleven Cather had undergone two major displacements and periods of adjustment. Until she went away to the University of Nebraska in 1890 (first as a preparatory student, then for college proper), the defining events of her life were displacements. The effects would be pervasive, shaping her emotional

responses and her ways of thinking about experience in ways both obvious and subtle. They appear in recurrent motifs of departure and return
and in her personal vacillation between a powerful homing instinct and
an at least equally powerful need to move, to go forth.[14]

In Red Cloud compensations again quickly developed. Until the family moved to town, Cather's only experience of school had been three
months at a one-room rural school near Catherton; for the most part
she had been taught at home by Grandmother Boak, her education consisting of being read to, taught to read, and given access to the family
library. After such a regime, being shut up in a classroom might well
seem onerous. She found her fellow pupils, though, if not the program
itself, keenly interesting from the first, and in her second year she had a
teacher she would recall as "a stalwart young woman with a great deal of
mirth in her eyes and a very sympathetic, kind voice," whom she very
much wanted to please.[15] Her transition to public education, then, was a
good one. Even so, she continued to learn mainly through her own
reading and observation and from well-read persons in the community.

Among these were Mr. and Mrs. Charles Wiener, Jewish immigrant
storeowners who spoke French and German and owned a sizable library
to which they gave her access. The Wieners later served as models for
the sympathetic Mr. and Mrs. Rosen in "Old Mrs. Harris." During her
college years, Cather reported on the state of Mrs. Wiener's health in a
letter to a friend in Lincoln, Mariel Gere, in which she also mentioned
another of her adult friends in Red Cloud, Lyra Garber, the model for
Marian Forrester in *A Lost Lady*. A year later she reported to Mariel that
Mr. Wiener (apparently now widowed) was boarding with Mrs. Garber
and was still very kind. It is unfortunate that when she reported his
death many years later in a letter to Carrie Miner Sherwood she managed
to make an anti-Semitic slur even while paying tribute to the culture
and graciousness of the Wiener family. She had been at their house frequently during his last illness and felt his death as a great loss. They
were a gracious, hospitable family, she wrote, so unlike the general run
of wealthy Jewish families. The kind of anti-Semitism represented here
was a trait Cather shared with many Americans of her time; indeed, in
comparison to the virulence evidenced by many others she was not so
much an anti-Semite as one who shared a poison in the air.[16]

The Wieners encouraged Cather to go to college much as the Rosens
encourage Vickie in "Old Mrs. Harris." Her earliest taste of German

and French literature (in translation) came to her in their home. But the Cathers' own library was also surprisingly extensive, with Dickens, Scott, Thackeray, Ruskin, and Carlyle, volumes of Shakespeare, Bunyan, Thomas Campbell, Thomas Moore, Ben Jonson, and Byron, and, among American writers, Poe, Hawthorne, and Emerson, as well as religious and historical books, a smattering of the Classics, and the popular romance novels Cather deplored in her college writings (Woodress, *Literary* 50–51; Slote, *KA* 38–40; O'Brien, *Emerging* 40, 78–79, 83). For working at the local drug store, she was paid in inexpensive translations of Tolstoy as well as novels by George Eliot and other Victorian authors. Her leisure reading, even before college, was strikingly extensive.

The young Cather's acquaintance with the Classics and her beginning studies of Latin were abetted by a British storeclerk, William Ducker, who had arrived in Red Cloud about a year after the Cathers. Ducker read Latin and Greek with her from then through her university years. Her recognition of how these early studies shaped her toward unconventional gender roles may be seen in *Shadows on the Rock* (1931), overtly a hymn to traditionalism, where Euclide Auclair (surely a portrait of Cather's own gentle father) is faulted for teaching Cécile Latin as if he had "forgotten that he had a girl to bring up, and not a son" (*SR* 40). Mr. Ducker's home laboratory also stimulated her interest in experimental science, as did the company of the two local physicians, Dr. McKeeby and Dr. Damerell, who took her along on house calls and presumably discussed anatomy and related matters with her. The two physicians had an effect beyond what is ordinarily called teaching and perhaps beyond their intentions, as she began to aspire to be a doctor and (notoriously) began signing herself William Cather, M.D. In addition, she began to develop a lifelong interest in serious music from listening to the oboe playing of Mrs. Julia Miner and the playing of an itinerant piano teacher named Schindelmeisser, with whom she talked about music more than she actually learned to play any. Mrs. Miner appears in *My Ántonia* as the impressive Mrs. Harling, who plays intently on the piano, while the piano teacher became Professor Wunsch in *The Song of the Lark*.

Yet another element in Cather's increasing pleasure in life in Red Cloud was the opportunity to participate in a lively culture of amateur theatricals as well as to see professional performances. She later recalled the excitement of going to the train station to watch companies of actors arrive (*WCIP* 185). Between such appearances, local people put on their own theatrical entertainments. Willa appeared as Hiawatha and as the trousered, top-hatted, and mustached father in *Beauty and the Beast*, along with her friends the Miner girls. She would continue to take part in plays when she went to the University of Nebraska, often but not always taking male parts—a practice less surprising then than now, since "trouser parts" for women were popular on the professional stage.[17] These experiences led not only to Cather's first assignment as journalist (theatrical reviewing) and a lifelong interest in drama but also, as Hermione Lee suggests, to her persistent "negotiation" between realistic and romantic modes (37). They did not so much lead to as become a part in a lifelong pattern of role-playing, of establishing a self or selves through performative experimentation.[18]

In this connection, Cather's early parlor rebellion against her mother's standards of propriety—"I'se a dang'ous nigger, I is!"—assumes added significance. It was perhaps her first performance of a role she would often choose as she neared adolescence and separation from family, the part of the free spirit in a hidebound world, the rebel against authority, the "dangerous" person who challenged prevailing assumptions and pieties. Who was this Willa Cather? She scarcely knew. But she seems at times, beginning as a spunky three-year-old, to have suspected that she was either an outcast (a "nigger," and a bad one at that) or a nervy swashbuckler ("dang'ous," a dandy, a scandal).

BETWEEN THE ages of eleven, when her family moved to Red Cloud, and nearly seventeen, when she went to the University of Nebraska as a "second prep" (having been excused from the "first prep" year typically required of students from small high schools), Cather acted out an intensified and somewhat idiosyncratic form of the adolescent rebellion experienced by many young people, today as well as then. We have seen an element of that rebellion in her appropriation of the name William, the common masculine form of her somewhat unusual first name. As strong-willed as her mother, who demanded orderly conduct and enforced it with sound whippings, but dead set against her mother's traditional conception of femininity and traditional persona as the southern lady, Cather set her sights on ambitions that would have been described as more appropriate to males or perhaps even as unavailable to females, and she adjusted her avowed interests and self-presentation accordingly.

She had her hair cut very short and adopted masculinized (though not necessarily masculine) modes of dress. In photographs taken in her early teens these modes of self-presentation, combined with her square-cut facial shape and features, give her a startlingly boyish appearance.[19]

We need to look again, however, at these frequently reprinted pictures. Together with her self-naming as William and her nickname Willie, they have generated a good deal of misinformation. Patrick Shaw, for example, not only discusses as fact her "adoption of conventional male attire" but implies that she may have continued to cross-dress in private as an adult (6–8). Carolyn Heilbrun writes that we "know" she "dressed as a boy when in college" (112). What we know is that as an adolescent and into her college years she dressed in masculinized styles that were in fact styles for females and were widely adopted by those who sought to define themselves as New Women. O'Brien points out that these boyish attires were often accessorized with a feminine scarf, ruffle, or ribbon (96). Or again, Emmy Stark Zitter writes, "During her adolescence and college years she dressed like a man, cut her hair short, and even called herself Willie" (291). But her family had called her Willie from early infancy, following common southern practice of pronouncing a terminal *a* as *ie*. The picture that Woodress labels "Cather with boy's haircut, about age 13" is clearly a studio photograph, indicating, as Wolff has argued, that her parents liked her appearance well enough to pay to have it recorded. Her hair, though it certainly does appear to be cut like a boy's, is brushed softly to the side over her forehead, and she wears a stand-up, round lace collar quite feminine in appearance (see figure 4). In the picture Woodress labels "Cather in Confederate Army cap" she wears a jacket whose extremely narrow shoulders and upraised puff sleeves were stylish for women and girls at the time, according to Severa (488). O'Brien errs in saying that she is "dressed in military garb" in this photograph (*Emerging* 107), except with respect to the cap (see figure 5). The commonly reproduced photo of Cather in top hat and trouser suit in the Red Cloud children's performance of *Beauty and the Beast* simply demonstrates that she was doing what many actresses were doing in the latter nineteenth century (see figure 6).

To those who see Cather as being in every sense a lesbian, the meaning is clear: she was manifesting her innate gender identity. When one notes the fervency of her later friendships with women and reads the few letters that survive from one of the more heated of those relationships, her

Fig. 4. Willa Cather at about age 13.
(Nebraska State Historical Society)

crush on Louise Pound in college, it is hard to resist such a conclusion, and I have no wish to do so. Still, other interpretations are also plausible, whether as alternatives or as collateral factors. It is interesting to note, for example, that her admired Aunt Franc also had her hair "shingled."[20]

Caught up as Cather was in a contest of wills that would continue well into her adult life, she must have known that these behaviors would nettle her mother. Yet, as Wolff asks (216), how could she have made these gestures without some measure of "complicity" from her mother? Was Jennie Cather, too, a person of doubleness? There is no evidence, at any rate, that her mother made any overt efforts to quash them. She

Fig. 5. Willa Cather as teenager wearing her uncle's Confederate cap.
(Nebraska State Historical Society)

Fig. 6. Children's performance of *Beauty and the Beast*, with Cather as father.
(Nebraska State Historical Society)

seems either to have enjoyed the image the young Cather was constructing or else to have been exercising a wise and admirable restraint
so as to take much of the wind out of her daughter's sails.[21] The male
masquerade, then, if it *was* that, was almost certainly in large measure a
device, a tactic employed in service of a strategy of rebellion and resistance against the repression and control that she would naturally have
associated with her mother. Edith Lewis, for example, does not identify
the cropped hair as a matter of gender but as "the mark of a rebel" (27).

The rebellion and resistance were also directed at the biological implications of her mother's conventionally feminine role. By the time she
was fifteen, Cather had seen her mother pregnant five times. (She may not
have remembered the first of these, which occurred when she was very
young.) One of these pregnancies, which led to a miscarriage, occurred
during the Cathers' first summer in Nebraska, when both mother and
daughter were miserably homesick. It was an event that must have been
greatly distressing, though in different ways, for them both. Jennie Cather's
other known pregnancies led to the births that crowded the Cather
household with babies and their needs: Roscoe in 1877; Douglass, 1880;
Jessica, 1881; James, 1886, three years after the family's move to Nebraska.

Another sister, Elsie, was born in 1890, the year Cather went away to do her year of preparatory study for the university, and John, always called Jack and a great favorite of Cather's during his childhood, was born in 1892, when Jennie Cather was forty-two years old and surely, like the mother in "Old Mrs. Harris," very tired of childbearing. It must have been a daunting spectacle of fecundity as baby after baby sapped her mother's strength and further strained the family's ability to maintain standards of gentility that already taxed their means, and it must have contributed significantly to the ambivalence with which Cather always regarded the female sex and sexuality itself.

In pondering the meaning of Cather's masculinizing of self during her adolescence (to the extent that it was that), we need to come back to the point with which we began: her admiration of the local physicians and her desire to be a surgeon. To dismiss the seriousness of her aspirations would be to disparage her capability and ambition. Woodress is both judicious and perceptive in his judgment that her "goal in life" must have seemed to her "not open to girls" and that as a result, with unassailable if futile logic, she "refused to be a girl" (55).[22] She went away to the university still affecting masculinized if not genuinely masculine attire. (She did, after all, wear skirts.) Her contemporaries remembered her as having been rather startling. But then not only did her ambitions undergo a sea change that she later attributed to seeing her words in print, but she must have begun to realize that such a persona was not entirely necessary and perhaps not even very helpful in getting on with those ambitions. And so, just as logically, she changed again.

The photographic record at this age remains interesting. Figure 7, taken fairly early in her college career, probably 1891 or '92, shows her with Louise Pound, later a distinguished folklorist and the first woman president of the Modern Language Association but then notable as the first of Cather's ardent infatuations. Both appear to be wearing some variant of a suit jacket, and both have close-cropped hair and boyish or mannish headgear, Pound's a light-colored cap, Cather's what appears to be a man's brimmed, creased hat. Cather is definitely the more "butch" of the two in appearance, if only because of her unmistakable square jaw, and wears, moreover, something of a smirk. Again, however, the cut of the jackets was a stylish one *for women*, as were the loose ties worn by both. (Photographs of women in the early 1890s show a great variety of neckwear.) Probably it is Cather's hat, more than any other single element,

Fig. 7. Willa Cather and Louise Pound at the University of Nebraska.
(Nebraska State Historical Society)

that, combined with her jawline, implies cross-dressing. She wears the
same hat in a picture taken slightly earlier, when she was sixteen (see
figure 8). Yet as figure 9 shows, hats of that very "shape and style" were
worn by young women who chose feminine dresses (Severa 435). Perhaps in interpreting Cather's attire in adolescence and early adulthood
we have read backward from our own assumptions in historically uninformed ways and as a result have rendered distorted or overstated judgments, such as that she was a "male impersonator" (O'Brien 225).

    There may indeed have been an element of cross-dressing in Cather's
choice of clothes. Coming from a fairly well-to-do family, she had options in her attire and could have chosen differently. It may well be that

Fig. 8. Willa Cather at age 16.
(Nebraska State Historical Society)

her choice of styles with a more masculine appearance sprang from a
developing sense of alternative sexuality. My point is that there are other
explanations as well, ranging from the fact that the clothes we see in
these photographs were consistent with women's fashions at the time,
so that they would not have been marked as male impersonation, to the
fact that they were consistent with her goals as an incipient career woman.
These factors are not mutually exclusive. Multiple impulses may have
converged to produce the persona she constructed.

Before she finished college, Cather would be performing the role of
Electra in flowing gown (in a tableau given in conjunction with a student production in Greek), wearing full sleeves and women's straw hats
for daytime, and blossoming out in an opera cloak and an ornately feminine (shall we say preposterous?) hat, as shown in figure 10. She always
had a taste for costume.

Fig. 9. Young women in shooting costume, with "schutzen-rifles."
Photo by Gerhard Gesell, Wisconsin State Historical Society, #(X3) 36722.
(Wisconsin State Historical Society)

Fig. 10. Cather in opera cloak, 1895. (Nebraska State Historical Society)

Another element in Cather's adolescent rebelliousness, equally important to the growth of her mind, related to the Christian piety and Baptist
Church affiliation of her upbringing. This, too, must have nettled her
mother; it may have been designed to do so. In contrast to the heavy
bent toward a language of providentialism evident in family letters, especially at times of grief, she espoused, toward the end of her high school
years and during her college and early postcollege years, a defiantly
freethinking rationalism. On the occasion of her graduation from high
school she gave an oration that was published in the *Red Cloud Chief* and
is reprinted in its entirety by Woodress (*Literary* 60–62). Firmly in the
grip of a commitment to positivistic science and scientific ambitions,
she titled her talk "Superstition *versus* Investigation." Superstition, she
maintained, whether "religious, political or social," had stood between
humankind and "the truth" throughout history, "retarding every step of
advancement." It had been a "curse" to the church, which would "never
realize" its "full strength" until it learned not to fear "scientific truth,"
because "there is another book of God than that of scriptural revelation,
a book written in chapters of creation upon the pages of the universe."
And more in the same vein, insisting on the rightness and glory of scientific investigation, even such seemingly cruel investigations as (though
she does not use the word) vivisection. The speech was, as Woodress
terms it, "a remarkable performance" and "an answer to the small-town
critics who had criticized her interests" (60). If the devout or nominally
devout in the audience (whom we would assume to have numbered in
the majority) were listening with any alertness whatever, rather than
merely sitting with glazed eyes and dulled ears while a young voice
droned on, they must have been greatly taken aback. It is surprising that
no outcry, either public or familial, seems to have resulted. Perhaps they
were all simply relieved that this youngster so disruptive of conventional expectations was at last about to go away, and they were willing to let
her go in peace.

IN SUMMARIZING the tenor of Cather's graduation oration, I have delayed
mentioning its first sentence: "All human history is a record of an emigration, an exodus from barbarism to civilization." It is entirely characteristic that she would enunciate her vision of "all human history" in
terms of movement. The "emigration" or "exodus" to which she draws
attention in the speech was a figurative one, but in her own life spatial

movement literally was often of great importance. Her experience up to the age of sixteen had been disrupted and shaped by literal, geographical movement—as well as that of the mind.

Joseph Urgo, who emphasizes the more positive outcomes of her "migratory consciousness," sees Cather as "a comprehensive resource for the demarcation of an empire of migration in U.S. culture" (*Myth* 5). That view is provocative and largely accurate, but it unduly minimizes the ambivalence of her view of migration, which arose from the fact that her own first migration, her dislocation from Virginia to Nebraska, was an involuntary one, causing an intense feeling of displacement and loss. Even so, she would later shape her adult life as a series of volitional departures on journeys of emergence, discovery, and self-fulfillment *even while maintaining a powerful homing urge.* That homing urge, I believe, is an extension of her sense of loss of the original home, the home in Back Creek, Virginia, to which she would return in *Sapphira and the Slave Girl.* In this as in virtually every other respect, she was a writer of dual and conflicting urges—an urge toward migration, in the largest and most figurative of senses, but also an urge toward enclosure, homing, and return. An insistently gendered vision of departure and spatial range, linked to freedom and fulfillment in work, characterizes much of Cather's writing. But that expansive vision coexists with an impulse of withdrawal to enclosed spaces, an impulse that becomes insistent in her later work. Mediating between the two urges is the open window, a thematically laden image that recurs throughout her fiction.

Cather's conflicted spatial desire, rooted as it was in her childhood displacement from northwestern Virginia to the flat, tree-less prairies of southern Nebraska, generated a long textual engagement with tropes of both departure and homing, an engagement also traceable in her later wish for escape from Red Cloud and the domain of her mother. It was an expression of her aspiration. Her adult departures on her solitary journey as writer-in-the-making would be made in large part as a separation from her mother, to whom she nevertheless kept returning in daughterly affection and duty. The complexity of this relationship set up tensions that would remain with her throughout her life and, as the late works *Shadows on the Rock* and *Sapphira and the Slave Girl* demonstrate, her work. Both of these novels are in part efforts to achieve reconciliation. Only late in life would Cather come to an understanding that her mother had been a helpful presence in allowing her to be "different" and in keeping "hands off" her soul.[23]

After an adolescence spent largely in groping for ways to evade conventional female decorum, Cather went away to the University of Nebraska. That departure is traced in "Old Mrs. Harris," where the mother appears as a blocking figure or at best an uninterested spectator, largely absorbed in her own imprisonment by sexuality, and the grandmother, representing Cather's own Grandmother Boak, takes the role of maternal advocacy and sacrifice. After completing her degree, Cather found it necessary to return home for about a year, writing newspaper columns and helping her family during a period of economic depression but largely marking time until an opportunity for escape presented itself. It was a discouraging period for her. As Marcus Klein writes, she had set her mind on professional fulfillment and was "markedly bent on escape" (ix).[24] Just how markedly, can be seen in her copious marginalia in Henrik Ibsen's play *The Lady from the Sea*, in a volume she acquired in 1893. In addition to checkmarks and such, showing her attention to the play's contrast of tameness and freedom, she wrote comments endorsing the sentiments of the passionate heroine. Ellida, she pronounced, would tolerate no barrier between herself and the unknown. There had to be, she added, a miserable carp for every great fish that swam free. Like Ellida, she felt herself to be one of those great, free fish. On May 2, 1896, she told her close friend from Lincoln, Mariel Gere, that she needed to see more of the world and would be unable to do anything significant, as her parents were clearly expecting, as long as she stayed in Red Cloud.[25]

The tension between Cather's great aspiration and restlessness and her profound homing urge is evident again and again in the patterns of her life. She became so securely settled in her home-base apartment at 5 Bank Street, which she occupied with Edith Lewis for fifteen years, that she was rendered almost physically ill by the necessity of moving out when the building was scheduled for demolition. She lamented to fellow writer and sometime friend Mary Austin that she was utterly homeless. Unable to face serious house hunting, she took refuge in the Grosvenor Hotel and made it her home base for five years, during which, however, she actually spent relatively little time in New York, due to her mother's final illness and her own retreats to Grand Manan Island, New Brunswick,

where she had built a house. But she needed the security of a single established home. She was in her very essence both an incessant traveler and
a homebody. Writing to Mabel Dodge Luhan to report renting a new
apartment at last, she exclaimed that she simply had to have a home and
familiar surroundings, and only then could she enjoy traveling and not
feel like a vagrant.[26] We can only suppose that the urgency of this need
for a stable dwelling place grew from her childhood sense of displacement in the move to Nebraska.

2

"Avid of the World, Always Wondering"

> Against all this, Youth,
> Flaming like the wild roses
> —"Prairie Spring"

> Hungry for distances;—her heart exulting
> —"Macon Prairie (Nebraska)"

EVEN BEFORE she left high school, the young "Willie" Cather had proclaimed herself, through her self-presentation and avowed interests, a member of a new generation of women. In addition to studying Latin and Greek (traditionally male preserves), cutting her hair short, dressing in a masculinized, or perhaps we should say a rationalized, fashion, taking an interest in dissection (in preparation for becoming Dr. William Cather), and assisting at an amputation, she had provided occasional assistance in her father's business. In 1888, still fourteen years old, she confessed in a letter to one of those adult mentors she was so quick to identify during her adolescence that she was reluctant to return to school after summer vacation because it would mean a loss of status. In the office she was in charge, but in school others held sway, and she was treated like a child. She added that to a person afflicted with human frailty (vanity) this was a significant difference.[1] The language of ruling power she used here would be important in her later metaphor of art as a "kingdom": a masculine domain.

Cather's pleasure in reigning (or imagining she reigned) over her father's office did not spring merely from self-importance. She preferred being in the place of the father. Asserting that preference again the next summer, she reported to Mrs. Stowell that she had arranged a study for herself in the office and was spending her time there reading Caesar.

She also listed her grades for the school year just ended: 95 in Latin, 90 in rhetoric, 100s in physics, astronomy, and ancient history.[2] Perhaps the rhetoric grade reflected spelling, which would never be her strong suit and was truly atrocious in these teenage letters.

Many of the adolescent gestures Cather made as she groped her way toward a comfortable expression of selfhood have been interpreted as idiosyncratic. But if we see these gestures against the larger backdrop of the changes in gender roles occurring in the late nineteenth century we can see that they were ways of casting herself as a New Woman. In a sense, she may be said to have become a New Woman before she became a woman. Her pursuit of interests and modes of self-presentation usually interpreted as a "butch" persona can be read not only as an indication of emerging lesbianism but also, with at least equal justification, as a conscious adoption of the markings by which the New Woman was then being defined, available to her in the national magazines that her family purchased and kept.[3] In appropriating them for herself, she was resisting traditional normative models and declaring herself—though only in selective ways—what would come to be called, by about 1915, a feminist.

Cather's determination to attend college was also a declaration of her identity as a New Woman. That determination was significant, of course, in multiple ways; her university experience had as far-reaching an importance in her life as the fact that she was born in Virginia and displaced to Nebraska. The fact that she set her face toward an unmarried life was also consistent with the role of New Woman—and indeed, was not unrelated to obtaining a college degree. Carroll Smith-Rosenberg points out that from the 1870s to the 1920s, the half-century during which Cather was born and grew to maturity, 40 to 60 percent of women college graduates remained unmarried, compared to only 10 percent of American women generally (253). Patricia Marks, in a study of satiric commentary on the New Woman in newspapers and magazines of the late nineteenth century, observes that the New Woman "asked for education, suffrage, and careers." Cather's goals in 1890, when she went to Lincoln to enter preparatory study for the university, encompassed two of the three (she never became active in the suffrage movement). Such women, Marks continues, "cut their hair, adopted 'rational' dress, and freewheeled along a path that led to the twentieth century" (2).[4]

It is informative to read in this context Woodress's account of Cather's appearance at the time she entered the university, when, he says, she was "still refusing to act and dress like a girl." Basing his description on the recollections of fellow student William Westermann, Woodress depicts a moment at which, as students waited for their instructor's arrival at the start of term, "the door opened, and a head with short hair and a straw hat appeared. A masculine voice inquired if this were the beginning Greek class, and when someone said it was, the body attached to the head and hat opened the door wider and came in. The masculine head and voice were attached to a girl's body and skirts. The entire class laughed, but Cather, apparently unperturbed, took her seat" (*Literary* 69–70). Woodress's language implies that he participates, in a mild way, in the ridicule conveyed in the account. Visually separating the (masculine) head from the (feminine) body, he foregrounds an act of intellect, the study of Greek, that was a marker of academic masculinity.[5] Other fellow students, he reports, also remembered her "mannish attire, short hair, and independent manner," her "high, stiff collars, string or four-in-hand ties, and mannish white cuffs," her "middy blouses with full skirts" (69–70). These descriptions duplicate rather precisely a description of the New Woman's style in dress that appeared in the *New York Chic* in 1881, which observed that above the waist the sexes "present an identical appearance (Marks 161). Cather was wearing "rational attire": above the waist, simple, quasi-mannish blouses and hats; below, light-weight flaring skirts that afforded freedom of movement (see figure 11). Perhaps her classmates were not so aware of innovations in dress as she was.[6] Perhaps her awareness of the satirical responses evoked by such innovations accounts for the aplomb, noted by Woodress, with which she went about her business.

Cather also adopted two other defining behaviors of the New Woman: cigarette smoking (which she would continue throughout her adult life) and bicycle riding. Again, we need to be cautious about assuming that these practices indicated cross-gendering. The influential *Godey's* magazine advised in April 1896 that "riding a 'wheel' did not interfere with being a 'true woman'" (Severa 466). Athletic exercise was often advocated by medical professionals, partly in connection with a concern for eugenics, that is, healthy motherhood (Garvey 66, 81–83).[7] In a study of the influence of Henri Bergson's vitalism on American culture, Tom Quirk refers to the nineties as a "muscular decade" and observes that the "'new woman' of the era had been urged toward a manly athleticism . . . years before Theodore Roosevelt formalized the attitude in 1900

Fig. 11. Cather as collegian in sensible attire. (Nebraska State Historical Society)

with his aptly titled book *The Strenuous Life*" (98). The "craze for bicycle riding" (Rudnick 71) in the 1890s was a manifestation of that concern. But it was more. A woman on a bicycle represented "both activity
and options" (Marks 175). Clearly, these were things Cather wanted. In
1895, following her graduation from college, she wrote to friends about
the good times she had riding her "wheel."[8]

CATHER ENTERED the University of Nebraska as a science student. Despite the focus on physics and astronomy indicated by the high school
grades she reported to her friend Mrs. Stowell, her primary scientific
interest seems to have been biology. Her dissection of small animals,
apparently taken up under the tutelage of her learned neighbor Will
Ducker, continued at least into the summer following her year spent as
a preparatory student in the Latin School of the university. While she
was at home for the summer, she wrote to her newfound friend Mariel
Gere (daughter of the publisher and editor-in-chief of the *Nebraska*

State Journal) urging her to set up a dissection laboratory in her father's newspaper office, where the roar of the press would drown out the animals' cries.[9] The disturbingly gleeful tone of this reference to the infliction of pain was perhaps intended humorously and should not be over-interpreted. Still, there is an undeniable casualness in her reference, in the same letter, to being ready to kill the frogs whose circulatory system she had been studying. One would not want to conclude that she was a budding sadist, but she seems to have been deriving pleasure from the exertion of power over her little victims. Indeed, we might well see it as an analogous satisfaction to that she found in governing, at her father's office, rather than being governed.

Although Cather's interest in biology, especially botany, would continue, her focus on scientific studies did not persist.[10] That, too, was not unrelated to gender. If we look back at her high school graduation address, we can detect a trace of community resistance to the young Cather's multifaceted disregard of proprieties and expectations customarily linked to gender. Her address was printed in the local newspaper without comment as to her future prospects, whereas success was predicted for the two males in the class of three. We cannot suppose she would have failed to notice this tacit reminder. She may have taken revenge in *The Song of the Lark* in her treatment of the brother who is successful financially but not celebrated so much as Thea. She wanted to join a profession, medicine, that was still almost exclusively a men's club, and she must have realized that this ambition, too, would evoke disapproval and discrimination. Patricia Marks (72) points out that a woman who wanted to pursue a career as a medical doctor "faced both discrimination and patronizing humor." It is little wonder that when Cather reached the university she changed her goals as soon as recognition in another field of endeavor came her way. Toward the end of her year as a "second prep" her instructor submitted an essay she had written on Thomas Carlyle for simultaneous publication by the *Nebraska State Journal* and, in a slightly variant version, the campus *Hesperian*.

Critics accounting for Cather's change in interest from science (medicine) to writing have usually followed her own lead in commenting, in an open letter to her former mentor at the *Nebraska State Journal*, Will Owen Jones, "What youthful vanity can be unaffected by the sight of itself in print!"[11] The swerve in her ambition has been seen as a sudden enlightenment, a "Peak in Darien" experience in which she saw, with a wild surmise, the literary life spread before her. It may well have been such an experience, but it was also a very rational decision, given the social climate. Moreover, it was not really her first time to see her words in print. Not only had her graduation oration been printed in the *Red Cloud Chief*, but an essay had appeared in the *Red Cloud Republican* (of which her father was part-owner and manager) in July 1890, preceding her departure to begin the University of Nebraska Latin School.

In her "prep" year Cather did well enough on a chemistry placement exam to be allowed into freshman chemistry. Taking "rather her own way with the curriculum" (*CSF* 475) like the heroine of her 1896 story "Tommy the Unsentimental," she initially pursued both the scientific and the classical curriculum, but her studies quickly gravitated toward the Classics (Greek as well as Latin) and French as well as English literature. She was allowed to take the junior-level Shakespeare course as a freshman. That experience yielded a two-part essay that appeared in the *Nebraska State Journal* in November 1891. Before the age of eighteen, then, she had appeared in the *Journal*'s pages twice. Her first fiction also appeared that year, the short story "Peter," based on the suicide of a Bohemian farmer (her friend Anna Sadilek's father) that would later figure in *My Ántonia*. Once again, the material had been sent for publication by one of her English instructors, this time Herbert Bates.

The placement of this story, in a magazine called *The Mahogany Tree*, is worth pondering for a moment. *The Mahogany Tree* had begun publication in January 1892 as an early *fin de siècle* "alternative" magazine in quality format, apparently created by students at Harvard and Princeton who had also founded the *Knight Errant*, a journal of the arts and criticism, with which it shared a clearly defined set of editorial principles: "an interest in early nineteenth-century literary ideology, including romanticism and transcendentalism, a reaction against realism, and an interest in contemporary continental European literature." According to a biography of Walter Blackburn Harte, a member of the so-called decadent set praised by *Mahogany Tree*, an editorial statement was printed in the first issue defining the ideal editor:

> He is a great reader, and fond of talking about books. . . . He is especially fond of novels, and his taste is decidedly for the romantic. He likes best, of present writers, George Meredith, with a large portion of admiration for Stevenson, and sometimes for Kipling. He does not care much for Howells; and he dislikes the followers of Howells, thinking that these

waste their pains in details, often without making their stories interesting. He reads the French magazines, and means to keep track of the best work done abroad. He is fond of poetry, and often writes verse himself. (Doyle 42)

Except for its masculine pronouns, the passage might have been written about Cather. Her literary taste followed the pattern laid out in this manifesto quite precisely. Even in this first story placement, then, initiated by a professor who was himself an East Coast aesthete, she was identified with an "alternative" school of literature and the arts that combined, in a curious way, avant-garde tastes with conservative ones.

The young Cather's involvement in journalism also began in her freshman year. Along with Louise Pound she served as founding coeditor of a short-lived campus literary magazine called *The Lasso*.[12] In her sophomore year she joined the otherwise all-male staff of the well-established *Hesperian* in the position of literary editor (see figure 12). As a junior she became managing editor, almost singlehandedly raising its standards, so that in Slote's words it gained "a flair and freshness unequalled in other volumes" (*KA* 12).

Fig. 12. The *Hesperian* staff. (Nebraska State Historical Society)

The editorial policy stated in her "Salutatory" as managing editor, on September 27, 1893, is an early indication of principles she would adhere to far beyond her days at the *Hesperian:* a devotion to "plain, unornamented language" and a willingness to take a stand on issues. "If there is any fighting to be done, we will be down in the line fighting on one side or the other, striking out from the shoulder" (*KA* 11). The language of combat here is characteristic, not so much, I believe, because she wished to adopt masculinity as because of her enthusiastic participation in the vitalism of the times. This same enthusiasm was evident less than two months later in a column on football and again in her exclamatory remarks on the Corbett-Mitchell heavyweight championship bout on January 28, 1894. The editorial "Salutatory" also gives early indication of her characteristic commitment to detailed workmanship ("we are . . . going to work with . . . a good stiff stub pen") and insistence on distinguishing public roles from private ones: "If a man says that the earth is flat, if he slanders a great book or writes an absurd one, we claim the right to pummel him as much as we please; it is within the province of liberal education and legitimate journalism. As to dictating whether our neighbor shall wear jewelry or not, we think this is none of our business." As a reviewer over the next several years, she would "claim the right to pummel" again and again.

It was in connection with the *Hesperian* that Cather got into a scrape in her junior year that interrupted her friendship with Louise Pound. A bitter and unnecessary experience, it might have taught her to doubt her initial impressions and to exercise discretion when sketching actual persons in her writing, but does not seem to have done so. On March 10, 1894, she published a send-up of Louise's brother Roscoe, then back at his alma mater as a graduate instructor in botany after a year at Harvard. The unnamed returning graduate is identified as a member of the "botanical seminar" by the "lengthy words" he "empties forth" on the unwary. He seems to have no function except to stand around "with an air of proprietorship and pleased condescension" (*W&P* 122). Continuing in much the same vein, the piece strikes verbal blows that must have smarted a good deal, calling Roscoe a bully in childhood and an intellectual bully now and predicting that he will never amount to anything but only hang around the university so people "may ask who he is and be told what fine marks he used to get in his classes" (*W&P* 122; in fact, Curtin notes, Roscoe Pound became dean of the Harvard Law School and a "world-renowned authority in the field of jurisprudence"). Though unnamed, the target was easily recognizable, and Cather was declared *persona non grata* in the Pound home. It was probably this affair that she was referring to when she wrote Mariel Gere that she would never have gotten through the Pound scrape without her. Or she may have been referring to her 1893–94 crush on Louise, recorded in a series of intense letters summarized by O'Brien in her account of Cather's development of a strongly gender-marked literary voice (130–31).[13]

The Roscoe Pound fiasco is especially interesting because there were similar episodes of recognizable portraiture later in Cather's fiction, though perhaps never such blatant ones. One of these caused another temporary severing of friendship, that with Dorothy Canfield, whom she also met while a student. In early 1905, as Cather's first volume of stories, *The Troll Garden,* was going to press, Canfield asked her to delete a story called "The Profile" about a woman with a disfiguring facial scar, on grounds that the character was easily recognizable as a friend to whom she had introduced Cather in France and who would be devastated by seeing her portrait in print.

> I have read the story and just as you thought I do ask that you do not pub-
> lish it—not for my own sake but so that you will not have done a cruel
> thing. . . . I beg you with all my heart . . . not to strike a cruel and over-
> whelming blow to one who has not deserved it, who has already lost her
> life's happiness through her deformity, and who was kind to you. I am
> quite sure you don't realize how exact and faithful a portrait you have
> drawn of her—her beautiful hair, her pretty hands, her fondness for dress
> and pathetic lapses of taste in wearing what other girls may, her uncon-
> sciousness—oh Willa don't do this thing.[14]

When Cather refused to withdraw the story, partly on grounds that the volume would then be too slight for publication, Canfield and her parents went to S. S. McClure's offices in New York to argue the case. The story was deleted. In its place appeared an equally close and directly disparaging portrait of Dorothy's mother, "Flavia and Her Artists." The friendship did not recover for almost two decades.

Even this second episode was not enough to deter Cather from sketching real people in her writing. In 1916 the husband of singer Lillian Nordica threatened to sue because the husband in Cather's story "The Diamond Mine" supposedly depicted him in insulting terms.[15] As late as 1923 the family of the deceased Lyra Garber, widow of the first governor of Nebraska, made rumblings of lawsuit upon recognizing her in Marian Forrester of *A Lost Lady*. The daughter of Burlington Railroad magnate Charles Elliott Perkins was equally incensed at what she regarded as a caricature of her family in the same novel, telling historian Frederick Jackson Turner that she "resented" the "absolutely false and arrogant impression of my mother and of me 'tho she would probably say she had never heard of us" (Billington 448). In another instance, the family of composer Ethelbert Nevin and other Pennsylvanians were reportedly "upset" about the "close parallels" between Nevin and the central character of "Uncle Valentine," published February 1925 in *Woman's Home Companion* (Byrne and Snyder 35). I am dubious, then, when Edith Lewis writes that Cather "never set out to do a portrait of anyone as a portrait" (24). It is not clear that she learned very well the lesson taught by the Roscoe Pound episode.

By the fall of 1893, when Cather became managing editor of the *Hesperian*, she was also working as a journalist professionally, doing a regular column for the *Nebraska State Journal* as well as miscellaneous reviews, primarily of plays—an assignment that allowed her to draw on an enthusiasm for the theater so ardent that it threatened to disrupt her degree progress. She was not yet twenty years old when her first column ran, on November 5, 1893.

Her motivation for taking the job with the *Journal* was in part financial. She was paid a dollar a column. Weather conditions had caused widespread crop failures in the state that year, adding to the impact of economic depression, and men like her father, who had been supporting his family on land speculation and loans to farmers who now could not pay, were hard-pressed. E. K. Brown says in his early but scrupulously researched biography that the newspaper job was her "chance to help" (65). Perhaps so. Perhaps she began to contribute to her own support and to send a little money to the family. Lewis states (one would suppose on Cather's authority) that later, after going to Pittsburgh, she sent her family "as much money as she could" (43). But in a letter to Mariel Gere written in 1896, a few months after her graduation, Cather herself referred to debts and spendthrift habits, including gifts of champagne and "diamonds" to actresses. She needed to cut back and get out of debt, she said, because she could not very well ask for any more help from her family.[16] That does not sound as if *she* had been helping *them*.

In any event, her move into earning money was consistent with her self-positioning as a New Woman, and whether it was due to keen judgment or to luck, in moving toward a career in newspapers she was riding a rising tide. The decade of the '90s was a time of "increased female participation in journalism, freelance magazine writing, and the writing of novels" (Doyle 10). She would not be ready to write novels for some time yet, but her course could scarcely have been better plotted toward success in the business of literature—a business in which (as her correspondence with her editor at Houghton Mifflin shows) she would be very interested indeed in maximizing her income, statements of disinterested aesthetic motivation notwithstanding.[17] According to Lewis, as a result of the drain on Cather's energies and a shift in interest toward professional achievement, the "whole current of her activities" shifted, and during her last two years at the university she "did very little studying" (33–34).

In her senior year Cather became involved in another *contretemps* when she chose to attack ladies' literary clubs. On October 28, 1894, in her column in the *Journal*, she poked fun at clubwomen's self-conscious efforts at "self-improvement" by way of weighty studies that did not "mix well with tea and muffins." They endured, she said, "a great deal of chaff to get a very little wheat" (*W&P* 115–16). In essence, she ridiculed the clubs as pretentious and inane. Her remarks evoked a response in print by Mrs. James H. Canfield, wife of the university chancellor and Dorothy's mother. It is easy to read the whole affair as an instance merely of Cather's brashness (of which she had plenty in those years) or, more damagingly, of a tendency to disparage women generally—an eagerness to separate herself from women who struck her as conventional or even a readiness to believe that with rare exceptions such as herself, women should stay in the home and not pretend to mix with their intellectual superiors.[18] Such a reading is not entirely amiss. She did at times employ an anti-woman rhetoric, most blatantly in a column in 1895 that has been so frequently quoted that it is sometimes taken as the essence of her literary judgment. "I have not much faith in women in fiction. They have a sort of sex consciousness that is abominable. They are so limited to one string and they lie so about that. They are so few, the ones who really did anything worth while" (*KA* 409). We can also read that rhetoric as evidence that she felt threatened by any association with women whose endeavors might stigmatize her as being frivolous or unable to compete in a men's world. On other occasions, she praised women writers.

In criticizing women's literary clubs, Cather seems to have over-looked the importance such clubs had for a great many women as a means of countering their relegation to domestic confinement, bridging the gap between private and public roles, developing solidarity with other women, and advancing their education in ways that did not place excessive demands on lives primarily committed to other efforts. Karen J. Blair, who enumerates these benefits, insists that the clubs "served as a first step for feminists determined to improve their status." Blair notes, however, that the clubs' format often facilitated avoidance of controversial issues and promoted a kind of stand-pat Americanism and stodginess of taste and that they "apparently failed to meet the needs of single professional women" (57–58, 65). As an incipient member of that group, Cather was impatient with the clubwomen's amateur status. Perhaps, too, as an aspiring "Bohemian" (to use her own half-facetious term for herself in those years) she wanted them to be bolder and to direct their attention toward artistic movements more nearly avant-garde than the nineteenth-century cultural status quo. Or perhaps she wanted them to leave her "Kingdom of Art" (a phrase she seems to have picked up from a professor of literature at Nebraska, Lucius Sherman, whose work she publicly ridiculed as dry pedantry) to herself and the like-minded exceptional few.[19] Probably she did not know precisely what she wanted.

Whatever the source of her objections, Cather felt sufficiently bothered by the literary clubs to resort to aggressive ridicule. She convicted them of shallowness and silliness as well as social and intellectual pretension, or snobbery. It is not at all clear, however, that this objection was an indication of democratic principle. If so, it is interesting that less than a year later she was attending parties given by what Slote calls the "most exclusive" of the Lincoln social clubs, including a masquerade ball—an occasion that might possibly have been characterized as silly, shallow, or even pretentious (KA 28). Already she was manifesting the conflicted interest in what Patricia Yongue calls "worldliness" that would ultimately lead to one of her most anomalous personal enthusiasms, that for decadent British aristocrat Stephen Tennant.[20] In Slote's words, Cather's "view of art in these years was both exclusive and inclusive"; she "believed in the aristocratic and she believed in the common, but with qualifications" (KA 51).

The two strains, the aristocratic and the democratic, were mixed together in the young Cather's activities and enthusiasms during her university years in a swirl that swept in far more than the masquerade ball. In the summer of 1893 she found delight in climbing a windmill with her brother Roscoe and watching the approach of a storm. She played cards and luxuriated in the greenness of cornfields high as forests. At the same time, she maintained demanding standards as a theater reviewer, and in March of her senior year, 1895, she signaled her affinity with the high arts by going off to Chicago for a week of grand opera. When she attended a dance in Red Cloud, she found herself unable to participate as an equal and sneered at the lumpy waxing of the floor, the rough benches for seating, and the sandwiches passed in a potato basket.[21] She was caught between cultures, not yet able to reconcile them as she would, temporarily, in *My Ántonia*.

If Cather entered her college years as a rebel in masculinized clothes, a mode of self-presentation sometimes described as cross-dressing, she ended them still a rebel but in less conspicuous ways, not having to do with dress (see figure 13). Photographs of her in her senior year wearing the cape and hat in which she went to the opera or her puff-sleeved gown for the graduation ball convey a theatrical flair in clothing of an indisputably feminine variety (see figure 14). What had happened to her masculinized persona?

For one thing, Mariel Gere's mother had intervened. In Bennett's words (216), Mrs. Gere "persuaded" her to let her hair grow longer and to dress with more femininity (and also, as Cather later recalled, to try to improve her spelling).[22] It is hard to believe, though, that anyone could have persuaded Cather to adopt a persona she did not want. More likely, as she gained worldly experience and moved into the world of professional journalism by way of her reviewing, two very important realizations came to her: first, that she could gain a reception among people who could advance her career, and thereby achieve her goals more readily, if she did not elicit hostility over something so unimportant as how she dressed or cut her hair; and second, that she, too, could be (indeed, had long been) a performer, an actor of roles, and not just in community theatricals.

Since the beginning of her junior year Cather had spent inordinate amounts of time in the theater, among actresses. It is probably not incidental that so-called trouser roles for women were very popular at the time.[23] In such roles, but also in their performances of female parts of all kinds, from ingenues to sirens to powerful and domineering figures

Fig. 13. Cather in cap and gown, 1895.
(Nebraska State Historical Society)

such as Lady Macbeth, actresses performed gender. Cather had observed and written about their clothing, their manner of walking, speaking, styling their hair, dressing, looking at others or staring them down, how they held their heads, their professionalism or "downright grit" (*W&P* 544), whether they were girlish or "womanly," powerful or only appealing, beautiful or so fascinating that beauty didn't matter. Just as she had performed the role of the masculinized girl (or what might be called the tomboy or butch)—which was more importantly the role of the New Woman-to-be—so she now performed the role of the elegant young woman.

Bennett notes that Cather got tired of the opera outfit, the "circular" trimmed in Persian lamb, worn with a boa. Her students a decade later

Fig. 14. Cather in graduation ball gown, 1895. (Nebraska State Historical Society)

would comment on her masculine appearance. Later pictures—such as the famous one taken by Edward Steichen–show her finding a comfortable middle way (see figure 15).[24] On the other hand, many other later pictures show her in sumptuous dresses and elaborate, feminine hats. What she developed in college and maintained in later life was an ability to move back and forth, in her self-presentation as well as in her activities, among degrees of what would be coded masculine or feminine. She also maintained a certain theatricality in dress. Look again at the senior-year photos: to what extent was she engaging in camp?

How ARE we to assess the growth of Cather's mind at this early stage in her life? She was an eager learner and one with wide-ranging interests and intellectual curiosity, but not a polymath. The scientific interests of her adolescent days—never so all-encompassing as Mildred Bennett's contention that "science claimed all of her attention" (109)—remained at an amateur level, she had little facility in mathematics, and it is doubtful that she had any extensive acquaintance with philosophy. But then, we do not usually expect all of this in the literary mind. Nor do we expect the literary mind to be formed primarily through formal instruction. Certainly Cather's was not. As Slote puts it, "In the end, Willa Cather's formal education does not explain how she happened to know what she did" (KA 37). Her adolescent and young adult years were spent learning, at a prodigious rate and with prodigious mental energy, from all aspects of her experience: from theater, from her engagement with the business of putting words onto paper, and primarily from her reading, which in both classical and modern literature, partly in the classroom but mainly outside it, was wide-ranging.

Susan Rosowski pronounces Cather's early reading "remarkable for both its diversity and its consistency" I am dubious about the consistency, but in diversity and extent it was indeed remarkable. She read, in Slote's words, "without logic and sometimes without discrimination," with an "eclectic, perhaps unorthodox, personal range" (KA 38). At fifteen she was reading (or so she reported) Caesar, the Latin Bible, astronomy, geology, history, Homer, Milton, Swinburne, Ouida (the pseudonym of English novelist Marie Louise de la Ramée, whose work William Curtin characterizes as "erotic and exotic" [W&P 273]), and George Sand. Even allowing for adolescent braggadocio, it is an impressive list. In 1892, after her freshman year at the university, she was effusing over the

Fig. 15. Edward Steichen's photo of Cather in 1926, at the age of 53. (Museum of Modern Art; reprinted with permission of Joanna T. Steichen)

Rubáiyát and in 1893 over the poetry of Ella Wheeler Wilcox. During the summer of 1894 she read Virgil with her brother Roscoe.[25] She read magazines. She was almost certainly, for instance, aware of Mary Hunter Austin well before Austin burst on the world of western American letters in 1903 with *The Land of Little Rain*, through having read (and by 1895 published in) the *Overland Monthly*.

Cather's reading embraced both ancient and modern, both the literary and the popular, both American and European. Markings in her books show painstaking study, almost certainly while in college, of Aristotle's *Poetics*, Shakespeare's sonnets, Browning's longer poems, Victor Hugo, Ibsen.[26] Authors mentioned either by Slote or by Rosowski include (and this is by no means a comprehensive list) Arnold, Bunyan, Carlyle, Virginia novelist John Esten Cooke, Marie Corelli, Daudet, Richard Harding Davis, Alfred de Musset, Dickens (the family owned a complete set), Dumas *père* and *fils*, George Eliot (mentioned in an 1891 letter to Mariel Gere), Emerson, Goethe, Sarah Grand, Hawthorne, Heine, Homer (of course), Hugo, Ibsen, Longfellow, Pierre Loti, Lowell, Ouida, Poe, George Sand, Scott, Shakespeare (in quantity), Stevenson, Thackeray, Turgenev, Verlaine, Virgil, Zola. More, many more, turn up in casual references in her reviews as gathered in *The Kingdom of Art* and the more inclusive *The World and the Parish*. What she read, she read with an intensity that made it part of her. Dorothy Canfield Fisher once wrote that at the university Cather "made it a loving duty to read every French literary masterpiece she could lay her hands on" (7, 9). A loving duty. After college she read French literature with her friends the Seibels in Pittsburgh. George Seibel recalled her as having "an eager mind" not only for books but also for "the study of human nature." She was, he wrote, "avid of the world, always wondering" (196, 203).[27]

Cather's broadening horizons during college and in the years soon after gave her much to wonder at. The "greatest cultural distinction" of Lincoln, in Slote's judgment, was professional theater, with several plays a week and the opportunity to see perhaps a hundred companies a year (*KA* 7), but there were also discussion groups and social clubs, a lending library, and three daily newspapers, plus two weeklies. The university's faculty included scholars from Sweden and England. Cather's favorite English teacher, Herbert Bates, was fresh from Harvard; he would serve as the model for Jim Burden's favorite professor, Gaston Cleric. The

student body, numbering several hundred when she entered and growing fast, included persons who would become dean of Harvard Law
School, head of the New School for Social Research, representatives at
the 1918 peace conference at Versailles, and Pulitzer Prize winners (*KA*
8–9). It was a stimulating atmosphere, its combination of cultural activity and frontier rawness an apt study in contrast for a thoughtful and
energetic young woman who would herself be such a study. She also had
opportunity, during her college years, to develop the interest in serious
music that would prove to be lifelong. Probably the fact that Herbert
Bates wrote music criticism for a local weekly, the *Courier* (for which
Cather would serve as columnist and associate editor for several months
in 1895), was influential in directing her interest in that direction.
Her March 1895 trip to Chicago to attend opera (having already seen *Il
Trovatore* in Lincoln) was one of the most important experiences of her
college years, heralding a lifetime of operagoing.

THE YOUNG adult Willa Cather was a mixture of restless free spirited-
ness, an active and inquiring mind, and self-construction as a New
Woman eager for a career, reluctant to follow the patterns of traditional
feminine charm and domesticity endorsed by her mother. When her
years at the university ended in June of 1895, she was poised for fulfillment of all these traits and eager to escape from the hinterland to the
metropolis and to the public sphere.[28]

Biographies of Cather have usually and with good reason emphasized her singularity and her amiability as a kind of maiden-aunt figure
(Katherine Anne Porter's characterization of her). But we also need to
see her in relation to the social and cultural history of her time. The
emergence of the New Woman at the end of the nineteenth century and
the first decades of the twentieth was one of the most far-reaching social
changes of the century, having profound effect on subsequent life in
America. Cather was a part of this emergence; she *was* a New Woman,
and as she entered her career, after a year of faltering overtures, she was
recognized as such.[29] The *Pittsburg Press* called her, in a brief article
published March 28, 1897, "a thoroughly up-to-date woman" and a
"pionee[r] in woman's advancement." An accompanying caricature captioned "A Woman Editor" shows her in no-nonsense attire typical of
the late-century "utilitarian movement" toward so-called rational dress,

stepping out on a surface drawn with slapdash marks suggestive of motion and activity, carrying, as an indication of the nontriviality of her work, a rolled manuscript of oversized proportions (see figure 16).[30] It is an amusing but also an appropriate image of Willa Cather, the young professional woman.

Fig. 16. Caricature of Willa Cather as a New Woman.
(By courtesy of the University of Nebraska Press)

3

ESTABLISHING A CAREER / ESTABLISHING GENDER

The days so short, the nights so quick to flee,
The world so wide, so deep and dark the sea
—"Evening Song"

Grandmither, think not I forget, when I come back to town,
An' wander the old ways again an' tread them up an' down.
— "'Grandmither, think not I forget'"

CATHER'S STUDENT years shaded into her early professional years by
more indistinct gradations than most people's. As a student, she worked
for an important regional newspaper; as a magazine editor and newspaperwoman she continued the eager learning of her college years; and as
a teacher (from March 1901 to May 1906) she continued to write for
newspapers. But it would be a mistake to see these continuities in her
transition from student to professional as meaning that she navigated
the crossing with ease or tranquility. Her young adult years were not a
seamless whole, and her progress was not uninterrupted or without
anxiety. She would later remember being sophomorically bitter in college,[1] and she continued to experience periods of disheartenment and
depression for the rest of her life.

Upon graduating, Cather was unable to establish herself immediately
in any employment that would enable her to live independently in Lincoln. From August through November 1895 she worked as associate
editor of the *Courier* for Sarah Harris, a woman Edith Lewis characterizes as "challenging" and "unconventional" [ix]). By January Cather was
back in Red Cloud at her parents' home, writing columns for the *Journal*
and making occasional trips to Lincoln but feeling out of the current of
events, banished from civilization. Her letters complain of being exiled

to Siberia. She lamented that friends were not writing to her and begged
Mariel Gere to keep her posted on Lincoln's theater world. On the other
hand, she reported hosting a wedding breakfast and going to dances, at
one of which she met the original for the later Lucy Gayheart.[2] Mildred
Bennett's description of these months as a period of depression and "enforced
vegetation" during which she "even hated to work on her manuscripts"
(217) is perhaps excessively solemn. It was a period of discouragement
and uneasy delay, during which the ambitious young graduate was trying to find her way and waiting for opportunities.

In February 1896, when Professor Bates resigned from the university
to take a position as music and literary critic with the *Cincinnati Commercial Gazette*, Cather, already vacillating between teaching and journalism, launched a campaign to replace him. Asking the respected Charles
Gere to champion her cause, she claimed total confidence in her ability
to handle the job and blandly pointed out that as a woman, she would
come cheap.[3] Her bid failed. But in June, Gere's efforts in her behalf
paid off. With his boosting and that of his managing editor, Will Owen
Jones, she was appointed editor of the newly established *Home Monthly
Magazine* in Pittsburgh. As Bernice Slote points out (*KA* 6), without a
knowledge of the writing Cather did during her student days we would
find it inexplicable that a magazine in a city a third of a continent away
would hire as editor-in-chief a twenty-two-year-old woman from a raw
midwestern town, fresh out of college. Cather, however, had in effect
begun her career while still a student. Building on an already established reputation, she began a career in journalism that would last until
1912.[4]

Her acceptance of the offer at the *Home Monthly* appears to have
been a case of the bird in the hand. Whether or not her family breathed
a collective sigh of relief, as Bennett intimates—and one can easily believe they did—they must have been glad that she had a job at last and
the hope of living up to expectations, her own as well as theirs. She left
Red Cloud for Pittsburg (as it was then spelled) in late June 1896, part
of a national cohort that by the turn of the century would raise women's
representation in the work force to 20 percent. The New Woman was
becoming "a sociological fact."[5]

Cather's early months in Pittsburgh were not entirely happy ones. She
called it the "City of Dreadful Dirt" and fell into renewed laments that
friends were not writing to her. Taken into the home of her employer,

James Axtell, until she could settle in, she found her hosts kind but excessively pious. Fortunately, she was able to take a humorous view of the situation, writing to Mariel, in letters that must have been at least partly spoof, that the daughter's room she was occupying was equipped with six Bibles, all the young woman's friends were devoted to church work, and a Baptist minister who lived next door was summoned the moment she told the Axtells she had been raised in the Baptist church.[6]

The irreverent attitude toward organized religion implied in these first impressions was not new. She had already established what she thought of ministers in a *Journal* column of April 7, 1895, in which she deplored the practice of public figures' letting their names and photographs be used for advertising purposes. Mentioning the celebrated Henry Ward Beecher as one of those who "sent out their photographs to advertise soap and bitters," she quipped, "Such cheap methods of advertising should be left to the clergy" (*W&P* 194). Probably she was happier leaving her new employer in ignorance of that particular column. But she trumpeted her rebellious "creed" in a letter to Mariel about a month after her arrival, when she was acutely weary of the Axtells' Presbyterianism. The true revelation of the one God was Art, she pronounced, and if need be she would follow that creed to a hotter place than Pittsburgh, for it summed up her very self.[7]

Cather quickly began to enjoy the cultural resources of the city, going to art museums, plays, and concerts, attending parties and supper cruises on the river, receiving and making calls, and becoming a member of a club. Her enjoyment of all this activity is clear from her letters. She gloated that when Dorothy Canfield and her mother were in town she introduced the self-consciously prominent Mrs. Canfield to a number of clubwomen. Imagine—*her* introducing Mrs. Canfield! It did her "wicked un-Christian heart good to get even, to pay off the old scores and make people take back the bitter things they had said" that hurt her so.[8] She felt vindicated and was taking a "satisfying . . . revenge" (O'Brien, *Emerging* 226).

However exalted her devotion to literature for its own sake, Cather always needed her Kingdom of Art to be peopled by admirers. She needed the reassurance of applause and a feeling of importance. Her letters in the early Pittsburgh days to the persons in Nebraska whose esteem counted most and who could be counted on to spread the word, the Geres, proclaim that importance and admit her satisfaction in it: she has a stenographer, she is writing most of the upcoming issue herself and handling all the correspondence with contributors, she is even overseeing the composing room. It all depends on her! Echoing her boast of a decade earlier that she "governed" at her father's office, she told Mariel twice in the same letter that she was the head of the enterprise.[9] If she was glad to be able to use her social success to prove herself to Mrs. Canfield, she was quite determined to use her appointment at the *Home Monthly* to prove herself to all those people back home who had doubted her. She would show them, she said, that she could work hard and be a success.

Success in the kind of publishing endeavor governed by circulation and advertising dollars was a very different matter, however, from success as the kind of writer she had learned to esteem in college. Conflict quickly developed between her writerly goals and the needs of her employers, and the mood of her letters vacillated from glee to a grim determination to grind out trash and domestic advice. She tried to get on with her "own" writing, but found it difficult to shift gears from the magazine work. Also, she quickly found that journalism was not a predictable and secure endeavor. As early as January 1897, only six months after starting her job at the *Home Monthly*, she reported to Will Jones that she was exploring employment possibilities with newspapers.

She had actually been writing reviews for the *Leader* since the previous fall. William Curtin lists, in the bibliography to *The World and the Parish*, twenty-five such reviews between September and June, when she went home on vacation. While she was there, the magazine changed hands, and she resigned, uncertain what she was going to do and worried that financial commitments (such as to her friend George Seibel) were not being honored.[10] Landing on her feet, she took a job with the *Leader* without knowing the nature of her responsibilities, which turned out to be those of daytime telegraph editor. She was paid $75 a month plus per-column fees for reviews and occasional pieces. Curtin lists seventy-five of these over the next two and a half years, during which time she also supplied material to the *Courier*, the *Journal*, and the *New York Sun*.

When Cather was hired at the *Leader*, she commented to Will Jones, using a colloquial expression thoroughly racist in its import, that it was really white of the editor to offer her a job when many newspapermen were unemployed.[11] She may not have felt quite so grateful when only a few months after she took the job she found her work greatly increased, with the outbreak of the Spanish-American War. The *Maine* exploded in Havana harbor on February 15, 1898, and Spain and the United States declared war on April 24 and 25. Telegrams poured in, and she had to postpone her summer vacation until August, due to the press of work.

Katherine Anne Porter once said that it seemed to her America had been going to war all her life, starting with that "disgraceful affair" in Cuba. Cather would seem to have had that "disgraceful affair" pressed on her attention much more insistently than Porter did, but she does not seem to have reacted to it so forcefully. Perhaps her strongest comment was a facetious remark somewhat along the lines of "good riddance" when a member of the Westermann family in Lincoln, the models for the Erlichs in *One of Ours*, departed for the war.[12] Yet we can guess that her experience dealing with war dispatches from Cuba must have contributed to a similar war-weariness when she later witnessed the spectacle of the Great War and World War II.

Shifting from one job to another would become a pattern for Cather over the next several years as she made her way through the intricate world of periodical publishing. She was often writing for more than one outlet at a time, sometimes under her own name, sometimes pseudonymously, sometimes without byline. In 1900 and 1901, for example, she sold columns to the *Leader*, the short-lived *Library* magazine, the *Lincoln Courier*, *Cosmopolitan*, the *Saturday Evening Post*, the *Index of Pittsburg Life*, and perhaps others. Despite occasional periods of gloom, during which she proclaimed her determination to go back to her beloved Nebraska and the people who meant the most to her, she seems to have been, on the whole, well satisfied with her life as a career woman earning her own way and making a name for herself. Her ability to move among this and freelance writing arrangements—including, for a few months in 1900 to 1901, a stint as a translator in Washington, D.C., that yielded a group of magazine sketches and the glimpse of Washington officialdom that appears in *The Professor's House*—demonstrates her practical savvy and survival skills.[13]

Cather seems to have been well satisfied, too, with her social life during these years. Her letters indicate a whirl of activities. In the spring of 1899 this whirl produced the most important single event in her personal life not only in these early career years but perhaps in her entire lifetime. Still moving in the theatrical world, she went backstage to the dressing room of an actress she had known in Lincoln and there met Isabelle McClung.[14]

Woodress describes Isabelle as "the tall, handsome daughter of a socially prominent and affluent Pittsburgh family" (*Literary* 139). Her father was a judge, her mother a member of the powerful Mellon family. Their home on Murray Hill Avenue, soon to be home to Cather as well, was a mansion where, Woodress continues, the McClungs "lived expansively and expected their children to conduct themselves as well-behaved young socialites." Isabelle's main interest, however, was in the arts. Although it is uncertain to what extent she overtly resisted her eminent parents' expectations, it is clear that to at least some degree she set herself apart within the family. In Hermione Lee's words (58), she challenged her father's "orthodoxies" by "hobnobbing with 'Bohemians'" such as actresses and writers.[15] By spring 1901 when Cather returned to Pittsburgh from her stint in Washington to accept a teaching job at Central High School, if not before, Isabelle invited her to move into the McClung home. There they shared a suite of three rooms perched above the main two floors of the house.

Although this move must have made a considerable difference to Cather financially, since it cannot be imagined that the prominent McClungs would suddenly begin to take in paying boarders, it did not relieve her of the necessity of working for a living. She continued in teaching for the next five years, initially as an emergency replacement at Central High covering classes in Latin and algebra, but by the next fall in the school's English department. There and at Allegheny High School, where she became head of the department in 1903, she was seen as a conscientious, demanding teacher who maintained a decidedly unconventional persona and related to her students in unusually direct ways. Her status in the McClung household afforded her the privilege of inviting a favored few to tea, and it is clear from published responses as well as from letters at the Willa Cather Pioneer Memorial in Red Cloud that being so invited was a memorable experience. Her students recalled her with great warmth.[16] She seems to have liked teaching, both for its association with young people and because it afforded her the intellectual stimulation of life on the fringes of cultural leadership.

A more important after-school activity was her writing. But like many others before and since, Cather found the time constraints of teaching unconducive to literary work. She told Dorothy Canfield Fisher many years later that during this period she taught all day, wrote at night, and made no progress.[17] That was an exaggeration. She did make progress, at least to the extent of publishing a number of stories in good magazines. "Jack-a-Boy" appeared in the *Saturday Evening Post* in March 1901, the month she began teaching and moved into the McClung house. Four poems were published in 1902, the year she made her first trip to England and France, and her vanity press volume of poems, *April Twilights*, in 1903. "A Death in the Desert" appeared in *Scribner's* in January 1903, "A Wagner Matinée" in *Everybody's Magazine* in February 1904, and "The Sculptor's Funeral" and "Paul's Case" in *McClure's* in January and May of 1905. These four stories plus an additional three (including the vengeful "Flavia and Her Artists") would make up *Troll Garden*, published in 1905. One can understand that in retrospect this production might seem like very little for so much effort, but she *was* making headway, and Isabelle McClung's admiring solicitude must have helped considerably.

Whether Cather's relationship with McClung was lesbian in a physical sense can never be known. If it was, it is little wonder that she would have wished to conceal its nature, since both the categorizing and the stigmatizing of lesbians greatly increased during the early years of the twentieth century. She had already, in a letter to Louise Pound, lamented the unfairness of defining friendships between women (she enclosed the phrase in quotation marks) as unnatural.[18] Such definitions and what Carroll Smith-Rosenberg calls a "taxonomical scrutiny" of sexuality became increasingly common in the 1890s in response to the work of Richard Krafft-Ebing in Germany, followed by Havelock Ellis, and reached a "crescendo" in the 1910s in concert with resistance to suffrage (265–80). Cather's concern for privacy may have been at least in part a response to the much-publicized scientific discourse on sexual deviance.

In a way, though, it does not matter whether the relationship of Cather and McClung was physically lesbian, since it is absolutely clear that it was emotionally so. They were devoted to each other. Even Woodress, who dismisses assertions of Cather's lesbianism as an "inference" based on no "external evidence," calls it "a great love that lasted a lifetime." Surely he is right on both counts. Nevertheless, his dismissal of the subject evades its importance, and his insistence that "there is not one reference to sexual relations in all the hundreds of [Cather's] letters"

(141) can be credited only if one takes it in the narrowest sense. The many letters she must have written to Isabelle over the years did not survive her determination to dispose of such documents, but her early letters to and about Louise Pound, speaking of her desire for a kiss and her excitement at driving one-handed or at times with no hand at all, as well as a much later letter to Edith Lewis (apparently the only one still in existence), are unmistakably ardent in tone. The relationship with Isabelle was at any rate conspicuous enough to attract snide remarks. After Cather had begun to achieve notable success, Will Owen Jones, her onetime booster from the *Nebraska State Journal*, complained to Mrs. Gere about his protégée's self-satisfaction and "her friend, the adoring young lady from Pittsburg."[19]

The two terms of Will Jones's dual barb may not have been unrelated. Even before the two met, Isabelle McClung had defined herself as a patron of the arts and a companion of artists. Cather had defined herself as an unconventional woman of literary aspiration and ability who wished to escape the gender roles embodied by her mother and what she perceived as the gaucheries of her upbringing and youth.[20] The two found their needs answered in each other. For the next seventeen years Isabelle's life would center on facilitating Willa's writing—dissipating the inconveniences of daily life, shielding her, charming her, resolving problems, providing admiration and affirmation. It is entirely indicative that when the problem over "The Profile" arose, shortly before New Year's Day 1905, when Dorothy Canfield urged Cather to withdraw the story from the *Troll Garden* manuscript because it might offend a friend with a disfiguring facial scar, Cather left it to Isabelle to reply before writing to Dorothy herself. The dedication of the book was to McClung, under whose "loving and protective eye" it had been written.

Lee has written that after 1899 Cather's work was no longer "at the centre of her life," for the "centre" was now "taken up" by McClung. She offers this in explaining that "Cather the schoolteacher is not as vivid a figure as Cather the ambitious, busy journalist" and that her experience as a teacher does not seem to have "made a mark on her fiction" except for the obvious example of "Paul's Case" and a single other story (57). In another and very real sense, though, as McClung's support, encouragement, and general removal of impediments indicate, we can see that Cather's self-definition as a career woman and a writer was at the center of the relationship. The same would be true of her later relationship with Edith Lewis, who replaced the "lost lady" that Isabelle became in 1916 by marrying violinist Jan Hambourg (thereby continuing her role as patroness of the arts).[21]

The relationship with Isabelle McClung demonstrates, once again, Cather's ability to move freely between roles. Just as she learned, toward the end of her college years, to vary her self-presentation and thereby avoid reactions on the part of others that would stereotype her and impede her success, so she demonstrated, in her Pittsburgh years, the ability to move between the roles of journalist and socialite, or friend, or lover —and so, between the public and the private; between the journalist and the withdrawn artist (another kind of movement between public and private); between the person in charge and the person needing to be taken charge of.

Cather's involvement with McClung may also have signaled an ability to move between heterosexual and same-sex romance; she seems to have had a proposal of marriage about two years earlier. In April 1897 she told Mariel Gere that a young doctor had proposed and she was considering accepting him, though she did not love him. She may also have had a more serious heterosexual involvement with a man who was unavailable because he was already married. Those in the know, or who thought themselves in the know, believed that she was in love with the composer Ethelbert Nevin. According to a transcription made by Slote, Frances Gere at one point wrote in a satirical tone to her sister Mariel that Nevin was writing romantic songs addressed to Cather and she was writing "love sick" poems. The idea seems to have struck Frances as absurd. She concluded that Cather seemed to be hard hit. We have no way of knowing whether the Gere sisters' gossip was true, but Cather's own letters of the period do betray a kind of excitement related to Nevin, who died at the age of thirty-nine in February 1901, about a year after they met. Whatever her feelings, these two flutters of heterosexual romance were not the only ones she ever experienced. Even before the young doctor, she had spoken of the attentions of charming men, and she would later fall temporarily gaga over a young man in Arizona named Julio.[22]

I believe that these seemingly unimportant incidents are, in fact, very important indeed, and precisely *because* they seem to have had no practical effect on Cather's life at all. They were not expressions of a hidden essence but experiments in what a different sort of self might do or feel.

Not only was she moving between gender roles, but she was doing so in a freely performative way, broadening her repertoire of how to be a woman.

THE PERFORMANCE of gender is at the center of Cather's journalism, especially her theater reviews, both those written while she was at the University of Nebraska and those written after she became a career woman in Pittsburgh. It is that aspect of her nonfiction writing before she moved to New York to work for *McClure's* that I wish to consider in the remainder of this chapter.[23]

My purpose is not to attempt to develop a theory of performativity and identity, or subjecthood. Judith Butler has argued a position at one extreme; the essentialist notion that the self is a preexistent entity to be discovered, rather than made, lies at the other extreme. I am happy to adopt, and I believe Cather enacted, a position somewhere between these extremes, in which the intuited self is defined by the interaction of performance, on the one hand, and a sense of the adequacy or satisfactoriness of one performance versus another, on the other.

The great preponderance of Cather's early columns—and there are over five hundred of them—relate to the theater and performers.[24] In part, this was a function of circumstance. During her last two years in college and through her twenties she earned at least part of her living as a reviewer, or more broadly a theater critic. First by assignment and then as a way of advancing her career by building on an established reputation, her journalism was primarily concerned with the theater and the world of the arts generally. This is not to deny that she had a genuine interest in the theater, going back to the days in Red Cloud when as a child she would read the playbills for road companies with "thrilling excitement" (Lewis 36).[25] We can guess that she would have spent much of her time attending plays even without the motivation of fees for reviews and that her own interest would have led her to write about them, but perhaps not to the extent that she did. The fact that her livelihood came partly from theater reviewing surely helped keep her writerly attention turned toward the stage. If we forget that—and the tendency to do so is, after all, also gendered—we risk forming a picture of her as even more of an aesthete than she actually was.

These early columns do show an eager focus on the concerns and activities of high culture. It was there that she located her center of emphasis and value. We see very little, during this period of escape from the rusticity of home, of her later sympathies (sporadic as they may have been) with rural life and broadly democratic values. Indeed, her language for the world of high culture is as directly anti-democratic as it could well be: a language of royalty.[26] The world of art is a *kingdom.* Within this kingdom there exists a nobility consisting of those performers or creators whose work is characterized by passion or emotional power. *Power*—a word fittingly associated with a kingdom and one customarily gendered masculine—is indeed her particular term of praise for women whose work she admired as well as for men. Such commonality between the sexes in her standards of judgment was readily extended to her columns about books, just as her working out of aesthetic principles by which to judge theatrical performance was readily transferable to her own writing of fiction. Her journalism served multiple purposes. That is particularly true of her writing about the theater.

In much the same way as Cather's adoption of masculinized styles— but styles *for women*—problematized assumptions about female appearance and behavior, so the performances and the societal functions of actresses, "women who imitated other women (and sometimes even men)" on stage, "demonstrated and disturbed essential notions of the female." Both in their performances and in their uncertain social status, actresses "filled a particular need" at a time when gender and the social roles available to women were undergoing radical shifts (Stokes, Booth, and Bassnett 7, 11). By writing about women's roles as performing and creative artists, Cather continued her engagement in performative self-definition—as she also would, in a sense, in her two major pieces of ghostwritten nonfiction, *Mary Baker G. Eddy: The Story of Her Life and the History of Christian Science,* in which she examined the sources and meaning of a woman's power, and S. S. McClure's *Autobiography,* in which she assumed the voice of a powerful male. (She would later attribute to that experience her confidence in undertaking the male narrative voice in *My Ántonia.*) We should read her theater reviews in particular, then, as serving a wider range of needs and purposes than merely that of fulfilling an assignment. They are directly pertinent to her thinking about women writers and women's writings—and indeed, with their language of masculine dominion (the *king*dom), to her own elusive gendering.[27]

Certainly the literary aspect of the theater—its engagement with words, the structuring of stories, and the eliciting of viewers' (readers') emotional responses—involved aspects of craft that she needed to master as an emerging writer of fiction. But Cather also saw in the theater the enactment of what it meant to be a performer. It is no great transition from performing artist to creative artist (writer) or from actress (a performer in a men's world) to career woman more generally. She saw, too, the performance of great ranges of masculinity and femininity and, in the trouser roles for actresses that were so popular at the time, ambiguous stages in between. A surge of interest in female performers has been seen by historians of the theater as being "parallel with the increased repression of women in society generally through the nineteenth century" and the need for a "more affirmative view of woman in contrast to the passive notion of the angel of the house." The actress was "emblematic" both of the possibility for a woman to be an independent professional and of the conflicting moral demands on her.[28]

Not only was Cather interested in assessing the avenues to career satisfaction and public influence available to women on the stage, but she sought to understand the importance of physical beauty and personal style in the construction of a gendered persona. What attributes projected a female (or a male) presence that could favorably impress an audience? What attributes did the two share? Her review of an October 1895 performance of Shakespeare's *Antony and Cleopatra* implies that her expectations as to appearance and manner were rather conventional. The actress in the title role, she wrote, was a "coy, kittenish matron" who sat "bunched up on a motheaten tiger stroking Mark Antony's double chin. . . . And the queer little motions she made when she put that imaginary snake in her bosom, it was so suggestive of fleas" (*W&P* 243).

> She fainted slouchily upon every possible pretext and upon every part of the stage. And it was no ordinary faint either, it was a regular landslide. When the messenger brings the tidings of Antony's marriage she treats him exactly as an irate housewife might treat a servant who had broken her best pickle dish. When she lavishes her affection upon Antony, she is only large and soft and spoony. To call her amorous would be madness, she was spoony, and it was large, 200 hundred pounds, matronly spooniness.
>
> Her death scene was done in the modern emotional drama ten, twenty and thirty-cent carnival style. . . . Was ever Shakespeare in this fashion played? (*KA* 293)

When she wrote lampoon, she was good at it. What she lampooned here was the failure to be slim, glamorous, and youthful, in addition to the failure to be graceful or convincing in the part. Her comments about the kittenish matronly Cleopatra show that she appreciated conventional female beauty and grace.

Cather saw many of the most famous performers of her day, and she seems to have been fascinated by them—even to the extent of assembling a book of open letters to actors and actresses to be called "The Player Letters." It was never published, but three of the "letters" were printed as columns. A few performers drew her prolonged attention and repeated comments. Although most of their names are now known only to specialists in theater history, I want to summarize her views of these few at some length in order to demonstrate continuities in her thinking about art, artists, and gender—and thus, about herself.

Among actresses she particularly praised (not surprisingly) Sarah Bernhardt (1844–1923), whom she first saw in Sardou's *La Tosca* in 1892 in Omaha, and Eleanora Duse (1854–1924). She also gave special notice to Clara Morris (1848–1925), who appears in *The Song of the Lark* and may have been the model for the actress Jim Burden and Lena Lingard see in *Camille* in *My Ántonia*; Helena Modjeska (1840–1909), who makes an important appearance in *My Mortal Enemy*; and Julia Marlowe (1866–1950). Among males, she gave particular attention to Richard Mansfield (1857–1907), pronouncing him "the foremost American actor of his time" (*W&P* 675); the comedian and romantic lead Nat Goodwin (1857–1919); and the popular Joseph Jefferson (1829–1905). Her comments on E. S. Willard (1853–1914) and Clay Clement (1863–1910) are also of interest, and she greatly admired Alexander Salvini (1861–96), famous for his performance of d'Artagnan in *The Three Guardsmen*, one of her favorite plays. In discussing these performers she seems to have found two issues particularly intriguing: whether their "power" was *emotional* or *intellectual* in origin and whether the artist's ego was submerged in the act of performance or enlarged.[29]

Joseph Jefferson was best known as Rip Van Winkle, a role he had played since 1865, and as Bob Acres in *The Rivals*, a role in which Cather saw him at least once. On November 9, 1896, she saw Jefferson as Rip at Pittsburgh's Alvin Theatre (that "kingdom of artifice") and praised the "rare perfection" that kept the role from becoming "hackneyed" (*W&P*

422). Both in this review and in an Open Letter published in the *Lincoln Courier* December 2, 1899, she emphasized qualities of emotional depth and sympathy that are often stereotyped as feminine. He gave, she thought, a "rich humanity" to his characters and conveyed an affinity for childhood and for the "hills and the sunshine" of the Catskills (*W&P* 681–84).

In praising Richard Mansfield, she emphasized quite the opposite: intellect. Whereas Jefferson was "genial," Mansfield was "brilliant" and "complex"; Jefferson's art sprang "warm from the heart," Mansfield's "white hot from the brain" (*W&P* 684–86). Reviewing a performance of Clyde Fitch's *Beau Brummell* on April 23, 1894, she called Mansfield "self-sufficient" and an "intelligent and educated man" and compared the play to Thackeray's novel *Henry Esmond*—high praise indeed, since as Curtin points out she then regarded that work as the greatest of English novels.[30] Her swerve from an emphasis on emotion is explicit: "Any actor with an emotional nature can play roles in which the emotions are simple and decided," but the "faculty of analysis" enables Mansfield to "touch chords that are not often struck." Intelligent, studious, technically brilliant, and idiosyncratic, Mansfield was able to get inside another's skin and convey the sense of that being to his audiences —the very achievement in which she would later exult as a writer. In the end, then, she saw Mansfield and Jefferson as drawing their "power" (*W&P* 54–56) from virtually opposite sources. In the less well known Clay Clement she saw a combination of the two, "scholarly and methodical mind" with "warmth of sentiment," as well as the craft to "make other men feel" (*W&P* 191–92). After several years on the stage, Clement had returned to school and completed a degree at the University of Chicago, and Cather extolled the feeding of imagination on "whatever is best in science, letters, or art."

She also contrasted Jefferson and Mansfield with respect to the issue of whether art was an endeavor of expanded or submerged ego. She found Jefferson "seemingly dormant in artistic ambition" (*W&P* 681–84) —a pronouncement that supports Rosowski's judgment that she prized selflessness in art.[31] Similarly, when she interviewed Clement she found his "modest unassertiveness" the "most impressive thing about him," rhapsodizing that he "subordinate[d] himself at all times" and had "a nature beautifully simple and sincere" (March 10, 1895, *W&P* 190–93). But beautiful simplicity did not usually strike her as the highest level of artistic mentality, and she did not—in reason, could not—admire this relative newcomer in the way she admired the complex egoist Richard Mansfield, whom she saw as an imperious Ulysses "forever roaming with a hungry heart" and a performer of strong individuality or "eccentricity" (489). It was Mansfield whom she herself would more nearly come to resemble.

Though personally aloof or even scornful of his audience, in character Mansfield could convey real humanity. The popular comedian Nat Goodwin also had a "gift of reaching out to the people and appealing to them" (*KA* 130). As Slote writes, Goodwin, too, held a place in the Kingdom of Art (127). Even a very fine court jester, though, was still only a jester. Cather found Goodwin skillful and enjoyable, a "graceful vagabond," but lacking in "sincerity" (131), or what Matthew Arnold would have called high seriousness. Yet she could not help feeling a certain fondness for Goodwin. Like Jefferson, Goodwin was usually modest enough not to overreach himself, and she applauded his good judgment. He could not rise to "legitimate drama," which required "a certain passion for intellectual problems, a taste for fine shades of interpretation, a consecration of purpose" that he did not possess (*W&P* 463).

In contrast, E. S. Willard, another actor to whom she assigned a lower place in the kingdom despite admiring his work very much, was "one of the keenest intellectual interpreters of modern drama, and as such [deserved] to be taken seriously." His dedication to "studious" preparation "rather renewed one's faith in the seriousness of the drama." But Willard lacked "warmth" and "magnetism," the emotional side of the equation. His appeal was solely to his audience's intellect, so that "you never for a moment feel that the man's whole self is speaking to you across the footlights" (*W&P* 487).

The quandary of intellect versus emotion was one Cather never resolved, any more than she did the quandary of craft versus personal presence. No one quality seemed to her sufficient to constitute "power." The great actor needed both, just as the great novelist did—and greatness was a quality that deeply concerned her.

Clearly, if Cather found these actors fascinating and significant, she found the female performer even more so. In the figure of the actress she confronted the nature and potential rewards of the woman artist and pondered issues that impinged on her aspirations as a writer, another kind of performer before the public. This is not to say that she did not watch male performers with a sense of self-discovery. My point is precisely that she did, that her fascination with actors of both sexes derived in large measure from their performing on stage the very role she was seeking to perform, that of the creative artist who could draw on traits commonly assigned to both sexes and personal resources defined as both intellectual and emotional. Despite her statement that women had only the "power" of love to draw on (*KA* 349)—an early pronouncement made with undergraduate effusiveness—it is clear that she expected more. One wonders if she was aware of Sarah Bernhardt's having attributed to women performers the quality of "intellectuality" (quoted in Horville 59).[32]

Bernhardt was Cather's primary touchstone of greatness in an actress, chiefly because she conveyed an intense and seemingly genuine "passion" that could never be confused with dripping sentimentality (*W&P* 39). In 1901, almost a decade after having first seen her on stage, Cather could still be moved to "trembles" by Bernhardt's intensity (820). She shared little of the public's fascination with the actress's private life, resisting, even at an early date, the common view that women in public roles should be uplifting and inspire the world to goodness. Demanding no higher standards of conduct for the female performer than for the male, she commented succinctly that "very few of the world's great artists have been desirable acquaintances"—an early germ, perhaps, of Thea Kronborg, in *The Song of the Lark*. She would like to sit and watch Sarah the Grand night after night, she wrote, "but heaven preserve me from any very intimate relations with her" (*W&P* 49).

Between Bernhardt and Duse, another of the most celebrated actresses of the time, Cather saw a contrast much like that between Mansfield and Jefferson. Once again she was devoted to both, Bernhardt the actress of the "grand gesture style" and Duse the artist of "contained gestures," "realist acting," and "careful control." She more than once compared the two—not surprisingly, since they at times pitted themselves directly against each other—and when their repertoires at competing theaters in London in 1895 included two plays in common she saw the situation as a deliberate challenge of Duse by Bernhardt for the allegiance of audiences and critics.[33] Bernhardt was fifty years old to Duse's thirty-five, but her "wrinkles did not trouble her," and she still had "her whirlwind of passion and her flawless art," her "power and magnetism" (*KA* 118). The London critics who had proclaimed Duse the greater of the two "now declared that [Bernhardt] alone was great and that there was none like unto her." Cather's impulses carried her both ways.

At its essence, the issue involved restrained versus flamboyant style as well as artistic ego. Is the greatest artist a figure of negative capability who effaces herself in her creation, opening herself to the inpouring of another being in order to pour it out again in performance? Or does the artist take imperial possession of the external world and use it to reflect and express her supreme self? Finally, Cather believed both. She exulted in Bernhardt's "physical excitement" and in Duse's "spiritual exaltation." For Bernhardt, art was "a sort of Bacchic orgy"; for Duse, a "consecration" (*KA* 119). It was impossible to admire one and not the other. Struggling with the issue, Cather invoked the significant and masculinizing term *power*: Bernhardt's "power" had a "royal" quality about it that made her like Cleopatra (118)—an assessment that incorporates her metaphor of the Kingdom of Art.

In a discussion of Verdi's *Aida*, an opera whose Egyptian subject links it with the figure of Cleopatra, Edward Said writes that the metaphor of royalty in definition of the artist "dovetail[s] conveniently with an imperial notion of a non-European world" (117). I argue later that Cather in fact participated in a mentality of imperialism—that is, American imperialism, where the language of royalty is curiously inappropriate, even incoherent, but perhaps all the more suggestive for that reason. Here, in her identification of Bernhardt as a latter-day Cleopatra, it is more that the idea of empire dovetails conveniently with a royal idea of the artist. We know that the comparison with Cleopatra would have come naturally to her because of her ever-present awareness of Shakespeare. It was almost precisely a year after drawing the comparison that she wrote the comic review of a performance of Cleopatra quoted above, published in October 1895. That review goes on to pit Lillian Lewis's clumsy performance against one by Bernhardt played with a "regal queenliness" (*W&P* 243). But the comparison of Bernhardt with Cleopatra may have arisen, as well, from her awareness of *Aida*, which premiered in Cairo in late 1871 and became fabulously popular in the United States, perhaps only because of the spectacle that has traditionally accompanied its productions but perhaps also because its display of imperial authority caught the ambitions of a country just entering upon an aggressive imperialist project.[34] Cather saw *Aida* in Chicago in the spring of 1895.

If Bernhardt was a Cleopatra empowered by queenly egoism, Duse embodied another kind of reigning power and authority, that of Christly sacrifice. Her "greatness came through her sorrow"; her art was a "martyrdom," a surrender of self to gain a greater self, in which she "takes her great anguish and lays it in a tomb and rolls a stone before the door" (*W&P* 208; *KA* 119). This notion of the cost of art in "anguish" arose naturally enough from the fact that in 1895 Duse continued to perform despite serious illness. But the idea served a considerably larger purpose than its personal reference. By way of her comments on the famous actress, Cather pondered the cost of art in general, a subject that would engage much of her deepest thought and effort for years to come. She was exploring what Curtin refers to as "the paradox that the bright medusa of art at once fulfilled the personality and destroyed it" (*W&P* 56).

Duse differed from Bernhardt in another respect that would be of persistent significance for Cather, her insistence on keeping her personal life private, separating the person from the artist. The result, Cather thought, though this was not in fact true, was that "we know as little of [Duse's private life] as we know of Shakespeare." Commenting in 1894 when she was only twenty-one and still a student, Cather thought that in this respect Duse was "greater than any other woman who has ever been before the public." She had "kept her personality utterly subdued and unseen and spoken only through her art" (*W&P* 57). It is an early trace of the insistence on her own privacy that eventually led Cather to ban, in her will, the publication of her private letters. Even so, she continued to share the public fascination with Bernhardt, producing an adulatory review of her performances in Washington in 1901 when she appeared in five productions, four of which Cather saw, including *Camille* and Rostand's *L'Aiglon*, in which she played the trouser part of the duke in "the grand manner" (*W&P* 815).

Also among Bernhardt's roles in Washington was Hamlet. Her 1899 performance of Hamlet in Paris had been a sensation, and she had returned to the part several times. Bernhardt had a penchant for trouser roles, as well as for glamourous roles like Cleopatra. She could do both: perform an overcharged femininity and perform the male. According to one count, she played nine roles in masculine dress in the first three decades of her career and eighteen in the last three. Importantly, the tradition in which she played these roles, the French *travesti*, unlike the

English breeches parts with which Cather would presumably have been more familiar, did not involve revelation of the truth beneath the disguise.[35] Thus it was particularly disruptive of gender conventions; it never demonstrated that, after all, women are women and must remain so. We can conjecture that such roles, especially when undertaken by a performer she admired, would have particularly engaged Cather's imagination. It is surprising, then, that she does not seem to have reviewed Bernhardt's Hamlet, which she later made a topic of conversation in *My Mortal Enemy.*

Clara Morris and Juliet Marlowe clearly belonged to a far less exalted order than Bernhardt and Duse, but in reviewing them Cather treated issues of great importance to her developing conception of herself and the art of writing, as well as the art of the theater. One would scarcely expect her to admire an actress whose style could be described, as Morris's was, as "extravagant," "bizarre," and at times "hysterical."[36] Even so, she pronounced Morris "one of the greatest actors of all time," despite acknowledging that the "school" imputed to her ran to "noise and intensity," "grotesque" writhing, and "weep[ing] and gagg[ing]" (*W&P* 44, 46–47). Like Bernhardt and Duse, or like Jefferson, Mansfield, and Clement, Morris could generate emotional intensity that caught up an audience into a different plane of existence. She, too, possessed "power." What Cather meant by that term remained a "thing not named" (to borrow the phrase she famously used in her later essay "The Novel Démeublé"), though its effects could be sensed. Perhaps it is defined by the "passion" of the phrase she liked to quote from the elder Dumas, "four walls and a passion," a passion that could cast its net over the audience. Clearly, generalities ceased to matter when she encountered a performer who possessed or could generate that passion. Of Morris she insisted that "a cataract has a right to roar" (*W&P* 197).

The considerably younger Julia Marlowe at first struck Cather as lacking such power. Her early comments (in 1894 and 1895) refer to a girlish or "winning" quality, a sweetness and daintiness or even mere "prettiness"—terms implying excess of femininity—that disqualified her for roles of greatness (*W&P* 35–37). For that reason, apparently, she condemned as "madness" Marlowe's attempt at the role of Prince Hal in *Henry IV* (205). Later, however, she became, in Curtin's words, a "positive supporter" of Marlowe (669), praising her for being "admirably in the spirit" of her role and for speaking Shakespeare's blank verse

"as though she meant it" (670). By this time, in 1899, Cather had become an enthusiast for Marlowe's "beauty, her melodious vocalization,
her personal grace and charm, . . . her whole unique personality" (671),
and particularly her "considerable intellect" (205)—a quality she also
discerned in Minnie Maddern Fiske, who acted the lead role in an adaptation of *Tess of the D'Urbervilles* for 88 performances in New York
beginning March 2, 1897, and an adaptation of *Vanity Fair* for 116 performances beginning September 12, 1899. Fiske, she thought, once
again summoning a language of imperial power, "simply conquers and
masters you by sheer force of intellect" (444). In disregard of traditional
formulations associating emotion with women, intellect with men, she
noted intellect in males (Mansfield, Willard, Clement) and females
alike.

     Cather's comparison of Clara Morris to a cataract, clearly meant as
praise, was written in 1895. One doubts she would have thought the
same by 1898, when, in her maturity as a drama critic, she celebrated
Helena Modjeska's "naturalness and simplicity" and "freedom from
exaggeration" (*W&P* 458). She saw Modjeska first in 1892 in the role
for which she would later praise Marlowe, Rosalind in *As You Like It*;
then in 1893 in *Henry VIII*; and not again until 1898, in New York,
where she interviewed Modjeska over lunch (37). She found her "grand"
and "queenly"—terms that place her among the (female) royalty of
the Kingdom of Art. Modjeska's acting conveyed, Cather thought, an
"undercurrent of passion" so subtly that its sources were not noticed
(36)—a hallmark of the "thing not named." Although she never took
on the more conspicuous behaviors of the free woman (194), Modjeska
espoused freedom so effectively as to be banned from Russian-controlled
sectors of her native Poland. One wonders if some measure of Cather's
admiration was not stimulated by her evidence that an artist could, by
dint of personal force, make her mark in the real, political world. When
she memorialized Modjeska in *My Mortal Enemy*, she emphasized her
patriotism.[37]

     It was Modjeska's art, though, not politics, that most impressed
Cather. In reviewing her 1898 performance in Schiller's *Mary Stuart* (a
queen portraying a queen) Cather emphasized the quality, dignity, and
authority of her presence on stage and the "freedom" of her work from
"all the customary devices of an emotional actress." She was "a realist in

the best sense of the word" (*W&P* 458)—one of the best possible summaries of what Cather herself would attempt to be in her fiction. In Modjeska she found united the queenliness of Bernhardt and the almost religious quality of Duse, so that she momentarily forgot, in her extravagant praise, her own commitment to reserve: "To me there has always been something of the mediaeval in this woman, something of that spiritual fineness and delicate reserve which the age of chivalry bred in women; something of that dignity which walked between the shadow of the cloister and the effulgence of the court, something that accords with the mellow notes of the lute, something that belonged to the days when men thought a woman's love worth sacrifices, and pilgrimages, and hard-fought battles, like the Holy Grail or the sepulcher of Christ" (459). We must believe that the impetus was powerful indeed for Cather to break into such empurpled prose so late in her development as this. Fully six months later she was still coming back to the experience, writing that there had always been, for her, "something of the chatelaine about this woman, something indefinably exquisite and patrician." Modjeska's, she summarized, was "an art which gives wings to the imagination rather than fire to the senses" (461). The measure of nobility in her Kingdom of Art had achieved definition.

Cather continued to write about the theater until 1901. By that time her newspaper columns were mainly devoted to books and authors. But important continuities link her theater reviews and her columns about writing. Gender is central in both, as is the challenge of establishing a style or voice. Her standards for the theater are by no means rigidly consistent. They might be described as radically empirical, emerging from the experience itself. Much as she valued craft, she valued even more an intangible and finally indefinable power or authority in performance. If she generally admired an art of restraint and performers of dignity and assurance in both their onstage and offstage presence, she could also value those who violated these standards if they managed, in whatever way, to achieve a compelling performance, one that caught up its audience, transported it, and wrung it emotionally. She demanded seriousness in the artistic endeavor, as well as something that might be called genuineness. Most often, she located the actor's power in an ability to lose the self in the creation. But that does not mean that she was unimpressed by the assertion of powerful egos such as Mansfield's or

Bernhardt's. Cather was interested in voice, but also in physical bearing and appearance, physical beauty. But beauty mattered less than magnetism or power—stage presence, we might say. Finally, and this is of great importance, the qualities she admired in female performers were the same as those she admired in males: power, emotional authenticity, intelligence. It is well to remember this fact as we consider her columns about books and writers, where the problem of gender becomes more pressing.

4

FINDING A VOICE / MAKING A LIVING

I had but a minstrel's torch
And the way was wet and long.
—"The Poor Minstrel"

To the old, old ports of Beauty
A new sail comes home!
—"Recognition"

PROBABLY MORE has been written about a column Willa Cather published in the *Lincoln Courier* on November 23, 1895, as a recent college graduate, than about anything else she ever wrote as a journalist. Addressing the issue of gender more directly than she had at any time before or (with a single exception) ever would again, she declared her distrust of women writers and called on women to write like men: "I have not much faith in women in fiction. They have a sort of sex consciousness that is abominable. They are so limited to one string, and they lie so about that. They are so few, the ones who really did anything worth while. . . . When a woman writes a story of adventure, a stout sea tale, a manly battle yarn, anything without wine, women and love, then I will begin to hope for something great from them, not before" (*KA* 409). This passage is sometimes regarded as the young Cather's definitive statement on women writers. But it needs to be read in context.

Cather's early journalism was the school in which she learned to be a writer. Both in the mastery of technique and in her development of a distinct voice, she came to professional maturity in her years in the newspaper and magazine business. She was also writing stories; twenty-seven were published in the decade 1892–1902. But it was primarily in her nonfiction that she became a professional. She learned to write fast,

yet with verve—skills that would carry over to her career in fiction. At
the same time, she thought *about* books and writing and incorporated
her views of others' books into her development of goals for the writing of
her own. These early professional writings allow us to trace her thinking on a range of personal as well as literary and public issues.[1] They
have generally been read as a collective mapping of an aesthetic realm.

Aesthetics—the Kingdom of Art—was enormously important to Cather
and would remain so. Both in her journalism and in the stories she was
writing at the same time, she was engaged in an effort to work out a set
of aesthetic principles. She envisioned art as an escape from life on the
prairie, a motif that appeared in her first published story, "Peter," and
would be insistent in stories of the next decade such as "Eric Hermannson's
Soul," "A Wagner Matinée," and "The Sculptor's Funeral." The title of
her 1920 collection, *Youth and the Bright Medusa,* referred to her own
youthful fascination with the (possibly treacherous) allure of art. Even
so, her feet were firmly planted on the ground of a real America, which
was neither a kingdom nor a culture primarily concerned with art. It is
important, then, to balance her engagement with the world of art against
other needs and interests that her journalism was serving. Because she
was working as a reviewer but was allowed by her newspapers to go beyond simply writing reviews—she was a columnist accorded a colum-
nists's range—her journalism had a high transfer value in helping her
define her goals and standards as a writer of fiction and practice her
craft. She thought and wrote about books, and in the process of doing
so, learned to write her own books.

Let us drop back for a moment to the first pieces Cather wrote as a
regular contributor to the *Nebraska State Journal,* in November and
December of 1893, a series of sketches or vignettes of the American
scene. Here we see her groping for material for the paying work she
now had an opportunity to do and trying out her hand at elements of
fiction writing: anecdote, visual scene, cameo characterization, dialogue.
These early sketches tend to be broadly sentimental, limning such stock
types as the unworthy father who weeps upon seeing his child. In some
ways they seem more amateurish than the stories she had already published, perhaps because of the need to strike an effect in little space,
perhaps because she was unsure of her audience's expectations. Death and
religion are recurrent themes, with several sketches launching a surprisingly aggressive assault on the falsities of organized religion. Together

with passing remarks in later columns and personal letters, they show us
a Cather in active rebellion against her Baptist upbringing and the general religiosity of her culture. She praised the noted "atheist and free-
thinker" (as Slote accurately labels him) Robert Ingersoll, calling him a
"man of letters" with "great beauty of language" and expressing no
trace of offense at his views (*KA* 210–11).

Another thread we see in these early sketches is a pervasive racism, a
habit of mind Cather shared with her culture.[2] Traces of racism are evident in her letters and fiction as well (for example, "The Affair at Grover
Station" and "The Dance at Chevalier's," where she denigrates Chinese
as "a race without conscience or sensibilities," with "amphibious blood,"
and Mexicans as "Greasers" who will "knife you in the dark") but never
more simplistically than here.[3] Even when her invocation of race seems
motivated by an intent to espouse some notion of "brotherhood of
man" (*W&P* 5), there is an underlying disparagement of nonwhites. A
Negro preacher stands up wearing two pairs of glasses: how can such a
detail not stigmatize him as foolish? A black child depicted with overt
pathos speaks in a grossly distorted approximation of dialect to a "woolly-
headed" companion (8). A "Chinaman" working in a laundry has glit-
tery eyes and, apparently for reasons of congenital incapacity, cannot be
"benefited" by "modern civilization" (23). Here as elsewhere, "civilization" means European civilization. In other columns the Chinese are
casually and gratuitously declared "dead inside," and the 1894–95 war
between China and Japan, which led to the independence of Korea, is
dismissed as a "mutual extermination of barbarians" (*KA* 199, 316).

Perhaps the most blatant retailing of stereotypes came in a piece
published in the *Journal* on November 26, 1893. A "peculiar-looking"
baby with the "unmistakable chin and the unmistakable nose of an unmistakable race" is shown to be, even in his carriage, "rubbing his little hands
together." When he cries, his mother, "a dark stout woman of her people,"
gives him a penny, which he grasps "eagerly" and examines "as though
seeing if it were genuine" before folding his fingers around it and set-
tling with a "long sigh of content" into dreams of future commerce
(*W&P* 21). Never again, even in her portrait of Louie Marsellus in *The
Professor's House*, would Cather express such crude anti-Semitism.[4]
There is plenty of brittle disillusionment and falsity to go around in
these earliest pieces; it is not as though she divided the world between
virtuous whites and inferior people of color, or for that matter happy

whites and unhappy people of color. The tarring by her still-adolescent brush is widely scattered. Yet the note of ethnic disparagement is conspicuous and troubling.

What are we to make of it? She was only a junior in college at the time, not even twenty years old. Very few writers would be well served by having their early efforts spread before the public eye and consulted in later years. Certainly Cather is not. Edith Lewis tells us that she "bitterly resented, in later life, proposals to collect and publish" her "student work" generally (33). Yet she did write these pieces; they were bought and published at a dollar a column; and they indicate an element in her mentality that was not at all oppositional to her culture, as she liked to see herself, but quite reflective of it. Perhaps the best we can say is that she learned quickly and turned to other forms and subjects. The worst we can say is that traces of ethnic slurring and typecasting would mar even her mature work.

Tone is an important issue in Cather's early journalism, and one directly pertinent to the "manly battle yarns" column. The apparent self-assurance of her writing contributed to her development of a reputation as an unflinching panner of performances she considered inferior. Her own editor said that she wielded a "meatax." Improbable as it seems, considering that she was still only a college student, she became known among theater companies for her "biting frankness" and was visited in Lincoln by a major impresario to discuss her attacks on his performers. Slote's account of these student writings (many of them done, however, in a professional capacity) emphasizes this quality of absoluteness and describes the youthful Cather as a person of certainty, free of self-questioning or inner dividedness, who "liked a good fight" and had a "conviction that she was right."[5] A more recent critic, following Slote, has characterized the Cather of the Lincoln years as "authoritative" or even rather godlike in her self-assurance (Peck 23). On the surface, the record of her newspaper columns and her work as editor of the campus literary journal would appear to bear out such a judgment. But I believe the early writing is deceptive in this respect, its assertiveness in some ways a screen or compensation for doubt, a gambit that will be recognized by anyone who has known very bright young people exploring their limits. She would later call her early brash tone "foamy-at-the-mouth" (WCIP 12). We should remember, too, that she often held dual or even multiply conflicting impulses *at the very time* that she was making such pronouncements. She spoke with a grandly Emersonian disregard for consistency.

Conflicting impulses are evident in her reading during this period as well, an arresting mélange of the ponderous and the ephemeral, the classic and the up-to-the-minute, the racy and the moralistic. To be sure, her literary sympathies ran strongly to romanticism. She would later espouse the value of literary "escape," but the escape she enjoyed was often of a sort not at all otherworldly or Emersonian, but more of the derring-do variety. Conflicting impulses are evident, too, in the contrast between Cather the aesthete and Cather the practical mover and shaker, the young woman wanting to get ahead in what was still a man's world. As Slote points out, she was "smart, advanced, eager to achieve" (*KA* 33). This is not to say that a romanticist cannot be smart, advanced, and eager to achieve. But her hands-on engagement in newspaper journalism, which included layout as well as column writing, seems to indicate a streak of practicality somewhat at odds with the image of the escaping artist. An interviewer in 1921 would say the trait that came most readily to mind for her was downrightness (*WCIP* 43); violinist Yehudi Menuhin called it her "let's-lay-it-on-the-table manner" (78). Edith Lewis as well described Cather as "downright" (*WCL* x). She manifested impulses toward both escape and involvement, toward the life of aestheticism and the life of the career woman.

For the most part, when writing about literature or the theater, Cather's tone was one of high seriousness, but several of her early pieces are humorous—contrary to her usual reputation as a sobersides. Besides spoofing the overweight Cleopatra, she tweaked the local Lansing Theatre by suggesting it exhibit its "pitiable" drop curtain (with a Latin inscription she defied any classical scholar to translate) for no more than fifteen minutes a night, on the agreement that playgoers would "all promise to look and suffer and get it over with" and could then be free to enjoy themselves (*KA* 173, 176). As befitted the editorial position of her paper,[6] she poked fun at the Populist Party in Kansas (March 11, 1894, *KA* 223) and, in a lighter vein, at a nautical melodrama whose plot had "two villains (both foiled)" and various other "dingy and disreputable persons who posed as the admirals of various fleets," all of whom were set to work "with kisses and curses and pistols and cutlasses and denunciations and explanations, till finally everything cleared up and things went universally well to the tune of 'Hail Columbia'" (253). A concert by the Sousa band produced "sounds that make angels—and certainly did make some babies—weep bitterly" (200). There is not enough of this sort of thing to justify labeling Cather a humorist, and there was less as time went on, though rare bits of humor do peek quietly out from around the edges of her mature fiction.

From the first, she tried to work out a coherent position regarding the place of morality in aesthetics—an issue of notorious elusiveness. In a piece in the November 1891 *Lasso* that she at least edited if not wrote, she was clear that social reform had no place in art. Tolstoy, she thought, would have been "a better writer" if he had not taken on a "mission to reorganize society and reconstruct the universe" (*KA* 377). In general she followed John Ruskin in linking bad art, bad taste, and bad morality. Precisely how that linkage worked she wisely left unclear, proclaiming (as a sophomore) that "a man can lie and cheat and sin with his brush as well as with his pen or tongue" and that "distorted art is an insult to nature and to humanity" (174). Most assuredly, good moral character could not guarantee good art, though bad character might manifest itself in bad art. The "cleverness" and "insincerity" of Oscar Wilde, for example, and his "malicious . . . claims that nature imitates art" (*W&P* 153–54) would inevitably produce an art lacking in honesty or genuineness. Although she left Wilde's homosexuality among "thing[s] not named" here, she seems to have believed that it made itself "felt upon the page"—or on the stage ("The Novel Démeublé," *OW*, 41).

Throughout her career Cather would continue to hold these beliefs —that morality, taste, honesty, and art are interrelated, but that it is not the business of literature to reform society. In the 1936 letter to *Commonweal* reprinted as "Escapism" she was still fighting "propaganda" in fiction (*OW* 23). She did not believe the "mission" of the artist was to "clean the Augean stables." Indeed, "no man, or woman, is ever justified in making a book to preach a sermon," for "art is its own excuse for being" (*KA* 406). The "or woman" here is noteworthy, since Cather generally used the masculine as if it were inclusive. By explicitly including females in the same aesthetic law as males, she discounted the traditional assumption that women were to be the special bearers of moral teaching or that such teaching was the only excuse for women's taking a public voice.

Even so, anything approaching salaciousness in the theater was likely to offend her (*KA* 274). She protested when a minister aspersed the morality of an actress merely because she performed on Sunday, but she expected serious newspaper reviewers to "disparage anything gross and vulgar" and thought some subjects inherently "not fit" for the stage (*W&P* 119, 233, 205). Similarly, she denounced Emile Zola repeatedly and at length for what she regarded as degraded subject matter and failure to redeem it with ideals (139–42). Yet the frequency with which she returned to Zola suggests she may not have been as certain of her dislike as she claimed.

When pondering the connection between private character and artistic performance, Cather was again inconsistent. She knew that somehow the person and the artist were connected, and she adopted biblical language to make the point: "A man cannot spend his life or even a few years of it among the husks and the swine and then go back clean and upright to his father's house"—or perform Romeo (December 2, 1894, *KA* 151–52). Yet two months later she insisted that people should go to the theater solely to see acting; the "personal character of the actor is none of their business and should not enter into the question" (February 24, 1895, *KA* 150). The world was "sick," she said, of the "boasted morality of the court of England" for refusing to knight a fine performer merely because he had done plays of a "risqué nature" (June 30, 1895, *KA* 191). When Oscar Wilde was a figure of public scandal, she burst out in what Curtin describes as a "harshly righteous" pronouncement (*W&P* 263): "A man who founds his art upon a lie lives a lie" (May 19, 1895, *W&P* 154), but her revulsion seems to have been at public notoriety itself as much as Wilde's "crime."

The tie between morality and art was a conundrum she pondered without finding an answer. She believed that at some point "evil affects and weakens art" (December 2, 1894, *KA* 151–52), yet remained convinced that the artist should not "write for a 'moral purpose'" because "art itself is the highest moral purpose in the world" (May 17, 1896, *KA* 378). As this sequence demonstrates, Cather was not nearly so assured in her judgments as she sometimes appears. She was forming her taste, even though individual pieces might sound as if it were already well formed. She was also formulating her goals, even though it might appear that she knew exactly where she was going.

In her theories of art and the artist, Cather was in many respects, as Rosowski and others have described her, very much the romanticist. She participated in what has been seen as a defining trait of the nineteenth-century romantic artist, the critique of industrialism (Rubin 2).

Her focus on individual performers in her theater reviews, consistent
with her lifelong interest in the exceptional individual, is also a typical
romantic stance. She emphasized mastery of craft, of course, but never
craft severed from passion. To poet Sara Teasdale she once confided
that the only reason she could see for writing poetry was to let an emotion blossom.[7] Like her comments on stage performers, her remarks on
writers emphasized emotional impact or power. It is a quality that seems
to have been tied in with the commitment to vitalism or a sturdy venture-
someness that would issue in her notorious praise of male adventure
stories as the measure of what was worthwhile in fiction.

WE RETURN, then, to the "manly battle yarn" column of November 23,
1895. Sharon O'Brien has developed her theory of the shape of Cather's
career as a move away from the position stated in that column—"I have
not much faith in women in fiction"—toward an identification with
women writers and attitudes of submersion and affiliation often identified as innately feminine. Only when she had "reconciled the woman
and the artist," O'Brien argues, could Cather "write from her own necessarily female experience without feeling that she was limited to telling
a woman's story" (*Emerging* 5). It is a powerfully persuasive argument.
Nevertheless, the rejection of women writers Cather announced in this
early column does not adequately represent even her *early* position on
women writers, let alone her later views. In typical fashion, she is not
entirely consistent, but by working backward and forward from the
notorious column and by placing it in its biographical context we may
be able to develop a better understanding of how she viewed the position
of women writers and female experience in literature in those years.

    If she lacked faith in women novelists, who, then, were the stars of
her literary firmament? It is impossible to say with certainty. We cannot
use frequency of reference as a definitive index. She was engaged in
commercial writing for the press, and her choice of subjects must have
been considerably influenced by her own or her editors' ideas of readers'
interests. Still, since she seems to have had a good deal of freedom and
to have enjoyed using it, frequency of reference is worth noting. Not
surprisingly, it was Shakespeare whom she most often invoked during
her college years. He was simply her measure of greatness. Beethoven,
for instance, is adequately measured by calling him "the Shakespeare of
music" (*W&P* 178). The value of French literature is defined by its being

"as necessary for a literary man" as Shakespeare (*KA* 60). After Shakespeare, the rest of her predominantly male list of literary greats would not be, by today's standards, self-evident: Balzac, Browning, Dumas (both *père* and *fils*), George Eliot, Henry James (whom she once called "the perfect writer"), Kipling, Keats, George Meredith, Ruskin, Robert Louis Stevenson, George Sand, Thackeray, Tolstoy. There were other names she mentioned frequently only to disparage them, or because she could not make up her mind: Hamlin Garland, Thomas Hardy, Howells, Ibsen, Zola. Indeed, Kipling might better be listed among this group than among her great lights; she returned to him with a frequency and manner that indicate he was worrisome to her: "sturdy, though scarcely classical," a lesser emulator of Stevenson but "of great promise" (*KA* 318, 192, 232).[8] Sturdiness was an important attribute at a time when voices of rebellion, in particular, were worrying that American literature was getting too "effeminate" (Shi 6).

Some writers Cather seldom mentioned nevertheless had a great importance to her. Jane Austen is one, Ralph Waldo Emerson another. Rarely mentioned in the journalism of her college years, Emerson served, when he *was* mentioned, as a measure of quality—a writer of "magnificent tranquility" who was to be numbered among literary "names to stir the hearts of men!" (*KA* 222). Notably, those listed in the heart-stirring roster that follows—Dickens, Thackeray, Emerson, Lowell, Longfellow, Hawthorne—are all male. Yet we know that both of the "great Georges," Eliot and Sand, were enormously important to her.[9] Curiously, in the notorious "manly battle yarn" column where Cather claimed she had "not much faith in women in fiction," she pronounced these two "anything but women" (409). It is a puzzling phrase that may have meant she was reserving the word *woman* for a category of person she could not esteem as she did them or that they were not women in any ordinary sense or the sense in which society in general understood so-called true womanhood. One wonders if she was aware of Sand's amorous life or her cross-dressing or of Eliot's irregular "marriage" to George Henry Lewes. If so, she could not have meant they were non-women because they did not engage in sexual love with men. Perhaps they were nonwomen in that they did not subordinate their writing to household duties? Or was it because they were free of what she called the "feminine . . . hankering for hobbies and missions," the urge to advance good causes (406)? She does not tell us.

We can see, at any rate, that the 1895 column was scarcely so encompassing as to constitute a summary statement of her attitude toward women writers. It was more of a momentary outburst. The very paragraph in which these statements occur gives them the lie by praising not only George Eliot and George Sand (though she pretends to exclude them as nonwomen) but also Brontë (which Brontë is not clear), who "kept her sentimentality under control," and Jane Austen, who was "in some respects the greatest of them all" (*KA* 409). Rather than a formulation of her considered position on women writers, then, we should read the column as a radically *unresolved* statement, even to the meaning of *them* in "greatest of them all." It was an effort to work out a troubling complex of feelings and judgments.[10]

One of those feelings—understandable enough in a recent college graduate casting about for employment, standing on the brink of a career in journalism but wishing to write fiction—was apprehensiveness about the severity of the competition. We need to keep that in mind when we read her disparagement of prolific woman writers: "I wish there were a tax levied on every novel published. We would have fewer ones and better." That anxiety, too, was gendered or indeed multiply gendered. Rather than fearing that as a woman she would be unable to achieve publication, she seems to have feared that with so many women being published she might be lost among them. Or perhaps that the popularity of novels by women such as Augusta Jane Evans and Marie Corelli, and their resultant labeling by defensive male powers as undistinguished, would mean that the competition for a place among the "names to stir the hearts of men" (here she was probably using the gendered noun with the intent of inclusiveness but may have meant it in its specific sense) would be loaded against her. That is, she may have been stirred to her outburst by real and on the whole sensible practical concerns.

She was assuredly stirred to it by her uncertainty over one writer in particular, the popular and sensational Ouida (Marie Louise de la Ramée). Cather's mother was a devoted reader of Ouida and other "melodramatic" writers, and Cather herself read them voraciously. In O'Brien's judicious words, however she might vilify Ouida and her peers (and we might add, however she might rebel against her mother), she had learned from the books her mother bought, borrowed, and read the important lesson that "writing as well as reading could be a female activity" (40). But as she defined her artistic standards in the course of her reading and writing during college, she came to believe that such writers as Ouida did not yoke their fertile and often thrillingly subversive imaginations to the discipline of craft.[11] Thus, by the standards of high art—the standards to which Cather increasingly gave her allegiance—they were not writers of greatness. They condemned themselves to membership in a category ("woman writer") that was both "limiting" and "belittled" by their failure to join the more "autonomous" and "celebrated" category of artist (Williams 215).

Here as elsewhere, Cather held exceptionalist views of her sex. As her royalist term the *Kingdom of Art* indicates, she was interested in the exceptional few, those of notable achievement, not the endeavors and the circumstances of the average. Many, even most, of the women writers she read presented the fearful spectacle of women who had the power to entertain but not to become members of the artistic elite. Moreover, they were marked by their readership as being of undistinguished status in the world of letters. Conversely, a fondness for Ouida, like bad taste in clothes, stigmatized readers as common, as belonging among "schoolgirls and ribbon-counter ladies" (*W&P* 696–97). Certainly Cather did not care to find herself among that group. In the notorious column where she laments that God "ever trusts talent in the hands of women," the diatribe against Ouida is launched by the sight of one of her books in the hands of "an elevator boy" (*KA* 408).[12]

Ouida is a painful example to Cather both because reading her may mark one as belonging among the lower classes socially (or among domesticated and frustrated women like her mother) and because Ouida herself is one of those writers who are so good that one wishes they could be *really* good. She has "great talent" and "the rudiments of a great style" but a style marred by "mawkish sentimentality and contemptible feminine weakness." Her lack of a sense of humor renders her unable, in effect, to be a good editor of her own work and thus, by Cather's emerging standards, a real professional. Because of that lack, she fails to perceive the "magnificently ridiculous" blotches on her work made by sentimental excess. But then, in Cather's view, such excesses are characteristic of "most women's pens" (*KA* 408).

We wince at the stereotyping. Yet it may be that the charge shows more good judgment than we first want to admit. Excesses would necessarily be characteristic of most women's pens if the ability to achieve restraint or balance, so that their efforts avoid unintended comic effects, is one that writers gain as they mature in their craft and if, as Cather seems to have believed, women's opportunities to do so were limited by male control of the profession and by cultural traditions that kept women's priorities focused on other, which is to say domestic, activities. Failure to "matur[e]" is indeed one of the flaws that evoke Cather's "disgust" with Ouida's books (*KA* 409). And to the extent that amateurish excesses can be traced to absence of a sense of humor, we might well regard them as one more mark of cultural gendering, since women in the High Victorian world, even more than men, were expected to be earnest.

Many issues were involved, then, in Cather's apparent betrayal of her sex in her column of November 23, 1895. Certainly she did not make a blanket dismissal of women writers. As we have already seen, she excepted from her diatribe the "great Georges" as well as Austen and one of the Brontës. Elsewhere she treated as an exception Mrs. Humphrey Ward, whom she perceived as the author of "really important novel[s]" (*KA* 375). Significantly, Ward had the "power" (that touchstone term) not only of invention but of artistic discipline, so that she could achieve structural "proportion." Yet Mrs. Ward, Cather thought, fell short of the highest levels of art because of failure to concentrate and minimize. She lacked "the power to make a whole picture stand out by a few masterly strokes," and in writing, as opposed to visual art, "detailed description has its disadvantages" (375). Already, in May 1896, though she had not yet named it, Cather saw the novel *démeublé* as the highest form of art in fiction.

We should note, too, that the "stout sea tale" column was written during a period of pronounced mood swings. Cather had graduated from the university in June. During the summer and again in December she wrote to the Gere sisters about how pretty and green Webster County was and how much fun she was having going to parties, talking with attractive young men, and riding around on her "wheel," or bicycle. But she was also feeling apprehensive and out of things. On January 2, she spoke of losing interest in everything, even suicide.[13] When we recall how prominent a motif suicide was in her early fiction, the jest loses some of its humor. Of the eight stories she had published at the time, counting one that very month in *Overland Monthly*, three include suicides or references to suicide: "Peter," "The Clemency of the Court," and "On the Divide." The remarks about good-looking young men in these letters signal that her anxiety about her future as a career woman included not a little element of anxiety about her future role as a woman in a heterosexual society more generally. "Married nightingales," she had written while still a student, "seldom sing" (*W&P* 176). It is scarcely surprising that her pondering of the achievements and the potential of women writers would reach a kind of crisis during this period, venting itself in her *Courier* column.

In the months that followed, Cather continued to ponder the woman writer and the woman performer—indeed, women's work in general; for instance, in a long column on the emerging nursing profession. One of her first projects for the *Home Monthly* was a column on the wives of the two presidential candidates, William Jennings Bryan and William McKinley. Scarcely over a week after her arrival in Pittsburgh and only four days after Bryan's celebrated "cross of gold" speech at the Democratic National Convention she wrote to Mrs. Gere asking for help with personal information about Mrs. Bryan. It is hard to know how much her sense of the magazine's audience and her eagerness to please her employer shaped the article that resulted. Even with its emphasis on both women's home involvements, however, and its sentimental gesture toward the McKinleys' deceased child, the piece shows a strong interest in the two women's intellectual lives and involvement in work. In the case of the plain-dressing Mary Baird Bryan, such an interest was an obvious one. An example of the "'New Woman' type at its best" (*W&P* 311–12), she was valedictorian of her college class, an avid reader, and an attorney admitted to the bar in Nebraska. With Ida McKinley, it would have been easy to stop with her personal charm and gracious social life, her willingness to let her own interests be subordinated to those of her husband "as every woman's must be," and her love for children. All of these qualities, which would surely have appealed to *Home Monthly* readers, are noted. But it is also noted that Mrs. McKinley worked in her father's bank "before the advent of the business woman, and certainly before the 'New Woman'" and "could do his work better and more thoroughly than any man" (309–10).

Over two decades later, in 1921, Cather would tell a reporter for the *Lincoln Sunday Star* that the "present movement of women into business and the arts . . . cannot help but be good" and would ask rhetorically, "As for the choice between a woman's home and her career, is there any reason why she cannot have both?" (*WCIP* 18). Her confidence on that occasion is notable but uncharacteristic. More typical are her pronouncements that "married nightingales seldom sing" and that every woman's interests "must be" subordinated to her husband's. It is not necessary to read the "must" in that comment as the optative; it may be simply descriptive: that's the way it is, that's what every married woman had better expect. A serious prospect indeed for a woman committed to her career and to the writing that could not yet be defined as a career, her fiction.

CATHER'S BOOK columns continued to be devoted primarily to James, Kipling, and other prominent males, especially of the vigorous outdoor sort—but not entirely. When she praised the "fireside style of book" that might appeal to a tired housewife (*W&P* 335), we can assume that the supposed preferences of the *Home Monthly* readership were guiding her pen. She continued to read and to find disappointing various writers in whom she saw "literary powers of the highest order" but failure to produce equivalent work (586). In April 1899 she briefly and dismissively took up her slightly older contemporary Gertrude Atherton, then (as Curtin notes) a writer of historical romances, saying that she doubted if Atherton would ever again do anything as good as her "unsubstantial" but "fairly good" *The Doomswoman*—left-handed praise indeed (696). Three months later she wrote one of the most memorable of all comments of one woman writer on another: a review of Kate Chopin's *The Awakening*.

The review tells us a great deal more than merely the fact that Cather did not like the book. O'Brien, who astutely links Cather's response to *The Awakening* with her dislike of the sentimentality and exaggeration she saw in such writers as Ouida, points out that in all such novels "the liberated, defiant heroine who deserts an uninteresting husband for a dashing love is still dependent on men for fulfillment" (181).[14] When Cather deplores Chopin's choice of subject, which she thought "new neither in matter nor treatment" (*W&P* 697), she may well be reacting to that fact. Comparing Edna Pontellier to Emma Bovary as a woman who "demands more romance out of life than God put into it," she in effect sounds, many years in advance of Rachel Blau DuPlessis, a call for "writing beyond the ending" of either marriage (as if that were the only possible satisfactory goal of a woman's life) or death. Edna's problem, Cather thought, was that she "really expect[ed] the passion of love to fill and gratify every need of life, whereas nature only intended that it should meet one of many demands." Such an expectation ruled out, for example, "what the arts and the pleasurable exercise of the intellect" had to give (698–99). Little wonder, then, that Cather regarded romantic passion with alarm and chose to spend her life in companionship with a supportive female partner rather than a husband, to whom any woman "must" subordinate her interests—even, apparently, in art and the pleasures of the mind.[15] Little wonder, too, that if even a writer such as Chopin, with her technical mastery, had to go on telling the stale story of obsession with love, she would continue not to have "a great deal of faith in women in literature." "As a rule," she confided in a November 1897 "Old Books and New" column, "if I see the announcement of a new book by a woman, I—well, I take one by a man instead." Since the "great masters of letters" were men, she preferred to "take no chances" (362). But once again she belies herself by going on to devote several long paragraphs to George Eliot, pronouncing several of her books "masterpieces." The problem remained a problem, and she obviously did "take chances" in her reading. She read, for instance, *The Awakening*.

At the same time as she was wrestling with the problem of women in literature, Cather was writing columns about women singers and actors. As we have seen, her appraisal of the actresses she most admired emphasized "power," a compelling emotional force combined with intellect. Looking for that same combination in women writers, she faulted both excessive emotionalism and excessive intellect (which she saw, for example, in Mrs. Humphrey Ward). Like the actress's power, that of the writer could be sapped by excess in either direction or by failure to convey much in little. Just as an actress had to convey great emotion or significance by a gesture or shift in intonation, a writer needed to establish a clear impression or force of meaning in a minimum of details. Her comments on singers continue in much the same vein. Those she admires, such as the American soprano Lillian Nordica, have "powerful," "all-conquering" voices (*W&P* 645), compelling stage presence, the artistic authority to make their audience forget where they are (526); those she does not admire lack "power to portray emotion of any kind" (393). "Personality," by which she meant the sense of a distinctive human presence inside the performance, is the "commanding" something (once again the language of governing power) that "counts" (756). This presence or vibrancy is an unanalyzable something because of which the performer *in toto* exceeds the sum of her skills (756)—in short, to borrow once again her famous phrase from "The Novel Démeublé," a "thing not named" or perhaps nameable.

Cather's music reviews were consistent with her theater reviews in that she was greatly interested in women's artistic force or "power," in voice, and in the mysterious connection between personhood and art. Just as that connection is felt though it can never be adequately explained, so does the connection between human voice and literary "voice" elude definition, though it is undeniably real. We can readily understand that at this stage in her professional emergence, as she struggled to establish her own voice as a writer and her own way of performing gender, she would find compelling interest in women performers and their voices.

CATHER HERSELF did not write the "stout sea tales" and "manly battle yarns" she called for in 1895, but she did experiment with masculine subjects of other kinds and with male voices. That she did so is in keeping with the versatility in personal gender roles she had developed during her college and early professional years, but it is also evidence of her continuing uncertainty about herself and her goals. The stories she was writing during the years when she earned her living primarily as a journalist, then as a schoolteacher, and finally as a magazine editor are characterized by multiple sets of unresolved dualities: between male and female, between Nebraska and the East, between the world of art and the world of ordinary human relationships and endeavors, between art as escape and art as immersion in familiar reality.

Such tensions, evident from her earliest stories, emerged from deep dualities in Cather's personal life. Torn between her desire to break free of Red Cloud and family, on the one hand, and the hunger for home evident in many of the letters she wrote during her early years in Pittsburgh, on the other, she plunged into a life that was itself torn between two kinds of commitments: to the everyday work she did to make her living (which was meaningful, however, in that it afforded her opportunities to think and write about art) and to the writing of fiction and poetry that she did in the evenings or whenever she could find time. There was a kind of inevitability, then, in the prevailing theme of her first book of stories, *The Troll Garden*: the opposition between art and crass reality. In a sense, she stood with a foot in each. But that is only a surface sense. More profoundly, she found elements of both in both worlds. Living a bifurcated life for a period of a decade and a half, she also lived a life of profound ambiguity. Perhaps that is the reason it has proven so difficult for critics to decide what the trolls and the goblins of the title and epigraphs of her first volume represent.

In the household of Isabelle McClung, where she lived from 1901 until 1906, Cather inhabited a kind of garden existence, as if behind a thick, ivied wall. Isabelle, with her fervent devotion both to art and to Willa Cather, constructed and safeguarded an environment in which Cather could write, but at the same time her very presence constituted a distraction from that work. Cather's teaching obligations distracted her in another way. When she took a train to New York on May 1, 1903, in response to a telegram from S. S. McClure stating that he was interested in her stories and wanted to talk with her, her production of fiction had dwindled. Before she began work on the *Home Monthly* in July 1896 she had published nine stories; from then until she began teaching in March 1901 she published sixteen, many of them done to fill pages; from the time she began teaching until the publication of her first story in *McClure's* in January 1905 she published only six. That first story in *McClure's*, "The Sculptor's Funeral," which she would later tell her niece Helen Cather Southwick was her first published story, heralded the appearance of *The Troll Garden*.[16] In the meantime, Cather had also written the poems that made up *April Twilights*, published by subsidy in March 1903. These, like her stories, show that she was groping for an authentic voice.

What do we mean by "authentic"? If the performance of gender is not a representation of an inner reality but the construction *ex nihilo*, as it were, of a mode in which to engage the world, how can one manner or voice be more "authentic" than another? I take these questions to be ultimately unknowable and only fleetingly germane to my purposes here. My interest in performativity and authenticity in relation to Cather's emergence as a major voice in American fiction is oriented toward praxis rather than theory and is grounded in two conceptual frames of reference, both of which were present in Cather's own thinking about authenticity in art.[17] One of these is experience; the other, the fact that she was female. Neither is an absolute. Her experience of the world was varied, and so were the ways in which the biological "fact" of sex might express itself behaviorally. We are still trying to understand this range of expressions and how the two supposed opposites may, in fact, overlap. The state that I believe she was working toward, which I am designating as authenticity of voice, was a mode of writing and of being-in-the-world with which she could be most comfortable, as reflecting the sum of her experience (and reflections on it) and her self-definition as a woman. The fact that self-definition emerged through performance of a range of personal styles does not, I believe, make it any less real or important for her writing.

As a poet, Cather seems not to have known *who* she wanted to be; one wonders why she tried to think of herself as a poet at all. Her subjects range from the ludicrously foreign, about which she had no direct knowledge and essentially nothing to say, to the immediate and experienced. Occasionally her language is direct and fresh, but more often she strikes conventional poses and adopts inauthentic language, shifting spasmodically from a supposed Scottish dialect to more formal archaisms and inversions to overwrought exclamations. A. E. Housman's presence is strongly if intermittently felt—for example, in "Poppies on Ludlow Castle" and "In Media Vita" (dropped from the 1937 edition) with its "lads."[18] During her first trip to Europe, in 1902, with Isabelle, she made a pilgrimage to Shropshire and met Housman in London by simply dropping in at his boarding house. Curiously, that visit would be the subject of one of her last pieces of writing before her death. For the most part, however, the derivative nature of *April Twilights* is not so much specific as a general emulation of what she conceived to be poetic language. In only one poem in the 1902 volume, "Prairie Dawn," does she escape the dead hand of Poesy to write in a truer voice about things she knows. Even here a "bright lance" gets hurled out of nowhere into Nebraska. Cather's friend George Seibel dutifully reviewed the little volume, but it made no splash. The main interest of the original *April Twilights* is its indication of her uncertainty as to a literary direction even at this stage in her advancing career.

Most of Cather's more memorable poems were added in later editions. "Poor Marty," a memorable folk elegy despite a switch to stilted inversions in its pious final stanza, was not added until 1933. The second edition, in 1923, although dropping thirteen of the original poems, added several stronger ones: "The Swedish Mother (Nebraska)," which rings true in feeling but is marred by an attempt at second-language dialect; "Spanish Johnny"; "Prairie Spring," a strikingly successful effort in free verse, with its heavy, honest monosyllables that break into lighter rhythms when "Youth" comes "flaming like the wild roses"; "Macon Prairie (Nebraska)"; "Going Home (Burlington Route)," which carries in its rhythm the sense of "how smoothly the trains run beyond the Missouri." One of the most interesting, both biographically and for its connection with her prairie fiction, is "Macon Prairie," with its portrait of a strong-willed woman who, despite being so ill she has to be carried on a makeshift bed, pours her energy into "Westward-faring." A version of Cather's Aunt Jennie, who died of tuberculosis not long after migrating to Nebraska from Virginia, this female "leader of the expedition" who takes "possession" of the "red waste" with her "burning eyes"— that is, with vision rather than through physical conquest—is given a journey not just across the continent, like the aunt, but across the ocean. Thus both she and the speaker, a niece or nephew "held . . . for a night against her bosom" in the covered wagon, become immigrants. For once, Cather speaks *as*, rather than about, one of the strong immigrants who intrigued her.

The figure of the female leader had appeared full-blown, of course, a full decade before "Macon Prairie" in *O Pioneers!*, the novel in which Cather said (in an inscription in the copy she sent Carrie Miner) that she "hit the home pasture."[19]

It is often said that until she did hit that home pasture she had been writing poor imitations of Henry James. But she did not begin her overtly Jamesian period until perhaps a decade after she began to publish stories. Her period of most obvious influence by James was 1903 to 1912, the year of *Alexander's Bridge*. Her very first stories, "Peter" and "Lou, the Prophet," drew on Nebraska materials, as did several others written during the 1890s. In those early works, however, she was not yet ready to write with assurance. Until *O Pioneers!* or perhaps "The Bohemian Girl," written in late 1911 when she was revising *Alexander's Bridge*, everything she wrote was, as she inscribed Carrie Miner's book, "half real and half an imitation." She was, after all, just learning to manage narrative, dialogue, and the challenge of igniting emotional power, and she could be forgiven the excesses of emotional coloring or the biblical intonations by which she tried to approximate Old World speech. Like her poems, her apprentice stories bounce about among styles and subjects so much that they are difficult to discuss in any coherent way. But until about 1903, when S. S. McClure took an interest in her, and later when she began editorial work at *McClure's* and became more sharply aware of both literary fashion and the ways in which fiction got itself published, that variability did not tend toward a Jamesian mode.

Thirteen of the stories before *Troll Garden* are set on the prairies. Even so, not all are the "home pasture." "The Clemency of the Court" (1893) was based on newspaper reports of prison atrocities, and "The

Affair at Grover Station" (1900) used knowledge of railroading gleaned
from her brother Douglass, then working as a Burlington agent in
Cheyenne, Wyoming. The home pasture is not just a matter of setting,
but of attitude and language as well. Yet characteristic ways of thinking,
such as attention to the power of the unstated and the dignity of reticence, appear even in some of the most amateurish and artificial of
them. For all its clumsy exoticism, for example, "A Tale of the White
Pyramid" (1892) develops motifs of secrecy and concealment that would
recur throughout Cather's creative life (O'Brien, *Emerging* 199–200).[20]
"The Sentimentality of William Tavener" (1900) demonstrates the
power of emotions held in reserve. "The Count of Crow's Nest" (1896),
laborious and uneven but a story in which a manuscript reader for *Cosmopolitan* showed an encouraging interest, elevates both the value of "the
indefinite" in "the domain of pure art" (*CSF* 453) and the dignity of
conducting oneself with reserve—a principle Cather would later carry
to the point of a kind of habitual secrecy.

Several of the early stories demonstrate the speciousness of rigid
gender roles and give favorable treatment to characters who undermine
conventions. The vigorous heroine of "Tommy the Unsentimental"
(1896), a girl with a boy's name, a face "like a clever wholesome boy's,"
"the lank figure of an active half grown lad," and a "peculiarly unfemi-
nine mind that could not escape meeting and acknowledging a logical
conclusion," prevents a run on a bank by riding some twenty-five miles
uphill on her "wheel."[21] A set of "old speculators and men of business"
undermines gender roles by "rather tak[ing] her mother's place" (*CSF*
473–74). In "The Sentimentality of William Tavenor" Hester can "talk
in prayer meeting as fluently as a man" and shows that it "takes a strong
woman to make any sort of success of living in the West" (353–55). The
stalwart Margie of "A Resurrection" (1897) has eyes "serious and frank
like a man's" (426), and another Margie, in "The Treasure of Far Island"
(1902), has "preserved that strength of arm and freedom of limb that had
made her so fine a playfellow" (278). In "The Professor's Commencement" (1902), a revelation of Cather's own fear that her "best tools [will]
have rusted" if she spends her life teaching high school, the professor
has hands "white as a girl's" while his sister is "the more alert and masculine character of the two" but also his "protecting angel" (284–85).
At the end, after he has again forgotten the memorized lines he meant
to speak, the professor confesses with shame that he "was not made to

shine, for they put a woman's heart in me" (291), but it is clear that we are not to accept that pronouncement at surface value. Even if the professor has not lived up to his own expectations, he *has* shone, for his colleagues see him, only half facetiously, as a Horatius who has "kept the bridge these thirty years." Like others of the early stories, "The Professor's Commencement" is not well resolved, but even so one wonders why critics have found the professor's love for literature "almost unnatural" (Meyering 204, summarizing Joan Wylie Hall, 142–50) and Cather's acceptance of his "emasculation" (a term that betrays the conventionalism of the critic's own definitions) a "dangerous" sign (Thurin 115).

The artist figures in these stories are vaguely androgynous. Given the common stereotype, of course, the yearning for beauty can itself be seen as a kind of feminizing touch, and since Cather certainly identifies with the characters who have that yearning, we can assume that she also identifies with their evasion of conventional notions of gender. In most of the stories before 1906 she centered her narrative attention on male protagonists or masculine activities, even football (in "The Fear That Walks by Noonday," written at the suggestion of Dorothy Canfield), though not literally the sea or battle. In several ("The Count of Crow's Nest," "The Treasure of Far Island," "A Night at Greenway Court"), she views events from a male perspective, a practice that Sarah Orne Jewett would label "a masquerade" (246). Again we see Cather moving between genders, reluctant to be typecast by conventions.

Contrary to the deep love for the Nebraska soil that would characterize *O Pioneers!*—long taken as the definitive expression of Cather's own feelings—several of the early stories convey a sense of deadness, harshness, or hostility in the prairie environment. Lou, the Prophet, in an 1892 story, is essentially driven insane by prairie drought. The "scorching dusty winds" in "On the Divide" (1896) "seem to dry up the blood in men's veins as they do the sap in the corn leaves," so that it "causes no great sensation there when a Dane is found swinging to his own windmill tower, and most of the Poles after they have become too careless and discouraged to shave themselves keep their razors to cut their throats with" (CSF 495). Her tone here may be grimly humorous, but the prevalence of suicide in her fiction of Nebraska is evidence that she was basically serious. When she speaks of the "awful loneliness" of the Divide, a country "as flat and gray and as naked as the sea," one hears an implicit contrast with the green hills and settled social relationships of

Back Creek, Virginia. In "El Dorado: A Kansas Recessional," where
Kansas is surely (as Woodress indicates of "The Sculptor's Funeral")
another name for Nebraska, a man from Virginia thinks "it would have
been better for us if we'd never left it" (496, 305; Woodress, introduction to *TG* xxi). In "A Resurrection" (1897) the town of Brownville,
which Cather wrote about directly and dismally in an 1894 *Journal*
article, is a place "without aim or purpose" (429). Although she would
sometimes insist that Nebraska was the only place she could live and be
happy (while she continued to live elsewhere), it appears in these stories
as a place to be escaped. The narrator of "The Joy of Nelly Deane"
(1911) recalls hearing the "faraway world . . . calling to us" (61), as it
called to Cather.

   Naturally, Cather offended people in the state by writing in this way.
A storm of public protest was evoked by "A Wagner Matinée" (1904),
which shows Nebraska not merely as flat, empty, and harsh but as a
trashed wasteland that shatters the spirit of the sensitive. Aunt Georgiana, a close portrait of Cather's own Aunt Franc, seems worn out and positively starved for beauty. Taken to an afternoon concert during a visit to
Boston, she is overcome by the music, begins to cry, and pleads at the
end, if the male narrator is right, not to go back to the "tall, unpainted
house, with weather-curled boards; naked as a tower, the crook-backed
ash seedlings where the dish-cloths hung to dry; the gaunt, moulting
turkeys picking up refuse about the kitchen door" (*TG* 101). Cather
told Dorothy Canfield that she had been barraged with angry letters
and that her family felt disgraced. When her old mentor Will Owen
Jones rebuked her in print she replied that she had not had the slightest
intention of disparaging the state.[22]

   By aligning the harshness of prairie life with its effect on a person of
artistic sensibility, as she does with devastating force in "A Wagner
Matinée" and "The Sculptor's Funeral" as well as such early stories as
"Peter" and "Eric Hermannson's Soul," she sharpens the opposition of
East (or Europe) and West running through much of her fiction and
poetry and links it to the opposition between art and a philistine world.
This dual opposition is customarily seen as the central structuring
theme of *The Troll Garden*. Hermione Lee, for example, points to an
opposition between "mid-Western philistinism" and the world of art as
the principle of the whole (75).

   Many critics have located that pervasive opposition in the two epigraphs to the volume. The first (with ellipses as shown here) is from Charles Kingley's introduction to *The Roman and the Teuton*:

> A fairy palace, with a fairy garden; . . . inside the trolls dwell, . . . working at their magic forges, making and making always things rare and strange.

The second comes from Christina Rossetti's "The Goblin Market":

> We must not look at Goblin men,
> We must not buy their fruits;
> Who knows upon what soil they fed
> Their hungry thirsty roots?

The two epigraphs set up, in Brown's words (113–14), a conflict between artists (the "industrious" trolls) and the enemies of art (the goblins). But even if we accept that art is the central theme, its import is by no means so simple. *Neither* goblins nor trolls, after all, are figures that usually evoke trust, and the trolls of Kingsley's parable are in fact considerably more sinister than Cather's elided quotation would indicate. When the ellipses are restored, we see that Kingsley labeled them "evil" and their garden a "fair foul place," that is, a place reminiscent of Klingsor's garden in *Parsifal*, a story whose importance for Cather would be manifest in *One of Ours*.[23] Klingsor's garden is mentioned, in fact, in "The Garden Lodge," where it denotes the artistic workshop, so to speak, the world of opera productions and concerts, in contrast to the "quiet nature" behind the walls of a real garden. It is alluded to, as well, in "The Marriage of Phaedra," where the walls of a garden have glass embedded in the top. Another problem with interpreting the epigraphs so rigidly is that *both* trolls and goblins produce, or at least possess, things "rare and strange." And if we read Kingsley's parable in full we see that the trolls' "rare and strange" products entice the "forest children" to corruption as surely as the fruits of the goblin men entrap Rossetti's Laura in an incessant hunger for more.

The epigraphs, then, as well as the stories themselves, show art as being dangerous. Yet its absence, in "The Sculptor's Funeral" and "A Wagner Matinée," is a kind of death. What *The Troll Garden* proposes is not a clear alternative in which one choice (art) is good and the other (a philistine existence) is not, but a duality expressing great personal ambivalence—as Cather's dualities generally do. That ambivalence is compounded not only when one story is compared with another, but when other pairs of dualities—East/West (or as Rosowski defines it, prairie/garden), male/female—are layered onto the opposition of art and philistinism.

The volume opens with "Flavia and Her Artists," an unmistakably Jamesian story about a woman who feeds upon art, and ends with two stories about sensitive souls who hunger for art, "A Wagner Matinée" and "Paul's Case."[24] In only one of the seven stories, "The Sculptor's Funeral," is the contrast between art and small-town philistinism clearly drawn. In the others, human values do not follow such a dichotomy. The sequence moves back and forth between East (New York, Boston, London) and West (Kansas, Wyoming, Nebraska). A linkage of the East with art or a specious appetite for art is established at the outset by the fact that Flavia has insisted on moving from a house on Prairie Avenue in Chicago to the Hudson Valley to establish her temple to art, which proves instead to be a temple to artificiality. The opposite, the West's artistic void, appears in the benighted narrowness of the Kansas town in "The Sculptor's Funeral," the sense of exile of the dying singer in "A Death in the Desert," the littered and barren Nebraska home where Aunt Georgiana longs for the musical joy of her Boston youth in "A Wagner Matinée." The sequence also moves back and forth between focus on male and on female characters, as well as focus *through* male and female observers. As O'Brien points out (275–80), a subtext of concern about "gender and vocation" runs throughout. Vocation, in the sense of career, was still Cather's great problem, inseparably tied to both her sense of the artist's vocation (literally, calling) and her misgivings about the marketplace for art. But it is not so clear as O'Brien claims that she develops a theme of male suppression of female creativity.

Flavia, in the first story, is one of the consumers in the artistic marketplace; indeed, she is a consumer in the predatory sense, the celebrities she attracts to her country-house salon being her "prey." A woman of no aesthetic or intellectual discernment, she is responsive only to whether a given celebrity's stock is rising. From the artist's point of view, then, to be boosted by publicity is to make oneself vulnerable to a predator like Flavia—again, evidence of Cather's concern for privacy. But if the desire for art can become a feeding frenzy, the opposite, an indifference to art, is even more deadening—as shown in the contrasting "The Sculptor's Funeral." Illustrating the artfulness of Cather's structuring of the volume, "The Sculptor's Funeral," second in order, is counterbalanced by "A Wagner Matinée," also about deprivation, second to the end, while "Paul's Case," where an appetite for the trappings of glamour that surround the world of the arts again lapses into an orgy of effete consumption, comes last, balancing "Flavia and Her Artists." Paul is more poignant than Flavia because of his youth, but his hunger for art has an equal speciousness. It is really a hunger for lifestyle.

In the three central stories of the volume the interplay of artistic creation and artistic consumption is more complex, though the stories may be less successful. In "The Garden Lodge," Caroline, the central character, has been reared in a household in which she and her mother were virtual servants of the husband-father, a composer and sometime piano teacher, while both parents carried on "a sort of mystic worship of things distant, intangible, and unattainable" that rendered them personally ineffectual. Caroline herself has narrowly escaped enslavement to the paternal taskmaster, not by suppressing her creativity, as O'Brien asserts, but rather by rebelling against his plan to make her a concert pianist. When she "came into the control of herself," she broke off her training for the concert hall and chose to build a career as an accompanist and teacher, further defying her father by refusing to have her pupils study his compositions. Since she is already well established in this career when she marries, the choice that O'Brien attributes to her of an "orderly controlled marriage rather than an artistic career" (275) is actually never posed. The conventionally feminine role of accompanist does not so much frustrate her creativity as afford her the satisfaction of doing something well and making her own way, just as a woman journalist might who successfully "accompanied" male publishers and editors-in-chief. Indeed, two other good accompanists in *Troll Garden* are male—only one of the many ways in which Cather undermines conventions of gender in these stories. One is the "lovable" Everett Hilgard, in "A Death in the Desert"; the other is Flavia's apparently inartistic businessman husband.

It is generally acknowledged that the husband in "Flavia and Her Artists" was modeled on Flavia Canfield's husband, Dorothy's father, but he is not presented as being *only* the husband of a foolish wife, as commentary on the story usually insists. It is he rather than Flavia who is sought out for conversation by the truest artist in the group of guests, and it is he who is sensitive to the feelings of the narrator, Imogen Willard (a name borrowed from Cather's Pittsburgh friends May and Mary

Willard). Cather did feel that Dorothy's mother dragged her about to museums without consideration of her feelings and seems to have preferred Dorothy's father, Professor Canfield.[25] It is the apparent philistine, then, rather than the supposed lover of art, who becomes "magnificent" at the end of the story, by defending Flavia in a way she does not even understand. The figure of Imogen, the Jamesian *ficelle*, is a sketch of Dorothy herself, who had recently completed a doctorate in Romance languages at Columbia after conducting research at the Sorbonne. Imogen "had shown rather marked capacity in certain esoteric lines of scholarship, and had decided to specialize in a well-sounding branch of philology at the Ecole des Chartes" (*TG* 7). But her scholarship is regarded with mild amusement (she is "brim full of dates and formulae and other positivisms"), and the third story in the volume, "The Garden Lodge," makes gratuitous reference to "withered women who had taken doctorate degrees." One wonders whether these barbs were added as revenge for Dorothy's interference with "The Profile" and whether she was offended. Her interference was actually beneficial to the volume, however, since the substitution of "Flavia and Her Artists" provided its strongest structuring element.

All but one of the artists in "Flavia" are boring egoists who hang about and flatter Flavia because they need a place to stay or plan to expose her foolishness in (presumably well-paid) print. Similarly, the artist in "The Garden Lodge," an opera singer named d'Esquerré, is a (sexually) parasitic egoist. In "A Death in the Desert" the artist is so utterly preoccupied with self that he uses his twin brother for errands and can be kind only when it costs little effort, and one gathers that his sponsoring of the career of his former pupil, now dying in the cultural desert of Wyoming, involved some element of sexual vampirism that drained her of her vitality. She is actually dying of tuberculosis—perhaps a pun on "consumption," since she is both consumed by her obsession with Adriance and eager to consume news of the New York art scene. Such is the insatiability of her hunger—like Laura's for the enticing fruits in "Goblin Market"—that she takes no interest in the actual life remaining to her, but only in the life she might have had. The life of the artist has unfitted her for any other. Similarly, when Caroline falls under the spell of d'Esquerré in "The Garden Lodge," she can think of nothing else and wishes to maintain the cottage as a shrine to his creativity and its covert sexual charge. In resisting that urge, she opts for a dry kind of existence, but a balanced one in which she can remain a free agent, within the limits of her marriage. The conclusion seems to indicate that for a woman, at least, there are no perfect answers, but she has steered as satisfying a course as circumstances allowed. For a schoolteacher trying to write fiction in her spare time, that was probably a reassuring conclusion.

In posing such unlikable artist figures as Adriance Hilgard, d'Esquerré, the backbiting Roux in "Flavia and Her Artists," and the overweening Hugh Treffinger of "The Marriage of Phaedra" (a story bearing the marks of James's "The Real Thing"), Cather was continuing to ponder an issue on which she had touched in her newspaper columns, the connection between private character and artistic performance, the mystery of whether art can be genuine when it emerges from personal shallowness. The question of genuineness, both in the artistic creation itself and in what Slote refers to as "the real desire versus the false," is recurrent.[26] Also recurrent and familiar to us from Cather's newspaper columns is a motif of gender-role fluidity. Some of these blurrings of gender boundaries—the women who speak in baritone voices in "Flavia and Her Artists" and "The Marriage of Phaedra," the diminutive Italian tenor with red lips, Paul's sybaritic unmanliness, the curious suggestion that Flavia's exploits might have "unmanned" her—are faintly disturbing, but others are accepted or affirmed. An actress who looks like a boy and is called Jimmy is one of the few likable characters of "Flavia"; in "The Sculptor's Funeral" the old father is feminized by his tenderness for his "gentle" son while the mother only feigns the conventionalized woman's role. The attentive reader is being asked to question assumptions about male and female.

BETWEEN *The Troll Garden* and *Alexander's Bridge* (1912) Cather did little writing. In 1906, the year she moved to New York to go to work for *McClure's*, she did not publish a single story. In 1907 she published four ("The Profile," "The Willing Muse," "Eleanor's House," and "The Namesake"), at least one of which had been written much earlier. None can be regarded as an artistic advance beyond *The Troll Garden*. She must have been very discouraged.

The influence of James reached its peak in the four stories of 1907 and *Alexander's Bridge*, with their recourse to aristocratic country houses and observer-confidantes, their European settings, and their elaborate and certainly, for Cather, artificial dialogue. They carry a sense of effete weariness and removal from reality. She later said that she had been trying to "sing a song that did not lie in her voice" (*WCIP* 37). Perhaps the voice in which her "song" did not lie was a masculine one. Both the central characters and the vantage-point figures are male in most of these stories, and she had adopted James's sense of the peril posed to sensitive men by women. In "The Willing Muse," the one story that undermines gender expectations, with a wife whose writing flourishes after her marriage while her husband's declines from even his earlier halting pace, this situation is regarded as deplorable, as if the wife *should* take the traditional role of muse—unless the point is even more covert than that and the wife really *is* her husband's muse, willing him to produce the two books a year that she energetically types up and publishes under her own name because he is too proud to let his be sullied by hasty work. Only in "The Enchanted Bluff" and "The Joy of Nelly Deane," among the stories of these years, does one get a sense of secure location and community, and only in these does she use the direct language that was one aspect of the voice she called the "real me."[27]

We have it on Cather's own word that the strain of managerial and editorial work in the frantic *McClure's* office took a heavy toll on her. Moreover, McClure himself discouraged her, telling her she should abandon the writing of fiction because she was never going to be much of a success in it.[28] Fortunately, her work on the magazine led to another new acquaintance who not only counteracted McClure's disheartening advice but pointed her in the right direction. Her first major assignment at *McClure's* was to turn Georgine Milmine's research materials on Mary Baker Eddy, the founder of Christian Science, into a publishable series of articles and ultimately a book. She worked on the project from December 1906 through May 1908.[29] Living in Boston for much of that period while verifying and extending Milmine's research, she developed a circle of Boston acquaintances. In February 1908, when she was taken to tea at the home of Annie Adams Fields, widow of James T. Fields of the publishing house of Ticknor and Fields, that circle was extended to include Sarah Orne Jewett.

Cather had long admired Jewett's work, with its quiet tone, its allegiance to the speech and manners of a specific place as unfashionable for literature as her own Nebraska, and its celebration of female friendship. As O'Brien points out, Jewett was also a writer whose "creative imagination was sparked by memory" (337), another aspect of her work that would have appealed to Cather as she came to realize the well-spring of her own strongest work. As O'Brien also notes, the example of Jewett's longtime sharing of her life with her friend Annie Fields would have been particularly significant to Cather at a time when she was making the decision to share living space and life with Edith Lewis. She had multiple reasons, then, to respond with gratitude to Jewett's expressions of interest and to respond with serious thought when Jewett urged her to make important changes in her career and her writing.

Jewett had written a letter *about* Cather even before their meeting. Responding to a copy of *The Troll Garden* sent to her by Witter Bynner, she praised the stories despite regretting their element of pessimism and said that she believed she and Cather would have a lot to talk about if they ever met (O'Brien 343–44). Apparently they did. Their meeting at 124 Charles Street gave rise to a series of remarkable letters in the brief time remaining before Jewett's death the next year. In response to Cather's confession of weariness and frustration with her work at *McClure's*, Jewett urged her to resign and devote her full energies to writing. As to the writing itself, Jewett told her with a gentle directness that it had not advanced beyond the level of the *Troll Garden* stories, a fact that Cather seems already to have realized, and advised her to turn for material to her own place and the subjects that had teased her mind over a long period and to treat those materials not as she thought readers expected but as she believed they really were. Finally, Jewett urged Cather to write from a female perspective rather than assume the voice of a male: "When a woman writes in a man's character,—it must always, I believe, be something of a masquerade" (Jewett 246–50).

Jewett's advice was the best Cather ever received. It freed her of the weight of needing to emulate James, while leaving her free to continue employing the technical expertise she had gained by studying him. Katherine Anne Porter, whose interest in Cather was longstanding, once wrote mocking marginalia in her copy of E. K. Brown's biography objecting to the notion that Jewett had counteracted, by her "example and her precepts," the "cult of Henry James": "Miss Jewett the carved cherrystone, trying to undermine Henry James the granite sea wall!!"[30] Porter entirely missed the qualities in Jewett's work that helped Cather recognize her own most authentic material—and voice—and the value of Jewett's personal example and supportiveness. At a time when Cather

Fig. 17. Cather about 1912, wearing a necklace given her by Sarah Orne Jewett.
(Nebraska State Historical Society)

was at a low ebb in creative energy and self-confidence, Jewett provided her with the living evidence that a woman could succeed while still maintaining her personal and artistic integrity. Cather would write to Jewett, later in 1908 while traveling in Italy, that she always kept a copy of "White Heron" with her.[31] More immediately, Jewett provided the direct encouragement to persevere in defining herself as a writer rather than a magazine executive (see figure 17).

Cather did not act on Jewett's advice until the fall of 1911, when she took an extended leave of absence, going to Cherry Valley, New York, with Isabelle McClung to live quietly in a cottage there while she finished *Alexander's Bridge* and wrote "The Bohemian Girl." Notably, McClure now supported her in her decision and even took the trouble to circle by Cherry Valley on his way to Michigan to encourage her. By waiting, she had gained, in effect, both the father's and the mother's permission. She would never fully accept Jewett's advice about masculine perspective, which she would use in many of her novels as well as stories, continuing to move freely among gender modes in fiction as she had already learned to do in fact. Nor would she immediately act on the advice to turn back to her home country for her fictional material. But by the time she finished her first novel, she was making that return.

CATHER'S ACCOUNT of the reorientation of her writing from the alien material and modes of *Alexander's Bridge* to her own, in *O Pioneers!*, can be seen as the work of an accomplished storyteller. Like her fiction, the essay "My First Novels [There Were Two]" is built on strong contrasts and evocative analogy and has a story-like turning point: her visit to Arizona and New Mexico in 1912, when her leave of absence from *McClure's* became her resignation. The "first" first novel, she said (though apparently there had been an earlier one, in Pittsburgh, which she destroyed), was artificial; the second, authentic. The first was a product of "arranging or 'inventing'" or, as she said in her preface to the 1922 edition of *Alexander's Bridge*, of construction; the second was as "spontaneous" as a ride "through a familiar country on a horse that knew the way." The first was like talking with someone she did not know well and found "not altogether congenial"; the second, like talking with herself (*OW* 91–97). But like a good story by a writer whose art is minimalist, this account leaves out a lot. It omits the fact that she had already taken the fictional road through familiar country in almost half of her published stories, though sometimes speaking, as she went, the stilted language of the uncomfortable conversationalist. She had turned away from that road in recent years, but it was an established one to which she was returning, now with developed powers. Her account also leaves out "The Bohemian Girl," a story in which she returned to familiar country precisely at the moment when she was completing her "first" first novel and preparing to turn to her second. And it leaves out the buried ways in which *Alexander's Bridge*, for all its artificiality and its attempt to use scenes and people who were not her own, is in fact a book very close to her own experience and concerns.

The story of Bartley Alexander, celebrated bridge engineer who has reached a point of midlife ennui, is told from the perspective of Bartley's former teacher and trusted confidante, Lucius Wilson. Thus Cather persists in taking the Jamesian road to the telling of a story about a male engaged in male-coded activities.[32] Bartley's story is classically masculine in centering on what has come to be called midlife crisis and an attempt to regain a sense of youth and virility through involvement with a woman other than his wife, an actress who had been his lover years before. The failed bridge, modeled on the Quebec Bridge, which had been under construction since 1900 when it failed on August 29, 1907, killing seventy-five workmen (March, *Companion* 8), becomes a metaphor for the bridge builder himself, torn in two by conflicting urges. It becomes in turn, as O'Brien has persuasively argued, a model both of Cather's own sense of dividedness and of her fears for her future. In taking up what was indisputably the reigning literary form, and certainly a male-dominated one, the novel, and in contemplating a radical change in direction in her career, she was, in O'Brien's words (388–89), changing both her "professional identity" and her "literary identity," and she feared failure. Would what worked "for an ordinary bridge" (story) "work with anything of such length" (*AB* 155)?

The failure that sends Alexander's bridge crashing into the river first appears as signs of strain in the lower chords of the partially completed structure, the very foundations. When the lower chord of the cantilever arm (it is to be the longest cantilever bridge in the world, as the Quebec Bridge was and still is) begins to settle, the whole structure cracks apart at the center, precisely (even too precisely) as Bartley's teacher had feared that he would himself: "a big crack zigzagging from top to bottom . . . then a crash and clouds of dust" (*AB* 15). Rosowski has pointed out the visual clumsiness of this and other images in the novel (*Voyage* 36–37). Perhaps that clumsiness is itself another trace of the self-referentiality of the text, as if pointing to Cather's sense that she was attempting to yoke dissonant impulses together by an act of will, or what she referred to in her 1922 preface as "building."

In part, her anxiety derived from her sense of the incommensurability between her work at *McClure's* and her literary aspiration. She found herself, as she said of Bartley, in a "network of great and little details" (*AB* 48). But the conflict is not so simple as that. The novel is not an allegory of art versus philistia. Rather, the split in Alexander reflects a composite of numerous conflicts that Cather had been carrying within herself. Certainly it involves East and West, with all their accumulated values. Bartley has come from the West (having been Wilson's student at "a Western university")[33] and now lives not only in that center of Brahmin culture, Boston, but on a street adjacent to Charles Street, where the Fields mansion was situated. Thus he is at the epicenter of the cultural life Cather associated with the East. But his allegiance to that world is no more complete than Cather's was. Near the end of the book, on his way to Quebec, he sees a group of boys around a campfire that "took his mind back a long way, to a campfire on a sandbar in a Western river, and he wished he could go back and sit down with them" (146). As Rosowski notes, these memories from Cather's youth are told "in her own voice, with confident, personal, clean prose" unlike that in most of the book (*Voyage* 38). Rosowski reads the passage as an intimation of youth. Certainly Cather's sense of the strains between youth and the maturing she desired, but also the aging she feared, are important in the novel. But the passage also expresses her wish to incorporate her western self into the eastern self that, with the act of writing a Jamesian novel, was reaching for success in the world represented by Charles Street.

Her sense of unreality or even deception—passing herself off as a publishing executive when she was really a writer, or as a writer when she was really a newspaperwoman, or as a member of the East Coast literati when she was really a midwestern up-and-comer, unless she was a Virginian—is evident in the text. Jewett had raised the specter of the "masquerade" and had urged her to write from her own center. Yet she was taking the risk of investing her scarce time and energy in "building" a novel precisely the way Jewett had warned her not to, "in a man's character." The title *Alexander's Masquerade*, under which it appeared in serialized form, had, then, an ironic appropriateness. Taken from chapter 9 of the text as Bartley thinks about the step he is about to take in leaving his wife and thereby making his life a mockery—"And for what? For a mere folly, a masquerade, a little thing that he could not let go" (143), it may also have been the sign that at some level Cather was thinking of Jewett's letter.[34]

Bartley Alexander's masquerade involves two women, his wife Winifred and the actress Hilda Burgoyne, but it is never clear which represents his masquerade and which his real self. Once he undertakes his deceptive double life, both parts are masquerades. The split in Bartley represented by the two women is also more complex than it at first appears. Certainly it does not represent, in any narrow sense, a "crack in his moral nature"; nor does Woodress, who uses the phrase, refer merely to his adultery (219). Like Cather, Bartley wants too many things, and they are incompatible. Nor is it plausible to identify the wife and the mistress as representatives of the spiritual and the physical (Rosowski, *Voyage* 35). Both are associated with art, which for Cather would usually mean with spirituality. It is more a difference of refinement versus energy, perhaps in relation to art itself: a difference between a mature (eastern? imitative? effete?) style and a youthful (western? freely experimental?) one. That issue was one of the most pressing aspects of the problem Cather was attempting to resolve.

When we consider how closely Cather's early career had been associated with the theater and reviewing, especially reviewing the work of actresses, we can see a special significance in Hilda's being an actress. To leave *McClure's* would be to go back to the early years when she made her living (in large part, at any rate) by her writing, often by writing about the theater and actresses, when she was younger, more energetic, and surely more hopeful and confident than she was now. At the same time, going back would seem very much like throwing away the gains of the intervening years in maturity, in understanding what she wanted to do, and certainly in income. It is little wonder, then, that the figure of the actress became at once enticing and dangerous, an inspiriting and an enervating force in Cather's at once Jamesian and personal, at once backward-looking and forward-looking, first novel.

5

Indoor / Outdoor
Writing What She Knew

The old West, the old Time,
The old wind singing through
The red, red grass a thousand miles . . .
—"Spanish Johnny"

As a teacher, Cather urged her students to "write out of their own experiences" (Byrne and Snyder 56). It was not an idea she had just arrived at. In a column in the *Leader* on March 4, 1898, three years before she took her first teaching job, she had enunciated a version of the same idea: "The artist is bound to his native soil more closely than the serf who plods in the furrow. . . . a man of letters must speak the message of his own people and his own country" (*W&P* 582). She did not always follow her own advice, either in her poetry or in her fiction. But in 1911 and 1912, with "The Bohemian Girl" and then *O Pioneers!*, she turned, as if with a re-awakening, to her own country—or at any rate to the one with which she would chiefly be identified throughout her career.

Cather always spoke of *O Pioneers!* in terms of ease and naturalness. We have seen her famous statement in "My First Novels [There Were Two]" about its being like "taking a ride through a familiar country on a horse that knew the way" (*OW* 92–93). She told an interviewer that she had "simply" decided to "give [herself] up to the pleasure of recapturing in memory people and places [she] had believed forgotten" (*WCIP* 21). She had discovered that "the main thing always was to be honest" and that "art ought to simplify" (8). But the appearance of simplicity in *O Pioneers!* is just that: an appearance. She was much nearer the truth of her own artistry when she went on to say that "from a kind of instinct of self-protection" you "distort" and "disguise" the things you feel most strongly about (11).

In setting her "second first novel" in Nebraska, she distorted and disguised her own sense of belonging. Simplifying meant, for one thing, leaving out—or seeming to leave out—the powerful conflicting pull she felt toward Virginia. If she had hit one "home pasture" in writing of the prairies she knew rather than the drawing rooms she had glimpsed (in person but also in the books of James and Wharton), she would not hit the other for years to come. Really to have left out the pull toward Virginia, however, would have meant leaving out her sense of herself as a person who *came to* the West, her sense of herself as, in effect, an immigrant. Instead, she wrote of that self covertly, in disguise. Her depiction of the Norwegians and Czechs in this first Nebraska novel is generally read in terms she laid down herself, as an expression of nostalgia for the interesting, kindly people among whom she spent that portion of her childhood when she was free to roam the prairie on her pony. It might more accurately be read as a kind of appropriation. Just as immigrants from northern Europe and migrants such as the Cathers who came from the older states appropriated the spaces of the Indians, so Cather appropriated the lives of the immigrants and used them as a means of writing about her own experience. It was easy to find a new country, she noted, perhaps thinking of her train trip from Virginia to Red Cloud, but "finding a new type of human being and getting inside a new skin was the finest sport" there was. It was that sport that consoled her at a time of dislocation.[1]

Hitting the "home pasture," then, was a more complex act than her comments make it seem. Not only was her sense of home more conflicted than it is represented in *O Pioneers!*, but the turn to writing what she knew meant both a geographical turn toward familiar settings that had "teased" her mind for years and a turn toward the writing of the self. From that time on, her writing became self-referential in very much the sense Leigh Gilmore designates by the term "autobiographics": self-writing that locates the reality of the self in the text rather than in fact.[2] That endeavor was by no means so easy as a ride on a horse that knew the way. She identified its difficulty in an interview statement that may have been the most honest she ever made, published in the *Omaha World-Herald* on November 27, 1921: "I could not decide which was the real and which the fake 'me'" (*WCIP* 37).

In late September 1911 Cather took leave from her job at *McClure's* for six months of vacation that she hoped would set her straight with the world. Being set straight meant, in part, regaining her exhausted vitality and redefining herself as first and foremost a writer. She had managed to draft *Alexander's Bridge* during the spring and summer while fully involved in her job at the magazine. Retreating to a cottage Isabelle McClung had found for them at Cherry Valley, New York, she could get long nights' sleep and enjoy life more than she had in years. She exulted to S. S. McClure that it was just what she needed. She revised the novel for serialization, wrote "The Bohemian Girl," and drafted a story called "Alexandra" that would become the germ of *O Pioneers!* During these few months the turn from borrowed material and scenes to a setting and a pattern of action she could regard as her own was directly tied to her sense of well-being.[3]

If *Alexander's Bridge* was a covertly self-referential work revealing in disguised form what O'Brien calls "the anxieties accompanying the woman writer's ambitious, risky decision to write and to publish a 'long story'" (386–87), the works she now undertook, beginning with "Bohemian Girl," were writings about herself in more profound but still indirect ways. She had been a "Bohemian" girl in her college and early professional days. In the meaning of a free-spirited aesthete, the word *Bohemian* dots her correspondence of 1896 and 1897, whether in denial or avowal.[4] By turning her attention to the ethnic Bohemians (a term commonly used in Nebraska for Czech and Slovak immigrants as well as those from Bohemia itself) she could bring together her sense of her aesthete self, her feeling of youth when she was making new beginnings in a career, and the delight she recalled feeling as a child in Nebraska when she visited in kitchens with old women from Europe who indulged her, who treated her as a favored person. Her story *about* the Bohemian girl who runs away in adultery is also a story *by* a Bohemian girl who has run away, but who, during summer visits and now in her creativity, has also gone back home. By taking the perspective of the immigrant, she identifies herself as a woman who is both at home in the prairie setting and an alien to it. This complex posture would allow her, in much of the work she produced over the coming years, to situate herself within the country she knew well and had come to love while avoiding the "erasure of personality" she had feared.

"The Bohemian Girl" was an enabling achievement; Elizabeth Shepley

Sergeant calls it a "springboard" (86). As O'Brien astutely sees, Clara's confident horseback riding in the story would reappear in Cather's horseback-riding trope for the writing of *O Pioneers!* Although she would self-protectively pretend to be surprised by the enthusiastic reception of the story at *McClure's*, she was pleased with it and was nerved to conceive another love story, "The White Mulberry," when she visited "the Bohemian country" near Red Cloud the following summer. That story would combine with "Alexandra" to make her novel. According to Sergeant, Cather said that the two suddenly "entwined" themselves together in her imagination, in effect presenting her with the difficult phenomenon of a "two-part pastoral" as a fait accompli (96).

Throughout her life Cather would rely on the supportive affection of women. It is significant, then, that as she made the transition to a differently structured, differently located, self-referential fiction she was supported by the solicitude and praise of three women: Isabelle McClung, who arranged for her retreat to the idyllically named Cherry Valley, shared her life there, and cleared practical difficulties out of her path; Elizabeth Shepley Sergeant, who read "The Bohemian Girl" in manuscript and urged her to submit it for publication; and Zoë Akins, whose enthusiasm for the story reinforced her belief in it.[5] A fourth, Sarah Orne Jewett, reached from the past to extend encouragement and advice. At this decisive juncture several such friendships converged. They coalesced into the powerful dream-figure in *O Pioneers!* that carries Alexandra, much as Cather sensed her creativity, the horse that knew the way, carrying her in the writing of the novel.

DESPITE CATHER'S insistence to an admirer that *O Pioneers!* was a direct account unembellished by art,[6] in turning toward scenes she knew from her own intimate experience, rather than from books or passing encounters, Cather made a circuitous approach by way of literary precedent, primarily Virgil's *Eclogues, Georgics,* and *Aeneid.* In both the fact of its indirection and the nature of her choice of precedent, the act signaled her affiliation, conservative as she may appear, with other modernists. Much as Pound and Eliot rejected the poets of High Victorianism in order to claim their heritage from poets and dramatists of England's sixteenth century, Dante, or predecessors even further off in language and time, Cather reached past her immediate forbears in English-language fiction, James and Wharton and Meredith, to writers further back or in other languages. These predecessors proved to be less controlling than James had been in her first novel. For all its semblance of reassuring simplicity, *O Pioneers!* is actually a work of rebellion, a rejection of the well-made novel in favor of formal innovation. It is an experimental work in subject matter and setting, in the nature of its protagonist and her relationship to the central male character (or characters), and in form. The extent to which these gestures replicate those of the writers, especially poets, we are accustomed to think of as High Modernists has not been adequately recognized.[7]

The epical echoes in *O Pioneers!* have been well explicated by David Stouck in *Willa Cather's Imagination.* The great theme of mass migration and the founding of a social order, a theme represented most clearly by the northern European immigrants Cather singles out but also by the westering of Americans and the nationalistic and imperial urges associated with that process, harkens back unmistakably to Virgil's epic of the founding of Rome (a parallel especially beloved in the South, Cather's first homeland). An American self-conception in Roman terms was, of course, reassuringly heroizing. It helped justify a rhetoric of Manifest Destiny as native inhabitants were shoved aside from the great spaces into which these heroic migrants poured. And it is clear, both in this novel and in such later works as *The Professor's House* and *Death Comes for the Archbishop,* that Cather shared that rhetoric and the assumptions in which it was grounded. Her celebrated statement, referring to Alexandra, that "for the first time, perhaps, since that land emerged from the waters of geologic ages, a human face was set toward it with love and yearning" (*OP* 64), is in fact a shockingly imperialistic misrepresentation. We cannot assume that the Sioux who ranged over this same space only a few years before the time of the novel's opening (as Cather well knew, though even in an essay on Nebraska's history she pretended to believe it had been an *empty* space) did not turn their faces toward it with love.[8] Only a writer blinded by the imperialist aspirations so dominant in her day as to be virtually irresistible could write that sentence.

After the *Aeneid,* with its account of migration and home founding in a new place, the Virgilian precedent that most decidedly shapes *O Pioneers!* is the *Georgics,* a group of poems celebrating country life and agricultural work (or as Cather put it in a letter to Sergeant, "crops and cows") from the perspective of the virtuous husbandman.[9] Rosowski argues compellingly that despite its commitment to the real work of the soil the vision of *O Pioneers!*, with its "desire for order," its insistence on "surround[ing] . . . moments of perfection" with "disillusionment and loss," and perhaps paradoxically its blurring of "harsh realities," is a pastoral one (*Voyage* 47–53). That is, she sees the novel as being closer to the *Eclogues*, poems of great artifice celebrating an idealized rustic life from the perspective of artistic and urban sophistication, than to the *Georgics*, or at any rate as being not so fully committed to the *Georgics* vision at it first appears. My point here is somewhat different: that only if one sees rather clearly the distinction between the two Virgilian forms can one perceive how Cather, who knew her Virgil very well indeed, was blurring that distinction. Moreover, she was blurring the distinction not only between eclogue and georgic, but between the Virgilian celebration of the countryside and the Virgilian epic of state founding: an act of literary resistance and innovation indeed. She may have claimed to be "let[ting] the country be the hero" and writing directly out of the sound of the long grasses on the Nebraska plains, as she insisted Dvořák did in his New World Symphony,[10] but for all her willingness to direct her fictive attention to such quotidian matters as the location of pigpens, she was actually writing of the land not directly but very indirectly, through Classical precedent which, at the same time, she reconceived.

Writing of what was familiar, Cather wrote by way of the unfamiliar. Writing of agricultural labor, she employed a "duplicitous" high-art form "liable to accusations of absenteeism, artificiality and insincerity" that has "never been written by shepherds" (Lee 90). Celebrating Nebraska, she mourned it as a time lost. Yet she did so without facing the most absolute loss of all, that suffered by indigenous people whose way of life was destroyed by colonizing agriculturalists. Nor did she face the unpastoral context of a "machine age" (91). It is scarcely surprising that Marxist critics in the 1930s accused her of being a nostalgic writer who ignored contemporary social issues. What they did not see was that such issues were tacitly present in her fiction through the very act of averting her eyes, a gesture as self-aware as her choice of the pastoral itself. Moreover, she uses a sly running joke at bathtubs as a gesture toward the material proliferation of the machine age—a gesture that anticipates the great detritus of rusting gadgets and implements in *One of Ours*.

Even as Cather was employing techniques of indirection to write about Nebraska and midwestern life, in writing about Alexandra she was indirectly writing about herself. David Stouck has written that "no specific prototypes have ever been identified" for the characters in *O Pioneers!*, who are probably, as Cather implied all her characters were, composites. But as he goes on to point out, she "transmuted" her own experiences into the novel; its materials were "remembered, not documented" ("Historical" 287).[11] That last phrase should be emphasized. "Documented" fiction might also come out of her own experience, but it would be a fiction of observation. To be sure, *Pioneers* is keenly visualized and replete with observation of differences of customs between social groups. But she does not merely look *at* the Scandinavians about whom she is writing. She translates herself into them, remembering her own migration to Nebraska in terms of theirs.

Numerous incidental details demonstrate self-referentiality; I will give only a few. The opening sentence of the first chapter evokes a time "thirty years ago." If we take as reference point the year in which Cather was writing, 1912, that would be 1882, or approximately the time Cather actually arrived in Nebraska (the spring of 1883). At that point in the story Alexandra is in her early twenties, not, obviously, the nine-year-old child Willa Cather was in 1882–83, but the world in which we first see Alexandra is the world Cather first saw as a "foreigner" to this harsh place where a little town had to "tr[y] not to be blown away." It is a "lead-colored" land under a "leaden" sky, an "iron country" (*OP* 26, 20, 169): metallic images that recall Cather's statement that she first saw Nebraska as a country "bare as a piece of sheet iron." Later in the novel when Alexandra is seen as a triumphant farmer and shaper of the land but one resented by her small-minded brothers, her age is given as forty. Cather turned forty in 1913, six months after the publication of *O Pioneers!* Wonderfully successful but, like Alexandra, not beyond challenge (perhaps by family, although I have found no evidence that they opposed her leaving her good-paying job at *McClure's*), Cather explored her present feelings as well as her childhood memories. In a sense, in writing this novel of approximately thirty years in her female hero's life, she was examining her own thirty years of becoming rooted in, and then growing away from, Nebraska and was asking whether she, too, was a product of that soil.

The "little Swede boy" (the bluntness of the ethnic labeling is characteristic) who sits crying in the opening scene represents Cather's brother Jack, younger than she was by nineteen years, just as Emil is nineteen years younger than Alexandra. Like Cather, Alexandra is the oldest in the family. Her father, the dying John Bergson, more good than effectual, is a sketch of the overly gentle Charles Cather, and we can well believe that the Willa Cather who enjoyed feeling important at her father's office would have taken satisfaction in being placed in charge and hearing her brothers told, as Mr. Bergson tells Lou and Oscar, to be "'guided by your sister'" (*OP* 32). The unconventionalities in Alexandra that draw Lou's and Oscar's disapproval—her unladylike suntan from carrying her bonnet "oftener on her arm than on her head," her resistance to abiding by the custom for "'all to do alike,'" the odd fact that "'she'd as soon be forty as not!'" (84, 88, 156)—are recognizable as versions of Cather's resistance to social conformity in her Nebraska years, especially with respect to gender roles.

Although Cather spoke of *O Pioneers!* as if it were her first time to write about Nebraska, it was simply her first time in the form of the novel. The view of Nebraska given in the early scenes of the book, the Nebraska she saw as a newly arrived (im)migrant, is the view she had given a decade earlier in "A Wagner Matinée," a story that angered her family, Red Cloud neighbors, and friends in Lincoln as well as strangers all across the state. The general bleakness, the flimsiness of the houses, and the "litter of human dwellings" that so offends old Ivar (*OP* 40–41) recall the ugliness of Georgiana's life there. But in *O Pioneers!* Cather turns away from this satiric mode of conceiving her "home pasture" to a mode of healing and celebration, the mode she would adopt again in *My Ántonia*. In a way, the novel's subject is the process of maturation into this benedictory mode, and the change is linked to recognition and acceptance of dual impulses toward home and toward freedom of movement. Alexandra may tell Carl, the friend from adolescence whom she ultimately marries, that she would "'rather have had your freedom than my land'" (*OP* 113), but we do not believe it for a minute. What she would really rather have had was both: freedom *and* fields—which is very much what she does have at the end. In imagining an agricultural West rather than an untamed frontier, Cather imagines a place that combines at-homeness with freedom of movement, and the Nebraska that affords such a combination is one she views with an eye of memory that is also a gilding eye.

Cather's decision to name her female hero Alexandra, the feminine form of Alexander, was a significant and surely purposeful one. Her own naming by the feminine form of a masculine name, William, was a sore point. She said a number of times in letters that she disliked such names, including her own. Given that fact, her choice of Alexandra's name is an especially strong signal of an intent to position the new novel in explicit parallel with *Alexander's Bridge*. Critics have often observed that Bartley Alexander's name recalls Alexander the Great. He is depicted as a great man, a conqueror of sorts, though one who falls into the confusion or inner conflict that is manifest in the cracking of his bridge/self. By feminizing his name into the name of her next hero, Cather seems to have posed the question of whether a woman could also be a great conqueror. It must have been very important to her to be able to answer that question in the affirmative. One is reminded of her exultation when reporting, in a letter to Elsie Sergeant, that Olive Fremstad had a powerful intelligence, despite having (like herself) grown up in the Midwest.[12] Establishing the possibility of heroism for a woman, and a midwesterner at that, was a kind of self-vindication.

The key to Alexandra's heroism is her androgyny. Her freedom from limitation by assumptions relating to gender is emphasized from the opening scene, when she appears as a kind of total being, strong, with a bearing "like a young soldier" (a young Alexander?), wearing "a man's long ulster" as if it "belonged to her," but so alluring that she attracts male notice. Refusing to play at flirtation, she darts "a glance of Amazonian fierceness"—that is, the glance of a woman with heroic strength—at the man who comments on her beauty (*OP* 15). Her size, strength, and freedom from conventions of gender are indeed Amazonian. Tied to home in a way that Bartley Alexander, the inveterate traveler between Boston and London, certainly is not, she nevertheless adopts a conventionally masculine freedom of movement when she goes to look over farms in the river valley as easily as she accedes in her father's charge that she is to have authority over her brothers in running the farm.[13] She is as much a builder as Alexander, not in the sense of constructing wonders *on* the land but as a worker *with* the land.

Alexandra is also a variant of the classic metaphor of the earth as woman or woman as earth. In its conventional form, of course, that metaphor is scarcely consistent with heroism. In a long-dominant critical tradition led by a succession of male scholars and critiqued by Annette Kolodny in *The Lay of the Land*, the American landscape has been constituted as a passive female body, or "virgin land," receptive to male penetration (exploration), male plowing, and male heroics. Such an identification ostensibly glorifies female life-giving, but it denies female volition and renders female autonomy antithetical to society.[14] In *O Pioneers!* Cather adopts the metaphor but, by accommodating it to an invocation of heroic androgyny, adapts it to her own purposes. At times, she writes, Alexandra "felt, as it were, in her own body the joyous germination in the soil" (183–84), and she identified in memory with a female duck she and Emil had seen when they took their trip to the river farms, an image of quiet contentment altogether at odds with the quasi-masculine drive and determination she displays in buying and cultivating farm land. Most conspicuously, Alexandra takes a passive role (almost like a Sabine woman being "raped," or carried off, by a Roman soldier) in her dream of a powerful male figure smelling of the earth who carries her "as if she were a sheaf of wheat" (185), an insensate product of the earth. It is significant, though, that Alexandra has this dream only when she is tired; her vigorous self thinks otherwise.

The passage, then, supports a range of meanings. As I have suggested elsewhere, we can associate this puzzling dream with Cather's own sense that in turning at last to her "own" material she could yield herself up to the material itself or to her own deeper imagination, to "carry" her act of writing. We might also read it as an inversion of the conventional gendering of artistic inspiration, the female artist being "carried away" (a common parlance for inspiration) by a male Muse. Moreover, since the gigantic male figure in the dream smells of the fields, it is he, rather than Alexandra, who is associated with the supposedly passive (but sustaining, or carrying) earth. In all these ways, Alexandra's dream, like the entire pattern of woman-as-earth in this novel, is a complex re-visioning. Alexandra may at times be the earth-woman, but she is more often a vigorous, imaginative, active presence.

Cather's transformative adoption of the earth-woman metaphor was not, in fact, original with her. An important predecessor in the literary use of the West, Mary Austin, had earlier used the trope of earth-as-woman for explicitly feminist purposes in a series of works almost certainly known to Cather, notably *The Land of Little Rain* (1903) and "The Walking Woman," published in *Atlantic Monthly* in 1907. It is clear that Cather took notice of Austin's work, and we can well believe she would have responded favorably to Austin's depictions of sturdy female characters who united in their "tawny" bodies the fertility of the earth and the self-reliance more commonly attributed to the American Adam.

The nature of Alexandra's relationship to her male employees as well as her sometimes resentful brothers is far from the passivity implied in the earth-woman metaphor. She takes a quasi-masculine initiative in running her own life. When her farmhands come in for dinner at noontime she sits at the head of the table served by kitchen maids whom she treats with great affection and amusement, listening to the complaints of her foreman and the others but telling them with sure authority what she means to do. She is firmly in control, as she is with old Ivar, the eccentric visionary who addresses her respectfully as Mistress. Ivar's quasi-feminine nature—his hatred of violence, his instinctual rather than analytic understanding of the natural world—is another indication of Cather's deconstruction of gender assumptions. Despised and ridiculed by her stuffy brothers, Ivar speaks for personal freedom to live differently from those around him. They, in contrast, worry incessantly about how things will look and what people will think. Lamenting their folly in "'letting a woman meddle in business,'" although in fact they had no choice in the matter unless they wished to defy their dying father's instructions, and asserting "solemnly" the ludicrous notion that "'the property of a family really belongs to the men of the family, no matter about the title,'" they evoke Alexandra's wrath. With a decisiveness far removed from the supposed passivity of the earth-woman, she defies them to "'go to the county clerk and ask him who owns my land, and whether my titles are good'" (152–53). Through the voice of Alexandra, Cather here asserts her commitment to equality of the sexes.

We see that commitment in every aspect of her characterization of Alexandra—in her respect for her mother's housewifely ways of preserving culture as well as her father's thoughtfulness, in her enjoyment of her women friends as well as her ways of conversing with males, in her strength and determination as well as her dreaming. Because she thinks for herself and behaves simply as a person, as competent as any other person, and because she assumes that the goals of all persons are more or less similar, she never has to play the coquette. Utterly free of the self-conscious ploys and vanities with which society constructs the sexual game, she openly displays her grief when Carl tells her his family is moving away, does not mind becoming middle-aged, and offers herself to Carl, when he returns, in a plain-spoken proposal that he refuses only because he is not equally free of conventionalism. "'How direct you are, Alexandra!'" he winces (112). Guilelessly telling Carl that the men in town "'seem glad to see me,'" she attributes their pleasure to the fact that she is "'clean and healthy-looking'"—and evokes from him a knowing chuckle, a response that by itself should eliminate readings of their marriage as a sexless companionship (*OP* 122).

Carl's chuckle also demonstrates that Alexandra's naivety about sex is not Cather's own, since it is she, obviously, who treats it with a degree of amused irony. Such naivety is pointed out, too, in connection with the illicit love of Emil and Marie, the doomed lovers murdered in sexual embrace under the orchard trees by Marie's husband. With scarcely believable imperceptiveness, Alexandra reflects that though she knew he "was fond of" Marie, it had "never occurred to her that Emil's feeling might be different from her own." He was, after all, "a good boy," and "only bad boys ran after married women." Moreover, she seems to suppose that being married would bar any possibility of sexual feeling on Marie's part, that the "mere fact" of being married "settled everything" (*OP* 253). Surely, we think, this is authorial irony, Cather detaching herself from her character to let the character's point of view stand revealed as inadequate. Yet we cannot be sure. Indeed, we can almost never be sure of Cather's irony.

On the basis of this and other passages, critics have sometimes read Alexandra as cold. Peck, for example, reads a passage about her doing her milking alongside Carl, "he on his side of the fence, she on hers" (*OP* 117) as showing that she "keeps even her prospective lover on the other side of the fence that surrounds her imperturbable composure" (Peck 89). Such a reading not only over-interprets but distorts, or perhaps simply misunderstands. It would be a foolish farmer indeed who would turn her cows into the pasture with the neighbor's simply to avoid having a wire fence between them while they milked. The problem in this passage is actually quite the opposite, since even the most ardent of friends are unlikely to do their milking in an open pasture at the edge of their property, from which they will have to carry heavy buckets back to the house, no doubt spilling some on the way. If anything, Cather is giving Alexandra an implausible degree of warmth toward Carl.

The passage in which Alexandra retrospectively ponders the disaster of Emil and Marie's love leads us, however, into other problems. Here is the passage, including a portion omitted earlier: "She knew that Emil was fond of Marie, but it had never occurred to her that Emil's feeling might be different from her own. She wondered at herself now, but she had never thought of danger in that direction. If Marie had been un-married,—oh, yes! Then she would have kept her eyes open." Why, we may ask, would she have regarded the possibility of a *licit* romance be-tween Emil and Marie as a "danger" and "kept her eyes open"? Not because she does not like Marie. On the contrary, she is very fond of her. The only reason supported by the text is that such a romance would not have been consistent with her ambitions for Emil. She has destined him for other and better things, things that build on a university educa-tion. Marie, it seems, would be socially inconsistent with whatever life that proved to be. In other words, we seem to have an indirect reference to social class, perhaps linked with ethnicity.

Although Cather is often thought of as exemplifying a kind of whole-some democratic sense that recognized and cherished the sturdy qualities of humble life, she also exhibited a pronounced taste for high culture and a love of affluent styles of living and aristocratic social tone. A society of wealth and cultivation was, of course, the world of *Alexander's Bridge.* It might seem, then, since she so emphasized her turn away from that novel's artificiality to her own fictional "home pasture," that class con-sciousness in the sense of a preference for members of the more affluent classes was a part of that artificiality and thus alien to her authentic self. But even those novels and stories set on the prairie, ostensibly celebrat-ing the beauty and strength of humble, uneducated people—the works that are taken to be her most characteristic—are pervaded by an aware-ness of social class. The generosity and goodness of the Burdens in *My Ántonia* reflects in part their sense of being among the established fam-ilies of the American democratic aristocracy—a seeming contradiction in terms. They manifest their superiority by giving things to the less for-tunate, who are expected to be appropriately grateful (as when Ántonia herself is taken into the Harlings' house in town as a domestic worker) or who can be gently laughed at when they show their eagerness for help in unseemly ways (as Mrs. Shimerda does when she grabs a cook-ing pot). In *A Lost Lady* Marian Forrester plays the role of the lovely patroness, taking cookies to little boys picnicking in her husband's grove of trees, ordering the lower-class boys out of the house when Niel Herbert is carried in with a broken leg, and buying fish at the back door from boys who recognize that their inferior position on the social lad-der compels silence about certain matters they have observed.

In *O Pioneers!* we see such a class sense in Alexandra's patronage (patronizing?) of neighbors once she becomes prosperous and in her statement to her brothers that they "*ought* to do more'" and have better foresight than their neighbors because "'our people were better people than these in the old country'" (*OP* 67). They are defined as part of what John Adams, arguing for social distinctions in the new republic against the more nearly equalitarian beliefs of Thomas Jefferson, called the "natural aristocracy." It was a concept in which Cather believed.

That this belief was linked to ethnicity and a rather rigid set of beliefs about the natural attributes of various ethnic groups is also hinted at in *O Pioneers!* and elaborated in later books. Cather may have "charted the emergence of a nation out of different peoples," as Guy Reynolds writes, but either in her own voice or in that of characters not clearly distanced she also invoked national stereotypes (47). An interviewer in 1921 (*WCIP* 22) reported that Cather's "foreigners" were "true to type": Czechs are "spunky" (*OP* 77), the "spirited and jolly" French like "a bit of swagger," Norwegians and Swedes are "self-centred, apt to be egotistical and jealous" (*OP* 192). The traits of "the Bohemians" are emphatically set off from those of the Scandinavians. It is an easy slide from ethnic stereotyping to Alexandra's casual assertion of inherited superiority. Accordingly, in *A Lost Lady* the Germans, whose customs are stigmatized as uncultured, know their place.

With respect to European immigrants, Cather's attitude was generally one of delight in variety. She was outspokenly opposed (in retrospect, at any rate) to the English-only policy that characterized the Great War period in the United States, condemning in a 1921 speech the "indiscriminate Americanization work of overzealous patriots who implant into the foreign minds a distaste for all they have brought of value from their own country." "No Nebraska child now growing up will ever have a mastery of a foreign language," she complained, "because your legislature has made it a crime to teach a foreign language to a child in its formative years" (*WCIP* 146–47). Sadly, she would reverse herself late in life, lamenting that her "gullible" country had let in so many immigrants of poor stock and ranting that for the past hundred years the United States had invited criminals and incompetents to come to America and live the good life, and now we were stuck with their descendants.[15] It is a harsh and intolerant statement not easily reconcilable with the welcoming vision of her plains novels.

IT IS ENTIRELY characteristic that immediately after the publication of
O Pioneers!, the first novel she set in her own place of Nebraska, Cather
took a trip to her own place of Virginia (see figure 18). She could scarcely
enact more clearly the dividedness of her sense of place. Writing to
Elsie Sergeant on September 12, 1913, from Winchester, where she and
Isabelle were taking a driving trip in the mountains near her childhood
home, she described the whole trip as something of a disaster and Winchester itself as dull and boring. She no longer cared, she said, about the
"holy and sacred peculiarities of the people she knew when she was little" and had no intention of making visits. The food available in commercial establishments could not have been worse "in the provinces of

Fig. 18. Cather during 1913 trip to Virginia.
(Nebraska State Historical Society)

Russia." Food was always a major item in Cather's sense of well-being. Although she still loved the mountains, the people she had cared about there were gone. Her claim that she no longer cared is belied, however, by the emotional pitch with which, in the midst of a complaint about the tiresomeness of long vacations, she burst into a diatribe against southern customs, especially of gender. Ten days later, when she again wrote to Sergeant, this time from the tiny hamlet of Gore, across the road from both the house where she was born and the house where she lived from the age of two until the family left for Nebraska, Willow Shade, she said that the trip into her home mountains had been wonderful after all.[16] The quick shift of intense reaction is as characteristic as her quick shift in focus from Nebraska to Virginia.

Cather would not write what she knew of that other home place for many years. After *O Pioneers!*, however, she did persist, though in fluctuating ways and with signal exceptions, in writing what she knew from firsthand experience; in both the "outdoor" sense of the scenes and people she overtly depicted and the "indoor" sense of covert reflexiveness, or self-writing. In *The Song of the Lark* Thea Kronborg may be a composite of singer Olive Fremstad and Mary Austin's actress figure in *A Woman of Genius*, but she is also, unmistakably, Willa Cather, with Cather's home town (though moved about three hundred miles to the west), her attic bedroom, traces of her mother, her younger siblings, her friendly town doctor, her determination, even her acquaintance with a railroad man killed in a wreck.[17] In portraying Thea's fatigue after a major performance and the quality of steel that has entered her soul as a corollary of her commitment to her art, Cather is examining the cost of her own commitment to her writing.

It is precisely this aspect of her self-examination that is most suggestive in the fact that *The Song of the Lark* directly followed *O Pioneers!* She was, in fact, well into thinking about her next novel by July 1913, only a month after publication of *O Pioneers!* If Alexander's bridge was a disguised reference to Cather's own effort to build an extended fiction, then the widely recognized conception of Alexandra as a kind of artist constitutes a linkage both backward to *Alexander's Bridge* and forward to *Lark*. Midway through *O Pioneers!* when Carl comes back to visit Alexandra after having been away, he pays tribute to her success as a farmer: "'Do you know, Alexandra . . . I've been thinking how strangely things work out. I've been away engraving other men's pictures, and you've stayed at home and made your own.' He pointed with his cigar toward the sleeping landscape" (*OP* 108). If in Cather's early stories set in Nebraska she had been sitting in the fields and howling for the world of art (or stage musicals), as she told Will Owen Jones, in *O Pioneers!* she was still displaying her insistent reach for art, even if she had stopped howling. But now she was doing so by defining the cornfield as itself a work of art.[18]

Such a definition may not be entirely plausible, but it seems to have pulled at her imagination rather persistently. Carrie Miner Sherwood recalled her saying, in a 1927 lecture in Red Cloud, that "the German housewife who sets before her family on Thanksgiving Day a perfectly roasted goose, is an artist," and so is "the farmer who goes out in the morning to harness his team, and pauses to admire the sunrise" (Bennett 168). Perhaps the idea appealed to her as a device for claiming solidarity, to counteract her growing sense of isolation from society in general and specifically from the people among whom she had grown up. In any event, the attempt so to define Alexandra shows us the impetus that would lead from her covertly autobiographical novel of a Nebraska farming woman to her conspicuously autobiographical novel of the midwestern artist who grows beyond the capacity of her originary place or people. Thea Kronborg is essentially the artist aspect of Alexandra that Carl recognized.

Fremstad—Swedish, midwestern, both earthy and artistic—was certainly a bridging figure, but there were others as well. One was the Swedish wife of a cousin Cather had been fond of, Howard Gore, who died in 1913, the year she began the novel. Gore's wife was named Lillian Thekla Brandthall: with the *kl* struck out, Thekla becomes Thea. Cather once described her as a regular Brunhilda who sang Grieg and read Ibsen "like the tragic muse"—attributes she assigns Thea Kronborg. Another bridge figure, curiously enough, was the model who posed for the frontispiece of Alexandra. Indeed, a reference to this shadowy figure in a letter from Cather to Sergeant virtually elides her with . . . Fremstad! In an excited exclamation, Cather wrote that she must remember to tell Elsie about the Swedish girl who posed for the picture and also about the wonderful Fremstad.[19] The intensity of phrasing is reminiscent of some of Cather's other accounts of the genesis of her novels in moments of discovery: the sudden twining of two stories into one to make *O Pioneers!* the abrupt seizing of the Taormina jar on Elsie Sergeant's table that helped her define her intended treatment of Ántonia, the discovery of a newspaper obituary that resulted, an hour later, in the conception of *A Lost Lady*.

Beyond Thea, Cather continued to write in an indirectly self-referential mode in *My Ántonia*, where Jim Burden's story draws on events and places she had observed in Nebraska, and again in *One of Ours*. Contrary to complaints by Ernest Hemingway and others that she was trying to tell a war story when she knew nothing about war, she was mainly occupied in that novel, much of it set in Nebraska, with writing about deeply personal matters. *One of Ours* reflects not only people and places she knew there (such as her Aunt Franc and her cousin G. P. Cather) but, in the central character's desperation to get away, her own feelings at the time she graduated from college. In *A Lost Lady* she once again wrote identifiably of a house and people she knew in Red Cloud, planting her own feelings in the confused narrator, Niel Herbert. In *The Professor's House*, in southwestern scenes comparable to those in *The Song of the Lark*, she looked outdoors at places she had known only as a visitor, though a repeated and very interested one, but in creating the professor himself she wrote with elaborate and troubling self-reflexiveness. And so forth, in varying degrees, culminating in the return to her family history, her first home, and her child self in *Sapphira and the Slave Girl*. Repeatedly we hear her asking in these novels, as she told the interviewer for the *Omaha World-Herald* in 1921, which was the real and which the false self. It was a quandary she was never to resolve.

6

Emergence / Nostalgia
What's a Woman to Do?

Who will wash the things away,
Wash them three times every day?
—"Poor Marty"

"Plenty of time for sleep," she said, "hereafter."
—"Macon Prairie"

As we have seen, Cather's problem of self-definition was in large part a problem of vocation. Defining herself from an early age as what might be called a Resistant New Woman, a New Woman committed to notions of personal singularity who refused to fit any prepared mold, she pursued the task of identifying a path of life very much as the task of defining a career path. At the same time, she required a path wide enough for expressive development. She needed both, achievement in a career and expression of individuality. Her work at *McClure's* had satisfied the first of these needs (and the concomitant need to feel important, evident as far back as the time when she helped at her father's office) but afforded little outlet for the second. Small wonder, then, that she found the work there enervating and sought a change, after almost six years as editor. Stepping out of her office role in 1912 was a gesture so dramatic and decisive that it redirected her life. In the most direct sense it led to the writing of *The Song of the Lark* and *My Ántonia* and their engagement with the problem of vocation, specifically a woman's vocation.

Cather's departure from *McClure's* enacted what Elizabeth Shepley Sergeant saw as "a truly gruelling inner pull between the opposites of East and West" (64). For E. K. Brown, that pull was expressive of the tension between her unconventionality and her veneration for "certain eternal values" (333). In her departure from *McClure's*, which was also a departure from the East to the expansive West, she also reenacted, in a sense, the Cather family's migration from the back country of the eastern seaboard to a sparsely inhabited frontier. But instead of retreating to Nebraska, she went on to Winslow, Arizona, where her brother Douglass was stationed with the Santa Fe Railroad. It was the most momentous trip of her much-traveled life. During what became an extended vacation not only from *McClure's* but from writing, she recovered from physical illness (she had been hospitalized in Boston for an unspecified "little surgical operation" in January)[1] and from what sounds very much like nervous exhaustion. In the rugged Southwest she discovered a new, vigorous, confident self. Relinquishing the underpinnings of employment security by which she had built a career up to this point, she took the heady step of defining herself as a freelance writer. She at last embraced the profession of novelist.

The story of that trip and of Cather's response to the high, rugged landscapes of Arizona and New Mexico has usually been told with reference to her development of an aesthetic based on the use of native materials. Much as the Anasazi women had once made beautiful pottery out of the deposits of clay they located about them, so Cather turned to the writing of a novel made out of the deposits (in memory) of her own experiences in her own place. Woodress calls the trip "a watershed in her career" (*Literary* 11). O'Brien identifies it as the enabling experience that led her to find her own voice in *O Pioneers!* Elaborating an argument suggested by Ellen Moers in 1976, O'Brien reads the creviced and folded landscape of the mesa country as an analogical female body that freed Cather to recognize her emotional affiliation with the female principle.[2] At the same time, its rocky outcroppings and heights that could only be explored by strenuous exertion implied and fostered a strong masculinity. More accurately, then, it was an androgynous body that freed her to recognize her own androgyny. The "unusual contours" of the Southwestern landscape, expressive of both male and female, offered Cather a "magical . . . balancing" and "integration of opposites" that "affected her emotionally, spiritually, imaginatively, erotically" (O'Brien, *Emerging* 403). There she rode and hiked, she recovered her health, she opened herself to subtleties of color and form with an almost painterly eye, and she went dancing with a younger man named Julio, about whom she rhapsodized in letters to Sergeant.

The letters about what O'Brien refers to as her "love affair" with Julio undermine prevailing notions of Cather as a sexless being. Woodress (*Literary* 125) believes she "sublimated her sexual impulses in her work." Yet she is so breathlessly exclamatory about the attentions and the physical presence of this "won-der-ful" younger man she has known only briefly that one can scarcely *not* see erotic excitement in her ravings. She breaks into talking about him when she says she had not meant to; describes his skin tones, the shape of his upper lip, the sound of his voice; confides that it has taken her "days to get over" the impact of an excursion with him in the Painted Desert. The fact that she chose to relay an amorous serenade sung to her by Julio, which according to him should be sung only by a married woman to her husband or lover— indeed, the fact that he sang her such a song at all—also implies an erotic coloring to their fling, as does the fact that Edith Lewis asked Sergeant to "reserve" one of these letters from reading by anyone else.[3]

Beyond her personal response, it is also notable that Cather *does* present Julio as a fling, the kind of passing erotic amusement that, as stereotype would have it, is indulged in by vacationing men. Turning that stereotype on its head, she apologizes for writing the kind of letter she herself hates that goes on and on about good-looking Latin youths. The implication is that such liaisons are a common occurrence, and the exoticism of the ethnic labeling suggests the attitude of imperialist romanticizing that Edward Said has taught us to call Orientalism. If Sergeant came to New Mexico, Cather assured her, she would be sure to find a Mexican lover. Her casting of the male in the role of muse, a role conventionally assigned to the female for the benefit of the male artist, while she, the artist, writes down the songs he spontaneously sings, takes the inversion of gender stereotype further. If brought back East he would be able to "make an easy living" not as an artist but as a model, that is, presumably by posing in the nude—another sidelong reference to an erotic quality in her interest.[4]

When she began to feel satiated with landscape and impatient for wider social contact (and perhaps ready to utilize the energy inspired by her male muse) she moved on to Red Cloud, arriving on June 11, ready to get back to work after an adventurous two months. The work she was ready to complete—*O Pioneers!*—was, she told Sergeant, the very story she had "always wanted to write."[5] But in another sense the work she was ready for was *The Song of the Lark*. The trip and her sense of herself as a woman on the verge of a hard-won artistic career gave her the impetus she needed for that at once introspective and socially observant book.

WE HAVE ALREADY noted that the creation of Alexandra—a woman strong, independent, and intelligent, and also, as Carl designates her, an artist—led directly to Cather's next heroine. Alexandra, with her monumentality and her determination, would modulate into Thea Kronborg. In addition, two other disparate and fortuitous events converged in 1912 to foster Cather's work on *Lark:* her ghostwriting of S. S. McClure's autobiography and the publication of Mary Austin's novel *A Woman of Genius.*

Cather's writing of the autobiography might seem less relevant to the coming novel and the one after it, *My Ántonia,* than her completion of the portrait of Alexandra, but it was, in fact, a directly contributive experience. She later told Will Owen Jones that her work on McClure's autobiography developed her competence in handling a male narrative voice. There were more immediate benefits as well. She agreed to the project in April, writing to McClure from her brother's house in Winslow, then wrote again on June 12, only a day after her arrival in Red Cloud, assuring him that whatever else she did that fall, she would indeed help with the autobiography and—an important point for the now impecunious McClure—would do so gratis, as a gesture of friendship. In part, she acknowledged, her offer was motivated by gratitude for the many favors he had done her. But it seems to have been motivated, too, by a realization of parallels between McClure and herself. Calling his personal history a remarkable one, even though his career might now seem to be ended, she assured him that considering the stresses of his work, it was no wonder he was exhausted, but even so, she had never felt his potential for accomplishment so powerful as it now was.[6]

Her assessment seems to have represented, to some degree, a process of projection. She, too, had had remarkable success, had become tired, and was now seeing her former career as being "over" while feeling in herself a power that she had never felt before. Her work on McClure's personal narrative could scarcely have been more timely for the process of self-examination and reorientation in which she was engaged. She might well have identified with his rise from an unlikely background; he had emerged from poverty as an Irish immigrant, she from the obscurity of the hinterland and the disadvantages of her sex. She must have recognized herself, too, in his determination to escape the scenes of his later childhood to advance his education and his sense of the "necessity to keep moving" (Cather, *Eddy* 182). Working on McClure's autobiography entailed reflecting on and putting into words all of these factors, all of which then entered into the story of Thea. The overriding theme around which they clustered was the story of McClure's building of a career, very much the process in which Thea would be engaged and in which Cather herself was engaged at the time. This theme reached back, too, to her earlier ghostwritten biography, *The Life of Mary Baker G. Eddy*, where she had presented another character of "masterful will and great force of personality" as an unlikely leader "groping for a vocation" (57, 62).

The other fortuitous event of 1912, the publication of Mary Austin's long autobiographical novel, represented an advance in the public reputation of an author who was considerably better known at the time than Cather. Austin's reputation was based primarily on her 1903 book about the far Southwest, *The Land of Little Rain*, but she was also a frequent contributor to national magazines. *Little Rain*, for instance, had first appeared in serial form in *Atlantic Monthly*. In addition, Austin had published a moderately successful first novel set in southern California, *Isidro*, and a second, *Santa Lucia*, that became something of a scandal when copies were removed from libraries and bookstores on grounds of immorality. There can be no doubt that Cather knew Austin's work; she seems to have borrowed from one of her stories as early as 1899.[7] The two were personally acquainted, probably by way of former *McClure's* staffers Lincoln Steffens and Ida Tarbell, by at least 1910. Cather would almost certainly have read *A Woman of Genius* soon after publication. It became another catalyst for the material she would soon begin working up into her own longest novel.

A Woman of Genius was by no means the only novel about the emergence of the woman artist that Cather could have taken as a model for the work gestating in her, but the similarities are too close to have resulted from happenstance or merely a shared engagement with the woman-as-artist figure.[8] The most salient of these is simply the fact that both central characters are stage performers, Austin's Olivia an actress, Cather's Thea a singer whose roles are notably well acted. Actresses had, of course, long been a center of Cather's aesthetic attention, her concern with the performance of gender, and her pondering of the problems, advantages, and ultimate feasibility of careers for women. Austin's novel, then, entered a space in her mind that was already well prepared.

By mid-August 1912 Cather was in Pittsburgh, reading the French historian Michelet with Isabelle and trying to settle her feelings about Julio. After two intense weeks in New York making arrangements for her next few months' work (which probably meant starting to listen to the reminiscences that she would shape into McClure's autobiography), she was back in Pittsburgh, turning her hand to *O Pioneers!* and some stories for the magazine. The novel was fast work. By January, having moved into a spacious apartment in New York at Number 5 Bank Street that Edith Lewis had located for the two of them in September, she was sufficiently at leisure to invest time and effort in decorating what would be their home until 1927.[9]

The fact that Cather and Lewis chose to live where they did alerts us to an aspect of Cather's life that has not been adequately recognized. From the time she moved to New York in 1906 she located herself in Greenwich Village. Before moving to Bank Street she lived for several years at 82 Washington Place, just off Washington Square, and before that at No. 60 Washington Square, on what was called Genius Row. The Village was already established as the home of the avant garde, although other groups (from immigrants to those of the well-heeled who enjoyed rubbing shoulders with artistic types) lived there as well. The Golden Swan Bar (known as the Hell Hole) where Eugene O'Neill and friends gathered was less than a block from her first apartment. Stieglitz's gallery 291 was within comfortable walking distance, as was, after 1912, Mabel Dodge's apartment-salon. When Cather and Lewis moved to their apartment at 82 Washington Place in the fall of 1908, she mentioned to Sarah Orne Jewett that they usually dined at the Brevoort Hotel four nights a week.[10] The Brevoort, then the "meeting ground for the moneyed and the bohemian" (Watson 124), was not far, but if they started from their apartment they would have been making it a point to go there. About six months after the move to 5 Bank Street the *Masses* took office space less than a block away; John Reed was already nearby. With only a few exceptions—one being Floyd Dell, whom Hutchins Hapgood called "the spokesman of the Village" (Watson 152)—there is surprisingly little evidence that Cather interacted with any of these people and groups, but it is clear that the atmosphere of bohemia was all around and that she chose to be within it. She was quite aware of and open to the new in painting, yet there seems to be no reference in any of her correspondence to the Armory Show of 1913. It is puzzling.[11]

Proofs of *O Pioneers!* started arriving in early April 1913. But even though Cather had said only shortly before that it was the story she had always wanted to write and had told her Aunt Franc in February that it was a great deal better than *Alexander's Bridge*, she was already feeling some reservations, confessing to Elsie Sergeant on April 22 that she was now wanting to do something of a very different sort. Signaling what that might be, she went on to say that she had gone to see Olive Fremstad the previous week and "ever since" had been "choked up by things un-utterable. If one could write all this battered Swede made one know, it would be a project well worthwhile."[12] By July 4, if not before, she was into the work on her next novel.

The Song of the Lark chronicles in disguise much of Cather's life up to that time and shows that its central thread was the struggle to establish a career. More specifically, in its crucial central section (the last chapter of Part III and the whole of Part IV) the novel is focused on her experience in 1911–12 of disengaging herself from *McClure's* and redirecting her sense of vocation. But the book also chronicles the artistic development of Olive Fremstad, whose life in some ways paralleled Cather's own. In effect, by representing Fremstad in a heroine who also represented herself, Cather had at last become the figure who had so long intrigued her, a performing artist.

DURING THE same period in which she produced *The Song of the Lark*, Cather also wrote several short stories about opera singers. Her interest in vocal art during these years, though by no means new, may well have been impelled by her awareness of finding her own voice in *O Pioneers!* In an interview only a few years later she would employ a metaphor of singing in referring to her work (*WCIP* 37). It is important to recognize, however, that these stories of women singers, usually read as a distinct group indicating "just how strong a hold opera singers had on Cather's imagination" (Meyering 215), are actually a subset of a group of stories about women's work and careers more generally, written during the years when Cather was redefining her own vocation. During these same years the Great War was causing dramatic changes in women's work lives throughout America and elsewhere. Mary Austin wrote in a 1919 essay that one of the three "sex superstitions" of which the war was ridding humanity was the belief that "the work a human being may do in the world is determined by sex" (*Beyond* 46).[13] Rather than turning aside from real-world issues to a rarefied aestheticism, Cather was addressing one of the great issues of her time.

All but one of the eight stories she published between "The Bohemian Girl" and *Youth and the Bright Medusa* (1920) are related in one way or another to women's work and careers. The one exception, "Consequences" (*McClure's*, November 1915), concerns the *lack* of a career. "The Bookkeeper's Wife" (*Century*, May 1916), "Ardessa" (*Century*, May 1918), and "Her Boss" (*Smart Set*, October 1919) depict work in offices and would have gone into a volume she was thinking of doing, to be called "Office Wives." It is clear from these three stories that Cather well understood the power structures in such work environments. Her typists and secretaries are not so much career women as functionaries. The remaining four are about singers: "The Diamond Mine" (*McClure's*, October 1916), "A Gold Slipper" (*Harper's*, January 1917), "Scandal" (*Century*, August 1919), and "Coming, Aphrodite!" (first published in August 1920 in *Smart Set* in a less risqué version called "Coming, Eden Bower!" and then in its present form a month later in *Youth and the Bright Medusa* [SPO]).

In "Coming, Aphrodite" it is a male who is presented as the serious artist, while Eden Bower might best be described as an entertainer. She succeeds in her career but scarcely has the sense of artistic vocation of a Thea Kronborg. But the central character of "A Gold Slipper" and "Scandal," Kitty Ayrshire, is a fine singer and a star. Both stories center on the shortcomings of the star system with respect to the artist's relation to her audience, in particular the public's readiness to believe titillating rumors or to think of performers as frivolous and shallow. But the Kitty Ayrshire stories also take up the issue of men's assumptions about women more generally. In a passage of uncharacteristically feminist import, Kitty complains that men consider women as (to use a term from a later day) sex objects. Men, she says, "'never see our real faces . . . never get more than one type through their thick heads; they try to make all women look like some wife or mistress'" (*SPO* 458). Ayrshire wants to be seen as an individual, not merely a member of a category defined by a single function, and she wants to be respected as a professional.

"The Diamond Mine," written in early 1916 but held up until late in the year by fears of a libel suit, is the most substantive story of the group.[14] Here Cather treated some of the issues dealt with in *The Song of the Lark*, particularly the woman artist's relation to her family and the emotionally draining nature of her work. Cressida Garnet, a soprano regarded by her "comfortable and indolent and vastly self-satisfied" family as a "diamond mine" or source of money for their own purposes, has two sisters and a brother who are jealous of her ability and doubtful of both her achievement and her judgment (*SPO* 404). In this sense, they are much like the Kronborg brothers in *Lark*, who feel disgraced by Thea's friendship with members of the Spanish community, and their sister Anna, who believes she is over-indulged. Considering the obvious parallels between Cather's origins and those she assigns Thea, and considering the bitterness with which the issue is presented in "The Diamond Mine," one wonders to what extent she felt herself estranged from or even used by her own family. But the most notable similarity of the story to the novel is the hard work and determination with which Cressida pursues her career: "For twenty years she had been plunged in struggle; fighting for her life at first, then for a beginning, for growth, and at last for eminence and perfection; fighting in the dark, and afterward in the light" (404). It is a powerful statement of what is entailed by a sense of artistic vocation.

By returning to the matter of a woman's vocation at a time when she was redefining her own, Cather also revisited the problem of her relation with her mother. As Merrill Skaggs has judged in an astute reading of the late and intensively domestic *Shadows on the Rock*, by writing about a girl who not only seeks and finds satisfaction in domestic order but does so precisely in accordance with her mother's instructions, Cather may have been performing an act of "ritual penance," giving a set of "idealized parents" the "perfect firstborn female" that she had not in fact been (Skaggs, "Good" 29). She had long since departed from her mother's way by remaining unmarried and pursuing her own living and the satisfactions of career advancement. It is not clear what Jennie Cather thought of all this, but it is known that at some points, at least, she had disapproved or even felt disgraced by certain of her daughter's behaviors. A letter she wrote to Dorothy Canfield in 1903 speaks obscurely of the Canfields' good influence and a hope that S. S. McClure's notice (which she seems to have learned of only through the letter from Dorothy that prompted this reply) might strengthen her daughter's resolve to use her advantages wisely. The implication is that she had not always done so in the past. About the same time, Cather herself wrote to Canfield indicating that there may have been an estrangement between herself and her mother. Dorothy's letter, she said, had prompted the first letter from her mother in two years that she could bear to read through. Its tone—as if this was remarkable—was almost free of hostility or reproach, and as a result she was beginning to think a peaceful adjustment might yet be possible between them.[15]

There is evidence, then, of sporadic tension between mother and daughter during the years when Cather was building her career. At the same time, there is also considerable evidence of daughterly care in Cather's continuing trips home and her efforts to leap into the domestic breach at times when her mother was ill (for instance, in 1916). Her feelings seem to have been sorely ambivalent. Throughout her life she was torn between a yearning for the securities of home (the place of the mother) and a compulsion to rebel against confinement and break free of a way of life that threatened her creativity.[16] The former expressed itself in the tributes to domesticity that have sometimes been celebrated as the essence of her work or even the whole of her fictive vision. But it was the latter, the rebellion against constraint that was also implicitly a rebellion against the figure of the mother, that was the stronger of the two. It was that impetus that chiefly powered *The Song of the Lark*, a text that defies many social conventions.

In reconfronting her maternal conflict, Cather cast herself in the novel as the inadequately loved and underappreciated daughter who must escape her mother and a constricting small-town environment if she is to fulfill her vocation as artist. O'Brien has conjectured that Mary Virginia Cather may actually have "identified with her rebellious daughter who was enacting the assertiveness and anger she could not express herself" (*Emerging* 105), but even if this was so, she still provided the lived example of the female role against which Cather's sense of vocation defined itself. Cather did concede to the fictional mother the first recognition of Thea's talent and a realization that the budding artist must work to develop such a gift. It is Mrs. Kronborg, rather than her husband, who has a conception of Thea's possibilities. Indeed, she so strongly conceives of talent as an obligation to work that Doctor Archie, Thea's opinionated friend, worries she is being overworked. Thea herself does not take that view. She knows that it is her mother who has made piano lessons available to her and who makes the decision to let her go to Chicago in accordance with Ray Kennedy's wishes (using the money left to her in his will). If she at times feels driven by the necessity to practice, she also centers her life on the opportunity that has been given her. The portrait of Mrs. Kronborg, then, is a mixed one.

Lark is autobiographical, of course, in other ways besides the mother-daughter relationship. The Panther Canyon sequence, a version of Cather's own flight from New York to the Southwest, is the most commonly recognized of these, but Cather admittedly transferred a good many of her own experiences to Thea's story. The small-town western setting, called Moonstone and situated in Colorado, is patently a version of Red Cloud, and the general situation of the family recognizably depicts that of the Cathers despite the recasting of the father as a minister.[17] The time frame of the opening action is almost precisely accurate in tracking Cather's life. If we take up the opening reference to "twenty-five years ago" and go back twenty-five years from 1913, when she began the book, the time would be 1888. In that year, until her December birthday, Cather would have been eleven, Thea's age at the opening, *if she had been born in 1876* as she claimed. The Cathers moved to Red Cloud in September 1884, not long before her *actual* eleventh birthday. Their crowded living quarters are reflected in the Kronborgs' house, where there is "no spare bedroom" (*SL* 5). Like Thea, Cather was one of seven children; the birth of the Kronborgs' seventh brings Doctor Archie to the house in the first chapter. Like Thea, Cather had to help with the younger ones as she was growing up. We can well believe that even if she did not say so directly, she felt herself, as Doctor Archie thinks of Thea, "worth the whole litter" (7).

The attic room that Thea fixes up as her private retreat was also drawn directly from Cather's own room, which can still be seen in the Red Cloud home with the wallpaper Cather put there herself. But the role of the mother in the creation of this private space is significantly altered. It was at her mother's initiative that Cather's room was partitioned off from an el-shaped space she had shared with two of her brothers. O'Brien, who writes that Virginia Cather "decreed" Willa should have her own room, regards that fact as important evidence of maternal encouragement (*Emerging* 84, 104). In the novel, Thea is simply "allowed" to use the money she earns by giving piano lessons to "fix up a little room for herself upstairs in the half-storey" (*SL* 45). The initiative seems to be entirely her own; there is no reference to any intervention on the part of her mother. O'Brien's account (85) of the fictional representation of events, that Cather "describes the acquisition of her own bedroom," obscures this significant revision. But O'Brien wishes to demonstrate maternal nurturance in Cather's imaginative growth. Why Cather muted her mother's role in so crucial an incident remains a mystery, but the effect is to accentuate Thea's difference from her family and particularly (by the simple fact of minimizing the mother's actual role here) her distance from her mother. If her pervasive impulse was to show Thea as a resistant heroine, as I have proposed, this deviation serves that purpose.

Thea's need for a private space reflects Cather's lifelong need for such spaces. Her possession of the room represents "the beginning of a new era" in her life" and is "one of the most important things that ever happened to her" (*SL* 46), affording her a place of retreat and reflection. At the same time, her eager gaze out the open window marks her as the aspiring woman whose enjoyment of indoor spaces is contingent on their having openings for vision and, by implication, for departure. Her imaginatively expansive gaze out the window conveys her need to escape the limitations of her small-town home, a need Cather identified in her preface to the 1932 edition: "What I cared about, and still care about, was the girl's escape." In assigning such an escape wish to a female character, she challenged conventional gender assumptions that accorded wanderlust to the male, and she emphasized that challenge by placing Thea in contact with such a wandering male. Thea's friend in the Mexican sector of Moonstone, Juan Tellamontez, called Spanish Johnny, is seized from time to time by the need to throw over the traces. He goes on binges of singing and mandolin playing at a local bar; then he hops a freight train and makes his way to Mexico, where he performs in bars and lives riotously. After Spanish Johnny returns exhausted and ill from one of these periods of vagrancy early in the novel, Mrs. Tellamontez attempts to explain her husband's urge to roam by reference to the roaring in a seashell. Just as one might be lured by that roaring to go find the sea itself, so he is lured by a little appreciation of his music to break out of his routine and go off seeking a free life as bar musician. It is a male thing to do. But it is Thea, not the male Dr. Archie, who immediately understands. Pressing the shell to her ear, she hears a sound "like something calling one" and thinks, "So that was why Johnny ran away" (*SL* 36). She, too, hears the call.

Escape is not easy. The lengthiness of Thea's preparation for her ultimate emergence as a powerful woman artist is reflected in the prolonging of the early structural sections of the novel, about her growing up and training, and the progressive shortening of the later ones, a speed-up effect that Cather's editor considered awkward but that Cather insisted was an integral part of her structural plan for the book.[18] Certainly from the vantage of 1913–14 the difficulty of the escape was autobiographically accurate. When Cather went on extended leave from *McClure's* in early 1912, it had been twenty years since she published her first work of fiction and still she was in doubt whether she could cast herself wholly on her resources as novelist. Her decisive trip to the Southwest was as reorienting for her as it is in the novel for Thea, who less than a year later (the delay being her unnarrated escapade to Mexico with Fred Ottenburg) resolves to go to Germany to continue her professional preparation. A year after her own return from the Southwest, Cather had crystalized the conception for *O Pioneers!*, completed it, seen it published to glowing reviews, and begun writing her next novel for an eagerly waiting publisher. It must indeed have seemed as if time were speeding up, as it seems to do for Thea in the accelerating structure of the novel.

Thea's first major opportunity is the chance to sing the part of Elisabeth in *Tannhäuser*, in Germany. Her determination to take advantage of that opportunity even at the cost of coming to her mother's deathbed (a refusal that she would repeat in her later novel *Shadows on the Rock*) is the clearest possible dramatization of the fact that her sense of vocation entails a kind of hard-heartedness that is itself a prolonged rebellion against conventional expectations.[19] Specifically, it is a rebellion against the mother's life-pattern, a statement that home and family relations do not invariably come first for every woman. The fact that Thea is a performing artist whose itinerary is controlled by production schedules and the availability of roles makes understandable her decision to stay in Germany and sing what amounts to her debut, rather than come to her mother. Mrs. Kronborg herself seems resigned to her absence, even proud of it, proving that she is, after all, a supportive mother, even if not always an expressive one.

For Cather herself, the necessity of staying away from home was less clear. As a writer rather than a performing artist, she might seem to be more fully in control of her own schedule and able to work wherever she happened to be. Yet she had for years felt unable to write at home. After all, it was after she went away to college that she began to write; her professional self-definition was bound up with departure; and whether her family understood it or not, she had to locate her work elsewhere. Even in 1912 when she went away to Arizona, she could not, with her brother in effect looking over her shoulder, take advantage of the time and space available to her. In a sense, she defied family once again. She wrote to Elsie Sergeant that she always felt rather paralyzed by the West, somewhat as she had felt as a child. Her brother's jerry-built "casa" was too confining for work; the whole atmosphere was wrong for it. He was not able to understand that, but it was true, and so she did not plan to stay long.[20]

Cather's vocation was tied to geographic mobility as well as to defiance of family, even though she maintained her ties to home and family while she pursued it. Escaping the pressure of *McClure's* had meant going west, but when she reached an outpost of family, at Douglass's casa in Arizona, she once again needed to go east. She wrote *about* the West, but she did so *in* the East—at Isabelle's house in Pittsburgh, at her Bank Street (or later, Park Avenue) apartment, and after 1917 at Jaffrey, New Hampshire. Her sense of vocation entailed defiance of expectation and connection with the world of high culture, and all of these drew her to the East Coast or beyond.

IN ASSOCIATING emergence with travel Cather was invoking both a long-established trope and a mode of experience and writing that was being energetically seized upon by women of her generation. Mary Suzanne Schriber has demonstrated that in the last third of the nineteenth century American women traveled abroad and wrote about their travels as never before. The total number of travel books published in the United States dramatically accelerated (from 325 between 1830 and the Civil War to 1440 between the war and 1900), while at the same time women were producing a larger share of the total. More important, women became travelers in their own right, for their own purposes, rather than accidental tourists accompanying husbands or fathers. Since travel was in various ways associated with identity, Schriber writes, women's "movement . . . out from domestic shores and into international spaces" served as an aspect of their revision of gender assumptions (2–4). Having been "set . . . moving through time and space as men had historically done," women who wrote about their travels cast them as a "liberating activity" (37–38). Their writing about travel was a "political act," particularly when they traveled alone or in the company of another woman rather than a custodial male (148). They were often "a type of the New Woman" (41).

Cather was one of those women who traveled abroad for her own purposes in the company of another young woman. In 1902 she and Isabelle McClung went to England, Scotland, and France, and she wrote about the experience in articles sent back to the *Nebraska State Journal.* That fact, as well as the articles themselves, has usually been seen—and rightly so—as an expression of her veneration of European cultural traditions. Brown writes of the trip as a "pilgrimage" of "intellectual and aesthetic discovery" (99–100). Woodress sees it as a reflection of the "compelling imperative" for the "educated American" to "water his or her cultural roots" (*Literary* 156). But it was also a public statement of her freedom to go where she wanted to go. By 1902 the spectacle of two young women traveling about together without masculine oversight was no longer so startling as it had been in the late 1880s when Lillian Leland, at the age of twenty-five, took a two-year global tour that she recounted in *Traveling Alone* (1890) and Elizabeth Cochrane Seaman (pseud. Nellie Bly) circumnavigated the globe alone, carrying her own luggage (one small bag), under the sponsorship of Joseph Pulitzer. Such women "used the figure of the solo female traveler in the interests of a woman's agenda" (Schriber 32–33, 159–64, 156).

Cather did not overtly pursue a "woman's agenda" in her writing. She avoided advocacy of causes. Even so, travel carried a well-established import of independence and defiance of convention, and it is clear in her travel dispatches (collected as *Willa Cather in Europe*) that she was aware of the gender issues involved. She noted, for example, that she and Isabelle stayed at a hotel that was not their preferred choice because it was "rather more reputable for women travelling alone" (*WCIE* 121). In another two decades such issues would all but disappear in the wake of women's wartime travels (in the case of American women, often for reasons of relief work), but in 1915, when *The Song of the Lark* was published, the war was only beginning to have an impact. Thea's solitary travels to Chicago, to Panther Canyon, and to New York and Germany, let alone her traveling with a man to whom she is not married, still defied conventional parameters for middle-class women's lives. They indicated Cather's realization that if a woman wanted to pursue an artistic vocation—especially in the performance arts, where Cather had long since observed the comings and goings of such admired but undeniably flamboyant performers as Sarah Bernhardt—she had to be able to go where she needed for training and for production opportunities. Thea stubbornly goes her own way and moves into an "antidomestic" pattern of life (Romines, *Home* 146).

Another convention Cather defied both in her own person and in her depiction of Thea as a woman who works hard in pursuit of a career was the conception of upper- and upper-middle-class women as creatures of cultivated leisure. We see this convention most clearly in late-nineteenth-century and early-twentieth-century American painting, with its insistence on depicting women in repose, often as innocents or angels or as idealized embodiments of high culture. Cather's interest in the work of French artist Pierre Puvis de Chavannes (1824–98), customarily linked only to *Death Comes for the Archbishop*, becomes pertinent here because it was largely under what Bailey Van Hook calls the "pervasive influence" of Puvis (along with James McNeill Whistler) that American artists turned to "decorative" painting characterized by a vaguely Classical decorum and an insistent presence of ornamental female figures.[21] It was a style that according to Van Hook reflected a widespread "construction of the feminine gender as leisure-bound" (12). Like notions of women's immobility, that style would soon die out. By the end of the Great War a preoccupation with qualities of naive loveliness would be perceived as "not only old-fashioned but negative" (212). But at the time Cather wrote *The Song of the Lark* such a change had not yet occurred.

Probably Cather first saw the work of Puvis de Chavannes during her 1902 visit to Paris; his mural *The Education of Saint Genevieve* at the Panthéon had been completed some two decades earlier. Certainly she would have seen his decorative paintings at the Boston Public Library in 1907 or 1908 (see figure 19). We can see what an appeal Puvis's painting would hold for her, with its idealized Classicism, its chasteness, its vaguely allegorical evocation of an "Arcadian past, uncomplicated by the moral and social dilemmas of the industrial nineteenth century," and its stylistic "synthesis of idealism and realism" (Van Hook 37, 96). Her own style can be characterized in similar terms.[22] Especially with respect to the insistence on leisure, however, her depictions of women bear little similarity to those of American artists influenced by Puvis.

The pervasive style of representation of the female during the decades preceding Cather's novel was the woman in repose—as in John White Alexander's painting *Repose* (c. 1895), John Singer Sargent's *Repose* (1911),

Fig. 19. Mural by Puvis de Chavannes, *The Muses of Inspiration Hail the Spirit, the Harbinger of Light*, Boston Public Library. (Courtesy of the Trustees of the Boston Public Library)

and countless others showing young and ideally beautiful women in quiet, restful leisure or serving graceful allegorical functions (see figure 20). Instead, Cather created a young woman who worked and who, when she went on vacation, hiked and climbed in rugged terrain. Thea's notion of leisure is active, even masculine.[23] Cather deconstructs the gendering of leisure as well as the assignment of upper-middle-class women to leisure rather than to work. The primary visual icon on which *The Song of the Lark* was modeled, Jules Breton's painting by that name, was a view of a peasant girl, sentimentalized to be sure but showing her with her tools of work (see figure 21). In her commitment to her work, Thea defies not only the expectation that a genteel woman will occupy herself in cultivated leisure but also the gendered assumption that the woman artist will be a cultivated amateur.

Thea also defies the prevailing assumptions of her time as to sexual behavior. Although Cather's presentation of Thea's liaison with Fred Ottenburg while he is still married to his first wife is scarcely explicit, she makes it clear enough that when they are together in Panther Canyon without chaperone their relationship is not lacking in eroticism.[24]

Fig. 20. John Singer Sargent, *Repose*, 1911. (National Gallery of Art)

Freedom to cultivate her art has entailed freedom to express her erotic emotions. Such behavior was, of course, commonly attributed to actresses, who were widely assumed to be loose women. The word *actress* was sometimes used as a euphemism for *prostitute*. Cather's interest in actresses, then, and especially her consorting with actresses during her college years, might be considered a defiance of the strictest moral conventions even though (as Cynthia Griffin Wolff has demonstrated) she was participating in a widespread craze among young girls, much like the later craze for movie stars. But Thea is not, after all, an actress; she is a musical artist, a category of performer that was regularly accommodated to respectability, as its association with church services at various points in the text makes clear.

When Thea and Fred are camping together, he freely touches her, kisses her, and whispers something that elicits her laugh and leads to their withdrawing into a place out of sight of the curious ranch hand

Fig. 21. Jules Breton, *The Song of the Lark*. (Photograph courtesy of
The Art Institute of Chicago)

who has been watching them. (As is so often true, Cather's narrative perspective moves around, sometimes disconcertingly, from one character to another.) Equally unconventional is Thea's competitiveness toward Fred. Rather than defer to male judgment and prowess, she wants to win when they engage in games of fencing and rock sailing and is "furious" when her rock does not sail as far as his: "'There it goes again! Not nearly so far as yours. What *is* the matter with me?" (*SL* 244). Her determination to excel at rock throwing, even in competition with a man to whom she is attracted, is analogous to her determination to excel as an artist. Similarly, when they are hiking and she wants to climb higher than he thinks is prudent, she insists, "'I'm not going to stop now until I get there . . . I'll go on alone'" (251). Going on (though not entirely alone) is what she does for years, in preparation for the career she can as yet only intuit. Like the eagle she sees flying above the rim of the canyon, she fastens her sense of self on "endeavour, achievement, desire, glorious striving" (*SL* 253).

When Fred mentions the possibility of "'a comfortable flat in Chicago . . . and a family to bring up,'" Thea finds the idea "'perfectly hideous!'" What she likes is "'waking up every morning with the feeling that your life is your own, and your strength is your own, and your talent is your own'" (250)—that is, with the independence usually assumed to belong to men, but not women. At the end of their visit to his father's ranch, Fred proposes that they go away together to Mexico. His unspoken intention to "make it up to her" by helping her get on in her career since he cannot marry her (262) makes it clear that he anticipates a sexual relation.[25] His deception in eliciting sex while letting her believe they can marry if she chooses is, of course, what he will need to "make up" to her. The novel omits any depiction of their time in Mexico; neither here nor elsewhere does Cather attempt to depict sex explicitly. (She comes closest to doing so in "Coming, Aphrodite!") But the scene between them after they return to New York confirms that Thea now considers herself a fallen woman who has been "'easy'" and has been "'take[n] . . . in'" (281). Her reason for refusing to borrow money from Fred for study in Germany is that she would regard herself as a kind of whore if she did so: "'If I borrow from [Doctor Archie], it's to study. Anything I took from you would be different. As I said before, you'd be keeping me'" (282).

Cather was aware that the episode raised eyebrows among readers, in Nebraska at any rate. She wrote humorously to Dorothy Canfield Fisher that Dorothy's admirers there (apparently more morally demanding than her own) were crying out that they *hoped* Thea had not lived in sin with Fred in Mexico. Mariel Gere was reported to be bitterly indignant at the immorality of the novel, which by not being obvious was all the more corrupting.[26] Although most readers would demur from Gere's judgment of immorality, her opinion showed astute understanding of the nature of Cather's writing. She realized that it operated through indirection and tacitness and that the touch of immorality in the novel was no less real, or perhaps more so, for not being blatant.

The same letter in which Cather reports her Nebraska readers' shock at her "immoral" novel includes a strikingly open avowal of what I have referred to as her rebelliousness or resistance to convention and her linkage of rebellion to physical escape. Commenting on Canfield Fisher's own recently published novel *Bent Twig*, she wrote that she would escape just as Dorothy's character did if she felt the powers of social conventionality closing in. She added that she liked the one vagrant sheep better than the ninety and nine that stayed obediently in the fold.[27]

NOT LONG after the October 1915 publication of *The Song of the Lark* Cather told Dorothy Canfield Fisher that the point of the book was not the development of a genius but Thea's relationship to Moonstone.[28] In most readers' experience, however, the point is Thea's development. Both Stouck (*Imagination* 183–98) and Rosowski (*Voyage* 69) identify its genre as the *Künstlerroman*. Rosowski's justification of this label is both concise and precisely correct: "The central relationship is between the major character's mind and art; secondary characters, setting, and action support that development."

Writers are, of course, notoriously unreliable guides to their own work. Cather may have been apprehensive that if she avowed a purpose of celebrating the development of genius, Canfield Fisher, who would have recognized many of the autobiographical elements in the novel, might think she had once again, as in the "Profile" episode a decade earlier, been overbearingly egocentric. In any event, she contradicted her statement of intention on other occasions. When Ferris Greenslet gently objected to the novel's structure, she replied that she was thinking of subtitling it "The Story of an Artist's Youth," a phrase that would seem to emphasize both the idea of the artist (or "genius") and the idea of preparation.[29]

Her focus was indeed on the arduous process of preparation, the question of how the artist defines herself, how she finds what it is that she needs to do and equips herself to do it. If Part IV (the Panther Canyon sequence) is the decisive point of reorientation, another "turn" almost as important occurs near the end of Part II when Harsanyi, Thea's piano teacher but in a larger sense her music teacher, urges her, in impassioned tones, to redirect her efforts. Significantly, it is at this crucial point (and I believe only here) that Cather introduces the key term *vocation*. Just as significantly, she identifies it with the emergence of selfhood: "'I believe that the strongest need of your nature is to find yourself, to emerge *as* yourself. . . . You have brains enough and talent enough. But to do what you will want to do, it takes more than these— it takes vocation. Now, I think you have vocation, but for the voice, not for the piano'" (166). Thea's voice, her vocation, is bound up with a "sense of wholeness and inner well-being" (172).

My point here is not so much to demonstrate that *The Song of the Lark* is a novel of the development of the artist, which I take to be obvious, as to point out how that fact demonstrates both Cather's preoccupation with the problem of a woman's vocation and her willingness to think resistantly, in ways subversive of the norms that governed assumptions about women's lives. These two casts of mind, her concern with vocation and the fondness for "naughtiness" or waywardness that she admitted to Canfield Fisher, are conjoined in the story of Thea, a heroine who gets angry, pushes, pouts, refuses to sing in the church where her own father is pastor but sings at a late-night party in the home of marginalized people, has a sexual relationship with a man to whom she is not married, indulges a large appetite for food and drink, refuses to come to her dying mother. Thea hardens herself against the softer emotions, demands others' subservience, and is headstrong ("'always drive[s] ahead'" [282]), all for the sake of her career. Measured by stereotypes of womanliness, these are unwomanly qualities. But Cather defines Thea both as a woman and as a person not restricted by such stereotypes. Her marriage, far from being the central event of her life, is such an inconspicuous detail that readers may well miss it. When Harsanyi urges her to pursue her vocation, he summons her to attend "'the *woman* you were meant to be'" (167, emphasis added). For her, womanliness is vocation—customarily the defining criterion of manliness. Becoming a strong, independent, accomplished, and conquering woman requires, in Rosowski's words, that she "follo[w] conventionally male narrative patterns" (*Voyage* 69).

How IS IT, then, that in Cather's next novel, *My Ántonia*, an equally strong and even more glorified female character finds her vocation by following what would seem to be conventionally *female* patterns? Ántonia becomes the quintessential wife and mother. In Jim Burden's idealizing —but, as I see it, reductive—view, she is a "rich mine of life" (342), fertility personified. Countless readers as well as numerous critics have accepted Jim's heartfelt tribute at face value. What, then, of Cather's espousal of a more subversive female vocation?

In the view of Merrill Skaggs, the explanation for such inconsistencies lies in Cather's dualistic pattern of thinking, giving her to an unusual degree an ability to see any given issue from alternative perspectives. This characteristic pattern of thought makes itself felt, Skaggs explains, in a reliance on structures of opposition and juxtaposition that clarify the alternatives and the counterbalancing of one work against another, exploring one perspective in one book and its contrast or complement in another (*After* 18). *My Ántonia* provides a kind of answer or riposte to *The Song of the Lark*. This persuasive reading of the large pattern of Cather's work has had an entirely positive influence on Cather studies in the past decade. Yet Skaggs does not, I believe, pursue the implications of her own position far enough. The dualism she sees is rooted in unresolved conflicts at the heart of individual texts, not merely alternations from book to book. To be sure, it is reflected in Cather's pairings and juxtapositions, but it is rooted in a deep ambivalence of response to a shifting, increasingly uncertain modern world. This pervasive dividedness of mind produces in Cather's work a fiction far more complex, subtle, and uncertain than its appearance either of simplicity or of *resolved* polarity would indicate.

In *The Song of the Lark* conflict occurs primarily between Thea and the rest of the world, making hers a story of finding her way through difficulties. The ambivalence I have referred to is seen primarily in patterns of spatial movement and stillness or withdrawal, a contrast between enclosure and free-ranging movement. In *Ántonia*, ambivalence is embedded in the narrative perspective itself. Jim Burden is identified as the narrator, yet Cather herself, or a fictionalized self, is present in the introductory frame, reminding us that Jim's narrative awareness is enclosed by hers, that however closely he may represent Willa Cather, his knowledge is less than hers. The result is an undercurrent of resistance to Jim Burden's voice and to his vision and judgment of Ántonia. He is presented in "an intermittently negative or critical light" (Skaggs, *After* 27).[30]

This does not mean that Jim is simply an ironic narrator; his celebration of Ántonia is also the book's celebration, reflecting Cather's memories of, and tribute to, the immigrant women she knew in Nebraska, especially Annie Sadilek Pavelka. Yet because she can see beyond his sentimentality—in part because as a woman she can see beyond the perspective of a man observing a woman's experience—she does more than celebrate.[31] She understands in a way that Jim does not the cost of Ántonia's life and the lives of women in general, and she sees alternatives. She shows us, despite Jim's failure to perceive it, Ántonia's desire that her daughters have the opportunity to choose among those alternatives. She sees the reassuring vitality and stability offered by a woman such as Ántonia, who takes as her vocation the nurturance of others, or essentially the emptying of the self, but she also sees the validity and the dignity of choices that mean expansion of the self.

This larger vision in *My Ántonia* is not at all inconsistent with the vision of *The Song of the Lark*. Determined as Thea is to "'go on'" and "'not . . . stop,'" identified as she is with "direction" and "expectant" desire (251, 209), she nonetheless retains a centering memory of home that she invokes at times of stress in order to locate herself spiritually in her place of origin, the symbolic space of the traditional woman, and she draws her sense of "higher obligations" from a more ancient past than any personal one (*SL* 243). With Ántonia, an equally persistent though not spatially wayward character, that ordering is reversed. Primarily identified with the past of memory and with the traditional central spaces of women's lives (the kitchen, childbed, the rocking chair, the garden and fruit cellar), she also has visions of larger horizons and a different future for her children.[32]

It is this latter aspect of *Ántonia* that is typically scanted, making it a paean to the strength of the mother, home, and a reassuring past. Woodress, for example, who argues that Jim Burden's memories are "of course" Cather's own (*Literary* 41–42, 290), effaces the distance between Cather's encompassing vision and Jim's limited one in order to hear a unitary narrative voice, making the novel a story rooted in universal values of nurturance and home. Ántonia, he writes, is a "heroic . . .

mother of races" and a "happily married . . . earth mother" (293–300). John Murphy raises these traits to "divine proportions" ("Biblical" 80). Rosowski's reading more convincingly insists that even while Cather employs Jim to establish mythic ideals of the domestic woman, she "builds tension against his account" (*Voyage* 89), revealing an Ántonia who is not subservient to men's purposes but strong in pursuing her own. Rosowski's insight into the shifting of values entailed in Ántonia's story, by which "conventional" masculine success is shown to be less powerful and less satisfying than success in traditionally female life-patterns, is a valuable one, making of Ántonia "a character a woman can admire" (Woodress, *Literary* 300). Still, this reading continues to envision Ántonia's triumph entirely in terms of domesticity and immobility—a traditional and confining view of woman's role. Despite arguing that Cather has transformed the act of abiding from "passivity" to a "vital sourc[e] of meaning," Rosowski does not extend Ántonia's vision, or apparently Cather's, beyond that of serving as a "center" of family life, happy to remain in her domestic space and wave goodbye to the wandering Jim, who plans to return to her and to "Cuzak's boys" whenever he wants another shot of reassurance and renewal (*Voyage* 90–91).[33]

Rosowski points out that the stories Ántonia tells her children are "domestic ones drawn from life" and illustrates by quoting Jim's listing of anecdotes about "the calf that broke its leg, or how Yulka saved her little turkeys from drowning in the freshet, or about old Christmases and weddings in Bohemia" (Voyage 90, *MA* 170). But this listing refers to an earlier time; they are stories she told when she was working for Mrs. Harling, not during Jim's return (the first time he has seen her among her children). By citing the stories told then as if they are still the same, Rosowski bypasses a different category of stories that Ántonia has told her children: stories of female departure and career achievement. The evidence is subtle. Two of the photographs particularly singled out during Jim's evening in the Cuzak living room are of Lena Lingard and of Frances Harling. The picture of Lena is identified as having "come from San Francisco last Christmas," and Ántonia emphasizes Lena's freedom of movement (or perhaps estrangement) by commenting that she "'hasn't been home for six years now'" (339). That photo passes without evaluative comment except for Jim's, which not surprisingly is focused on Lena's appearance. But when the picture of Frances Harling is shown, the daughters (but not Leo; the son is pointedly "unmoved") unite in praising her. "One could see," Jim notes, "that Frances had come down as a heroine in the family legend" (*MA* 339). Clearly, the source of such legends has to be Ántonia; it is she who has established Frances as a "heroine." And Cather has already shown that she is an unconventional one: an astute businesswoman who manages her father's office when he is away, "read[s] the markets," and talks with him about grain cars and cattle "like two men" (145).

The point is not that Frances is unsexed; she later marries. But she is not limited by conventional expectations of gender. She relates to "women who seldom got to town" so well that even the "most reticent and distrustful of them would tell her their story." She takes an interest in the weddings of neighbor farmers' daughters. These are traditionally feminine traits. But she understands traditionally masculine lore as well; she is "as good a judge of credits as any banker in the county" (146). Her role is an androgynous one, and she is successful in identifying and fulfilling it. What is more to the point, she is affirmed for doing so *by Ántonia*, who is glad her daughters will not have to work as domestics and glad that the children of a neighbor woman who has prospered will "'have a grand chance'" (338).

Frances, Lena, and Lena's friend Tiny Soderball become the novel's subtext of alternative lives for women.[34] Lena, usually spoken of as an embodiment of female sexuality, is also an embodiment of independence, determination, and achievement. She sets her sights on a career early, stating confidently, "'I'm going to be a dressmaker'" (*MA* 156). Explicitly defying domesticity in pursuing that goal, she refuses to be distracted by the erotic attentions poured on her by men, clear-sightedly telling Frances, "'I don't want to marry Nick, or any other man. . . . I've seen a good deal of married life, and I don't care for it. I want to be so I can help my mother and the children at home, and not have to ask lief of anybody.'" Significantly, her attitude is endorsed by the person Ántonia later holds up to her daughters as a heroine: "'That's right,' said Frances" (157). Although Jim insists after he has a sexual fling with Lena that "of course" she will get married, she holds firm to her determination to be "'accountable to nobody.'" Seeing domestic life as a matter of "'always too many children, a cross man, and work piling up'" (282–83), she successfully pursues her career and lives as she wants to, moving freely to larger and larger venues.

Tiny, who also gains independent wealth and "lives in a house of her own" (*MA* 318), has an even more unconventional life. Although Jim

remembers her from his Black Hawk days strictly in terms of her high heels and her pert look and seems to agree with local gossips that her adventures will "ruin her," she in fact goes west "quietly" with "very definite plans" (290) and succeeds through alertness, daring, and hard work. While running a boardinghouse in Seattle, she hears that gold has been discovered in Alaska and immediately sells out and starts for Circle City, then pushes on to the Klondike and quickly opens a hotel in Dawson City. When a Swedish prospector dies after having his frozen legs amputated and leaves her his claim, she sells out again, invests half her money in town property as a hedge against bad luck, develops the claim on her own, buys and sells, and returns a wealthy woman. It is Tiny who persuades Lena to move on from Lincoln to San Francisco— one woman encouraging another in her career. Jim, of course, disparages such rejection of proper feminine roles, pronouncing Tiny "hard-faced" and bored with life (293–94). That may indeed be Cather's judgment as well. At any rate, no other is given. But it is Cather, after all, who chose to include these stories of alternative female lives, and it is Cather who affixed the preface that establishes a distinction between Jim's point of view and her authorial presence.

The interpolated tale of Tiny Soderball's adventure in Alaska is in effect a miniature travel book. That is, it invokes a genre that was both popular and, as we have seen, subversive in its implications when written by a woman recounting the adventures of a female traveler. Indeed, a possible source for Tiny's story was a specific example of that genre, written by a woman adventurer in Alaska who consistently flouted gender expectations, Mary E. Hitchcock's *Two Women in the Klondike: The Story of a Journey to the Gold-Fields of Alaska* (1899). Mary Hitchcock was by no means a poor girl seeking her fortune alone, but a woman of wealth traveling with a female friend on a lark and seeking profit on capital investment. Still, there are striking similarities. She goes to Circle City, takes one of the first (rather than last) boats upriver to Dawson City, stakes claims, walks the Skaguay Trail in a "blinding snowstorm" (Tiny also reaches Skaguay in a snowstorm), goes over the Chilkoot Pass or the nearby White Pass (Tiny goes over the Chilkoot), and returns to Seattle on her way to San Francisco. Hitchcock offers both a description and a photograph of a hotel in Dawson and mentions the eagerness of Klondikers for good food (Tiny feeds 150 men a day). She encounters a woman who has made money staking out and selling claims and a man who has suffered frozen feet and legs (Hitchcock 88, 439, and *passim*; cf. *MA* 291–93). Many other travel books also reported the excitement of the Alaska gold rush, of course (one of them is advertised at the end of Hitchcock's book), and Cather may not have known of *Two Women in the Klondike* at all. But she did import the genre, if not this particular example of it, into her novel of nostalgic glorification of domesticity and by so doing introduced a subversive note of female adventure.[35]

The stories of Tiny, Lena, and Frances, all stories of career development and geographic mobility, comprise a distinct contrast to the story of Ántonia. They widen the horizon within which she is anchored and contest Jim's certainty that the ideal female life is one of fixity in place, fixity in traditional roles, and nurturance of others. This does not mean that Ántonia's life is not valued or that critics who read the novel as a celebration of a female center in the home are wrong. Clearly, Ántonia is a powerful emotional center of nostalgic import. At the same time, she herself points toward other possibilities for women.

How can the book be both? Cather grasped, long before the evacuations of identity associated with postmodernism, the idea of the plurality of the self and the falsity of unitary conceptions of meaning. Ántonia can epitomize an ideal of domestic centering and the maternal source *and also* point beyond that role to wider horizons. As Cather herself said of the choice between home and career, "Is there any reason why she cannot have both?" (*WCIP* 48). Jim Burden celebrates the preciousness of "the incommunicable past" (*MA* 360), but he also distorts the past. As Rosowski states, there is "a certain ruthlessness" about his devotion to Ántonia. One might say, a certain manipulativeness.[36] When the facts of her life conflict with what he wants to believe, his "allegiance" remains with his own wish-fulfilling ideas (*Voyage* 89). Cather anticipates narratively, then, the point made by Leigh Gilmore in *Autobiographics* that "we can never recover the past, only represent it." Reading *My Ántonia* as a conflicted, pluralistic text, at once in tension and in harmony with *The Song of the Lark*, we also demonstrate Gilmore's point that in feminist readings "incoherence" is itself a "significant" expression of the "historical instability and political volatility" of women's lives (80–86).[37] Cather, who experienced that instability and volatility during a period of dramatic social change, reflected on it in connection with the problem of women's vocation in these two novels written during a time when "sexchanges" were particularly earthshaking.

7

Coming to America / Escaping to Europe

Twisting a shoestring noose, a Polack's brat
Joylessly torments a cat.
. . . .
With hate, perhaps, a threat, maybe,
Lithuania looks at me.
　　　　　—"Street in Packingtown"

"Oh, how high is Caesar's house,
　Brother, big brother?"
　　　　　—"The Palatine"

IF ONE of the great themes of *My Ántonia* is gender and the nature of women's lives in the American *polis*, another is the status of the ethnic other, particularly the status of ethnically diverse European immigrants. When Cather reported to her publisher in early 1917 that she had begun a new novel—the earliest trace of her work on *My Ántonia*—she said that it was not the "Blue Mesa" story as expected (material that would later go into *The Professor's House*) but a western story with a background similar to that of *O Pioneers!*[1] She meant, of course, the Nebraska setting and agricultural life that formed the milieu of both books, but she could equally well have been referring to the treatment of immigrant groups. Both *My Ántonia* and *O Pioneers!*—and indeed *The Song of the Lark* as well—convey an affectionate vision of an ethnically diverse America. Susan Rosowski has written that Cather was "the first to give immigrants heroic stature in serious American literature (*Voyage* 45). Yet she did so only within limits whose exclusions reflected those of widespread popular opinion. Focusing primarily on the Scandinavian and Bohemian settlers that she had written about in *O Pioneers!* and a

number of short stories, she produced a novel that has been recognized for
its re-creation of personal memories, but one that is also deeply engaged
with contemporary politics, the debate over immigration.

Cather had earlier been involved in this debate when as managing
editor of *McClure's Magazine* she either acceded to or actively participated in the publication of a series of articles written by fellow editor
and *McClure's* staffwriter George Kibbe Turner, which expressed bitter
hostility toward certain immigrant groups, specifically Italians and
Jews. It might seem surprising that *McClure's* would pursue an exclu-
sionist editorial policy, since McClure himself was a member of a once-
despised immigrant group, the Irish. By the early twentieth century
that prejudice had considerably diminished; in Noel Ignatiev's terms,
the Irish had become white; and McClure, now simply an American and
carrying the cachet of the successful self-made man, joined the chorus
of suspicion toward later-arriving groups.[2] Both he and Cather (whether
actively or by co-optation) became participants in the public outcry that
culminated in the Immigration Act of 1924, a law that, as Walter Benn
Michaels writes, "brought to an end the tradition of unrestricted European immigration" and made "eligibility for American citizenship . . .
dependent upon ethnic identity" (30).

Turner's articles, one of the "muckraking" series for which *McClure's*
was known, were directed at exposure of urban corruption but repeatedly targeted Italians and Jews, which were the two most disfavored
immigrant groups. By calling Italians a source of social disorder, Turner
identified them with a bête noire of Progressive public spirit, and his
labeling of Jews as a "new Oriental population" linked them with a
group long subjected to exclusionary measures (Michaels 144, n. 13).[3]
Cather would reinforce that linkage in "Scandal" (1919), describing a
Jewish character as looking "Mongolian" (*YBM* 166).

In "The Daughters of the Poor," in November 1909, Turner named
Jews as the masterminds of organized prostitution in New York, charging
that "Jewish commercial acumen"—a familiar stereotype—had developed prostitution "to great proportions" and thereby promoted corruption in the political power structure. By seizing on the folklore of "the
licentious or lascivious Jew," he presented the Jewish male to the public
imagination as an "amalgam of sexual and political power, perverting
gentile bodies and the body politic with a single gesture" (Freedman
94). (Miles Orvell points out [48–50] that in *The American Scene*, only

two years earlier, Henry James, always a useful comparator with Cather, had described the Jewish masses of New York's Lower East Side by reference to "innumerable fish, of over-developed proboscis.") In the May 1910 number Turner referred to "a pawnbroker named Mose Levish" as the "commanding genius" of vice in Des Moines ("Tammany" 121), while Burton J. Hendrick, identified as the author of "The Great Jewish Invasion," attributed to the "average Russian Hebrew" a range of "sufferings" physical, moral, and "psychical" (47).[4] The anti-Semitic note was being struck repeatedly in the magazine's pages.

Probably of greater significance as a clue to Cather's thinking was an editorial that appeared at the back of the November 1909 issue, a diatribe of ethnic hostility bearing the name of McClure himself. Given the frequency with which Cather spoke for McClure in conducting business for the magazine and the fact that she would later assume his voice in the ghostwritten *Autobiography*, it is entirely possible that she either wrote or revised the article herself. Neither this nor her more general role in the involvement of *McClure's* in slurring Jews and Italians is by any means clear.[5] Quite apart from the question of authorship, we cannot take this article lightly, knowing as we do from the comments of her contemporaries as well as her own letters how greatly Cather admired McClure.

In keeping with his interest in German society during those years (according to a letter written by Cather in 1911, he regarded it as greatly superior to that of the United States),[6] McClure's article credited the "Germanic races" with having "built up slowly and laboriously, the present civilization of the West" that "now lifts the whole race above barbarism and bestiality." The "great masses of primitive peoples from the farms of Europe" pouring into American cities, he warned, constituted a threat to that civilization. Commending as "competent" the judgment of a trustee of the City Vigilance League that "'a fraternity of fetid male vermin (nearly all of them being Russian or Polish Jews)'" were managing vice, McClure went on to denounce the impunity of murderers among "the Italians of New York." The "northwestern countries of Europe," he proclaimed, were the "only nations worthy of comparison with the United States in their civilization" ("Tammanyizing" 117–18, 125).

These same northwestern countries were, for the most part, the source of the immigrant culture Cather depicts in *O Pioneers! and My*

Ántonia. The celebrated ethnic variety of Jim Burden's experience in Nebraska, reflecting Cather's own, is not *too* various. The immigrants who stir his affection are not only like himself in being newcomers but also in being white—a term that then meant not only not-black but also not-Italian, not-Asian, not-Jewish.[7] Besides reflecting personal memories, Cather's tributes to Nebraska's immigrants reflect fairly accurately the prevailing preferences in the United States at the time at which she was writing. They also reflect the actual demographic makeup of Nebraska's Divide at the time the story takes place—or actually, reflect it with one major exception. That exception, I believe, is tied up with the wartime context in which she was working—a topic to which I will return and one that links *Ántonia* with the novel that would follow it, *One of Ours.*

WE KNOW that Cather took a strong interest in the human variety she encountered when her family moved from the stable society of Virginia's Blue Ridge to the Nebraska prairie. She later reminisced about times spent in kitchens with old women who spoke little English but understood her homesickness and gave her "the real feeling of an older world across the sea" (*WCIP* 10). From her first published story she showed an interest in the fictional possibilities of such groups and in *O Pioneers!* gave warm treatment to the industry and folkways of Swedish, Norwegian, Bohemian, and Acadian French settlers. The life of Jim Burden, in some ways her autobiographical double, gains interest and vitality from the presence of Danes, Norwegians, Russians, an Austrian, and again (significantly) Bohemians. One reason Jim is so ready to establish friendly relations with these varied neighbors is that they are, like himself, newcomers. A Virginian trying to learn to think of Nebraska as home, Jim can feel that his sense of displacement is shared, as intermittent loneliness and homesickness provide a common, if unspoken, language. Another reason is that he associates these neighbors with the earth and nurturance, just as he does Ántonia herself, whose eyes are like "the sun shining on brown pools in the wood" (22–23). Many years later, he views her in her final apotheosis amid a riot of vegetal and animal life, jars and jars of preserved food, and kolaches baked by the dozen. Ántonia's kitchen recalls Grandmother Burden's, a uterine center of consolation where he had been fed and immersed in warm bathwater as a child. This association of Bohemians with primal essences of earth and food was one that Cather made in her own voice as well, writing exultantly about vacation weeks spent in the Bohemian country during wheat harvest, when the whole countryside smelled like bread baking.[8]

It is this autobiographical context that is usually invoked in discussions of Cather's vision of frontier immigrants—a context that is, to be sure, both interesting and important. Accordingly, the novel was long read as a nostalgic celebration of the past and an escape from current issues. But more is at issue here than her affection for people who eased her transition to a new land or her delight in distinctive customs brought from Europe. Just as a glow of nostalgic affirmation disguises problematics of gender and what I take to be Cather's desire to subvert traditional assumptions about women's lives, so does a nimbus of personal affection blur her participation in the widespread public concern about immigration.[9] *My Ántonia* was, in fact, very much a novel of its time, responding both to the war then devastating Europe and to a contemporary discourse about "hyphenated Americans."

The impact of wartime makes itself felt in *Ántonia* in a variety of ways: in an awareness of the vulnerability of peace and a tone of nostalgia for a more innocent time (a factor that would later contribute to Cather's enthusiasm for Oliver LaFarge's Pulitzer Prize novel of Navajo life, *Laughing Boy*, which also reaches back toward a time before the disillusionment of the war) but also in the novel's de-emphasis on German immigrants in Nebraska in favor of Bohemians. To be sure, there were compelling biographical reasons. Bohemian settlers did live near the Cather ranch, and after the family moved into Red Cloud the young Willa did come to know Annie Sadilek, the model for Ántonia, who worked as a domestic for her friends the Miners. Even so, in singling out Nebraska's Bohemians, Scandinavians, and even (despite their small numbers) Russians, she obscured the fact that Germans were by far the largest single group of immigrants in the area.[10] By 1916, when she was writing *My Ántonia*, these German immigrants were being subjected to intense suspicion of disloyalty, while Germany itself was being demonized as a warmonger.

Cather stood in relation to popular attitudes toward Germans and German culture very much as Jim Burden stands in relation to people in Black Hawk who look down on immigrants. Just as Jim is more enlightened than his prejudiced schoolmates who think of them as "ignorant ... foreigners" (*MA* 194), so Cather was more enlightened than those of her contemporaries who suspended the production of German operas in New York or demanded that the teaching of the German language be dropped from schools.[11] In a 1921 speech in Omaha she mocked the foolishness of aggressive "Americanization" that eradicates ethnic customs and language learning (*WCIP* 147). By then, to be sure, the war fervor that provided a powerful incentive to de-emphasize Germans in her portrayal of the human patchwork of Nebraska had dissipated.

If it is fairly clear why Cather avoided the presence of Germans in writing *My Ántonia*, her reason for favoring the Bohemians, or Czechs, is less obvious. But that, too, is traceable to wartime politics. The Czechs were "the most Western and consequently least threatening of the Eastern European peoples toward which the government was willing to extend the promise of self-determination," a promise much vaunted by Woodrow Wilson in his war aims (Fischer 41). Cather's emphasis on the Bohemians in *My Ántonia*, then, accords not only with the ethnic preferences we have seen in the *McClure's* discourse on immigration but with what was essentially a wartime stance taken for propaganda purposes. The Czechs served as a useful "ideological figuration of American tolerance, eliding the racism that characterized the United States's relationship to non-Europeans" or, indeed, its own nonwhite citizens (42).

Domestic racism, another aspect of the general culture in which Cather participated, also disrupts *Ántonia*'s celebration of inclusiveness. It does so in two ways, by presence and by absence: the presence of the African American other, objectified as being at once exotic and freakish, and the novel's silence or near silence with respect to the Native population that was displaced by newly arrived migrants and immigrants alike. Both of these disruptions of inclusiveness are intertwined with the novel's response to the European other.

The stigmatizing of African Americans enters the novel in the person of Blind d'Arnault, a traveling pianist who comes to Black Hawk to appear at the hotel. Depicted in denigrating caricature, he is described as having a "negro head . . . almost no head at all; nothing behind the ears but folds of neck under close-clipped wool"—that is, a head that implies mindlessness. As stereotype would have it, he is all rhythm, "happy" and governed by "sensations"; playing his "barbarous" piano, he "enjoy[s] himself as only a negro can" (*MA* 183). This last phrase, with its demarcating "only," places Blind d'Arnault in a category defined solely by race while it privileges the speaker as a person whose ground of superiority —not belonging to the category negro—qualifies him to understand the behavior of the subordinate other and make pronouncements on it. We cannot suppose this positioning was Cather's conscious intention. But neither does she indicate any disavowal of Jim's perspective at this point. Moreover, the reader who knows even a little about the original from which she took this portrait—Thomas Greene Bethune, a blind savant piano player born into slavery in 1849 whose performance she reviewed in 1894—realizes that the only way "a negro" can enjoy himself with such abandon is by denial of his exploitation by whites. The Bethune family (his former owners) who managed Blind Tom's concert appearances from about 1860 until 1904 had charge of all the money he brought in.[12]

Disruptive as this caricature is of Cather's semblance of an ethnically diverse America, the shadow of the displaced Indian that falls across her midwestern and southwestern novels is perhaps even more disturbing, for the simple reason that Indians were in fact a far more numerous presence there. To ignore them and to ignore the history of their displacement in novels that avow their historical foundation is a major distortion. Cather can well be seen as the lyrical voice of Manifest Destiny. In *O Pioneers!* she takes unalloyed satisfaction in the transforming of the prairie into agricultural land, and in *My Ántonia*, adopting the comforting theory of an empty land awaiting settlement, she sees through Jim Burden's eyes "nothing but land: not a country at all, but the material out of which countries are made" (*MA* 7).[13] Jim feels "outside man's jurisdiction." But this can be true only if the Sioux or Lakota people recently displaced from the Nebraska prairies are defined as not-human —as indeed they are in *O Pioneers!* when Cather writes with reference to Alexandra that "for the first time, perhaps, since that land emerged from the waters of geologic ages, a *human face* was set toward it with love" (*OP* 64, emphasis added).

Cather has been castigated for her fictional erasure of the Native presence by Mike Fischer, who reminds us that as recently as 1868, only five years before members of the Cather family began to arrive in southern Nebraska, Chief Red Cloud held a war council "aimed at expelling white settlers from the lands north of the Platte River" that had been guaranteed to his people. The town of Red Cloud, established in 1870 at the very time when Chief Red Cloud was in Washington completing a treaty that supposedly guaranteed the Oglalla Sioux possession of the Black Hills in perpetuity, was "the first permanent town in what had been one of the Indians' last buffalo hunting grounds south of the Platte" (32–34). Fischer's point is that the Sioux presence had ended so shortly before her family's arrival that Cather must have been aware of it and that her virtual erasure of them is a knowing one. But in fact he understates the case. The Indians were still very much in evidence when her uncle George P. Cather and his wife, Frances, arrived. In a letter written in 1876 to his sister Virginia Cather Ayre, G. P. Cather reported that about two hundred Omahas passed in sight of his homestead the previous week.[14] The silent procession of this sizable band across the horizon enacts the vanishing of the Vanishing American, a phenomenon in which Americans of the late nineteenth and early twentieth centuries wanted very much to believe and a phenomenon that is very much at work in Cather's writing.

The phrase "Vanishing American" is itself misleading, of course, since the Indians did not simply vanish; the process was not nearly so innocuous as that. But the notion became widely accepted because it so soothed the national conscience. Belief that the Indians were vanishing and all trace of their languages and way of life would soon be lost paved the way for an intense anthropological interest toward the end of the century. It also made the Indian readily available for romanticizing. The naming of the town of Red Cloud was an episode in that process. Cather demonstrated her awareness of the outlines of the historic presence of the Sioux in a 1913 interview in which she stated that her hometown was "named after the old Indian chief who used to come hunting in that country, and who buried his daughter on the top of one of the river bluffs south of the town" (*WCIP* 9). But her language evades the reality of Indian life by making it sound as if the frequenting of the southern Nebraska hunting range was occasional and individual, rather like a vacation trip, and sentimentalizes it by focusing on a story of a dead child. She noted in an article in the 1923 *Nation* that west of Lincoln "the tall red grass and the buffalo and the Indian hunter were undisturbed" before 1860 ("Nebraska" 236–38).

Cather's renaming of Red Cloud as Black Hawk in *My Ántonia* is a parallel act of nostalgic tribute to the vanished American chief who in the 1830s had led the last Indian War east of the Mississippi and whose "autobiography" was, in Fischer's words, "one of the first texts in the nineteenth-century cult of nostalgia that would increasingly come to surround white perceptions of Native American peoples" (35).[15] Her

nod at the history of European expansion into the plains is equally sen-
timentalizing. When Jim tells Ántonia, Lena, and Tiny about his belief
that Coronado ventured as far north as Nebraska, he makes it a story of
heroic relics and the conquistador's broken heart, occluding the fact of
aggression (*MA* 236). A small and significantly female countervoice is
heard in the girls' demurral that "'more than him'" has died in the wilderness of a broken heart.

The vanishing of the Native American people was only too real, however, and was directly tied in with one of the most recurrent presences in
Cather's work, the railroad. Since the railroad was also one of the most
powerful forces in the process of immigration into the Midwest, it
serves as a direct link between the presence of the immigrants Cather
celebrated and the absence, both from the plains and from her work, of
Indians. Railroads such as the Burlington, the system that ran through
Red Cloud and on to Denver, were among the primary forces that
caused that vanishing. Cather herself arrived on the Burlington, as do
Jim Burden and the immigrating Shimerdas in *My Ántonia*. The railroads, in particular the Santa Fe, participated in promoting the ideology
of the Vanishing American through the artworks they sponsored
showing lone Indians, "dignified but aloof," whose eyes "stare vacantly
into the distance" at what might well be "a vision of the coming white
man."[16] The building of the railroads, of course, was accomplished
largely through a vast transfer of public lands (in other words, land that
sustained the Native populations) to private hands. Through the gift of
these lands, which they then sold to settlers or speculators, the railroads
were able to build up vast reservoirs of capital used to construct track
and purchase rolling stock, and the settlers who took up the land and
established farms and businesses became the railroads' customers as
they purchased goods shipped in from the East and sent their agricultural products out to market. It was a system that worked quite effi-
ciently to develop the rail system across the country, enrich a small
number of investors, and deprive Indians of their way of life and means
of survival. Not only did settlers come to possess land that had provided
game for the Indians' sustenance, but their clearing of land as they
plowed and planted destroyed necessary habitats and disrupted migration patterns of game even as trains brought in professional hunters
who took buffalo hides and left the carcasses to rot or passengers who
shot the great animals for pleasure.

To the extent that she idealizes the railroad, Cather is endorsing this process. But in *My Ántonia* it is not entirely obvious whether she is idealizing the railroad or not. The train by which Jim arrives in Nebraska, which also brings the Shimerdas, is endowed with a glow of nostalgia and adventure through its association not only with the start of their glowing story but with the much bemedaled and pinned conductor and the book Jim reads on the way, "Life of Jesse James." Ironically, the real Jesse James was a robber of railroads whose hostility had been aroused by the exploitative ways of their land operations. Moreover, the notion of the West that Jim gleans from reading about this often-heroized gunman is quickly debunked, as the West he experiences is not so much a place of derring-do as of homebuilding.[17] Even before this ambiguous appearance of Jim's train ride to Nebraska and his childhood notions, railroad heroism has already been brought into question in the prologue, where we meet the adult Jim Burden before we meet the child. We learn that he grows up to become an attorney for the Burlington but gets no satisfaction from his incessant traveling, which is undertaken at least in part to escape an unhappy marriage. Instead, he turns for satisfaction to his nostalgic and reconstructive imagination of Ántonia.

Another way in which the railroad is significant in *Ántonia* is its promotion of a false lure. In order to sell their vast land holdings and thereby bring in both immediate cash revenue and long-term customers, railroads advertised aggressively throughout the United States and in Europe. Directly or indirectly, it was in response to such advertising that people like the Shimerdas came, expecting a far more comfortable home than they actually found. Essentially, the railroads ensnared such people with false promises. It may be no coincidence, then, that the man who lures Ántonia away with him under false promises of marriage and leaves her pregnant is a railroad man. It is not that Cather overtly opposes the railroad to the interests of her immigrant characters in *My Ántonia*, any more than she opposes railroads to the well-being of Indians. The linkage I am proposing remained an undercurrent until she brought it nearer the surface in *A Lost Lady*, five years later. On the other hand, her sympathetic identification with the immigrants pouring into Nebraska over the recently built Burlington is overt. The fear expressed by Jim's traveling companion Jake, that they bring diseases, is patently set up as a straw man to be knocked over by Jim's—and the novel's—perception of Ántonia's liveliness and innate goodness. However objectionable

Mrs. Shimerda and Ambrosch may seem at times (in class-linked ways associated with cultural patterns not understood by the native-born Burdens) Ántonia and her gracious father are always affirmed. So, to a less personalized extent, are the other Bohemian and Scandinavian characters.

It is surely true that Cather wrote about "a greater variety of European peoples than many of her contemporaries" and that she regarded them with "attentive sympathy (Reynolds 81). She was, in fact, *too* sympathetic to suit some readers. Historian Frederick Jackson Turner, growling about the "stress" that Cather and certain other writers placed on "the non-English stocks" in the Midwest, assured the daughter of Burlington railway builder and executive Charles Elliott Perkins that the "constructive work of the men of means, bankers, railway builders, etc. will also be recognised again after the present criticism of all things American has died down" (Billington 365). Cather herself, in fact, "recognised" the work of such men, though in a possibly duplicitous way, in *A Lost Lady*, only a year before Turner wrote.

Cather's sympathetic, even celebratory attitude toward immigrants was extended, however, within a narrowly selective range of ethnic origins and a hierarchical vision in which immigrants were marked—perhaps inevitably, given the economic plight they generally encountered—as lower class. In spite of Jim's easy fondness for Ántonia and the significantly undifferentiated Bohemian Marys and Danish laundry girls, a fondness that was clearly Cather's own, it is patently evident that they are all assigned positions of menial labor while the native-born hold themselves superior. Even Jim's kindly grandparents see the Shimerdas, who seek to establish the kind of seigneurial relationship they had experienced in Europe, as a source of amusement, and in general the immigrant groups are viewed most positively when they show that they know their place. Worse, the boys and men of Black Hawk use immigrant girls as a supply of convenient sex, implying no responsibility. A steady turnover of hired girls is generated by the regularity with which they have to withdraw to their parents' farms to bear the babies of their employers or employers' sons, who for all their infatuation with these strongly bodied young women firmly expect to marry "Black Hawk girls" (*MA* 195). Being a girl and living in Black Hawk does not, it seems, make one a Black Hawk girl any more than living in America and having American citizenship made one, in the view of nativist polemicists, an American

(Michaels 9). The immigrant girls are present and they are liked, but they are not equal.

Even Jim, who congratulates himself on his superior social vision, clearly realizes that he is destined for better things. Ántonia's warning to him not to "go and get mixed up with the Swedes" (*MA* 217) is scarcely needed; he leaves for the university and an upper-middle-class life at the first opportunity. When he later assures Ántonia that he'd "have liked to have [her] for a sweetheart, or a wife, or my mother or my sister—anything that a woman can be to a man" (312), we know that he is indulging false retrospective illusions. Cather would later tell a reader that Jim was never in love with Ántonia.[18] His statement that she is "'really . . . a part of me'" is America's assertion of its (selective) absorption of European peoples in the melting-pot process that denied their separate identities and value.

If Jim's appropriative claiming of Ántonia as part of himself is an ironically self-delusive assertion of love, Cather's similarly loving statement that Ántonia had embodied all her feelings about the early immigrants to the Great Plains would seem to have been far more ingenuous. Her faithful support of Annie Sadilek Pavelka's family and others during the Great Depression, when many of them faced real want and were in danger of losing their farms, indicates a lasting and generous affection. It is the very warmth and apparent genuineness of those feelings (albeit a warmth exercised, as years went on, very much from a distance) that make all the more startling some of her later pronouncements on the presence of the foreign-born. In letters of the late 1930s she began to complain about "brassy young Jews and Greeks," dreadful New York University graduates whose behavior was as foreign as their names.[19] In *Ántonia* she had seemed to delight in foreign names and manners and in families who kept their languages and their customs. In her October 1921 speech in Omaha she had praised differentness itself (*WCIP* 46–52). Such receptiveness to diverse others had eroded by the time she wrote to Sinclair Lewis in 1938 deploring America's historic willingness to admit outsiders, whom she had come to regard as ruffians and simpletons. But when we take a longer view of her response to ethnic otherness, and when we look closely at its limitations, it is not clear that her vision of American inclusiveness had ever been quite so simple as it may at first seem in *My Ántonia*.[20]

IN *One of Ours*, four years after *My Ántonia*, Cather reversed the direction of her concern with European cultural richness. Rather than Europeans who came to America seeking a better life, she wrote of the desire of the dissatisfied American to get away from a culture that looks all too much like a wasteland—indeed, very much like T. S. Eliot's broken heaps of rubbish as well as the trash-heap life Cather had earlier depicted in "A Wagner Matinée." In this way, *One of Ours* forms a revisionist complement to *Ántonia*'s vision of the American magnet, much as *A Lost Lady* revises its theme of housewifely satisfaction.[21]

Seeds of the reversal can be found in *Ántonia*'s glorification of the rich diversity of customs and cultural sensitivity brought by Scandinavian and Bohemian immigrants to an America scarcely equipped to recognize much less appreciate them. Jim Burden's grandparents, depicted as admirable and kindly people but rigid and culturally unsophisticated, do not recognize even the edibility, let alone the delight, of so foreign a culinary embellishment as mushrooms. Recalling Cather's statement apropos *Shadows on the Rock* that a civilization begins with the salad dressing (*OW* 16), and knowing from her letters how highly she valued her French cook, Josephine Bourda, we know that she did not share the Burdens' caution in this respect. (This and other points at which Cather's perspective differs from that of the Burdens demonstrate that a space for irony exists in the novel.) Cultural depth and sensitivity springing from complex European origins are especially seen in the person of Ántonia's father, a craftsman and a lover of music and gentleness and all things beautiful. In *One of Ours* these tributes to European cultural depth blossom into a desire to turn back east, to escape to Europe.

It is not only her misled hero's desire but Cather's own. If her apparent warmth toward immigration from a European source was a limited one that would later cool, her response to European culture was and would remain ardent. Indeed, her adulation of Henry James during a considerable portion of her literary apprenticeship may well have been stimulated as much by James's Europhilia as by questions of technique. Her first visit to Europe, in 1902, had been a powerful emotional experience, a cultural pilgrimage that represented her whole sense of herself as an outsider wanting in. Letters written during subsequent visits convey an undiminished sense of, or eagerness for, cultural affiliation. In *One of Ours*, however, that sense of the beauty, authority, and allure of

Europe becomes compounded with equally powerful complicating elements. Cather's complex feelings about life in Nebraska versus life in the metropolis (the East, Europe), her response to the trauma of the war, and her participation in the general postwar disillusionment make this not only the first of her "dark middle novels," as Richard Giannone has labeled it (126), but probably the most ambiguous and ironic of them. She later wrote in Carrie Miner's copy that the writing of *One of Ours* was more draining than any of her other books.[22]

The irony and the breadth of the novel's concerns were missed by such sophisticated contemporary readers as H. L. Mencken, Edmund Wilson, Sinclair Lewis, and Ernest Hemingway. Even now criticism founders on the rock of Cather's seeming glorification of military heroism. It is a response that she foresaw. When the novel was in proof she told Canfield Fisher, who was providing help and advice as she struggled to finish her work on it, that she knew it would be seen as a war novel and that she had never wanted to write such a thing but had found it unavoidable, something she had to deal with before she could go on to work on anything else.[23] The fact that the book *was* read as a war novel probably contributed to its large sale and its winning of the Pulitzer Prize. But such a reading is problematic and entirely too narrow.

IN A SENSE, Cather had already written a war novel. In the March 1917 letter to her publisher that first mentions *My Ántonia* she stated that she had begun work on the book a few months before, in November 1916. According to Elizabeth Sergeant's recollection, her work on it had begun by the spring of 1916. Either dating places *My Ántonia* as a novel of, even if not about, the Great War. By that time, although the United States would not enter the war until April 1917, public sentiment, which had at first been isolationist and either neutral or fairly evenly divided, had shifted toward the Allies, and agitation for war was strong. In June 1916 Congress voted to increase the size of the armed forces and in September voted a seven-billion-dollar appropriation for the military, the largest in history to that point. Interception of the Zimmermann telegram in January 1917 stirred the fire, Germany's declaration of unlimited submarine warfare tipped a reluctant Wilson, and war was declared on April 6.

None of this would seem to have had the least bearing on Cather's novel, with its air of inviolate timelessness, nostalgia, and celebration of maternal womanhood. Yet the serenity that readers usually recall as its strongest quality is in fact broken by irruptions of violence not once but at several points.[24] Mr. Shimerda goes quietly to the barn and kills himself; a tramp waves goodbye and hurls himself into a threshing machine; Jim Burden is set upon in Ántonia's bed by a lusting Wick Cutter and beaten; Cutter later commits murder and suicide merely to keep his wife's relatives from inheriting their wealth. The world of the novel is one whose peacefulness is vulnerable to senseless violence. Sergeant's anecdote of the spring day when Cather came to her apartment after a walk in Central Park and broke off their discussion of novelistic form by reaching for a Taormina jar and likening its position on the bare table to the centrality of her new heroine is prefaced by these words: "She had not been able to forget that, in these war days, the youth of Europe, its finest flower, was dying" (Sergeant 148). "But," Sergeant continues, as if to dispel any impression that she meant to suggest a connection between the two, for Cather the new project "took precedence" over such matters; her worry over the war was swept aside by her engagement with her heroine. One might almost read that account as indicating that Cather tried to invest her attention in her new book *in order to* sweep aside her worry. She would later extol the value of art as "escape" (*OW* 18). But issues that were in the air in that war-conscious time left their traces in *My Ántonia*, not only in its awareness of the threat of violence and its nostalgia for the past, but in its concern with the relationship of Europe to America.

Cather's letters confirm Sergeant's belief that the war weighed heavily on her mind. As early as September 1914, less than two months after the invasion of Belgium, she lamented that news of the war reaching her during her late-summer retreat to New Mexico sorely broke up her contentment and caused her to feel uneasy and fearful about the danger to everything she found most precious. What that "everything" was can be inferred from the essays she wrote during her 1902 trip to Europe, which convey a strong sense of western European cultural origins. France, in particular, she saw as a center of both natural beauty and high-art treasures. The outbreak of war also quickly aroused her humanitarian concerns. In November 1914 she mentioned to Sergeant that she had heard there was starvation in Belgium, and after attending a lecture on the Belgians' plight she told her aunt that she was planning to donate to a relief fund rather than send Christmas presents that year. She wished

there were some way to induce every family in Nebraska to donate a
dollar or a half-dollar. "History would be ashamed of America," she
wrote, "if it acted niggardly."[25]

Her correspondence with Ferris Greenslet, at Houghton Mifflin,
also kept the war before her. Taking a characteristically jocular tone,
Greenslet wrote on December 15 that he would be going to England in
February and hoped to "succeed in putting a stop to this horrid war."
Falling into step with his tone, she replied yes, please do stop it, and
added that until it was stopped there could be nothing pleasant in the
world. In July 1915 she wrote that the reason she was lagging with the
proofs of *The Song of the Lark* was that she had been distracted by plans
for a trip to Germany and Austria with S. S. McClure to interview leaders
of the Central Powers. Isabelle McClung was to go along for propriety's
sake, but the trip had been canceled because of Judge McClung's fears
for their safety. It was just as well, she said, since she doubted she could
have maintained a neutral tone without seeming pro-German. Greenslet,
fearing the United States might soon sever diplomatic relations with
Germany, was relieved she had not gone. Rightly so. The boldness of
the idea becomes clear when one realizes that this was two months after
the *Lusitania* was torpedoed. Greenslet must have been relieved, too,
that she resumed work on the proofs. But advance sales of *Lark*, published on October 2, did not come up to the expected four or five thousand, and he had to point out that with the war on, the book trade was
"rather backward." A flurry of letters about publicity strategies ensued,
but sales remained disappointing. Government controls and shortages
of paper meant copies were often unavailable even when there were
buyers. A planned German translation seemed "likely never to come off
. . . owing to the war." In April 1917, back once more "from the submarine front," Greenslet inquired about her progress on the new book, by
then clearly identified as *Ántonia*.[26]

All during the time she was working on the novel, Cather was keenly
conscious of the war and depressed by it. Perhaps that in itself impelled
her imagination toward wishful celebration of nurturing, abundance,
and security. In March 1916 she wrote Dorothy Canfield Fisher that
total misery had been let loose on the world. Surprisingly, she considered going to Italy that spring but was apprehensive about submarines.
When McClure, who had sailed aboard Henry Ford's Peace Ship in
December 1915 (an undertaking that Cather along with many others

thought ill-advised), returned from his extended trip to Germany, Turkey, and England, she planned a dinner party so people could hear his reports about the war. After seeing the daughter of a friend off for ambulance service in France that same month, she opined to Mary Rice Jewett that a pall of discouragement would lie over everything until the war ended.[27] This was December 1916, only a month after she had, by her own report, begun *Ántonia*.

McClure's trip would have strange results. Accused in the press of being pro-German (or even a German agent) and a militarist, while in fact his convictions were for neutrality and his sympathies apparently pro-Allies, he struggled to regain credibility but succeeded only in attracting additional bad publicity when he was interned in England and violated official directives by going on to London (Lyon 371–79). In reaction, his public rhetoric took on a militarist shading that colors even the quasi-documentary style of *Obstacles to Peace* (1917), the book he assembled from available documents and his own many lectures. Generally well received, it today reads like an assemblage of atrocity tales. Cather found it "thrilling."[28]

In June 1917, two months after the April 6 declaration of war, with work on *My Ántonia* proceeding more slowly than she had optimistically predicted three months before, Cather reported to Greenslet that Nebraska was impatient for war. In July 1918, still at work on proofs of *Ántonia*, she asked whether he had seen the *Times* notice of the citation posthumously awarded to her cousin, Lieutenant Grosvenor Cather, killed in action May 28 at Cantigny.[29] The seed for *One of Ours* had been planted.

LATE IN LIFE Cather wrote to Chicago book critic and former bookstore owner Fanny Butcher, in response to a kind of survey Butcher was conducting, that she would rather have written *War and Peace* than any other novel she knew. In a sense, she did.[30] *One of Ours* is really a novel of war *and* peace, with the emphasis on the conjunction, the *and*. Whether it is more the one or the other is a continuing debate but a false one. Despite charges that it is structurally broken-backed, the two are not separable. To be sure, it is not a novel that can be regarded as a masterpiece; critics have been almost unanimous in conceding that it is a seriously flawed work, perhaps even an incoherent one.[31] Cather's wish to Butcher might be read as a wish that *One of Ours* had turned out to be the equal of *War and Peace* and her realization that it had not. Even so, it is a novel of great interest and richness because of the intensity with which its contraries of thought and feeling are realized. It depicts what is for its main character, Claude, a war peculiarly filled with inner peace and a peace back in Nebraska that is filled with strife. Cather told Greenslet that the novel was all West and War.[32]

Perhaps *One of Ours* is most persuasively read as a novel about why someone like Claude Wheeler would so willingly go to war. The answer implicates America's project of westward expansion and technological innovation (producing a proliferation of junk such as that piled up in the Wheelers' basement), the question of whether beauty really is truth and truth beauty and, if so, whether that is all we need to know, and issues of gender and of religious belief. One result of Cather's writing it, I believe, was that the world really did break in two for her; she looked at the completed novel and realized how fully she shared the postwar disillusionment she had spared her hero. Even twenty years later she was still looking back to the happiness of life before 1914.[33]

The central and driving concern of *One of Ours*, like that of *My Ántonia* and the two novels that had preceded it, is life in Nebraska and its effects on the young person who grows up there. For Claude Wheeler, the result is a disaffection that inspires in him a yearning to get away, to go to Europe. More than that, he wants to *belong* in Europe. Just as Georgiana of "A Wagner Matinée" wishes she did not have to leave the concert hall that serves as the antithesis of her unbeautiful life at home, so Claude fantasizes, after he has reached France, that he may "never go home at all" but "buy a little farm and stay here for the rest of his life" (327).[34] That is, he wants to reverse the pattern of emigration/immigration that Cather had earlier celebrated. In Reynolds's words (119; cf. Urgo 156–57), in Claude's vision "an Edenic America, originally projected by Europe onto the new world, is reprojected by the wondering American onto France."

The centrality of Claude's escape wish in Cather's conception of the novel is evident in her letter to Dorothy Canfield Fisher in which she expressed regret that it would be read as a war novel. There she explained the genesis of the book not by the fact of her cousin's death but by her awareness of his fierce desire to "escape the misery of being himself." She had seen him in the summer of 1914, had in fact been visiting at his father's farm when the war broke out, and for the first time they had been able to get past his envy of her and "contempt" for her means of escape

Fig. 22. Grosvenor Cather and field crew—the life he wished to escape.
(Nebraska State Historical Society)

and could really talk. At that time, she said, he asked her about the
geography of France. The elements of the novel are all there: the young
man who feels himself provincial, the wish to escape, the war, France.
Attempting to explain her curiously emphatic sense of compulsion to
write the book, she stated that she was "mixed up" with Grosvenor "by
accident of birth," so that a part of her "was buried with him" in France
and "some of him left alive" in her. But the letter makes it plain that the
reason for her sense of identification was not only blood kinship but
their shared wish to escape what they felt to be cultural deprivation (see
figure 22). It was precisely to escape from the likes of Grosvenor, she
told Dorothy, that she wrote at all.[35] I believe we are to read this to
mean, from the beginning.

The great difference was in their ways of escaping. Why her cousin
would have been contemptuous of her way is not explained, but she regarded his way as leading to nonsense. Whether she meant by this her
cousin's ways of escape *until* the war came to release him or meant to
include his going off to war is not clear. It is at any rate the sharing of
the escape wish—indeed, a shared yearning toward France—but the
dissimilarity of their ways of escaping that she referred to when she

wrote, still in the same letter, that they were "very similar and at the same time very different," a statement that captures the ambivalence of the novel's narrative voice, an amalgam of identification and distance.[36]

The theme of escape from the periphery to the cultural center, then, can only be discussed in relation to the war. Or to put it another way, Cather discusses Claude's departure to war only in relation to his masculine wish (as distinct from her own) to escape from the quotidian to the splendid. For him, because his vision is limited by patriarchal assumptions about how he should conduct his life, the only way to reach the splendid is military heroism. Such a belief is patently unreasonable. Cather's own life demonstrates that there were other ways of escape that could lead one to the same splendid destination: Europe, France. But for this particular young man, limited in both will and imagination, the war provides the one opportunity to get away and to find, despite the spectacle of destruction all around him, the "something splendid" he has always wanted (*OO* 86).

What it is that Claude wants to escape is hard to say only because there is so much. Life as he experiences it has a general ugliness, from the "dark sediment" left by thoughtless fellow users of the family wash basin to the tobacco stains around his father's mouth and the necessity of hauling "stinking hides" to town in company with "coarse-mouthed men" when he wants to be dressing decently and going to the circus (*OO* 3–6). Clearly, Claude is oversensitive to such unpleasantness; not surprisingly, given his age, he suffers from false pride and vain self-consciousness.[37] But these defects do not entirely invalidate his views. His brother Ralph's discarded "mechanical toys" in the basement (19) are presented from a central narrative perspective clearly distinct from Claude's. His distaste for them is the novel's own and presumably the reader's as well. Besides this ugliness and crude materialism of life, the general harshness of climate and work, and the coarseness of most of the people around him, Claude also suffers a frustratingly limited opportunity for education that provides him just enough cultivation to perceive what he is missing. His mother is so sunk in unthinking piety that she insists he attend an intellectually benighted Bible college, and his father merely tolerates his educational endeavors until he takes a whim to yank Claude home to run the farm.

Part of what Claude wants to escape, then, is his family—more specifically, his "patently abusive father."[38] Such a reading is well sustained by such moments in the text as when Mr. Wheeler refuses to let Claude drive the car into town on circus day after Claude has washed it for that very purpose or when he malicious chops down his wife's treasured cherry tree. (It is scarcely incidental that Claude first sees Mme. Joubert, the Frenchwoman who will become a mother figure to him and whose husband participates as an equal in domestic life, sitting under a cherry tree.) Male aggression and oedipal rivalry drives the son to rebellion and the wish to kill; it drives sons to warfare. But Claude also wants to escape his mother. Despite his devotion to her and his feeling that she understands him better than anyone else, he is irritated by her piety and her refusal to assert herself in opposition to her husband. Not that he welcomes opposition from his own wife, of course; his marriage to Enid is another of the dissatisfactions he wants to escape. He imagines a marital relationship compounded of witty interplay, sex, and good home cooking, and Enid provides none of these. Issues of gender are indeed pervasive in the novel and have been intertwined in the critical response to it from the beginning.

Writing about war is one of the most strongly gendered of all literary traditions. Anthologies of war poetry still appear that exclude women poets altogether or represent them by only the most grudging of tokens, despite the fact that both world wars brought major outpourings of verse by women on the tragedy being enacted around them. It is as if "war poetry" meant only poetry about the battlefield. Even if the term did mean only that, we would need to examine our assumptions that only those who have been there have anything worthwhile to say, a standard that would exclude many male writers who were not in battle but whose words have nevertheless been accepted as convincing and compelling.[39] Such a narrow definition of war writing makes no sense. Not only is *battle* a term whose meaning is unclear in the twentieth century, when bombs and artillery shells fall on civilians far from the battlefront, but *war* includes a whole complex of social experiences, from the manufacture and delivery of matériel and the resulting shortages of domestic goods to the displacements suffered by refugees to the medical and relief work required for combatants and noncombatants alike to the losses suffered by families whose sons and daughters are wounded or killed. War is all of that. War also entails moral and intellectual dilemmas about which women are fully as qualified to write as men. As Patricia Yongue argues, "how women feel war and feel about war ought, from a

human and moral viewpoint, to matter as much as how men feel it and
feel about it," and Cather had "every right and, more important, every
obligation to write about it from a thinking and articulate woman's perspective" ("For Better" 144). But the response to *One of Ours* did not
accord her that right. It was a response that reflected, she said herself,
prejudice.[40]

Like many other women writers of her time—Dorothy Canfield
Fisher, Gertrude Atherton, Vera Brittain, Edith Wharton, and others—
Cather emphasized in her writing about the war the great range of
women's roles.[41] That women both suffer from and are active in modern
total warfare is made evident by such glimpsed characters as the old
woman and little girl shot by a German sniper, the indefatigable relief
worker Mlle. Olive de Courcy, and the woman fighter pilot shot down
by Claude's friend (*OO* 234). Claude's realization that "to be alive, to be
conscious and have one's faculties, was to be in the war" (336) could well
be Cather's own statement of her right and obligation (to borrow
Yongue's terms) to write of the great cataclysm.

Gender issues are important in the novel in other ways as well. Indeed,
One of Ours is an unusual war novel in the abundance and range of its
female characters. One of the most important of these is Mahailey, the
beloved domestic servant of the Wheelers, slightly retarded but an
abider and the last voice heard in the novel. Another is Mrs. Erlich, the
lively and gracious and tolerant mother of one of Claude's friends, not
at his own college, but at the University of Nebraska, where he takes a
history course. Another is Gladys, a childhood friend who becomes a
teacher and a woman able to construct a gracious life despite limited
finances. Like Claude, Gladys believes that life can be splendid, that it
can be made up of "love and kindness, leisure and art," though these
"beautiful" things are stifled by money-grubbers such as Claude's brother
Bayliss (129). Not surprisingly, Gladys, who is associated with European
origins through her grandfather from Antwerp, has the appearance and
the "musicianship" of a woman of culture (90).

Clearly, Gladys is the woman Claude should have married. She is his
soul mate; their two names are the male and female versions of the same
name (Schwind 68). Instead, he marries Enid Royce, a figure all readers
find disagreeable. Enid is by her own confession "not naturally much
drawn to people" (*OO* 110). Her nature is only too well indicated by
the sharpness of her features, the limpness of her handshake, and the

"suggestion of flight" or "gliding away" in her air (104). Unrelenting once she makes up her mind, she is a vegetarian and a prohibitionist—two causes for which Cather had no sympathy. She leaves Claude cold dinners while she drives to far-flung meetings, and she not only withholds sex on their wedding night but perhaps later as well, finding a man's embrace "distasteful" (147, 172–73). Comically enough, she also disapproves of sex among her barnyard fowl, resolutely keeping her laying hens penned off from the flock's one rooster. In short, Enid is treated with amusement and disdain throughout.

Still, Cather's intentions with regard to Enid are far from obvious. Most of the disapproval directed at her reflects the perspective of hostile males. The chicken episode, for example, is told mainly by a male neighbor who seems to feel the need to stand up for the rights of roosters even though Claude himself points out that infertile eggs keep better. The neighbor's wife says she "really didn't see any harm" in Enid's poultry raising (167–69). Claude's own resentments reflect his disappointed expectations. Wanting a woman with the sparkle of Mrs. Erlich who would provide responsive sex and home-cooked meals, even though nothing in Enid's behavior before marriage justified such expectations, he is naturally frustrated.

Enid herself is quite clear what she wants to do until she is persuaded by her (male) spiritual adviser that her duty lies in marrying Claude to try to bring him to Christ. The first time he proposes she tells him frankly that her "mind is full of other plans" and she believes that marriage may be for most girls "but not for all" (127). Certainly we recognize this as a sentiment Cather would and did approve. What Enid wants is to go to China as a missionary. Once again Cather has created a female character with a sense of profession. But no one pays any attention to her wishes. Claude must bear considerable blame for marrying her in the knowledge that marriage is not what she wants. When the opportunity presents itself she escapes, just as he does and just as Cather did herself.[42] Not only is her scapegoating in the novel, then, of doubtful justification within the text, but it can scarcely be taken as reflecting any simple intentionality on Cather's part. As we have seen, her views on gender as well as on the war were complex, and her narrative perspective in the novel is fluid and problematic.

The complex ambiguity of the text is illustrated by Cather's treatment of the most important of the female characters, Claude's mother.

Disagreeably doting and vapidly devout, Mrs. Wheeler is nevertheless shown as a person of sensitivity. It is she who understands, at the end, how Claude had deceived himself and how miserable his life would have been if he had returned to lose his illusions. Gelfant argues that Claude's mother must bear some of the blame for sending him off to the war, since it is her "impassioned advocacy of the war" that influences him to enlist, "an irreversible decision that leads to his untimely death" ("What" 92). But the text does not support such a reading. True, Mrs. Wheeler is so ardent for helping the Allies that even Claude reproves her for getting "worked up" over it (*OO* 178). But it is Mr. Wheeler, not his wife, who first mentions the war, expressing his glee at the rise in the price of wheat. Claude is immediately interested enough to wait in town late for the newspaper. Only later do we see him engaged in conversation about it with his mother, and at that point he is already at least as intent as she, hoping the French will make a heroic stand in Paris or else burn it down, while she hopes for moderation (139). Contrary to Gelfant's statement that she "evokes silent assent" when she asks whether he believes the prayers of the French will save the city, he does answer, saying that he supposes the Germans are also praying. In other words, he doubts that the conflict will be resolved by prayers. True, after reading the barrage of propaganda pouring out of the nation's presses, Mrs. Wheeler does define the issue as a moral one demanding sacrifice. But in that, too, she is more a victim caught up in a process driven by profit motives (such as her husband's) than an instigator. A reading that blames her and women like her for sending their sons to war is no more acceptable than one that poses Mrs. Wheeler as the voice of peace.

How, then, are we to read passages in which Claude exults that "life had after all turned out well for him, and everything had a noble significance" (*OO* 332) because he had gone to war? And how does this issue relate to Cather's vision of Europe?

An early hint is the motif of masculinity versus passivity, belligerence versus self-doubt that pervades the opening section, "On Lovely Creek." In these chapters Cather exposes the speciousness of available models of masculinity. Claude is surrounded by guffawing hired men who think it is smart to mistreat horses, peers who try to settle issues with their fists, brothers who either grasp at pennies or throw money away on junk, and a father who likes to roam around, talk big, and play practical jokes. In response, Claude worries about his manhood, fearing that his name marks him as a weakling or a "sissy" and consoling himself that he at least has good muscles. Little wonder he is happy to get into uniform! As soon as he joins the army, that most masculine of institutions, he begins to notice machinery and take an interest in tinkering with the car, which he has previously despised. Men, it seems, like machines, and now that he can consider himself a real man, Claude does, too. It is not so simple as that, of course. Claude is, after all, the (pathetic) hero of the novel, and as he matures he finds alternative models of masculinity and becomes less limited by dichotomies of gender, though never entirely free of ingrained notions. Working with Dr. Trueman (true man), he serves well as a nurse on the troop ship and gives up worrying that his wristwatch is a "sissy" affectation, since it proves so useful. This extended critique of prevailing assumptions about masculinity (an echo of her earlier critiques of prevailing assumptions about femininity) lends plausibility to the idea that Cather is also critiquing masculinity's drive toward war.

Another hint is provided in the paragraph of summation, set off both typographically and by its switch to present tense (implying reliability), that marks Claude's departure for college. Summarizing his hopes and fears, the paragraph ends with an emphatic pronouncement: "He is terribly afraid of being fooled" (*OO* 30). The idea will be reasserted after he gets to France: "It was the Wheeler way" to fear "being fooled" (327). We are reminded yet again when Mrs. Wheeler recalls at the end how he was "so afraid of being fooled!" (370). But Claude *is* fooled, again and again. He is fooled on the way over, on the *Anchises*, by a new acquaintance named Victor (as it turns out, not a winner at all) who sends him to Dr. Trueman for a prescription for venereal disease without telling him what it is (250). Claude never quite understands that the delightful woman Victor keeps talking about, who will be sure to "receive" him if he gets to London, is a prostitute. He is fooled in the first scene on French soil by a shopkeeper who overcharges by "two-and-a-half times the market price" and regards the Doughboys' presence less as a rescue than as another "invasion," this time an assault on "integrity" (263–64). He is fooled in Rouen when, determined to maintain high standards in his sightseeing, he goes "hunting for the Cathedral" and thinks he has found it when in fact he is in a parish church (276). Most emphatically, as David Gerhardt realizes with affectionate amusement, he is fooled when he opens the locket of a just-killed German sniper and, finding the picture of a beautiful boy, takes it to be "'probably a kid brother'" (349). At the end he is (mercifully) fooled by being told that David Gerhardt has survived the artillery barrage, when in fact David is dead.

Claude is fooled in his entire attitude toward the war. But the diffuse irony of Cather's writing does not allow us to say what a correct attitude would be. Clarity is exposed as reductive. Unwilling as she was to adopt the view of modernists who wrote of a world lacking all meaning, she instead created a succession of limited and illusory meanings, false floors that keep dropping us, if not into the nihilism of a Hemingway ("Our nada who art in nada . . ."), at least into radical uncertainty. A single meaning may be there somewhere at the bottom, but we cannot quite detect what it is. And so the irony that surrounds Claude's more general misconceptions is less crisp, less clear in its import, than the limited ironies of his "foolings." He has envied Alan Seeger (the poet of "I have a rendezvous with Death") the "fortunate" chance to fight for an ideal, but we know, from our perspective as heirs to all that followed the Great War and readers of unnumbered recountings of its filth and horror, that even Seeger's sense of doom was overly pretty. Aboard the *Anchises* Claude thinks that being a part of the American Expeditionary Force is a "golden chance" (*OO* 253), but the evidence is all around him that it is only a "chance" at a miserable death. Those who escape the flu will be immersed in filth, both in the trenches and in a "picturesquely situated" shell hole Claude and his men find to bathe in. When he loosens a German helmet from the bottom, releasing the gas of decomposing bodies, they prove to have been bathing in putridness. The scene is a telling one and almost certainly a direct response to Rupert Brooke's 1914 sonnet that envisioned soldiers as "swimmers into cleanness leaping."[43] Claude leaps, but not into cleanness.

The novel's depictions of the war as a glorious thing, depictions derided by a chorus of male literati at the time, are consistently identified with Claude's point of view and are juxtaposed either to images leading readers to question it or to questionings voiced by other characters. Claude's friend David, drawn as a paragon of sophistication and honor, offers repeated correctives. Regarding the war as the inescapable doom of his generation (if it "didn't kill you in one way, it would in another") and finding Claude excessively "sensitive to any criticism of this war," David knows that whatever the war was fought for, it was "certainly not to make the world safe for Democracy" (*OO* 286, 295, 330). Cather's irony is rarely so direct as this echo of Woodrow Wilson's war message. More often it is a muffled kind of irony that sets up narrative distance without subjecting her naive hero to obvious derision. Characteristically, she prefers not to spell things out clearly on the page, but to make them felt there. And there are many moments at which irony is felt. When Claude sees the "great dump-heap" of war damage and recognizes that there was "nothing picturesque about this, as there was in the war pictures one saw at home" (307), but still insists on believing that "no battlefield or shattered country he had seen was as ugly as this world would be if men like his brother Bayliss controlled it" (339), the sentiment is hyberbolic, belying the human cost as well as the visual ugliness of the battlefield. It is also both an exposure and a concealment of the direct connection between the profit hunger of men like Bayliss and war's ruin. When Claude looks out over No Man's Land somewhere "east of the Somme" and decides to "enjoy the scenery" (OO 294), we recall the many pictures of that eerily ugly strip of devastated land and wonder what he can be thinking of. The fact that he does so at dawn aligns the scene with one of the most frequently used ironic tropes in all of World War I poetry. When Claude believes that "life had after all turned out well for him, and everything had a noble significance" (332), we recall Wilson's abandonment of his touted war aims, souring Europeans and Americans alike on the whole peace process and leading millions to believe that there had been no real significance to the war at all.

It is to Claude, not the (intermittently) distanced central narrative perspective, that the guns sound "pleasant" (OO 339). The "romantic vision of war" throughout is Claude's, not Cather's (Schwind 55). Still, her irony is one that results from genuine multiplicity of meaning, not a clear opposition of truth and untruth. The world a Bayliss would make, even without war, *is* ugly; we have already seen the evidence of that. The hope that "ideals were not archaic things" but "real sources of power" *is* appealing. It really would be nice if "lads" could go off to war as if to a football game (a recurrent trope of the early war that Cather knowingly deploys when Claude ships out). But they cannot. And as long as they think they can, more of them will keep going into wars that shred them up into appalling pieces like the hand that will not stay buried (361) or the severed and mutilated body parts that so troubled war poet Wilfred Owen up to and during his hospitalization at Craiglockhart.[44] Mrs. Wheeler is right to believe that Claude's death may have been more merciful than a prolonged disillusionment, though it is hard to imagine a mother's thinking so. The feeling shows how clearly she recognizes the inevitability of such a disillusionment, which causes Claude's returning friend Hicks, for example, to wear a "slightly cynical expression" (369). But Mrs. Wheeler's faith that her son's ideals were "beautiful beliefs to die with" (370) implicates her in the social structure that continues to perpetuate warmongering. So long as such beliefs are thought beautiful, humanity will continue falling into the delusions of a Claude Wheeler —the easy use of dehumanizing epithets such as "the Hun" for equally misled enemies, the love of a pale blue color when seen in cornflowers but not when seen in the eyes of a misbegotten infant (a *Kaiserblume*, indeed), the belief that the "face of danger" is "bright" (339).

Claude, then, is both validated and disavowed. As Cather admitted to an astute early reader, he is a version of the legendary Parsifal, at once hero and fool. Praising her reader for recognizing the Parsifal theme, she said that she had considered using as an epigraph the oracular prophecy in Act I of Wagner's *Parsifal*, "The blameless fool, by pity enlightened." Having decided against doing so, apparently for reasons of not wanting to be too explicit, she thought she had buried the Parsifal theme too deeply to be recognized.[45]

The parallels created by this mythic and operatic precedent are indeed not obvious but, once noted, are intriguing and powerful. Claude has been shielded by his mother much as Parsifal was "removed from the world by his mother . . . lest he fall into sinful ways." The young Parsifal "fights without knowing why," leaving the mysteries of the opera greatly veiled in silence and unknowing. Both the weaknesses and the strengths of the mythic characters (Kundry and the wounded king Klingsor as well as Parsival himself) are bound up in their "unbridled confusion" (Rienäcker 62, 65). The spear that wounds Klingsor also heals, as the war that wounds and ultimately kills Claude "heals" him of the affliction of chronic dissatisfaction. In caring for his men, the fooled Claude fulfills the prophecy of being "made wise through pity." If he is a fool, he is at any rate a "blameless" one.

Rather than the prophecy from *Parsifal*, Cather used as epigraph and also as title of the last section "Bidding the eagles of the West fly on," a line from Vachel Lindsay's poem "Bryan, Bryan, Bryan, Bryan." When we recall that the poem is a tribute to William Jennings Bryan, the Silver-Tongued Orator, and recall Cather's conservative politics, the choice rings with irony. Although she felt considerable interest in Bryan and even a certain affection from having been welcomed into his home as a student in Lincoln, she and her father were Republicans.[46] In "Two Friends" (1932), "The Best Years" (1948, written 1945), and *O Pioneers!* she showed supporters of Bryan as foolish enthusiasts or extremists. The opponent of Bryan in "Two Friends" bears the same name as the admirable army doctor in *One of Ours:* Mr. Trueman.[47] Her reuse of the name in the short story was probably a tribute to her father, the "true man" of her life whose Republican sentiments had been anti-Populist and anti-Bryan and whose business in farm loans had placed him in a group particularly hated by the Populists. Even without this information, however, we catch an indication of the sense in which she appropriated Lindsay's line if we look at the passage from which it comes:

> Oh, the longhorns from Texas,
> The Jay hawks from Kansas,
> The plop-eyed bungaroo and giant giassicus,
> The varmint, chipmunk, bugaboo,
> The horned-toad, prairie-dog and ballyhoo,
> From all the newborn states arow,
> Bidding the eagles of the west fly on,
> Bidding the eagles of the west fly on.
> The fawn, prodactyl and thing-a-ma-jig,
> The rakaboor, the hellangone,
> The whangdoodle, batfowl and pig . . .
>
> (Lindsay 97–98)

It is hard to imagine Willa Cather reading these lines as anything but foolish blather.

One of Ours appeared at a time of disillusioned reassessment of the war, its aims, and its outcomes. John Dos Passos's *Three Soldiers*, published the previous year, had shown "a battalion of veterans sporting the red badge of cynicism" (Griffiths 261). Popular music, that barometer of the mood of a time, reflected the nation's determination to forget about highflown ideals and have a good time. As early as 1919 a Cole Porter musical called *Hitchy-Koo* featured an ex-soldier's lament that the girls don't like him as much anymore since he no longer wears a uniform—a deflation of war aims indeed. Chillingly, from our present perspective, the soldier's proposed solution to his amorous problem is to "start another war." By 1920 composer Charles Ives expressed a different kind of disillusionment in a song called either *Nov. 2, 1920* or *An Election* that deplored both public cynicism and the fact that the "hog heart" of greed had betrayed the war aims once thought noble (Houtchens and Stout 92). One of the biggest hit songs of 1926 would be the Peerless Quartet's recording of *My Dream of the Big Parade*, in which a patriotic celebration turns into a parade of wounds, dismemberments, and grieving mothers.

There can be little doubt that Cather not only was aware of this souring of the public mind but shared it. In a letter to Zoë Akins in October 1919 congratulating her on the success of her play *Déclassée*, Cather wrote that since the advent of trench warfare a "triumph" was possible only in the theater. By enclosing the word "triumph" in quotation marks, she distanced herself from the very concept. Earlier in the year, while the Versailles Peace Conference was in progress, she had wondered to Greenslet what the English could be thinking of Wilson, and in 1920 when she wrote home from France to her Aunt Franc, Grosvenor Cather's mother, she was careful to distinguish between the French people's love for American soldiers and their opinion of the president. In 1922, shortly before publication of *One of Ours*, she wrote Dorothy Canfield Fisher, "We knew one world and knew what we felt about it, now we find ourselves in quite another."[48]

The derision with which male intellectuals greeted *One of Ours*, despite its enthusiastic popular reception and winning of the Pulitzer Prize, indicates that they did not recognize Cather's distancing of her own perspective from that of her character and the irony or ambivalence it created. Perhaps because she had constructed the bases for irony with her usual light touch, while accentuating the masculine delusions that she held at arm's length, such undeniably intelligent readers as Wilson, Mencken, Hemingway, and Lewis seem to have seen only the accenting, not its undercutting. But there is another possible explanation for their response. She had shown the soldier himself as deluded and the women who surround him as being more knowing than he. Perhaps these male powers of the literary world preferred to see the male soldiers, not their women, as the perceptive ones, able to see and judge the bankruptcy of outworn notions. Hemingway may have perceived more than he realized, however, when he ridiculed "that last scene in the lines" as having come straight out of *The Birth of a Nation*, "Catherized."

The cleanness of Claude's death, "three clean bullet holes" through the chest (*OO* 367), in a war characterized by mutilation and filth, may well have come out of the death on the parapet in *Birth of a Nation*, with its visual reminder of the World War I battlefield. That is, it may have been another ironic touch, well in keeping with the conflicted vision of the novel as a whole. But it is hard to understand how these men of letters could have missed the narrative endorsement of Mrs. Wheeler's recognition, at the end, that the war had been only a "flood of meanness and greed" and "nothing ha[d] come of it all but evil" (370).[49]

Cather's implied invocation of the trite notion of a fate worse than death in connection with the disillusioned survivors of the war was not, after all, an idle one. Among the unsolicited letters from readers that she sent to Carrie Miner, now kept at the Willa Cather Pioneer Memorial in Red Cloud, is one dated December 22, 1922, that confesses poignantly,

> I have not felt [such emotions] since I went through Hoboken, Newark & Elizabeth on a troop train & heard the people cheer. . . . This seems to be the great land of bunk. . . . So far as I know you are one of the few living persons who would understand if you heard me curse Hiram Johnson, Henry Ford, or Col. Harvey, & I curse with a depth of bitterness that I never felt toward any Fritzie. . . . Those who died in action are lucky, but what of us whose military fortune gave good safe jobs & who have also the bitterness of knowing that better men are buried in France? How shall we carry on in a place that is bunk?

Cather, often charged with escapism and nostalgia, seems to have spoken a language understood by this embittered veteran.[50]

She had written her "manly battle yarn" at last, but as a questioning of both manliness and battle and with none of the rollicking simplicity of a "yarn."

THE COMPLEX movement between irony and a desperate idealism in *One of Ours* does not in any event vitiate its picture of the American's longing for a Europe that is taken to represent cultural maturity, beauty, and enlightenment. In part, that is because (notwithstanding the polluted swimming hole) Cather minimizes the filthiness of the war experience so far as place itself. She has been accused of having written a disinfected or squeamish version of the war. Sergeant observed that even though there are "a few smelly corpses," there is "no profanity, no sex, no rebel-lion, no chaos" (191). John Murphy derides her "soldier dialogue," which includes that powerful exclamation "Pshaw!" ("One" 238). Such criticisms are to some degree justified—though in fact there *is* chaos: Claude's battalion "outrun[s its] provisions" (343), in the final battle scene communications are cut off and he does not know where some of his men are, and several men are killed or wounded because a new doctor drew fire by switching on a light to check a wound. But squeamishness about the coarse behaviors of soldiers (if that is what it is) pertains only to the writing of a war novel, which as we know is not what Cather had set about doing (though she knew people would call it that, and we may question her candor on this point). Restraint in depicting the ugliness wrought by the conflict on France itself, the land and the civilization, was another matter.

Two distinct processes seem to have been going on here. In accordance with the creed she announced in 1922 in "The Novel Démeublé," she seems to have been struggling to compress the scenes in Europe in order to pose them against the clutter of the scenes in Nebraska. The effort to do so would account for the omission of many realistic details that we can be sure she knew about from her conversations with soldiers in hospitals. The number of decaying corpses (some of them going *glup glup* as they emit gases) is quite sufficient to make grotesque horror "felt on the page." It is more the grubbiness of the war that she omits—the omnipresent vermin, the problem of urinating and defecating in water-logged trenches (particulars that we cannot suppose she would have thought suitable for a novel). These details of the general misery she simplifies to two rats and the fact that men coming out of the line are given clean clothes (a shorthand version of the elaborate delousing measures actually employed).[51] In addition, it was important to her to show that however fooled Claude had been in his sweeping idealism and in many particulars, he was right to believe that in France he had glimpsed the "splendor" he most wanted from life. Accordingly, in the depiction of Mlle. de Courcy's village she shows that despite the "ugly . . . ruin" caused by the war, resembling the "dump-heap[s] . . . which disgrace the outskirts of American towns," beauty in the form of wild-flowers keeps coming up "spontaneously out of the French soil," and people go on maintaining, where they can, neat patches of vegetable gardens and sheltered spots of beauty (*OO* 307–9). In the dawn scene on the battlefield when Claude looks out over devastation, his determination to see what "scenery" he can may be foolish, but it reflects his insistence on the validity of the European lure.

In his feeling for France, Claude is Cather. She indicated as much in a letter to Canfield Fisher during her work on the proofs of the novel, stating that Dorothy had never understood how uncultured she felt when they were in France, but Claude would show her. In the summer of 1920 she wrote letters from France whose tone confirms the point. Paris, she wrote, was more beautiful than ever, with the green and gold Luxembourg gardens like a symbol of youth; she was enjoying the city even when the weather was bad, and she had found the French countryside, too, more beautiful than ever before. This was at a time when the destruction was still so unrepaired that it was almost impossible to travel about the country. In the flush of her Europhilia, she could even accommodate the war itself to a justifying vision of cultural continuity. The sight of crippled soldiers on the streets being helped around by veterans of the Franco-Prussian War, while little boys helped both, reminded one that the beauty of French civilization had always been preserved at a cost.[52] The beauty, it seems, was at least as real to her as the cost.

Europe remained Cather's refuge. In 1923, smarting from adverse reviews of *One of Ours* and dragged down by influenza, she wrote to Canfield Fisher that she could hardly wait to get away to France.

8

FACING A BROKEN WORLD

Where are the loves that we have loved before
When once we are alone, and shut the door?
    —"L'Envoi"

The times are bad and the world is old . . .
    —"The Palatine"

THE REVIEWS that greeted *One of Ours*, essentially saying that she should have known better than to venture onto ground not her own, struck Cather a hard blow. She had fallen into depression even before the book was published, writing to Dorothy Canfield Fisher in April that having lost the joy of Claude's company (as if he were a real person), she felt drained of her ability to take an interest in things.[1] The reviews genuinely unnerved her. Even her handwriting during that period became scrawly and slack.

She had been apprehensive all along, apparently for reasons that proved prophetic. As early as June 1919 she warned Ferris Greenslet not to tell anyone that her new book had anything to do with the war. It cannot have helped her cooling relations with Houghton Mifflin to learn that he had already done so. When negative reviews began to appear, she wrote Dorothy that she wished she could have published the book anonymously, but Alfred Knopf would not hear to it. He had made a commitment to her work for the long haul, and this was the first book of hers he would publish on which he could hope to make a profit, since *Youth and the Bright Medusa*, in 1920, was in large measure a gesture of good will, four of its eight stories having already appeared in book form.[2] Understandably, he wanted the benefit of her established name on *One of Ours*.

In retrospect, Cather would convince herself that she had also had bad reviews on *My Ántonia*. Fanny Butcher, for many years the book review editor of the *Chicago Tribune*, later echoed that notion as if it were fact, writing that *My Ántonia* "was not well received by either the critics or the public" (365). In fact, H. L. Mencken called it "one of the best [novels] that any American has ever done," and Randolph Bourne, a critic Cather particularly respected, praised its "artistic simplicity" and said it took Cather "out of the rank of provincial writers." W. H. Boynton, in the *Bookman*, called her "an accomplished artist." Sales of *My Ántonia* were unremarkable, but that was partly a matter of its being released in the last days of the war, when public attention was riveted elsewhere and book sales in general were depressed. By 1922 sales had strengthened, and *My Ántonia* remained a secure source of income for the rest of Cather's life.[3] At a stroke she had demonstrated that she was a major writer, not so much in a commercial as in a literary or artistic sense. With the strong sale of *One of Ours* and the award of the Pulitzer Prize, her position in the world of letters was confirmed. Ironically, she was "recognized as one of America's foremost writers" (Rosowski, *Voyage* 130) even as the book was being mauled by the literati.

Cather herself believed that *One of Ours* surpassed her previous level of work. Alfred Knopf either agreed or was determined she would think he did. After reading the final proofs he telegraphed her that it was "masterly, a perfectly gorgeous novel, far ahead of anything [she had] ever done" and would make her "position" "secure forever." He added that he was "proud to have [his] name associated with it." Cather quickly shared the telegram (perhaps a planned publicity device) with Fanny Butcher and with her old friend in Lincoln, Dr. Julius Tyndale. Even after it was clear that most reviewers disagreed, she continued to regard the book as a technical achievement and, at any rate, one that she had to write, a book that thrust itself on her and dominated her life until she completed it. Subsequent readers have more nearly agreed with the reviewers, while rejecting their egregiously sexist tone. *One of Ours* is usually regarded, even by the most devoted of Cather scholars, as an interesting failure.[4]

It is much more than that, however, in its importance to Cather's evolution as a writer and in what it tells us about her mind. Technically, she had indeed advanced with each book. After establishing her voice and her fictional milieu in *O Pioneers!* and *The Song of the Lark*, she had consolidated her identity in the business of letters with a work of unassailable power and finish in *My Ántonia*, a deeply characteristic work in its propensity to look back toward childhood but also in its use of an uncertainly distanced, only partially validated narrative voice. She was working her way toward a narrative strategy that would afford multiplicity of effect, so as to convey a sense of the complexity of being, unclarified by direct statement.

In *One of Ours* the gap between authorial voice and the perspective of the observing and narrating character widened to a radical ambiguity. The observer of France and of the U.S. Expeditionary Force was always Claude, Cather insisted, not herself.[5] The author had seemingly abandoned her authority, with results that are at times undeniably awkward. Combining sympathy with irony, shifting perspective with less apparent intentionality than we expect in modern fiction, the narrative hovers between special pleading for Claude and distancing of the reader's engagement. For many readers it simply does not work. Cather is attempting to render, on this side of the war experience, attitudes that existed on the other side. She is reaching back to a previous and generally outmoded aspiration, a lost idealism. Even if we regard the idealist not yet enlightened by pity (and disillusion) as a poor fool, of course, we do not have to regard the author as one for having tried to convey the poor fool's state of mind. The ending of the novel demonstrates her awareness and indeed her sharing of the postwar disillusion that invalidated Claude's naïveté. But by adhering to her principle of not making direct statements in fiction, she left herself open to the charge that she shared that naïveté. In fact, the central intellectual thrust of the novel is not advocacy of either vision but revelation of the disparity between them. *One of Ours* reaches toward a past that it acknowledges to be inaccessible and suspects to have been of dubious worth. The suspicion that the longed-for lost past was, after all, unworthy would shape much of what followed.

With the recognition of postwar disillusionment and despair that ends *One of Ours*, Cather found herself facing a world seemingly jarred loose from all its moorings—intellectual, moral, and aesthetic. The novel she quickly turned to is a fragment stored against its ruin. Often considered her finest work, *A Lost Lady* was termed by no less a literary figure than Sinclair Lewis "about the finest thing that has ever appeared in American fiction."[6] It is also a novel that addresses the problem of facing a world that had, as she would later say in the prefatory note to *Not under Forty*, broken in two.

Certainly Cather was not alone in sensing a break from the past. Virginia Woolf famously stated that human nature "changed" on or about December 1910.[7] Vera Brittain was convinced, in 1916, that the war would make "a big division of 'before' and 'after' in the history of the world" (317). Herbert Read, attempting to define modernism, would speak of "a break-up, a devolution." The year in which Cather located the break, "1922 or thereabouts," has usually fixed critical attention on *One of Ours* because of its publication in 1922 and its winning the Pulitzer Prize "thereabouts," in 1923.[8] But the novel she actually wrote in 1922 was *A Lost Lady*, a very different work though equally dark and equally concerned with the severing of the present and future from the past. It is the first of a grouping of three—*A Lost Lady* in 1923, *The Professor's House* in 1925, and *My Mortal Enemy* in 1926—designated by Bernice Slote as Cather's "problem or conflict novels of the 1920's" (*KA* 110).

These novels do indeed form a "dark" trio occupied with discontent and misgiving. *Death Comes for the Archbishop* in 1927 is conventionally seen as being something else altogether, a book of serenity or "heroic perfection" (Giannone 185). Cather herself fostered such a view, proclaiming in numerous letters that the writing of *Archbishop* was an utter pleasure, giving her a happy and peaceful sense of actually working alongside her archbishop himself.[9] Rarely do we see so clear an example of a writer's formulating the direction of subsequent critical interpretation. With *Archbishop* marking her emergence from a "dark" period, the boundaries of a clear periodicity are established and her career can be seen under the guise of a shining schematic that affirms some of the most closely held of western culture's idealizations of itself: a three-part triumphal progress from youthful sunniness into and through the slough of middle-aged despond to triumphal religious certainty and historical affirmation.[10]

Yet so schematic a view of Cather's career is not finally tenable. *Death Comes for the Archbishop* is not serene, nor are the novels before *One of Ours* sunny. The dark middle novels of the mid-1920s differ from the rest of Cather's work only in degree, not in kind. What draws them together as a group is not their conflictedness—Cather's novels are all "'conflict' narratives" (Shaw 95)—but their focus on the sense of rupture, the break in time. The three so-called problem novels share a fixation on the past from the perspective of a present so deteriorated that it forces a reassessment of what had seemed to be a clear contrast between the two sides of the breach. The reach toward the past across the abyss of brokenness is problematized by a suspicion that the past was not, in fact, idyllic. The past, then, is doubly lost, severed from the present by the Great War's breaking of the world and rendered unavailable, or of doubtful availability, for recuperation by nostalgia. In *My Ántonia* the past was "precious" and "incommunicable," but it could be shared, "possessed together" (*MA* 360). In 1921 Cather still felt that she and Canfield Fisher possessed together a past most of which they could regard as precious, in contrast to the disordered present.[11] But in the three "problem" novels the past is possessed, if at all, only in isolation and is precious only in being possessed, in being a part of the possessor. Intrinsically the past seems to have been no more precious—or, to use Claude's word, splendid—than the all too sorry present. The idea was stated in embryo in the letter to Canfield Fisher; only most, not all, of the past was delightful to remember. Such doubts would grow larger but would be submerged, entering the novels in unacknowledged forms.

It is this sense of cultural divorce that is the largest significance of these novels' concern with what Patrick Shaw singles out as their central theme, "the phenomenon of American marriage and domesticity" (95). The broken marriages with which they are ostensibly occupied—Marian Forrester's status as trophy wife of a hero who leaves her a penniless widow, Professor St. Peter's marriage to a woman he can only vaguely remember having loved, Myra Henshawe's marriage begun in flamboyant romance that ends in regret and recrimination—are metaphors for the world's larger brokenness. The uncertainty with which past love is regarded conveys Cather's doubt about a past now only glimpsed on the far side of the divide. Treating unconventionally the conventional device of a marriage plot, she asks to what extent we can be married to the past world and whether we want to continue the union. In her earlier novels irony sprang from the contrast between a splendid past and a deteriorated present. Now she asks whether the past was all that splendid.

ACCORDING TO her own account, Cather conceived the idea for *A Lost Lady* in the summer of 1921 while she was in Toronto visiting Jan and Isabelle (McClung) Hambourg. In a packet of newspapers from Red

Cloud she found a notice of the death of Lyra Garber Anderson, widow of Silas Garber, the founder of Red Cloud and a two-term governor of Nebraska. After reading the notice she went upstairs to rest, and the story of Marian Forrester came to her in an hour's time with perfect clarity. Once again she was drawing directly on people she had known, not only Lyra Garber, whose portrait was close enough that the family threatened lawsuit, but also Annie Pavelka, the original of Ántonia, who, Cather later told Ferris Greenslet, had worked for the original of Mrs. Forrester.[12]

The Garbers had been the social elite of Red Cloud during Cather's adolescence, and she had been just as charmed by the young second wife of the aging prominent citizen as Niel is by Marian Forrester (though never, she insisted to her mother, fooled by her).[13] Silas Garber's varied career had included most of the activities Cather attributes to Captain Forrester: military service at the rank of captain, early settlement in southern Nebraska, and banking, but not railroad construction. For that she may have been thinking of Charles Elliott Perkins, who built the Burlington tracks across Nebraska and served as president of the line from 1881 to 1901. Perkins's daughter recognized herself and her mother in the disagreeable Ogden mother and daughter who come to visit the Forresters and succeed in luring Marian's lover, Frank Ellinger, into marriage. By adding railroading to the fictional captain's résumé, Cather links him to an image of the late pioneer days that (contrary to Alice Perkins Hooper's bristling) she insists on regarding as generally heroic. But Forrester's railroad construction activities also link him to the land grabs, specifically from Native Americans, that ultimately call into question the heroic stature of those past pioneers.[14]

This concern with money and the gaining or losing of wealth is another characteristic that distinguishes *A Lost Lady*, along with *The Professor's House* and *My Mortal Enemy*, from Cather's work more generally. She declared in "The Novel Démeublé" (1922) that novels properly had nothing to do with finance: "Are the banking system and the Stock Exchange worth being written about at all? Have such things any proper place in imaginative art?" (*OW* 37–38). Yet the three gloomy novels that soon followed her declaration had a great deal to do with the effects of money management and asset gathering, and not a little with the processes themselves.[15]

Cather's account of the newspaper notice that generated the idea of

A Lost Lady strikingly resembles her story of the origin of *One of Ours.*
One day in June 1918 she chanced to see a newspaper reporting the
death of Grosvenor Cather, killed (or, as commonly said, "lost") in action
in France (Woodress, *Literary* 303). Three years later, again on a summer day (her letter describing the event specifies that it was very hot),
she looked into a newspaper and saw the notice of Lyra Garber's death.
Both were "lost." Both novels grew from a sense of loss. But the loss at
the origin of *A Lost Lady* was doubled, indeed trebled, and the biographical resonance of the novel compounded, by the fact that Cather read
about it where she did, at the Hambourgs' home in Toronto. Isabelle,
who had already been "lost" to Cather by virtue of her marriage, was
soon to leave Canada and move to Europe—indeed, to France, where
Grosvenor had also been lost.[16]

The linkage goes further. Cather wrote *A Lost Lady* during the time
when *One of Ours* was in production and newly released, when the postwar disillusionment was, because of her engagement with it, very much
on her mind. It was 1922 or thereabouts. Although her frequently quoted
statement about the world's breaking in two would not be made until
1936, it was not merely in retrospect that she felt that way. She expressed
a sense of the broken world in June 1922, when she was well into the
writing of the new book: "'We knew one world and knew what we felt
about it, now we find ourselves in quite another.'"[17] In "The House on
Charles Street," published in the *New York Evening Post Literary Review*
of November 4, 1922 (retitled "148 Charles Street" for its reprinting in
Not under Forty), she speculated that a reshaping of literary sensibility
itself had taken place in the war: "Was it at the Marne? At Versailles,
when a new geography was being made on paper?" (*SPO* 848). The
break had occurred.

Even the *form* of *A Lost Lady* is related to this sense of brokenness.
Rosowski writes ("Historical" 191–93) that the two-part structure and
"backward-looking" narrative perspective embody Cather's stance on
the hither side of the Great War and the "disillusionment in its aftermath," from which she looks back to lament the loss of a pioneer world
that did not know what devastation lay ahead of it. There is great poi-
gnance in that sense of unsuspecting innocence. The narrative perspective of the novel, however, reflects not only her sense of severance from
a time that was good but her severance from an assurance that it really
was. One of the most tightly structured of Cather's novels, *A Lost Lady*

exemplifies the principles of concentration that she had recently enunciated in "The Novel Démeublé" (published April 1922), an essay that might serve as a manifesto for minimalist modernism.[18] It is structured by a central and quite functional break of two years. This silence at the center expresses Niel Herbert's expectation that he can return from college and find nothing changed, that he can take up his life at Sweet Water and his idealizing of Marian Forrester just as before. He looks back and wants the past to go on being just as wonderful as it was. But Cather's own backward-looking perspective includes *both* the world forever stranded on the other side of the chasm *and* Niel's regretful view of it. She sees, though Niel does not, that the world he regrets was also a flawed world whose very flaws constitute the bridge over the chasm of brokenness.[19]

My invocation of a bridge metaphor here reflects Cather's own, immediately prior to the end of Part I and the structural gap that breaks the book in two. Standing on the bridge between the Forresters' land and the town of Sweet Water on the night before he leaves for college—the same bridge where, muttering Shakespeare's line about lilies that fester, he had earlier thrown his freshly picked bouquet into the mud after discovering Marian Forrester's adultery—he bitterly asks himself where such a woman puts her "exquisiteness" when she is "with" a man like Ellinger and whether she can "recover herself" and again give such a perceiver as himself the sense of a "tempered steel" sword that could "fence with anyone and never break" (*ALL* 95). The implication is that Niel, at any rate, does not believe she can. In one sense, that is the central, but I believe not the most important, question of the novel, and it remains unanswered. The break drops us along with Niel into unknowing. When he returns two years later after an absence to which we are never privy, he still wants to see his lady in terms of dazzling charm; that is, he wants a mended past to continue as it was before. But it becomes increasingly difficult and finally impossible for him to see her that way.

Marriage and a "considered speculation" on "female sexuality" (Skaggs, *After* 66) are not, however, the essential issue.[20] Rather, they are used instrumentally toward the asking of a larger question about continuity. Niel's image in pondering the immediate question of Marian Forrester while standing on the bridge, the image of a fencing sword, is a very odd one to invoke with reference to a woman. Although it is an image of quality, to be sure (the "tempered" blade is adequate to any occasion of

ceremonial conflict), its phallic association seems misplaced, and its bare-
ness scarcely accords with Niel's usual delight in Marian's rings and
swirling petticoats and ruffles and veils. But another import carried by
the sword image is precisely apposite: an association with the past, when
fighting was done with swords instead of, say, machine guns and poison
gas. At the site of spatial connection, Niel ponders the possibility of
temporal connection, whether the past can carry over into (be bridged
to) the future. When he returns he will be forced to realize—or at any
rate, we readers will be forced to realize—that not only does the past *not*
provide guidance to the future, he did not understand very much about
it even before. A gap of uncertainty as well as time opens in the middle
of *A Lost Lady*, breaking it in two. Along with the chronologically larger
but typographically less emphasized gap preceding the epilogue, this
gap introduces into the text the space of the unsaid and the unexplained.

Such fractures are instances of one of Cather's favorite narrative
devices, the vacancy or "vacuole" (Middleton). She had employed that
technique in *O Pioneers!*, but there it served less as a site of ultimate uncertainty than as simply a device for the passage of time. In *My Ántonia*
such vacancies occur in the two-year lapse between the "Lena Lingard"
section and "The Pioneer Woman's Story" and in the more drastic
twenty-year lapse preceding "Cuzak's Boys." In *One of Ours* the emptiness is not so much a matter of gaps of time as gaps in perspective and a
refusal to clarify the relation between the authorial point of view and
Claude's. These vacancies fracture the text, opening it to indeterminacy
and leading us to ask questions for which answers are not supplied.
They are perhaps the most visible manifestation of Cather's affinity
with modernism, and they would become more insistent with each successive novel.[21]

In *A Lost Lady* Cather combines vacancies of time with partial narrative
disjuncture. It is this state of partialness, this simultaneous identification
with and skepticism of her flawed male center of consciousness, that
keeps her own perspective so elusive. Because her detachment from
Niel's point of view is not complete, so that even while she reveals the
limitations caused by his naivety she nevertheless shares his regretful
yearning, it may be that we perceive ironies she did not consciously
intend. She moves back and forth across a space of narrative indeterminacy without resolution, partly sharing Niel's feelings, partly showing
their tensions and inadequacy.[22] The crafting of that disjuncture would

seem to account for the difficulties in the writing process that Rosowski summarizes ("Historical" 189–91). She began the story in the third person, started it over in the first person, and then went back to the third. Both she and Edith Lewis explained that she was seeking the clearest way of presenting the effect that the lady in question (the actual Lyra Garber) had on those who "knew her," in just the way Cather "remembered" it (*WCIP* 77; Lewis 124–25). A first-person narrative might have conveyed that effect, but it would not have afforded her so clear a space for irony as the more detached third-person perspective.

What Cather was groping for does not seem to have been the clearest way to convey a particular effect or emotion so much as the clearest way to convey the impossibility of knowing what the lady's effect was. Niel's effort to know the elusive (always already lost) lady becomes a trope for the effort to know anything at all—or at least anything beautiful and charming; in the wasteland world the unbeautiful and uncharming are so obvious as to require no effort. It is precisely this that is the importance of the time setting of the novel: not the postwar but the prewar world. By moving the shabbiness and uncertainty back into the time before 1914, she questions whether the emptiness and shabbiness were not, in fact, there even before, even in the world for which Niel wishes Marian Forrester would "immolate" herself. What he "most held against" her was her unwillingness to "die with the pioneer period to which she belonged" (161).

The elusiveness of narrative voice in *A Lost Lady*, then, is linked to uncertainty about the past. The novel looks across a gap of social transformation and loss to a past that may have been more monumental and more virtuous than the present, or may only seem to the immature viewer to have been so—an uncertainty that impinges very directly on the novel's questioning of who will be the determining stakeholders in American society. We will take up that question more directly in the next chapter, but we need to touch on it here in order to see how Cather leads us to ask, without ever being able to resolve, the question of whether the present is really so different from the past after all, or perhaps whether certain elements in the seemingly noble past did not in fact anticipate the deteriorated present.

Just as the beauty of the past is represented by the lady herself, so its dignity and heroism are embodied by Captain Forrester. (The title of captain is an honorific retained from Civil War days.) He and his

cronies, the railroad elite who visit his house, have become the author-
ities of the social world seen in miniature at the start of the novel. To the
extent that it is a naive narrative identified with Niel's point of view, the
novel would have us believe that the Captain and his lady (before she
was "lost") belonged to the elite of a meritocracy now disrupted by
social climbers and money-grubbers lacking a sense of honor. Nothing
in the book ever entirely invalidates that view. Captain Forrester is seen
as a gracious, kind, dignified man who honors his obligations. But he
is also seen by the central narrator—not Niel, whose perspective is
blandly masculinist—as a man thoroughly enmeshed in the patriarchal
power structure. Moreover, Cather's elusive language, with its tantalizing inclusions and exclusions, leads us to question though never entirely
erase the contrast drawn between the heroism of the past, represented
by Forrester, and the brash materialism of the present, identified with
the singularly repulsive young lawyer Ivy Peters.

In the postwar years of the 1920s, when Cather was writing, a "materialistic civilization" was "triumphant" in America. Electrification of
factory machinery increased from perhaps 5 percent of horsepower at
the turn of the century to 80 percent or more by 1929, a transformation
in process paralleled by increased productivity. One result was wider
availability of consumer goods. Household electrification, a rarity in
1910, was becoming common in urban areas, making new mechanical
devices available and, we can well believe, widely desired.[23] Cather was
reacting to real changes in American life. We know that she felt uncertain about this increased availability of household conveniences from
pronouncements about one such convenience, the telephone, recorded
in her letters: She was trying to get one and could not, she would not
have one because it interrupted her work, she would go out and use a
telephone elsewhere in the afternoon, she was having it disconnected
for the summer to save money, she was keeping her telephone number
secret, and so on. Clearly, she was personally discomfited by mecha-
nized modernity and a society in which things were in the saddle, and
this discomfiture is expressed in her fiction. But it does not follow as a
corollary that she found prewar American society idyllic.

The opening paragraphs of *A Lost Lady*, one of the most subtle and
meaning-packed passages in all of American literature, introduce a
questioning of the established commercial elite. "Thirty or forty years
ago, in one of those grey towns along the Burlington railroad," the novel

begins, quickly establishing the backward view and associating the rail-road with a time more pleasant than the "much greyer to-day" (7). Here the narrative voice shares Niel's nostalgic values. Then comes the rest of the sentence: "there was a house well known from Omaha to Denver for its hospitality and for a certain charm." Again the tribute to the past, but with an overtone faintly suggestive of a house of prostitution—a harsh suggestion and certainly an overstatement of the way Forrester uses his beautiful wife to attract the attention of male business associ-ates, but perhaps not an entirely farfetched one.[24]

These powerful men are not builders like the Captain but are organi-zation men. The railroad has moved out of the building phase and into a phase of industrial consolidation. The present railroad men are an "aristocracy" (*ALL* 7), and the quality of life established in this opening paragraph is one of a pleasantly prosperous but perhaps stodgy class consciousness: "In those days it was enough to say of a man that he was 'connected with the Burlington.'" Enough for what, the novel does not say. Enough for anything, perhaps; or enough for such a man to be regarded as a person of privilege. Such persons had (free?) annual passes for travel on the road, unlike the "homesteaders and hand-workers" who made a living in its territory and lived there. Forrester is one of the elite, a person of privilege who "had to do" with an enterprise related to the railroad business. But it is clear from the pronouns that the narra-tive voice itself belongs to the others. The investors and organizers who come in by train are "they" in opposition to "us": they came to "invest money and to 'develop our great West,' as they used to tell us" (7). Along with the pronouns, the quotation marks around "develop our great West" set up a class distinction between these moneyed outsiders and the homesteaders and workers who belong to the place. Together these details create a tone of skepticism.

It is because of Cather's delicate management of narrative perspec-tive and tone in the first paragraph that the alert reader sees an ironic qualification in the ensuing summary of Captain Forrester's earlier work. Despite his being defined throughout as a man of impeccable business honor whose words had "the impressiveness of inscriptions cut in stone" (*ALL* 51), he had built those hundreds of miles of road "over the sage brush and cattle country, and on up into the Black Hills" (8). That is to say, he had been complicit, by virtue of his construction work, in one of the most shameful episodes in the history of American dealings with Native peoples. At the very time of the founding of Red Cloud in 1871 Chief Red Cloud had been negotiating a treaty that guaranteed the Sioux perpetual possession of the Black Hills. The federal government entered into that treaty in the belief that white America would never want the area. But when gold was discovered in the Black Hills in 1875, the treaty was abrogated and the Sioux were again shifted and reduced in range. Forrester, a good man but not one to challenge the assumptions of his day, participated, however indirectly, in the exploitation of the Indian.

How the novel regards that fact is not clear. Forrester's own integrity is never open to question, unlike that of the repulsive Ivy Peters who, when he begins to manage Mrs. Forrester's investments, "'gets splendid land from the Indians some way, for next to nothing'" (*ALL* 117). Here, there is no evasion; Peters is in the most direct way an exploiter. Mrs. Forrester admits as much when she concedes that she does not "'admire people who cheat Indians'" but lets him manage her small sums because "rascality" (as Niel terms it) "'succeeds faster than anything else'" (118). Still, the fact is that both men got land from the Indians. If Ivy's dealings are "rascality," why were Daniel Forrester's so different?[25] Having first seen the site of his future home when it was "an Indian encampment," he had driven willow stakes into the ground to mark the location and returned, after "helping to lay the first railroad across the plains," to buy the property from the railroad (50–51)—which had, in the meantime, acquired that "splendid land from the Indians" through a process of national appropriation and distribution: a perfectly legal process but no less exploitive in its outcome than Ivy Peters's methods.

The appropriativeness of the white male is conveyed, whether deliberately on Cather's part or because she unconsciously recognized and transmitted what was inevitable in her culture, in the language of possession that permeates the opening chapters. The house is on "Captain Forrester's property" entered by way of "the Captain's private lane"; "he" had chosen it; "he" was "well off for those times" and "could afford to humour his fancies"; "he" did not have children (*ALL* 9).[26] The same word is used for his pride in his wife as for his pride in his livestock: it "gratified him" to hear his cattle admired, and it "gratified him" for his wife to wear jewels (9, 38). We cannot suppose Cather was unaware of how her language was setting up an equivalence. This is the way of things, she says; white males take things and own things, including wives who are assets when doing business with the likes of Cyrus Dalzell, the president of the Colorado & Utah, "that great man" (10). The phrase "great man" carries an inescapable ring of mocking overstatement. Great or not, the class of men to which Dalzell and Forrester belong represents the stakeholders in America who, in the crassest terms, matter: it is theirs.

Cather had her own "fondness for *gentilesse*" and a taste for such expensive comforts as "travel, fine clothes, and fine foods and wines" and "the best china, crystal, and linens for her table" (Yongue, "Aristocrats" 1:46–47).[27] Her class affinities were those of Captain Forrester and his friends, a peculiar combination of pioneering self-reliance and aristocratic comfort. But however important prosperity was to Cather, her tastes and affinities did not extend to the conspicuous grab for money that she saw in the postwar period. If she reveals for what it is Niel's snobbery in deploring Mrs. Forrester's hospitality to a commoner class of people, the new up-and-comers, she also shares in the ridiculing of these commoners. Near the end of the novel, when Mrs. Forrester's social set has been reduced to lower-middle-class youths whose manners she hopes to polish while fending off her own loneliness, it is the larger narrative voice, not Niel's, that points out Annie's "bad complexion" and inability to maintain a conversation, and it is Marian Forrester, not Niel, who remarks on how "vulgar" they are in their management of their wine glasses (153–54). Yet one of those vulgar boys, perhaps having benefited from her tutelage, succeeds to the point of traveling in South America and greeting her courteously as a social equal.[28] If *A Lost Lady* reflects Cather's distaste for the speeded-up money-making of the '20s and her preference for a past decorum, it also reveals that the financial powers of the past got hold of money and influence just as effectively as those of the present—and, with the buried story of Ed Elliott, that a lady who was "lost" to polite society could help a young man of the lower classes join it. It undermines the very distinctions that it sets up.

Such distinctions are associated with race. In the old ways of doing business, when it was clearly understood who should rise and who should stay subservient, the "difference between a business man and a scoundrel was," Judge Pommeroy expostulates, "bigger than the difference between a white man and a nigger" (*ALL* 88). Men of honor made enough money to look after the interests of those who did not, and the have-nots who had to be looked after are characterized as racial others:

"Poles and Swedes and Mexicans" (87). But the implication is that the old absolutes are breaking up. Successful men of business in the novel's present, the Ivy Peterses of the world, *are* scoundrels—implying that the racial difference may not be absolute after all. It is Captain Forrester who calls Black Tom merely "Tom" when he thanks him for his services (135), thereby erasing the most visible marker of the difference between them, and it is Forrester who concludes his peroration on the pioneers' dreams with "a sort of grunt" like the "lonely, defiant note that is so often heard in the voices of old Indians" (53). These gestures do not disguise the fact that Black Tom is still stigmatized by his race and the Indians have been pushed off their land. The old aristocrat can afford to relax social distinctions because everyone knows that the distinctions go on, courtesy or no. But the note of Indianness in his voice is something else, a sign that Indians, now effectively wiped out by the forces epitomized in the railroads, have become a complex symbol representing the essence of an ideal America that exists only in nostalgia, with no actual power in the present. The "lonely" old Indian is in effect the dying Indian. As in *The Song of the Lark*, the dead Indian can be inspiring, though the live one can only be cheated.[29]

When Niel returns to Sweet Water at the opening of Part II, elaborate parallels with the opening of Part I force the reader to recognize continuity within change. Confronting an obviously changed world-in-miniature, Niel returns on the same train as Ivy Peters, with the narrative perspective fluctuating oddly between them. If Niel, the nostalgist, the would-be old-line aristocrat, looks (with the same distaste as ever) at Ivy, Ivy, one of the hoi polloi, the disrupter of the past, also now looks at Niel. Moreover, Peters takes evident delight in knowing more than Niel knows about the fortunes of the Forresters during the two-year gap in Niel's (and the novel's) awareness, telling him that they need money, which he, Ivy, provides; that he has drained the Captain's swamp; that he now hunts there (in Part II he had recognized the Captain's prohibition on hunting); and that Mrs. Forrester is now working hard and taking good care of her husband but taking more consolation from the bottle than ever. Niel and the reader are prepared for deterioration. But even as these details demonstrate the difference of the present from the past, they show likeness. If Mrs. Forrester now drinks *more*, she also drank then—as we, though apparently not Niel, have realized. Pondering the deterioration from pioneering "adventurers" to

"men like Ivy Peters" who "never risked anything," Niel thinks indig-
nantly that this whole "generation of shrewd young men"—himself
not included, of course—"would do exactly what Ivy Peters had done
when he drained the Forrester marsh" (*ALL* 102). *Niel* ponders this. But
in the first chapter of Book One the *central* narrative voice had told us
that even in those lost pristine days "any one but Captain Forrester"—
anyone, not just a shyster—"would have drained the bottom land" (9).
Comparing the two passages, we question Niel's judgment of Ivy and
whether things have changed so radically after all.

When Niel goes to visit, he finds the Captain in the garden watching
the moving shadow of his sundial (the visible lapsing of time) and talking
of his railroad magnate friend Dalzell. Mrs. Forrester is in the grove,
lying in her hammock. Catching her up in his arms, hammock and all,
Niel momentarily thinks of her as the same charming woman he had
once idolized, still laughing and slender "like a bird caught in a net"
(105)—or like the bird trapped under Ivy Peters's hat in the corresponding chapter of Part I, the bird cruelly blinded and released to fly
against the trees. He wishes he could "rescue her and carry her off"
(105)—as the younger Marian (we learn later) had been "caught" when
she fell off a mountain ledge and then rescued, "carried" off by Forrester
and his men (157–58). In effect, Niel wishes to be Forrester—the Forrester of old. But to the extent that Forrester and Ivy Peters have been
conflated, this means that he partly wishes to be Peters. A puzzling continuum is set up among men, while specious distinctions are set up
among women, with talk about whether "nice women" were now smoking after dinner. Mrs. Forrester (the doubly fallen woman) objects to
such a practice; Niel is amused at this attitude from another "generation" (107). But the hard fact of women's lives in general, to which she is
now falling, knows no generation. "That house!" she laments. "Nothing is ever done there unless I do it, and nothing ever moves unless I
move it. That's why I come down here in the afternoon,—to get where
I can't see the house" (107–8). Niel, it seems, is struck dumb. He makes
no reply.

The reason Mrs. Forrester now laments the housework that used to
seem like delightful play (as she waved her "buttery iron spoon" [*ALL*
10]) is that she can no longer afford help. Her husband's sense of honor
was such that he divested himself of his wealth in order to pay out a hundred cents on the dollar to depositors when his bank failed. Probably,

we think, Marian would not have had it otherwise, at least not until later, when regret struck her. But we will never know, because she did not have a chance to say. He assumed her consent without asking. The difference between her present sense of enslavement and her former delight in her home is attributable to changed circumstances. But how do we know she *did* delight in it? Perhaps that impression, too, was over-idealized by her male observers. She never stayed at home much; she had plenty of time away. Again we are led into uncertainty. Her appearance in frowsy housedresses after she is widowed (in dishabille indeed), carrying buckets of water, destabilizes the contrast Niel once held dear between, on the one hand, her graciousness and the beautiful order of her home and, on the other, the slovenliness of his visiting aunt, who read books rather than stick by her washing tubs. The furnishings that once made the Forresters' house seem so stable and gracious become, in the end, only an accumulation of things very heavy to push around for cleaning, and the beautiful glassware that made their table a delight now tempts local women to speculate about buying some of it at auction.

The relics of the (possibly) heroic era have become detritus, like the junk piling up in the Wheelers' basement in *One of Ours*. They are the junk of the wasteland consciousness, a symbol of trashed modernity that Cather would offer her readers again in *The Professor's House* in the gaudy kitsch of the Marsellus house and in *My Mortal Enemy* in the dusty velvet curtains the Henshawes lug with them from rooming house to rooming house. Cather's images of junk and litter are domestic variants of the modernist image of trash or shattered ruins that we see in T. S. Eliot, mostly in architectural and verbal forms, and in Ezra Pound, with the "two gross of broken statues" in "Hugh Selwyn Mauberley."[30]

DURING THE late summer of 1922 Cather taught briefly at the Bread Loaf School in New Hampshire. She seems to have enjoyed the experience. A familiar photograph shows a surprisingly portly figure standing on a walk, smiling broadly. At the end of the summer she made her first visit to Grand Manan, the island off New Brunswick where she would later build the only house she ever owned—in Edith Lewis's name, at that (Woodress, *Literary* 414). *One of Ours* was published in September, bringing on a spate of activities as well as disappointment. Late in the fall, but too late to be there for Thanksgiving, she went to Red Cloud

for a prolonged visit with her parents and the observance of their fiftieth wedding anniversary. The concern with marriage in her fiction of
the mid-1920s, including the unhappy marriage in "Uncle Valentine,"
her only short story of those years, may have been stimulated in part by
this event.

While at Red Cloud she seems to have been in good spirits. On
December 6 she wrote whimsically to her old friend Will Owen Jones
asking him to run a notice of her parents' anniversary in the *Nebraska
State Journal*, and that same day wrote Zoë Akins that she had been
riding around to the Scandinavian and Bohemian settlements with her
father in his car, enjoying the spectacle of human continuity. Red Cloud,
it seemed, counteracted the sense of brokenness. On or about December 10 she dashed off a short note to Ida Tarbell saying that she would
not be back to New York for several weeks and exulting in how good
winter was in the country. In a postscript, she sent greetings to another
old friend, Mary Austin.[31]

On December 27 Cather and her parents joined Grace Episcopal
Church, a site around which emotions of yearning for simplicity and
assurance would center for the rest of her life (see figure 23). They were
confirmed by George Beecher, the bishop of Nebraska, with whom she
would maintain a relationship of mutually respectful friendship, regularly signing her letters to him as one of the devoted of his flock. Long
years after the fact, she assured him that their confirmation had meant a
great deal to herself and her parents. There is no reason to doubt her
statement. Still, the frequently made claim that she was a deeply religious person or that at this time in her life she undertook a serious quest
of religious belief seems unwarranted. She had just written *A Lost Lady*
with no religious overtone whatever; indeed, she made final changes in
January, within weeks of her confirmation.[32] Not long afterward she
wrote "Uncle Valentine," in which she drew, with surprising directness
after two and a half decades, on her days in Pittsburgh when she had
been indisputably freethinking and rebellious against organized religion. Her next novel, *The Professor's House*, would be about a man whose
focus as he sets his face toward death is strictly on this world and who
takes considerable pleasure in tweaking the religious establishment
(despite denying that he does so). A language of religion rarely appears
in Cather's correspondence even in letters to Bishop Beecher, where it
might seem de rigueur. When she wrote on various occasions to console

Fig. 23. Grace Episcopal Church, Red Cloud, Nebraska.
(Nebraska State Historical Society)

Beecher for illness or loss or to say that she hoped his health was improving, she did not say she would be praying.

Only during the gloom of World War II did Cather's letters become overtly religious in tone. A Christmas card of 1943 addressed to Bishop Beecher, showing a picture of Canterbury Cathedral, bore handwritten messages calling Christianity the sole light of world civilization and expressing a fear that its light was being extinguished and that there would be nothing left but ultimate darkness and the gnashing of teeth.[33] But even in her letters of that troubled time, such a tone remains rare and when it does appear is usually perfunctory. Her conversion to the Episcopal Church, the most socially elite of the Christian denominations, may have been as much a confirmation of social status and a desire to please her aging parents as an expression of a newly religious orientation. To be sure, religion and the relatively formal Episcopal Church may have provided, as John Hilgart has written, a "cultural axis" serving as the locus of "values she sought elsewhere in life: discipline, formal structure, and stability" (378). She would maintain her membership in the church in Red Cloud and send regular donations for the rest of her life. But it is probably significant that her church membership did remain in Red Cloud, not where she was actually living.

After the confirmation Cather lingered in Red Cloud on into January 1923. In a letter to Zoë Akins apparently written the first week of the new year she reported happily that she was going ice skating on the river. It is one of the earliest traces of *Lucy Gayheart*. (The skating would be repeated during her Christmas 1927 visit.) She returned to New York by January 13 and made plans to sail for Europe to visit Isabelle and Jan Hambourg but fell ill with influenza and had to be hospitalized. She scheduled her departure for March 24 but had a relapse and postponed the date to early April. It was in Paris, on May 14, that she learned she had been awarded the Pulitzer Prize.

In their new house in the Paris suburbs, the Hambourgs had planned a study for Cather's use, and they now invited her to make her home with them. But she found herself unable to write there and ultimately refused the offer. The decision may have occasioned tensions between them; a note to Irene Miner sounds perfunctory in its report that their home was lovely and she had met delightful people there.[34] Late in the summer, tired after a hectic pace that included getting her portrait painted by Léon Bakst at the behest of the City of Omaha, she went to Aix-les-Bains for rest and mineral baths, hoping to relieve neuritis in her right arm and shoulder. The ailment may have been partly psychosomatic. There were plenty of reasons for anxiety expressing itself as pain. She had been troubled by the critical response to *One of Ours*, and visiting in the Hambourgs' home, where she saw daily evidence of their stable relationship, must have renewed her sense of exclusion and loss (O'Brien, *Emerging* 240; Stout, "Autobiography" 209).[35] She returned to New York in the late fall, tired, apparently depressed, and facing her fiftieth birthday, and quickly began a novel about a depressed middle-aged professor of history who is the prize-winning author of eight books (the same number as Cather's at the time, not counting her poetry or her ghostwritten works) and who refuses to move from his shabby old study to a fine one in a newly built house. It is little wonder that the tone is one of weariness and disheartenment.

Plunging into a new novel seems often to have served Cather as an escape from personal demons. In a letter written in early 1924 to the editorial staff at the *Yale Review*, which had been soliciting a contribution, she said that she was concentrating on the newly begun novel because she found that if she scattered her energies she became personally decentered and life itself began to seem a hateful chore.[36] (Cather appears in a photograph thought to have been taken in Red Cloud during 1924 in figure 24.) Her professor finds himself hating living and thinking it a chore. Like Cather, he conceives of his desk as a "shelter one could hide behind" or a "hole one could creep into" (*PH* 161). Both are tired, depleted, and oppressively aware of aging and the approach of death. Both are trying to find graceful ways of saying goodbye to love. Indeed, one wonders if it was a sense of having revealed too much of her own state of mind that led Cather, shortly after its publication, to refer to the book with distaste.[37] She also expressed surprise that it sold so well, though it seems easy to understand that book buyers would be attracted to an author who had won the Pulitzer Prize two years before, whose next novel had sold well and been made into a movie (the first film version of *A Lost Lady* premiered in Red Cloud in January 1925), and who had recently had a longish story in *Woman's Home Companion* ("Uncle Valentine," in February and March).

"UNCLE VALENTINE" makes clear the close link between *A Lost Lady* and the two novels that followed it. Not only does Cather's preoccupation with the brokenness of the world and the breaking of the present from the past continue with a singular explicitness in this "long, melancholy story" (Miller, "Margie" 133), but the narrative voice of the bedazzled youngster looking at the older, charming, but already corrupted central character resonates of Niel Herbert. In "Uncle Valentine" the voice is that of a sixteen-year-old girl whose gaze is fixed on an older male—a reversal of the gender structure of *A Lost Lady* and thus an illustration of Skaggs's theory that Cather tended to write mirror reversals in successive works. The male in question, Valentine Ramsay, is referred to as "uncle" (as are his brother, uncle, and father), but that title, like Forrester's "captain", is honorific. Cather seems to have been greatly occupied, during this period, with issues of the genuineness or speciousness of human distinctions and bonds. As the insistent self-reflexivity of her writing in the 1920s indicates, she was also occupied with problems of the self, and so perhaps with the problem of whether she herself was (artistically, emotionally) genuine or specious. "Uncle Valentine" is a remarkably evocative, retrospective, and certainly self-referential story.

The few critics who have written about it have recognized that the figure of Valentine is based on the composer Ethelbert Nevin, whom Cather knew in Pittsburgh and remembered as a person of charm and

Fig. 24. Cather at a picnic in Red Cloud, probably summer 1924.
(Nebraska State Historical Society)

grace. But this explanation scarcely begins to convey the emotional power of the flood of remembrances that pour through the story. Cather did not merely know Nevin, she was thought by some to have been in love with him. At any rate, she seems to have loved the idea of the life he led. But there is more. The story opens in Paris, where during her several-month stay in 1923, the year before she wrote the story, Isabelle had offered her a home.[38] In the opening frame, the narrator of the story proper, Marjorie, witnesses an exchange between a singing student and her teacher in which the name of Valentine Ramsay comes up. The teacher, a woman who still keeps her beauty, had long ago loved the now-dead composer. Loves and losses are compounded.

The story proper relates the events of a "golden year" (*SPO* 242) when Marjorie was sixteen years old and when Uncle Valentine returned to his home next door to her aunt's country house. The opening sentences enunciate the lostness of the past and the breaking off of the present: "Yes, I had known Valentine Ramsay. I knew him in a lovely place, at a lovely time, in a bygone period of American life; just at the incoming of this century which has made all the world so different" (210). The "lovely place" is a village called Greenacre, a close sound-alike for the Nevin estate, Vineacre. The fictional Greenacre is indeed located near "a big inland American manufacturing city, older and richer and gloomier than most." Cather, who found Pittsburgh gloomy at first, met Nevin in 1897, shortly before the turn of the century. Not long afterward she met Isabelle and by October 1899 was visiting the big McClung mansion, where she would later have a study in the attic. When the house was sold and Isabelle married in 1916, the loss of that retreat, where Isabelle had served as a combination muse and facilitator and where Cather was able to work so effectively, was a great grief, reinforced in 1923 when she visited Isabelle in her Paris home. In the story, then, mainly set in and around two large old houses and their studies, the sense of loss and of a past never to be restored has multiple resonance. At the end a third house nearby is bought by Valentine's former wife— once again a broken marriage, the breaking off of love, is invoked in connection with severance from the past—and Valentine goes back to Paris, never to return. Even the song he composes, which he and Marjorie sing on Christmas Eve, is about a time long gone. It begins, "From the Ancient Kingdoms, / Through the wood of dreaming . . ."

It would seem that the past is idealized. As in *A Lost Lady*, though, an odor of sexual corruption hangs over it. The brilliant Valentine is also the corrupt Valentine. Not only did his divorce result from an affair, with a woman he insists was "pure in heart" though she was regarded as fallen (or "lost"), he has also had some kind of sexual embroilment with Marjorie's aunt that causes her embarrassment when words like "innocent" are mentioned. The past is less golden than it at first appears; it is ambiguous, perhaps gold and perhaps not. Valentine and his brother and uncle are heavy drinkers, given to passing-out binges. When he leaves Greenacre, he gives Aunt Charlotte the key to his study in the Ramsay house. But when the key is found after Aunt Charlotte's death there is "no door for it to open," because the Ramsay house, with the study where he worked, "was pulled down during the war" when a "wave of industrial expansion swept down that valley." Now "roaring mills," the diabolical emblems of the present, "belch their black smoke up to the heights where those lovely houses used to stand" (*SPO* 249). Aunt Charlotte's house, too, is gone and with it the wall where her husband grew the red climbing roses that inspired Valentine's "I know a wall where red roses grow." Loss is absolute—both Isabelle and Nevin, the McClung house and Vineacre (and the house next door where Cather also visited and enjoyed musicales), Valentine and Greenacre. The study key—the key to Cather's study at the McClung house in Pittsburgh, the key to the study she could have had in France—fits no door.

Roses are important in Cather's imagistic lexicon. In attributing to Valentine Ramsay a song beginning "I know a wall where red roses grow," she was responding to the frequency of roses in Ethelbert Nevin's songs. According to the *Grove Dictionary of American Music*, his two best-known songs were *The Rosary* (1898; a sound-alike title) and *Mighty lak' a Rose* (1901). Others were *Deep in a Rose's Glowing Heart* (1888) and *The Rosebud* (1892). Cather's invented song line is a reasonable extrapolation. But it also evokes the bouquet of wild roses Niel throws into the mud in *A Lost Lady* after he learns Marian Forrester is sexually impure, a gesture keenly expressive of bitter disillusionment. The depth of emotion that flowers, beauty, and transience carried for Cather personally is evident from brief references in two particular letters from the mid-1920s. In February 1925, the month in which the first part of "Uncle Valentine" appeared, she admitted in a note thanking her friend Irene for a bouquet of red roses that she did not know anyone who could be so overwhelmed or "hard hit" by flowers as she could; even the most ordinary of roses gave her pleasure, but spectacular ones like those impressed her the way special personalities did. It is a striking linkage of flowers and persons. Two months later she used the same phrase, "hard hit," in responding to a letter from F. Scott Fitzgerald saying he hoped she would not think he had plagiarized from *A Lost Lady* in *The Great Gatsby*. What was amazing about personal charm, she replied, was how the effect exceeded the cause, so much so that all a writer could do was to write about the effect rather than the person who caused it. In just that way, all we could say about beauty was just how hard it hit us.[39] The red rose is a conventional symbol of female sexuality, and in both cases beauty is evanescent; one has only the emotion or the memory left, not the thing itself. With women and with roses she dwells on the fleetingness of beautiful things —on loss itself.

"UNCLE VALENTINE" was the bridge across which Cather moved from *A Lost Lady* to *The Professor's House*, another story of houses, an old study and a new one, a garden, lost love, and lost innocence. Once again, as with *One of Ours* and *A Lost Lady*, she seems to have had a sense that the material imposed itself on her, that she was compelled to write it or could not escape it—a statement we may take to mean that these works arose from her deepest feelings, her unconscious.[40] The opening words, "The moving was over and done," carried enormous resonance for Cather, who associated movement with personal and intellectual freedom but also with displacement. Accordingly, Godfrey St. Peter is paralyzed by uncertainty. It has been said that ambiguity is at the heart of the novel (Rosowski, *Voyage* 139). There is considerable irony in the fact that St. Peter is a professor, someone who is supposed to know and to enlighten others, yet he so little understands himself or what is bothering him.

As in *My Mortal Enemy* a year later, the severance from the past is signified by the loss of love in marriage. The St. Peters' marriage has become a polite formality from which the professor sees "no way out" (*MME* 46). He thinks about how much in love he and Lillian had once been and how happy their marriage had been, but he does so entirely in the past tense; that feeling is gone. Even his language toward her is acerbic. Feminist critics who sympathize with Lillian and find St. Peter less than "charming" have been accused of bias (Tanner 109), but it scarcely seems farfetched to detect misogyny in a scene such as the following: Godfrey has returned tired and disgusted from a shopping expedition to Chicago with one of his married daughters, prompting Lillian's heart to "ache" for him. She makes him a cocktail, they have dinner, and afterward they sit reading.

> "What are you thinking about, Godfrey?" she said presently. "Just then you were smiling—quite agreeably!"
>
> "I was thinking," he answered absently, "about Euripides; how, when he was an old man, he went and lived in a cave by the sea, and it was thought queer, at the time. It seems that houses had become insupportable to him. I wonder whether it was because he had observed women so closely all his life." (156)

Apparently it is rare for the professor to smile "agreeably," but if it is rare for him to speak insultingly to his wife we are not told.

Why Cather would make a character so plainly patterned after herself a misogynist is difficult to say, but we might start by noting that Godfrey St. Peter is, after all, not *entirely* modeled after herself. She has made him male and an academic and married, none of which she was herself. Yet she had, after all, sometimes defined herself in quasi-masculine terms, at least to the extent of adopting masculinized attire and calling herself William. Like her transfer of her feelings for Lyra Garber to the male character Niel, or her feelings for Annie Pavelka to Jim Burden, her transfer of autobiographical impulses to a male character here may reflect her longstanding elision of gender and gender roles. Or she may have imagined herself in the guise of a man, loving or not loving a woman, in order to cover her engagement in the novel with her feelings for Isabelle McClung. Their friendship had weathered difficult years following Isabelle's decision to marry Jan Hambourg, but there may have been a coolness following Cather's 1923 visit. If she was feeling hurt or angry, it is not surprising that she would put wounding, even unloving, finally self-hating words into the mouth of a character who in part stood in for herself.

A more important question, perhaps, is why the St. Peters have fallen into estrangement after years of affection or even passion. When did he stop loving her? When did he stop sleeping with her? The book gives no hint; Godfrey himself does not seem to know. But he speaks of his amorous feelings as a thing of the past, and as he avoids moving into their new house he interacts with Lillian in a dutiful way at best, comfortably accepting her suggestion that they have separate bedrooms and bathrooms. Bodiliness is being obscured as they reduce their relationship to mental and social dimensions only. Two flesh that became one have been severed. Their present is cut off from their past. With respect to his daughters as well, Godfrey's loving feelings are located in the past. He enjoys remembering them as pretty little girls (a way of thinking that goes far toward objectifying them as pleasant things to look at) but now finds both of them unpleasant to be with and tiresomely obsessed with possessions. It is as if the adult daughters bore no relation to their child selves.

Finding no satisfaction in reaching back to his marital and fatherly past, Godfrey reaches further, to his childhood self, when the complications of such relationships did not exist. Recalling a day long past when he was sailing along the coast of Spain, he thinks of it as the one perfect day in his life, the day he found life most satisfying. It was a day spent, significantly, in the company of other men, having nothing to do with his present life or his family; his wife "was not in it" (PH 95). Subsequent to the good times he remembers, the professor has indulged his escapist academic interests virtually without limit, writing eight volumes about a subject associated with masculine, imperial adventuring free of domestic entanglements, the Spanish incursion into North America. Refusing to leave his study in the upper story and move to the new one on the ground floor where he will be, as James Maxfield has pointed out (75), on a plane of equality with his family, is an act of clinging to his intellectualized escapism. We can read in this, perhaps, Cather's suspicion that she, too, may have demonstrated a dehumanizing commitment to her writing over the years, especially when she refused Isabelle's offer of a home and a new study on grounds that she would not be able to write there. In 1924, when she was well into the novel, she said that she could scarcely stand company any longer but wanted only to be alone.[41]

Although the professor has achieved professional recognition and has been a successful teacher for years, he claims to see it all as "commonplace" (PH 62). What, we wonder, would have given him greater satisfaction? Refusing to move into the new house he and his wife have built, refusing to be more than sporadically pleasant to his family or his colleagues, he turns all his emotional energy backward, centering it on the loss of Tom Outland, the one student whose memory redeems what has now come to seem a teaching career amounting to nothing but drudgery.[42] Outland is dead, having gone away on patriotic impulse and died with the U.S. Expeditionary Force. Once again the Great War has broken the world in two. It was a tragic waste of an inventive and emotionally rich young life. Yet the professor (much like Mrs. Wheeler at the end of *One of Ours*) insists to himself that Tom is probably better off dead. By dying young he "escaped" having to deal with money and "worldly success" and having to be "the instrument of a woman who would grow always more exacting" (*PH* 261)—another slur at Lillian, though she does not seem particularly exacting.

However far back one goes, there is always the trace of human fallibility and venality. Despite the professor's self-pitying effort to see his life in terms of deterioration from past happiness, there was no such perfection in the lost time. Loss was always already there, preceding memory. Loss of home: his move to Kansas as a child so distressed him that he "nearly died of it" (*PH* 30). Loss of his parents. Loss of his French foster parents and foster brothers. Tom Outland's story parallels the litany of St. Peters's own losses: migration with his "mover people" parents (115), then orphaning, then the loss of his friend Roddy and the artifacts he had so hoped to preserve. He, too, in the first-person story set into the middle of the novel like one of his own turquoises set in dull silver, looks back—to a time preceding America's written history and a people now dead who lost not only their homes but their recorded identity, the Anasazi.

"Tom Outland's Story" brings the breath of fresh air and the sense of open spaces that Cather spoke of when she likened it to an open window in a Dutch painting of an interior scene (*OW* 31). In contrast to the story of Godfrey's aging and disheartenment and weariness, it is a story of youth and excitement and discovery. It is a story, too, of aspiration and hope, as Tom first finds the lost city and its artifacts and then conceives of getting them preserved in the Smithsonian. But the government officials he goes to see about the project have many other fish to fry, and he returns to the Southwest in disheartenment, only to discover that Roddy has sold the artifacts to a German collector. At this point Outland reveals that his own supposed idealism is tainted by what amounts to merely a different version of the German collector's urge to possess. Claiming the Anasazi relics as the rightful property of the American people and the American government, he implicitly asserts claims founded on imperialism, since the American government is the power that dispossessed the rightful heirs of the Anasazi. Little wonder Godfrey St. Peter, the scholar of the Spanish conquest, feels so strong an affinity with Tom Outland! As if in confirmation of his commitment to an imperialistic model of civilization, Tom devotes himself to the study of Virgil, the celebrant of empire, and hands out pieces of Anasazi pottery as if he really did own "the pots and pans that belonged to my poor grandmothers a thousand years ago" (*PH* 243). His sentiments about the mesa are marred by nationalist assumptions rooted in the very "imperial model" that would "play itself out in the ghastly climax of World War I, in which Tom would die" (Crow 56).[43]

The "rift in the family" in *The Professor's House* indeed "corresponds with a rift in American civilization," but despite Cather's objection to postwar materialism, it does not lie between "a noble idealistic past and an ignoble materialistic present" (Tanner 113). The past St. Peter wants to idealize and into which he wants to escape does not support such idealization. The Spanish incursion (or as he calls it, adventures) about which he has written eight volumes was an expedition of unexcelled cruelty. Cather knew that, even if she did choose to let Jim Burden dwell on Coronado's "broken heart" in *Ántonia* rather than the sufferings of the *indigènes*. (We know she did, because in *Death Comes for the Archbishop* she acknowledged, though with a light touch, the atrocity at Acoma, when Juan de Oñate sentenced all males of fighting age to have one foot cut off.)[44] It was a process of empire building no less motivated by greed than the much-maligned Louie Marsellus, with his showy house named after Tom Outland in token acknowledgment of the source of his wealth, or Professor Crane, the chemistry professor who wants his share (*PH* 147). St. Peter himself, for all his deploring of the moral shabbiness around him, is not above bringing Spanish sherry into the country through Mexico to avoid import duty (99). Even before the Spanish incursion, the time of beauty represented by the Anasazi ruins was seemingly also marred by domestic violence (evinced in the frozen scream of the mummy Tom calls Mother Eve) and by whatever it was, hunger or disease or war, that drove the Anasazi away from their cliffside fastness. Tom's idyl on the mesa was marred by commerce, betrayal, and anger.

Linked with this theme of successive ruin is the war, the "one great catastrophe" that "swept away all youth and . . . almost Time itself" (*PH*

260). The Great War intruded on the dream of an innocent life by taking Tom away and continues to intrude on the tranquility of the professor and his extended family, the Cranes, and the Cranes' lawyer by generating a military market for Tom's patented invention and thus a source of the money that corrupts and divides them.

Cather's deployment of the technique of the vacuole or vacancy in *The Professor's House* expresses and emphasizes this division much as it does in *A Lost Lady* and would again in *My Mortal Enemy*. As a historian, the professor is "a professional rememberer" (Crow 53), but he cannot (re)member the past as a seamless whole and join it to the present. However accurately he retraces the footsteps of a Spanish diarist, he is still only retracing them; the footsteps are gone, and retracing them cannot recover their meaning. The French phrases and references to France that intrude so insistently into the text are like dead objects in a museum, ripped from their context and displayed to do the work of cultural keepsakes and marks of cultural refinement. But in this postwar world they point inescapably toward death—Tom's death and more generally the death of a generation on European, often French, battlefields. The central irony of the book is that the past is irrecoverably severed from the present by a vast graveyard, but even if it were recovered, it would not redeem us.

The novel's vacancy is in part, then, a vacancy of time, but in a different way than the lapses of years in *A Lost Lady*, *My Ántonia*, and *O Pioneers!* Indeed, one of the most remarkable aspects of Cather's work is the extent to which she experimented from novel to novel, not in the radical sense of a Gertrude Stein or a James Joyce, but with a conscious reaching for newness in structure. The vacuole of silence representing passage of time also serves as an emblem for lapse of connection. Cather's image explaining the tripartite structure of *The Professor's House*, the open window in a Dutch genre painting of an interior scene, is an image of interruption and juxtaposition. The open window breaks the solid interior wall of the painting to juxtapose a contrasting scene. In much the same way, her interruption of the novel with the open window of "Tom Outland's Story" forces an awareness of contrast. What we are called on to do as readers is to read not only the two contrasting blocks of text but also the space between them, the fact of the disjuncture. To construct a false coherence by finding explanations for the insertion may be to misread the break.

During the time she was working on *The Professor's House* Cather also made a selection of Sarah Orne Jewett's work for reissue by Houghton Mifflin and wrote a preface for it. Her willingness to undertake this task can be explained by her respect for Jewett's work (or some of it) but also by her personal devotion to the writer who had been, for a while, her mentor. In the course of doing this edition she explained to Greenslet her arrangement of three extraneous stories that she (notoriously) inserted into *The Country of the Pointed Firs* by saying that this arrangement would indicate the passage of time.[45] Clearly, the passage of time was a thought that weighed heavily on her mind. The fact that she reassessed Jewett's work at this time, deciding what to include to represent her finest achievement and what to exclude, may in itself have intensified her impulse to reconsider the past, to ask whether it was as fine as she had thought.

The explanation that she gave for inserting a contrasting story, "The Queen's Twin," between two stories about William's love for the shepherdess in *Pointed Firs* does not apply, however, to her insertion of "Tom Outland's Story" between the two sections of her novel centered in Professor St. Peter's study. She does not supply any simple explanation for breaking the text by introducing contrasting material. We are left to wonder not only whether our conjectures about the structure of the book and the relation (or fragmenting) of its parts are adequate but also, at the end, whether life itself—St. Peter's continued life after he is rescued from his half-accident, half-suicide—is of any value. On that gloomy question, which Cather seems to have been asking about her own life during the time of its writing, the novel remains silent, as it does on the question of why the professor has so abruptly changed, in his wife's judgment, from an "impetuous young man" into a "lonely and inhuman" one (*PH* 162). The only answer, Cather concludes, is to accept what *is* (the "real") and define it as "enough" (281). The brokenness of the text—its experimental structure that moves without strong rhetorical linkage from present time in Illinois to Tom Outland's telling of his adventures in Arizona several years before, when he discovered the remains of an extinct culture, and back to present time as the professor ponders the future—is emblematic of brokenness of meaning and broken relationships as well as brokenness of history.

Many readers find that despite the work's structural beauty it does not make a humanly satisfying statement. Yet this, too, is evidence of

Cather's participation in the modernist mentality: to insist, in a kind of inversion of the notion of organic form, that if the times are inorganically broken and cold, so must be their art, however much we may wish, like the professor, to recover more.

AFTER *The Professor's House* Cather returned, in *My Mortal Enemy*, to the brokenness of the world and an apparent contrast between past and present, a contrast that on closer reading is called into question. Once again she devised a binary form shaped by a central breach, this time the silent passage of ten years. Another experiment in form, *My Mortal Enemy* is a work so brief, so empty of any sense of continuity or density, that after a negative review in the *New York Times* she stopped her publisher from calling it a novel, lest book buyers feel cheated. The advertising was changed from "novel" to simply "Miss Cather's newest book." Only eighty-three pages, it nonetheless more resembled a novel *in posse* than a novella and is usually referred to by the more expansive term. Fanny Butcher, whose review in the *Chicago Tribune* pleased Cather hugely, called it a novelette but one that plumbs the depths of its main characters' entire lives, a "masterpiece of tragedy."[46]

Despite its compression, *My Mortal Enemy* spans some thirty-five years. At the beginning the fifteen-year-old narrator, Nellie Birdseye, meets Myra Henshawe, a figure whose romantic elopement she has heard about throughout her childhood in the town of Parthia. Immediately, the second chapter moves back twenty-five years to the time when Myra's "good looks and high spirits" had, in a word whose connotations resonate with those in *A Lost Lady*, "gratified" her uncle's "pride" (*MME* 11) until she eloped from his house. The narrative then returns to the present but shifts to New York for four concise chapters before skipping across a temporal and geographical gap marked by emphatic white space to Part 2, which takes place not only ten years later and a continent-breadth away, in California, but across a breach of deterioration both personal and social. The geographic location is significant. Cather often spoke of California as a soulless place. In 1937 she would tell Yehudi Menuhin's sister Yaltah, who was living there, that one of the disheartening things about California was that it attracted all the failures of the whole country—a statement that could well have applied to *My Mortal Enemy*.[47]

On two separate occasions Cather stated that the book was about an intense and dazzling love and also about the New York of 1904, when she had first known the city, in a better time than the present. In fact, references to actual events locate Part I in the winter of 1900–1901. It is all the more significant, then, that she transferred it in retrospect to 1904, which for her had been a time of opening possibility, initiating her wonder years in magazines. In May 1903 she had gone to New York at the behest of S. S. McClure and heard him say he would either publish every story she produced or place them for her elsewhere and would bring out a volume of her stories the next year. She found herself launched; her life opened before her. Twenty years later when she wrote *My Mortal Enemy* she saw New York as a deteriorated and threatening place; the only way she could keep a grip on her own soul was to stay away at least eight months a year. The New York winter of 1927, she complained, was particularly depressing.[48] In returning to the time before the break, she evoked the city and its high-art dimensions with richness and depth despite the novel's brevity.

In New York the Henshawes live amid beauties of architecture, decor, floral displays, jewelry and beautiful clothes, sculpture, music, and theater. The St. Gaudens statue of Diana that did, in fact, stand on top of the Madison Square Garden tower until 1925 (another loss) "step[s] out freely and fearlessly into the grey air" near their apartment (*MME* 21), and Nellie's Christmastime visit brings her into the company of a circle of artists that includes the great Helena Modjeska, with whom Cather had lunched in New York in 1898. Shortly after the New Year's Eve party at which Nellie hears a private performance of the *Casta diva* aria from Bellini's *Norma*, she gets to "go alone with Oswald to hear Bernhardt and Coquelin" (41)—that is, in *Hamlet*. The celebrated French actor Constant Coquelin played the First Gravedigger to Sarah Bernhardt's Hamlet in New York in 1900–1901, in repertory with *Cyrano de Bergerac* (Brandon 399).[49] The Henshawes show Nellie a magically glittering life of beauty and glamour, excitement, and, it would seem, emotional depth.

In contrast, the world of Part II is improvised and shabby. In a "sprawling overgrown" city on the West Coast "in the throes of rapid development," Nellie works at a college "as experimental and unsubstantial as everything else in the place" and lives in a "wretchedly built" apartment hotel where even a cough next door is clearly audible (*MME* 49). She finds the Henshawes living at the same apartment hotel (the

improbability of this coincidence is ignored in the starkness of statement that makes it seem like iron fate) in "shabby, comfortless" quarters
that recall only by contrast the charm of their life in New York. Myra is
tormented by the noise of the people upstairs, and Oswald, still devoted
to her despite what is now her bitter hostility toward him, is reduced to
dry-cleaning his own ties on Sunday morning. Once again the broken
world is epitomized by the ruin of a marriage; the decay of the marriage
compact is a synecdoche for decay of the social contract. Once again, if
we accept Cather's location of the New York scenes as 1904 as she said
(despite details in the text that point to an earlier date), the breaking in
two of the world is associated with the Great War, since a lapse of ten
years would put the second part in 1914, the year of the guns of August.
Her imagination kept circling over the great catastrophe of her time.

There would seem to be an absolute contrast between then and now,
there and here, Part I and Part II, a contrast sharpened by the minimalism with which it is posed. But again, the book undercuts its own opposition with an accumulation of troubling details that bring the charm
and beauty of the Henshawes' earlier life into question. These begin in
the opening scene, when Nellie Birdseye (whose bird's eye seems to
miss a lot) first meets them. Into a bit of amusing patter about a half-
dozen missing dress shirts that seems to indicate Myra's admiration of
Oswald's looks, Cather smuggles a warning of "the poorhouse" awaiting them if Myra doesn't curtail her extravagance (she has given away
the custom-made shirts because she did not like their fit) and an indication that Oswald, after twenty-five years of marriage to his redoubtable
wife, feels a futile "bitterness" (*MME* 8). When Nellie and Aunt Lydia
arrive in New York for their visit, Myra's humorous reference to their
hotel's being only a stone's throw away from her apartment "if at any
time a body was to feel disposed to throw one Liddy!" (17) pointedly
calls attention to the possibility. And we quickly see that someone might
feel so disposed. Myra is an intrusive matchmaker despite claiming to
"hate old women who egg on courtships" (25); her conspicuous donation of "a coin" to a poor newsboy scarcely compensates for his having
"no overcoat" in the snowy weather (22); and Oswald puts Lydia into an
ethically false position by asking her to cover the fact that he has received a gift of jewelry from another woman (28). The longer Nellie
and Lydia stay, the more evidence they see that the Henshawes' marriage is not the romance it had seemed. Oswald drinks surreptitiously.

Myra courts moneyed friends to make up for his lack of success in business but secretly hates their having more money than she does and foolishly compensates by overtipping her cab driver. "It's very nasty," she complains, "being poor" (34). As unforgiving as she is imperious, she lives buffeted by strong emotions, a woman of "tremendous passion, tremendous joy and rage" (Fisher-Wirth, "Queening" 38). She had been carried out the door of her uncle's house on a wave of infatuation; now she is swept into bitterness by jealousy and by regret at having thrown away a fortune. In the last chapter of the New York section Nellie walks in on a poisonous quarrel between the Henshawes, and at the end of Part I, as the visitors leave by train for Parthia, they see Myra, going as far as Pittsburgh, leaving Oswald.

We are scarcely surprised, then, when in Part II we see that the Henshawes, after the lapse of ten years and reverses in Oswald's work, have "come on evil days" and are "wandering about" among temporary lodgings—a life that would have struck Cather with fear and misery. In an apparent reference to her youthful romance, Myra complains that the "darkest" days of life "come early"—a striking reversal of the Virgilian epigraph to *My Ántonia, Optima dies . . . prima fugit.* Even in Oswald's presence she calls their elopement "the ruin of us both" (62), though she admits it is a "great pity" to "spoil the past" (71–72). Angry and immobilized by heart disease, she accuses the husband for whom she gave up wealth and religion of being her "mortal enemy" although he has stood by her with what Nellie sees as "indestructible constancy" despite hints of infidelities.[50] Shortly afterward Myra stages her own death on a cliff overlooking the sea that she has christened (after *King Lear*) Gloucester's cliff, "gorgeously or chillingly histrionic" to the last (Fisher-Wirth, "Queening" 38).

Which is better, the book asks, to face the harshness of it all with bitter courage, like Myra, or to console oneself, like Oswald, that the past was splendid enough to make it all worthwhile? Oswald's view is confided to Nellie after the funeral: "I don't want you to remember her as she was here. Remember her as she was when you were with us on Madison Square, when she was herself, and we were happy. Yes, happier than it falls to the lot of most mortals to be" (*MME* 84). Yet Cather has shown us with concise clarity that they were not happy, or at any rate that their happiness was severely tarnished. With Oswald's word "mortal" she pointedly invokes Myra's own summary statement, "alone with my mortal enemy," and thereby compels us to see the evasion in his determination to hold on to the good times at all cost.

Between these two extremes, where does Cather stand? That is always the question, and we can never say with certainty. It is surely not irrelevant, though, that she has written herself into the story, not in the explicit way she would later in *Sapphira and the Slave Girl*, where the intrusion of the direct autobiographical presence raises a question of where textual reality is grounded, but in the form of a girl of eighteen "overgrown and awkward, with short hair and a rather heavy face" and with "something unusual about her clear, honest eyes," who "worked on a newspaper" (64). A more accurate picture of the eighteen-year-old Cather, just beginning to write columns for the *Nebraska State Journal*, could scarcely be drawn. This girl admires Oswald, listens to him, and courts his help with her writing. What is at stake for this budding writer is what, in retrospect, Cather seems to have seen as having been at stake in her own earlier experience: the mentality that she would take into her future work. The question is, will the young journalist follow Oswald in his tenacious grip on the sunnier view of experience? Or will she remember that in knowing him she knew a man whose world had broken in two, who had been let go from jobs and let down when employers went bankrupt, the love of whose life had come to wish she had never known him?

We know that Cather was much occupied in those years with the issue of art's tie to reality. In the same year that she wrote *My Mortal Enemy*, the year *The Professor's House* was published, she also wrote a preface for Knopf's reissue of Gertrude Hall's book *The Wagnerian Romances*, paying tribute to "noble, mysterious, significant dramas" that can keep coming back to one in recollections evoked by the "delicately suggestive pages" of books like Hall's (*OW* 65–66). A decade later she would still be asking, "What has art ever been but escape?" (18). It was an issue she grappled with as she tried to face a broken world and as she looked back on her own work from the vantage point of mastery: the issue of whether, from the beginning of her career, when she was a budding journalist at the University of Nebraska, she had set her face too determinedly toward the romance, whether she should have been more like Myra—harder, more ruthless, more direct in her acknowledgment of the breakup around her.

9

Whose America Is This?

Conquest on conquest pressed
By these marching, arrogant masters,
Who could have hoped for the West?
    —"The Gaul in the Capitol"

Alack, it was poor Caliban who sang.
    —"Paradox"

The figure of Caliban, the racial other, haunts Cather's writing as effectively as he haunts the play in which Shakespeare brought him before a London audience in 1611, *The Tempest*. At that time the English were, in Ronald Takaki's words (25), "encountering what they viewed as strange inhabitants in new lands."[1] Embodying an imagined version of a people erroneously called Indians, Caliban has also been read as a representation of the African. Referred to in the play as a slave, he is prophetic of the African in America: Africans would first be sold into America eight years later, in 1619. That is not to say that the "ideology of 'savagery'" (Takaki 44) being constructed in response to New World encounters has subsequently been restricted to these two groups, either in American experience generally or in Cather's writing in particular. Nor can we suppose that Cather had a racial iconography in mind when she wrote her poem "Paradox," where the speaker expects Ariel but sees Caliban. But whether such symbolism was conscious or not, it is clear that she was concerned with the threat posed by the savage who "sings" to her in Ariel's stead. Such concerns in her work usually cluster around the Native and the African presence.

Two decades after "Paradox," with its "poor Caliban," Cather's novels of the 1920s raise persistent questions about the location of power in

American life. When both Captain Forrester and Ivy Peters "ge[t] splendid land from the Indians some way" (*ALL* 117), it is because America is manifestly destined to belong to whites, not Indians. Yet the very fact that Cather poses so strong a parallel between the two men, despite insisting that one is worthy and the other not, indicates some uneasiness about the processes of expansionist nation building, if not the collective destiny itself. Both by family experience and by her participation in the prevalent views of her time, Cather was identified with the concept of Manifest Destiny, a national ideal embracing "a myth of 'virgin' territory and new beginnings for the stalwart and brave" and of Anglo entitlement (McDonald 29). She was also a reader and admirer of nineteenth-century romantic historians such as Francis Parkman and H. H. Bancroft (very much the kind of historian her Professor Napoleon Godfrey St. Peter is) and generally adopted their conception of American history as a heroic adventure carried out by strongly individualistic, and inevitably white, men. Even so, her vision of history is not without ironies and unresolved misgivings about the course of American empire in making its way westward. Deeply submerged beneath apparently serene or affirming surfaces, these ironies and misgivings often relate to differences of race as well as class. Caliban is heard singing behind Ariel.

According to the most widely held model of Cather's development, the three "problem novels" of the mid-1920s formed a distinct phase ended by the reassurances of *Death Comes for the Archbishop*, as if somewhere between the writing of a book published in 1926 and one published in 1927 she had turned a corner and seen brighter skies. But in fact a strong engagement with issues of national ownership, building from some of Cather's earliest work, links all four. In order to demonstrate this continuity, I want to return to the three so-called problem novels, this time to consider issues of race, class, and economic power, before turning to *Archbishop*.

RACE AND its intertwining with social class is a difficult issue throughout Cather's work and one that can easily disrupt our response to its beauty. This is not to say that she was a racist, but that she participated in a racist culture. Despite her much-touted fondness for certain of the European immigrant groups that poured into the United States around the turn of the century, she did not entertain a genuinely democratized or inclusive political vision, even for Americans of European stock. Some, in her view, were more equal than others. At times and in ways perhaps traceable to her southern roots, her social vision was fundamentally aristocratic.[2] In Hermione Lee's persuasive formulation, she was at once "a democrat and an élitist" (16).

In book after book, especially in her novels of the mid-1920s, Cather entered the discourse of group empowerment within the American *polis*. Raising questions of whose America this is, both politically and in the sense of actual possession or ownership, she seems to give generally conservative answers. Yet the frequency with which her fiction leads us to these questions indicates that she was herself uncomfortable with such answers, to the point of entertaining resistant strains implying a "critique" of the conservative consensus, even while she resisted the image of what is usually called the "engaged" writer (Patricia Clark Smith 120–21).[3]

In *A Lost Lady* Cather presents a vision of a white America controlled by a stable upper middle class, at the moment of its lapse into instability. The class structure of Sweet Water is a hierarchical one in which the Forresters are at the top as long as they have money. It is possible to belong to "good" society for reasons of kinship or descent, but status unsupported by financial reserves is a slippery thing. Niel feels socially endangered by the failure of his poor-relation mother-substitute to adhere to genteel standards of housekeeping, and when Marian loses her money, her status spirals downward as she begins to associate with the wrong people and fails to maintain "nice" patterns of behavior. So long as her failings were supported by a secure fortune, they could be disregarded as the peccadilloes of a privileged class. The Blum boy, son of a working man who knows his place, turns a blind eye to her sexual dalliance with Frank Ellinger in the woods. But the Blums, with their vestigial ties to Old World class stability, are the exceptions. Far more numerous in the social order of *A Lost Lady* are those for whom class status is not fixed but a matter of constant aspiration and struggle. These members of the unreconciled lower middle classes exemplify the restless volatility of American society and its definition by externals such as clothes and possessions. Not that they reject the system, only their own consignment to lower rungs on the ladder. The women who come to the Forresters' house during the Captain's illness, ostensibly to help Marian but really to snoop and to gloat over her fall, anticipate buying her fine glassware as if it will give them her quality of life. In the meantime, they hover about the spectacle of her decline as relentlessly as jackals over a carcass.

Cather seems to give her allegiance to the stable upper-middle-class society threatened by uncultivated manners and the forces of economic boom and bust. Yet for all its conservative satiric surface, her attitude toward this volatility is not entirely negative. If the less cultivated classes behave in envious and unbeautiful ways, the story of Ed Elliott, the son of one of the women who gloat over Mrs. Forrester, reminds us of the possibilities the unstable American system affords for the rise of the exceptional.

Race is a more absolute division. Judge Pommeroy's manservant, Black Tom, is straightforwardly, unapologetically positioned as an appendage to the people whose views and activities matter. As isolated in his blackness as Blind d'Arnault of *My Ántonia* and as isolated as must have been his actual prototype, a handyman and domestic worker named John Foster who was Red Cloud's only African American resident (March 766), Black Tom is given no last name. He is a functionary, the Good Negro of white racist desire. When planning a dinner party, Mrs. Forrester asks the judge (another title that seems to be purely honorific) to "lend" her Tom (*ALL* 33); when Niel proposes to rescue Mrs. Forrester from the cadre of gossipy volunteers helping during her husband's final illness, he, too, asks the judge to "let [him] have" Black Tom, who is then "put" in the kitchen (134). Cather's grasp of the place of the African American in the social structure is all too accurate. The silence of her nonquestioning of that structure, perhaps reflecting her "white burden as a writer from the South," is a loud one indeed (Zettsu 96).[4]

If the African American is excluded from ownership of America, the Native American is dispossessed of it, reduced to a textual shadow. The invocation of the Native American's absence participates in the implicit structural irony created by a dual narrative perspective and thereby, like the story of Ed Elliott, participates in the novel's tacit questioning of the American power structure that Cather seems, on the surface, to endorse. Niel sees Ivy Peters as being utterly unlike Captain Forrester, but we as readers see similarity in their dealings with the Indians. Although no direct guilt attaches to Forrester for purchasing what he wanted from a railroad company that according to law had every right to sell it, the result is that the white male gets what he wants and the Native people are dispossessed. Clearly, it is not their America. Nor is it the America of the working classes, whose "great West" is subjected to what is called "development" by moneyed easterners who buy up land, draw on their capital to establish profit-making ventures, and return the assets of the poorer classes when banks fail only if they happen to be exceptionally honorable, or perhaps exceptionally patriarchal.

The term *patriarchal* indicates another aspect of whose America this is: men's, not women's. Skaggs writes (*After* 50) that Marian, called Maidie by her husband, is "a full-fledged member" of Forrester's band of associates, but the point is precisely that she is not. She is only an ornament for the amusement of the merry men. When her male protector falters, she is as hapless as the female bird trapped under Ivy Peters's hat in the opening scene, though finally more ingenious in making her way out of the woods.

This is not to say that Cather conceived the novel as social criticism. Her comments on *A Lost Lady* locate it exclusively in a sense of affection for a lost time and a person she found fascinating. Similarly, her various comments on railroad aristocracy indicate nothing but admiration. Yet the text itself militates against so unitary or so exclusively emotional a reading. Unless we suppose that Cather was either a very careless writer or so obtuse as not to notice problems that are evident to us in the fictional structure she created, we have to believe she was reticent about her intentions to the point of disguising them (which may be true) or else that unconscious or unacknowledged impulses were at work that were at variance with her conscious (or at any rate, stated) purposes. It is essentially this latter view of her fractured and multiply textured—and thus very modernist—writing that I am arguing here. Her conscious affiliation with a white, upper-middle-class America of rural landholding and conservative business was strong enough, and her wish to admire that group compelling enough, that she tried to pursue a literary project advancing that affiliation; but she was too intelligent not to see the problems with such a view of her society and too fundamentally honest not to acknowledge those problems in some way. The tensions in Cather's fiction running counter to its surface meanings occupy a finally indeterminate continuum ranging from, at one extreme, evidence of insensitivity to such social issues as anti-Semitism, through various degrees of purposeful insertion of submerged hints, to relatively overt designation of problems in American society that disturb the benign view Cather wished she could believe in.[5]

Cather was always "acutely conscious of class distinctions" (McDonald 11). We see that in *My Ántonia*, for example, in her attention to such matters of material culture as the ownership of wooden versus sod houses and the possession of good agricultural tools and household equipment. We see it, too, in the ability of persons of a higher class to behave generously as compared to various comical grotesqueries and manifestations of grasping envy attributed to the lower-class Mrs. Shimerda, who at one point memorably attempts to shove a cow behind concealment to keep it from being taken away by its owner, Mr. Burden. He forgives her debt and lets her keep the cow. Being prosperous enables one to be more beautiful in a behavioral as well as a physical sense.

To be sure, Cather saw room for exceptions. Pondering the effects of economic and social deprivation and the mystery of the beautiful exception, she once penciled on blank flyleaves in the back of a book her observations of a poor family sitting near her on a train. After detailing the dirty fingers and cheap ornaments of the mother (labeled as being of the servant class) and the filthy personal habits (presumably nose picking) of the children, she noted with amazement the presence among them of a little boy as fastidious in behavior as he was beautiful in person. Even in his solicitude for the others he was unlike them. What, she asked, would happen to such a child? Probably he would become a preacher or a store clerk or an elevator operator.[6] These notes are captioned "Train, June 2, 1916." We recall her *Courier* column of November 1895 in which a diatribe against the fiction of Ouida is launched by seeing one of her books in the hands of an elevator boy. In the lapse of twenty-one years she had learned to regard that fate, at least for a beautiful few, with regret.

The problematics of *The Professor's House* are very much tied up with the issues that fracture the surface of *A Lost Lady*, including the dissatisfactions of women relegated to roles of ornamental housewifery. Tom Outland is another example of a natural aristocracy given opportunity to manifest itself by the fluidity of the American social and economic system. Yet for the most part economic and class distinctions result in unbeautiful behavior. The professor's daughter Kathleen envies her sister, who inherited Tom's patent on a discovery that proved to be the key to advances in aircraft engines; the low-salaried professor who helped with the research has become mean-spirited in his pursuit of a share of the profits. But prosperity brings its own ungraciousness. Rosamond,

the daughter whose husband handled the technology transfer that led
to the Outland engine, has become acquisitive and hard. Rosamond and
Louie Marsellus have profited by the same war that killed Tom, since it
was the war that stimulated interest in the development of aircraft.
When the hard-working seamstress Augusta tries to buy her own share
of ownership in America, stock in a speculative copper company, and
loses what is for her an enormous sum, Rosamond refuses to help
make it up to her on grounds that Louie had advised her against the
investment and she needs to learn to listen to her betters. But in an
economy where the rich seem to get richer at a fantastic pace, what
wonder is it that the poor would hope to get a piece of the pie by imitat-
ing them? The dour St. Peter, whose name places him as a kind of ur-
Christian though he has none of Augusta's devoutness, is disappointed
by Rosamond's lack of sympathy. A distant and less wealthy version of
Captain Forrester and perhaps also of Cather's father, he holds to values
other than acquisitiveness. The true elite of Cather's world, it seems,
were those who combined financial competency with tasteful decorum
and innate superiority.

Ethnically, the novel's social problematics center on the Jewish
Marsellus, who is painfully (for most readers) stigmatized by stereotyp-
ical associations with moneymaking, showy spending, and (like the disagreeable Stein of Cather's story "Scandal," written in 1916) social
climbing. Apparently a delayed venting of resentment against Isabelle
McClung's Jewish husband, whom Cather at least initially suspected of
fortune hunting, Marsellus is overly ingratiating and given to displaying
his possessions.[7] Naming his new house Outland, as if it were a kind
of monument to the Tom Outland he never knew, is simply tasteless.
Yet Louie is also a person of surprising good-heartedness, so free from
resentment when he is blackballed from the local men's club by his own
brother-in-law that the "vanquished" Godfrey (abashed? humbled?)
can only think of him as "magnificent" (PH 170). Innocently rapacious,
he shops for furniture on a grand scale and, utterly unembarrassed,
plans how he will bring his European purchases into the country
through Mexico to avoid paying import duty (as the Professor does his
sherry). That is, he plans to evade the law—a moral failing that no one
in the novel seems to notice. Perhaps Cather meant that detail as a revelation of the shabby way things were being done during the money-
mad, Prohibition-bound postwar years. Or perhaps she did not notice it

herself. She, too, brought in alcohol in her luggage during Prohibition and on at least one occasion asked Blanche Knopf to have her New York grocer falsify the value of goods he was shipping to her in Canada in order to reduce the amount she would have to pay in Canadian taxes.[8]

Louie Marsellus has been seen by Walter Benn Michaels as a version of Ivy Peters, whom he calls a "proto-Jew" (46). That is perhaps too severe. To be sure, Cather sometimes engaged in calumnies against Jews. One of the worst moments in all her work is her labeling of Miletus Poppas in "The Diamond Mine" (1916) as a Greek Jew and a "vulture of the vulture race" with "the beak of one" (*SPO* 402). Yet it is hard to imagine that she would intentionally have painted so derogatory a picture as Michaels's comment suggests at a time when she was enjoying a productive and mutually affirming relationship with publisher Alfred A. Knopf and his wife, Blanche. *The Professor's House* was the third of her novels published by the Knopfs, whom she highly esteemed both professionally and, so her letters indicate, personally. Her friendships with them and with the musical Menuhin family were among the most important relationships of her late-middle-age years. Both families were Jewish. Marsellus, labeled a Jew, has an attractive personal generosity. Even so, he reflects anti-Semitic stereotypes that may have been so deeply ingrained in Cather and in her culture that she was scarcely aware of them.[9]

Cather was a thoroughgoing exceptionalist. In her response to members of ethnic groups, as in her conception of the social roles of women, she was always more ready to imagine the quality and success of the exceptional individual than to think in collective terms. But such exceptions did not necessarily dislodge the generalization. Only a few years before enacting, in her friendship with the Knopfs and the Menuhins, an unwitting parody of the familiar joke "some of my best friends . . . ," she was capable of such scurrilities as her remark to Elizabeth Sergeant, after attending a performance of John Galsworthy's "Jew play" (her term) *Loyalties* and seeing the author there, that she wondered whether Galsworthy might not like to revise the text a little after sitting between two corpulent Jewish women on such a hot night.[10] Difficulties arose when she tried to sort out the conflict between her feelings toward the general and her feelings for the exceptions or when she had positive feelings for both sides of a pair of opposites, such as affection for rural life and people like Annie Pavelka but an urge toward social and artistic sophistication and expensive urban comforts. The world was too complex to yield easy answers.

As in *The Song of the Lark*, Cather's treatment of Native Americans in *The Professor's House* turns toward the past and the American who was not merely vanishing but vanished. Despite Tom Outland's years as a cowboy in the reaches of the Southwest where he would be most likely to encounter actual Native Americans (probably Navajos or Utes), the Anasazi are the only Indians in the book. To be sure, they or at any rate their relics are venerated, after a fashion. If Tom had succeeded in displacing the relics to a museum in Washington, he would have enacted precisely the kind of removal that is now being redressed under the Native American Graves Protection and Repatriation Act of 1990. Instead, his partner sells them to a private collector from Germany. The removal of the mummified female quaintly called Mother Eve, which miscarries when the case in which she is packed forces the pack mule off the trail and mule and all are smashed on the rocks below, seems to have been inserted into the text as a warning against the evil of profiteering from the sale of such relics. Not that Mother Eve would have been left in her burial place if Tom had had his supposedly honorable way. In any event, his esteem for the Anasazi relics entails no equivalent esteem for living Native Americans. As Elizabeth Ammons trenchantly puts it, the Anasazi are "dead, the favorite white version of Indians" (Ammons, *Conflicting* 133). In *Death Comes for the Archbishop*, two years later, Cather's emphasis would again be on the death or the dying of the Indians. They have no more role in her vision of contemporary America than do African Americans, Jews, or immigrants from countries outside a restricted part of Europe.

In the third of the three "problem novels," *My Mortal Enemy*, the question of who would possess America is answered strictly in terms of money and big business. Here, even more than in *The Professor's House*, Cather shows us "the incorporation of America."[11] At the fondly remembered turn of the century, two elites, one of beauty or high culture and the other of business, seemed more or less balanced in social influence. In what is offered as a momentary ideal (comparable in import to the parties in Virginia Woolf's *Mrs. Dalloway* and *To the Lighthouse*), Myra's New Year's Eve party, the two elites come together to produce a genuinely aristocratic culture. But the alliance is illusory. To the members of the social set to which the Henshawes cling, the poor seem scarcely to matter. Marginalized and grateful for small favors, they occupy the inconspicuous perimeter of the novel's stage set. Yet even in this marginalized position, there are glimpses of newsboys and old men selling flowers coatless in the snow, destabilizing the elitist vision. The rest of the novel after the party scene shows the breaking apart of the moneyed elite from the aesthetic elite and the apparent triumph of business over beauty.

In part 1 Myra is unbeautifully preoccupied with maintaining a footing in New York's moneyed class despite dwindling resources. She makes grand gestures, sending the florist's most expensive holly tree to Mme. Modjeska for a Christmas present (*MME* 25), tipping the delivery man a whole silver dollar for taking it (26), overtipping the hansom driver to assuage her own discontent with being "poor" (though not in comparison with the cab driver). But these gestures gain her only momentary stays against meanness, both of spirit and of circumstance. In running away with a young man of no capital, she has given up an independent fortune and, by marrying a mere employee, has placed herself in the power of a rapacious business structure that cares nothing for human beings. When the railroad for which her husband works goes into receivership and is "taken over" by a larger one (*MME* 51), she and Oswald are cut adrift into a free fall from the upper-middle into the lower-middle class, a precipitous drop indeed. (In contrast, in an early example of the now-standard principle that CEO's fare differently than workers, the deposed president of the railroad goes to live in Europe.) We see no great artists in Myra's company after she takes refuge in a cheap apartment building a continent away. Her young man, no longer young, has gone west indeed, but scarcely in the way of the pioneers.

Clearly, Myra regrets her early romantic gesture and wishes she had kept money while she had it. That in itself is disillusioning enough for the reader who expects Cather to affirm the romantic escape. But any illusion that the old ways were better than the new (the illusion fostered by references to the jerry-built urban sprawl in which the Henshawes find themselves) should have been forestalled early on with the explanation that her uncle's fortune, the basis of the life Myra now regrets giving up in a stodgy little town in America's heartland, had been built by business methods just as rapacious as the corporate power structure that has ground her up along with her unfortunate husband. John Driscoll had "made his fortune employing contract labour in the Missouri swamps"

(*MME* 10). Contract labor would almost certainly have meant convict labor. Cather does not tell us that such a method of profiting was cruel and a kind of slavery, any more than she tells us explicitly that the business methods of the railroads that make no pretense of providing security for the Henshawes of the world are systems of dehumanization based on greed, but she does not have to. We are invited, in this novel démeublé, to imagine for ourselves what life was like for those laborers in the swamps and for the office workers "riffed."[12]

In this last of her so-called problem novels, then, Cather completed what might be seen as a trilogy of increasingly bleak works pondering the grimness of middle age for characters whose belief that America was theirs ends in despair and impoverishment. In two cases (Marian's and Myra's) that impoverishment is financial, in one case (Godfrey's) emotional. In all three the central figure has a kind of splendor, so that the reader, and surely Cather herself, perceives the fall as a tragic one. But in each case the lost claim of ownership is shown to have been based on complicity in a process of despoilment by the white upper middle class, the class with which Cather herself identified and whose claim she overtly endorsed. No wonder she felt the need for an escape to a new fictional world with an invigorating "lightness" in the air (*DCA* 273).

THE ROOTS OF *Death Comes for the Archbishop* reached back to Cather's first visit to the Southwest in 1912 and even further back to the familiarity with magazine literature that began in a professional sense in 1896 but in a readerly one long before that. A familial devouring of magazines in the Cather home is demonstrable, and well before the turn of the century southwestern culture was featured in large-circulation magazines such as *Harper's Weekly.* The popularity of the Southwest surged during and after World War I. In the aftermath of the war "people increasingly felt that an unbridgeable gap had opened between tradition and the modern world" and in reaction turned to the synthesizing of "stylized" celebrations and locales, as a supposed alternative to the decadence of Europe. As a part of the nativist spirit that propelled Americans toward celebration of a domestic exoticism derived from nativist roots and "yet another wave of xenophobia against immigrants," a flood of articles appeared in national magazines emphasizing the indigenous character of Santa Fe, in particular, and describing its pueblo style as "'strictly American'" (Wilson 205, 140).[13] Cather's interest emerged from this widespread cultural phenomenon.

The more immediate stimulus for the novel was a return trip to New Mexico and Arizona in 1925. It is perhaps not incidental that only the previous year Cather had been deeply involved in making selections and writing the introduction for a two-volume edition of Jewett, immersing herself once again in her mentor's tranquil tone and decidedly regional orientation. It is also perhaps not incidental that less than two weeks into her 1925 trip she stopped at Lamy, New Mexico, a village named for Jean Baptiste Lamy (1814–88), the first bishop of Santa Fe and later archbishop.[14] Drifting about, as she described it to Mabel Dodge Luhan, she and Edith Lewis stayed for a while at the La Fonda in Santa Fe, then at a ranch at Alcalde, near Española and Georgia O'Keeffe's Abiquiu. Abiquiu was the birthplace of the historic Padre Martínez, who would be another important character in *Archbishop*.

While at Alcalde, Cather read proofs of *The Professor's House*. She and Edith Lewis went on long horseback rides in the Sangre de Cristo Mountains, visited Acoma and Laguna Pueblo (where they seem to have bought snacks in a little grocery store and café operated by the great-grandfather of novelist Leslie Marmon Silko), and stayed briefly in one of Mabel's guest cottages at Taos. According to Lewis, they enjoyed being there, especially riding about the countryside with Tony Luhan in his car. Cather reported that throughout the trip she was hot on the trail of her old priests, a phrase that may have meant the priests of the Southwest in general or may have meant specifically Lamy and Machebeuf, who became Latour and Vaillant in the novel. Lewis said Cather pursued Padre Martínez, who appears in the novel under his own name, through every book she could find at the local museum and they stayed up nights reading about priests.[15] It was during this time that she happened across William Howlett's *The Life of the Right Reverend Joseph P. Machebeuf* (1908). Written by a priest who had worked under Bishop Machebeuf in Denver, the book is a virtual hagiography, which Cather took as fact. Indeed, the readiness with which she accepted as truth Howlett's account of Machebeuf and his friend and spiritual leader Lamy, despite the fact that she herself so often destabilized the truth by the use of individualized narrative perspectives, is one of the most surprising aspects of Cather's long and thoughtful career.

She began work on the new novel soon after reading Howlett's book, fully nine months before correcting proofs of *My Mortal Enemy*—an overlap that by itself calls into question the idea that she put her dark period behind her when she turned to the "eirenic" *Archbishop* (Reynolds 150). In October 1925 she reported good progress and the following January exulted to Irene Miner Weisz that she simply loved her Bishop. In the same letter, she crowed that Professor St. Peter (that is, royalties from *The Professor's House*) had bought her a mink coat.[16] One recalls her greeting Stephen Tennant at her door wearing black satin pajamas and a flamingo-pink tunic (Hoare 212). Such moments disprove the misconception, fostered by Cather herself, that she was impervious to the pleasures of wealth.

In May 1926 she again set out for the Southwest, the landscape she associated with vigor and adventure and now with her two French priests. Before leaving, she hurried to complete revisions of the introduction to *My Ántonia* for a new edition proposed by Houghton Mifflin as a means of increasing its sales by capitalizing on her current reputation. Using the new edition as an opportunity to improve the introduction, she made cuts that freed its salient features from a clutter of extraneous details and brought them into sharper focus. She seems to have completed, by the time she started west, at least part 2 of *Archbishop*, "Missionary Journeys," describing it to her agent as having a more solemn coloration than part 1.[17] Perhaps so, but it also features a singularly comic episode in which Vaillant exerts spiritual pressure in order to gain possession of a splendid pair of white mules (in Howlett they are bays), which then virtually become characters in the story. The incident initiates a series of episodes in which Vaillant shows himself to be an astute fund-raiser, no doubt a needed attribute in a missionary priest but one that sometimes runs counter to his depiction as a servant of the people.

Shortly before she left New York Cather received a telegram from her father that led her to stop off in Red Cloud (with Edith Lewis, though usually she went there alone) before hastening on to Gallup, where she was expecting to receive proofs of *My Mortal Enemy*. On the way she enjoyed meeting the movie dog Rin Tin Tin (and would later report going to a Rin Tin Tin movie), but she found Gallup a "hell of a place." Located between the great Navajo reservation to the west and north and Zuni to the south, with other tribal lands nearby, Gallup was a place of bars and pawn shops with an annual exposition featuring Indian dancers and knickknacks, the epitome of American disruption of Native culture. While there, she and Edith visited Zuni, a pueblo noted for its strong spirituality, and the Canyon de Chelly, sacred to the Navajo, which Cather rejoiced to report could not be visited by car and was thus relatively safe from tourist pollution. The sentiment is ironic, considering her own enjoyment of the very Fred Harvey facilities that in conjunction with the Santa Fe Railroad promoted the tourism to which she was objecting. While herself a tourist in Santa Fe, she mocked the Harvey-run Indian Detours whose object was, except for its literary outcome, little different from her own.[18] Both her writing of *Archbishop* and the curiosity of the Indian Detourists, as she called them, were products of the romanticizing of the Southwest that had begun in the late 1800s.

The proofs of *My Mortal Enemy* did not arrive until June 3. Cather left for Santa Fe the next day, taking them with her. From the La Fonda Hotel she wrote to Mabel Luhan inquiring whether the pink cabin that she and Edith had occupied the previous summer might be available for two weeks, until Edith's scheduled departure on June 23. Instead, they stayed on at Santa Fe. While there, Cather fended off the request of an editor at Scribner's by telling him that she was on her way to Mexico and would not be back in New York until October, none of which was true. Claiming travel in isolated places was one of her favorite evasive strategies during the years of her fame. Starting around June 19 she went daily to Mary Austin's new house, finding it (so she wrote the absent Austin) quiet, peaceful, and conducive to working. Later, after Austin publicly boasted that Cather had written *Archbishop* there and exhibited the very chair in which she had sat, she would deny having done so, telling Mabel Luhan that letters were all she had written at Austin's house and she had done even that only to be polite. Both her note and the inscription she wrote in Austin's copy of the novel indicate otherwise.[19] The episode shows once again how she hated having her privacy intruded on.

Moving on, around the first of July, to Denver and making a stop in Red Cloud, where her mother was unwell, Cather returned to New York long enough to meet with her agent and arrange for serialization of *Archbishop* before going to the MacDowell Writers' Colony at Peterboro, New Hampshire, where she worked intently for six weeks (Woodress, *Literary* 395). She seems to have taken a break in September for a quick

trip to Grand Manan Island, New Brunswick, where she bought a piece
of land, identified the spot for a cottage, and hired a carpenter. (Possibly
Edith Lewis may have done these things without her, though it does not
seem likely.) The cottage, featuring an attic work space but no indoor
plumbing, would be ready for occupancy when they returned the following July. On September 22, back in her familiar rooms at the Shattuck
Inn in Jaffrey, New Hampshire, her fall retreat for a decade, she wrote
Blanche Knopf that she would send the full manuscript for the typeset-
ter in November. Two weeks later she moved that date up to the end of
October.[20]

Cather's ties to Jaffrey and Grand Manan are well known and often
mentioned, especially the fact that she wrote part of *My Ántonia* in a
tent pitched in a meadow near the Shattuck Inn. Yet relatively little has
been written about the quality of her life in these two places beyond
O'Brien's observation that she constructed environments of "intimate
immensity" (70–71) and Woodress's brief notes that living conditions at
the cottage were "primitive" and at Jaffrey she took "long walks through
the countryside and up Mount Monadnock" with a field guide to wild-
flowers (*Literary* 414, 286). In fact, her long walks were often quite strenuous. As she did during her visits to the Southwest, she delighted in hiking
and climbing, taking considerable pride in her ability to scale rugged
heights. From the rocky cliffs at Grand Manan she watched pods of
whales and once tried writing a letter to Zoë Akins on white birch bark,
an attempt that did not work very well but enacted her wish to incorporate into her writing the freedom and authenticity of the outdoors.[21]

Both at Grand Manan and at Jaffrey she was a remarkably close observer
of plant life. The copy of F. Schuyler Mathews's *Field Book of American
Wild Flowers* (1902) that Woodress mentions is heavily marked, with
checkmarks or lines in the margin at some 156 distinct varieties that she
had apparently identified at Jaffrey or Grand Manan or, in a few cases,
Virginia. A few are noted as having been seen in Nebraska as if, seeing
Mathews's descriptions, she remembered them. Frequently she noted
the place and sometimes the date of her observation of a particular plant;
such markings range from 1917 to 1938. Occasionally she added details
to Mathews's already detailed descriptions.[22] Clearly, she was more of a
naturalist than has generally been realized.

For all the complexity of *Death Comes for the Archbishop*, Cather wrote
it with what appears to have been astonishing ease and speed. Despite

confessing in a letter to one of her sisters that she found the form very difficult and that the closeness to historical and biographical record hampered her freedom of creativity, for the most part she spoke of her work on the novel as a blissful escape from the problems of the world. She told Ida Tarbell that writing it was "the most unalloyed pleasure" of her life and gave her a "happy and serene" mood, and she exclaimed to Fanny Butcher that she had loved doing it. While reading proof, she wrote her niece that she felt somewhat depressed to think that she could not expect ever again to have such fun working. But though her references to escape assert the delightfulness of the experience, they also demonstrate that she felt a *need* to escape. Whatever its origin, that need seems to have been inner as well as external. She had once told Elsie Sergeant that she was less a problem to herself when writing than at any other time, and in 1922 had spoken of Claude, clearly a surrogate self, in terms of his wish to escape his sense of self.[23] It is often noted that she was disaffected from the materialistic excesses of the 1920s (despite her own enjoyment of material pleasures), but she seems also to have wanted to escape her self. A photograph glued into her personal copy of the 1929 illustrated edition of *Archbishop* (now at the University of Nebraska) indicates that she may have sought to do so by burying her identity in that of Bishop Lamy. Showing her on horseback in the New Mexico desert, the photo is affixed to the title page of Book One just below the words "The Vicar Apostolic" (see figure 25).

Readers have usually found the book tranquil and assuring. The actress Cornelia Otis Skinner called it "a benediction."[24] Yet beneath its apparent tranquility it betrays a troubled sense of social conflict and unplumbed, even unplumbable, ambiguity. The cruciform tree that Bishop Latour sees when he is lost is the desert, in the opening scene, is an emblem of divinely assured meaning conveyed in the language of nature, but it is balanced at the center of the book by an equally powerful emblem of ultimate *un*meaning, a cave of indeterminate depth haunted by mysteries that disturb and bewilder him. We also see the countercurrents of Cather's conflicted vision in the social dimension of this most assured of her masterworks. Her misgivings about the process of enlightened dominion that she overtly celebrates are so strong that she litters the text with occasions for doubt. Even in this novel of apparent tranquility, she continues to raise the question of who will possess America.

Fig. 25. Cather in New Mexico, snapshot pasted into her personal copy of the illustrated
edition of *Death Comes for the Archbishop* beneath the words "The Vicar Apostolic." (By
courtesy of the University of Nebraska–Lincoln Archives/Special Collections Department)

Death Comes for the Archbishop opens at a moment of national appropriation of the territory of another country and focuses on the issue of the
Americanization of those who are thereby dislocated across a national
border. The first words of the introduction, an imagined scene in Rome
when the new bishop is chosen, locate the time setting as "one summer

evening in the year 1848" (*DCA* 3). On February 2 of that year, under the Treaty of Guadalupe Hidalgo, the United States gained almost half of the territory of Mexico under force of arms. By specifying this imperialistic moment, Cather placed the book squarely within a highly politicized situation. Her language in a letter to her agent, Paul Reynolds, referring to the historic moment as the time when New Mexico was "taken over" from Mexico, confirms that she saw that fact quite clearly.[25]

Her valuation of the historic event is less clearly negative, however, than her language might imply. She seems, indeed, to write as a proponent of Manifest Destiny. Likening Latour's errand into the southwestern wilderness to the heroic journey of Odysseus and comparing the United States government to Hercules, ready to cleanse the Augean stable of this backward territory (*DCA* 7), she invokes originary texts of the western tradition.[26] The two heroic forces of church(man) and state will operate as one. When Latour and Vaillant ride into Santa Fe they may be "claiming it for the glory of God" (22), but Latour frankly declares that he means to "help the officers at their task" of making "these poor Mexicans 'good Americans'" (37). His paternalistic assertion that it is "for the people's good" is the classic claim of the benevolent imperialist. But the Mexican people themselves, who, except for a 12-year hiatus following the Great Pueblo Revolt of 1680, had lived in New Mexico for 250 years since the colonizing incursion led by Juan de Oñate in 1598, and who now find themselves transferred willy-nilly to citizenship in what they perceive as a hostile nation, have a different view of the matter: "'We want our own ways and our own religion'" (27).[27] That fact—and thus a resistant current—is also established in Book One of the novel.

The contrast between the statement of Lamy's colonialist intentions and the protest of the colonized illustrates why we cannot finally be certain how to assess Cather's intentions in this novel. Was she glorifying the political and religious process of appropriation she chronicled? I believe so. But her glorification was not without misgivings. In keeping with the concept of Manifest Destiny, she wrote of U.S. expansionism as a process of enlightened betterment and an inherent right of the American people. Yet she also placed in the text the protesting voice of the humble resident of Agua Secreta, where the newly appointed bishop found succor when he was lost and thirsting in the desert. In return, this José with the "sullen eyes," who boldly speaks of Americans as "infidels," is called,

in traditional clerical address, "my son" and is blandly assured that he is
mistaken, there are many "devout Catholics" among the Americans (*DCA*
27). True enough, no doubt. Still, the country of which José is so suspi-
cious is indeed predominantly Protestant and intolerant of Catholi-
cism, and the wish to maintain local ways and religion will go unheeded
as Latour proceeds to depose Mexican priests in favor of clergy from
France and occasionally Spain, dismaying his flock and provoking a
schism led by the defiant Padre Martínez. Latour takes an essentially
ultramontane position on church authority. Locating correctness as
well as power at the center, Rome, he devalues the practices and beliefs
of the margin. He takes, and Cather seems to endorse, a Eurocentric
view of cultural practices that have grown up in New Mexico over a
period of hundreds of years. Surprisingly, she asserted some years later
that the tradition left by the French priests was one of tolerance and
sympathy for the people.[28]

Among the localized religious practices disapproved by Latour (as they
were in fact by Lamy) are the devotional observances of the Penitentes.
Here Cather's novel engages a murky historic quandary. The *Terciarios
de Penitencia*, or Penitentes, were a localized brotherhood practicing
fasts, self-flagellation, and Holy Week processionals including a crucifixion, sometimes to the death. A greatly esteemed local historian, Fray
Angelico Chavez, has emphatically denied that the "gory" practices of
this group had any connection except by confusion of name with the
original Third Order of Penance founded by St. Francis in the thirteenth
century, which allowed secular men and also women (unlike the strictly
male Penitentes) to participate in his mission. Oñate himself is sometimes
said to have been a Third Order Franciscan. But this group, according
to Chavez, had all but disappeared from the area a century before the
appearance of the "flagellant Penitentes," whose bloody excesses were
condemned by church hierarchy well before Lamy's arrival—contrary to
Murphy's belief that they were condemned "with the coming of Lamy
and later" ("Historical" 449). Even so, the respected resident priest at
Taos, Antonio José Martínez, served as an officer of the brotherhood.
Asked by the regional superior of the Franciscan order to supervise
any remaining remnants of the Third Order in New Mexico, Martínez
accepted, so Chavez believes (36–37), partly out of confusion, believing
that the official was referring to the Penitentes with whom he was
familiar, and partly as a way of "extending and solidifying his personal

influence" over the area north of Santa Fe.[29] This was, of course, an important part of the diocese over which Lamy was charged with establishing his own authority. As Cather depicts the conflict between the two, the challenge to the bishop's authority is direct and possibly threatening. Pointing out that Latour knew "nothing about Indians or Mexicans," Martínez warns him, "If you try to . . . abolish the bloody rites of the Penitentes, I foretell an early death for you" (*DCA* 155).

Martínez's tie to the Penitentes was only one of a range of conflicts between himself and the new bishop. Another, much emphasized by Cather, was his rejection of the doctrine of priestly celibacy. In developing her book achronologically "in the style of legend" and by analogy with the stately and stylized manner of the Puvis de Chavannes frescoes she had seen in Paris and Boston—that is, "without accent, with none of the artificial elements of composition" (*OW* 9)—she seems to have realized that she needed some narrative thread to draw her disparate incidents together. These conflicts serve that purpose. Despite her later insistence that it was not necessary to think of *Archbishop* as a novel but simply as "a narrative" (12), any book by her not classifiable as nonfiction or a collection of short stories would naturally be read as a novel.[30] She might wish to emulate the style of the legend or the visual style of Puvis and not "hold the note" but "touch and pass on" (9), but she needed to make at least some gesture toward readers' expectations of linearity and character development. The bishop's conflicts with Martínez allowed her to make such a gesture while elaborating the theme of conflict between European cultural authority and New World primitiveness, a theme also explored in *The Professor's House*.

In choosing to accentuate the conflict with Martínez, however, Cather blackened the old padre's character far beyond Howlett's version, her source. She endorses Lamy at every turn, while her treatment of Martínez borders on the scurrilous. Disregarding both contrary evidence of which she was certainly aware (since, according to Lewis, every book she found about Martínez told the story differently) and Howlett's natural bias in favor of his mentor, she painted Martínez as utterly corrupt. Besides relaying rumors that he had fathered many children and an old canaille that he had masterminded the killing of Charles Bent, the first American territorial governor of New Mexico, as well as "some dozen other whites" (*DCA* 11), she pictured him as being physically repugnant, even bestial, with shoulders "like a bull buffalo's," a large head "set

defiantly on a thick neck," a "full-cheeked, richly coloured, egg-shaped
Spanish face," a full-lipped, sensual mouth expressive of "violent, uncurbed
passions," and yellow, "distinctly vulgar" teeth (147, 156). Ethnic aversion seems implicit.[31]

Ethnic marking extends beyond Martínez to the treatment of the
Mexican populace generally. In part, Cather may have absorbed a denigrating or at best condescending attitude toward Mexicans from
Howlett, who incorporates a lengthy quoted diatribe against Mexicans
of the region in 1846 as dirty, thieving, lazy, treacherous, and "liars by
nature" (259–63). Howlett adds a formulaic disavowal that they were
not really so bad but were only a simple, childlike people considerably
improved by "half a century of Americanizing influences" (402) and at
any rate were beloved by the saintly Machebeuf. Cather's version closely
approximates this ameliorated but still disparaging view, romanticizing
Mexicans as innocent and quaint. Yet even Vaillant, while asserting his
loyalty to his Mexican parishioners, calls their ways "foolish" and claims
that work among their "poor natures" does not require intelligence
(*DCA* 217). Although most are indeed poor, owning "nothing but a
mud house and a burro" (272), the novel reports without comment that
Vaillant "could always raise money" among these deprived people. The
wealthy Olivareses, whose house is a center of charm and cultivation
very pleasing to Latour and Vaillant, are nevertheless painted as being
frivolous, flirtatious, and vain, the wife shaving eleven years off her age.
(Sra. Olivares is only one of several female characters in the book, belying Cather's quip that it was a novel without a woman in it except the
Virgin Mary. Gender is a subdued but not unimportant issue.) One of
the Olivareses' friends, Manuel Chavez, perhaps suggested by Howlett's
quoted account of the Mexicans' being "but one degree removed from
the veriest savage," is a vengeful scalper of Indians who in his youth
hunted Navajos for "sport" (*DCA* 193). Intelligence, maturity, and good
judgment are qualities associated with white (that is, non-Hispanic)
Europeans. It is they, not New Mexico's "fickle" (117) Mexicans or His-
panos, who will shape the course of the American Southwest toward
civilization.

Cather's treatment of Indians in *Archbishop* is equally bothering, assertions of her "great affinity" and "sympathy" for them notwithstanding
(Stouck, "Indian" 433; McDonald 77). As in *A Lost Lady*, her import is
far from clear. Although she indicates respect for the Indians' "ecologi-

cal awareness" (Stouck, "Indian" 435), paying tribute to their ability to "pass through a country without disturbing anything" (*DCA* 246), and presents the Navajo Eusabio as being impressively wise and thoughtful, she vilifies the Acomas from the perspective of Latour himself as "something reptilian . . . rock-turtles on their rock" (109). They are dehumanized by both terms, the comparison to reptiles and the word "some*thing.*" Similarly, in the central incident of the cave, an affinity is implied between reptiles and yet another pueblo group.

In Book IV, "Snake Root," Father Latour sets out with his faithful guide Jacinto to reach Vaillant, who lies ill with "black measles" at a village near Las Vegas. Jacinto is one of the last members of the dying pueblo of Pecos—historically, already dead; its last seventeen inhabitants moved to Jemez Pueblo in 1838. Cather resurrects Pecos only to emphasize its dying. Jacinto is consistently shown as an independent thinker and an astute observer of character; his view of the bishop himself is endorsed by the novel. Yet despite being a married man and a father, he is consistently addressed by Latour as "my boy" and is called "boy" by the narrative voice as well. It is as belittling a locution as that used for his home at Pecos, a "lair" (*DCA* 127).

Pushing their journey hard, Latour and Jacinto are caught in the open by a heavy snowstorm until, recognizing where they are, Jacinto insists that they abandon their mules and climb a steep mesa to a cave. Entering between "two rounded ledges, one directly over the other, with a mouth-like opening between" like "two great stone lips, slightly parted and thrust outward," they enter a "fetid" cavern that strikes the bishop with "an extreme distaste" (*DCA* 134). He is aware of rumors that the Pecos people worship or once worshiped a huge snake kept in some secret place, to the point of practicing infant sacrifice.[32] The implication is that their own primitive beliefs, and not solely the diseases brought by Europeans, have contributed to destroying the Pecos people. Now "the Indian boy" tells Latour that the cave is a secret place used by his people "for ceremonies" and that he is not sure he should have brought the bishop there. Ignoring Latour's plea for a fire, Jacinto first makes "a minute examination" of the floor and, stick by stick, a pile of firewood stashed there; then he thoroughly seals up a hole in the back wall. Only then does he build a fire that disperses the "disagreeable" smell (136). But now Latour becomes aware of a mysterious roaring or humming. In explanation, Jacinto leads him along a tunnel to a crack in the stone floor plastered with clay, which he digs out. Placing his ear to the crack, he listens; then Latour listens. They agree that it is "terrible." As long as the bishop is awake, Jacinto avoids so much as glancing toward the plastered-up hole in the wall. But when Latour wakes during the night he sees the Indian "standing on some invisible foothold, his arms outstretched against the rock, his body flattened against it" and "supported" there "by the intensity of his solicitude," his ear over that patch of fresh mud, "listening; listening with supersensual ear" (139).

This sequence is absolutely central to a reading of the novel that proposes to deconstruct its apparent certitude and is also central to the issue of Cather's ethnocentrism toward Native Americans. The geographic space haunted by the unknown is emblematic of radical ambiguity. Conflicting images cancel each other out. The uterine cave with its vaginal passages is reached by way of an opening between thrusting lips blatantly resembling genital labia. (The offensive smell in the cave is perhaps an allusion to an old canard against women.) But it is located within a blatantly masculine landform, the up-thrusting butte. Within the cave itself may or may not lurk the hugely phallic sacred snake and perhaps smaller snakes among the piñon fagots. It is cold yet warmed by fire, a refuge yet sinister. In its space the authoritative representative of Christianity confronts the imputed presence of the pagan serpent god, the serpent also being a Judeo-Christian symbol of evil. The superficially Christianized devotee listens through the night, perhaps in fear but perhaps in devotion, in a posture of crucifixion. The snake cannot be there, because it is preposterous; yet it may be there, since Jacinto proceeds with such great caution. In the story told to Latour, the snake is a cruel divinity; yet we know that in prevailing southwestern Native beliefs the snake was (is) associated with rain, a good. It was also seen as a messenger to the lower worlds (as rain soaks into the ground) and therefore a potential threat if it overheard one telling the sacred stories incorrectly. The roaring under the stone may be terrible or may be a sound of "majesty and power" (*DCA* 138).[33] Identified by Latour as the sound of underground water, "one of the oldest voices of the earth," it may be a naturalistic sound or the ancient "voice" of an immanent god. The Native presence represents a pueblo Cather claims as alive while acknowledging it (in the strangely unfictive device of a footnote) as dead. An emptiness within a mass, with depth under depth, level under level of rock falling away to the nonmeaning voice of the oldest existence, the cave profoundly discomfits the benevolent imperialist who cowers while the dark subaltern takes charge and refuses to give "comment or explanation" (136).

Possibility cancels out possibility. As readers, we are dropped from uncertainty to uncertainty, like the layers under layers of hollowness inside the butte. No wonder the bishop, the messenger of absoluteness, is glad to get away from this sexualized, paganized space. He had "made" Jacinto say the Lord's Prayer with him before going to sleep (*DCA* 131), but the words are only lip service compared to the devotion to ancient mysteries displayed during the night. Jacinto is revealed as far more than the complaisant helper he has seemed. The European Latour can no more fathom what Jacinto thinks than he can fathom the mysteries of the cave. It is clear that Jacinto represents an Other that is dying off; his village is mostly deserted, his only son sickly. But like the running water consigned to a "sewer dungeon under stone / In fetid darkness" in Robert Frost's poem "A Brook in the City," he and the submerged river with which he is associated can be expected to trouble the unconscious of the conquering Euro-American:

> I wonder
> If from its being kept forever under
> The thoughts may not have risen that so keep
> This new-built city from both work and sleep.
>
> (Frost 285)

Cather's subterranean stream may, in fact, have been prompted by Frost's, whose poetry she knew and admired. Book publication of "A Brook in the City" in *New Hampshire* (1923) preceded that of *Death Comes for the Archbishop* by four years.

Twice in *Archbishop*, once near the beginning and once very near the end, Cather makes direct pronouncements on the history of imperialism in the Southwest, acknowledging the mistreatment of the Native people but in language so mild that it is in effect a misrepresentation. To say that "the Spaniards had treated [the Acomas] very badly long ago" (*DCA* 56) is a considerable understatement.[34] After the Spaniards destroyed the pueblo in 1599, with great loss of life, in retaliation for the killing of one of Oñate's aides, Oñate sentenced five hundred males of the pueblo to have one foot chopped off and to serve twenty years of hard labor. The sentence, so barbarous that some of the Spanish colonists found ways to help Acomas escape, was actually carried out on twelve (Spicer 157). Similarly, her protest of the expulsion of the Navajos by Kit Carson (through systematic destruction of their food sources) and their exile via the Long Walk is couched in ameliorating terms. Latour, now archbishop, regrets that his "misguided" friend had become involved in that cruel business and is thankful to see the Navajo people restored to their own place (308–13). But his response (and apparently Cather's) is more one more of sorrow than of outrage for the starved-out, driven Navajo, and his faith that God will "preserve" them side-steps the issue of human responsibility and only minimally recognizes their rights as a people. The war-chief Manuelito, another actual historical figure imported into the story, sees clearly that Latour is "the friend of Christóbal, who hunts my people" (311). Latour will no more involve himself in protesting the government's actions than he will intervene in behalf of the illegally enslaved Mexican woman Sada, finding it "inexpedient to antagonize" those who hold political power (226) and merely exhorting both to submissive goodness.

Ammons, who accuses Cather of racism, describes the Indians of *Death Comes for the Archbishop* as "decorative details" (*Conflicting* 133). It is perhaps a severe statement, but not far wrong. Cather's interest was in creating an aesthetic effect of serenity and balance, and in the process she drained real human issues of their intensity. By implying a kind of acceptance of historic inevitability in her account of the Americanization of the Southwest and the suppression or demise of racially different populations, she contributed to the development of a palliative "rhetoric of tricultural harmony" (Wilson 148). *Death Comes for the Archbishop* is the culminating text of Cather's participation in the romanticizing of the Southwest, a process in cultural history that included not only the boosterism of a Charles Lummis but the sometimes manipulative antiquarianism of a Mary Austin, the emotional mysticism of a Mabel Dodge Luhan, and an intensively mythicizing architectural effort centered at Santa Fe.[35]

CATHER'S AMALGAMATION of history, legend, and fiction in *Archbishop* raises difficult issues of authorial responsibility. In choosing to interweave history and traditional legend (for example, the legend of the Virgin of Guadalupe) she blurred the distinctions among these genres and their varying claims of truth. Such generic blurring places her representation of Padre Martínez, in particular, on uncertain ethical grounds. The use of a real name would seem to entail a special obligation to maintain historic veracity, yet Cather knowingly ignored the existence of conflicting versions of the historic record, choosing to present a one-sided version as if it were only a novelistic truth about created characters. She was writing fiction, after all, and she exercised the novelist's art in posing Martínez as a foil for her archbishop, while also leading her reader to question Latour's rightness at times. But since she chose to use his actual name in a context in which generic distinctions are blurred, her aesthetic heightening implies reportage. In the view of some who take a different view of the historic Martínez, she became guilty of a kind of posthumous libel.[36] Her account of Padre Martínez still rankles among many New Mexicans.

In later years Cather would claim that she had "followed the life story of the two Bishops very much as it was" and had reported incidents almost precisely as they happened (*OW* 12).[37] Such statements, with their assumption that one person can ever overcome the limitations of individual perspective, the inadequacy of records, and differences of cultural circumstance, imply a strikingly naive view of history. Her emulation of Howlett has been termed "uncritical" (Weidman 60), but it was in fact more serious than that, given Lewis's revelation that she was quite aware of the disputed nature of the record regarding Martínez and given her own indications of awareness of the politicized atmosphere in which Lamy and Machebeuf worked. It is especially shocking in that she chose to use his actual name in painting him as a corrupt villain, while substituting fictional names for Lamy and Machebeuf.

The opposite problem might be cited with respect to Kit Carson, who also appears in the novel by name. In this case Cather chose to depict a historical personage *cum* legend and a disputed figure historically as if he were a paragon of gentle virtue. There is much in the historical record (for example, his adoption of several children) to indicate that Carson *was* a kindly person. On the other hand, he was a grizzled mountain man, scout, and Indian fighter who led a process of systematic starving-out that resulted in one of the great atrocities of American history, the Long March and the imprisonment of the Navajo at Bosque Redondo (Fort Sumner), in the course of which thousands, not the "hundreds" Cather mentions, died.[38] By whitewashing the historic Anglo character and vilifying the Mexican priest, she defined in exaggerated terms the conflict between the two cultures they represented, further loading the terms of her legend of enlightened American expansion.

Cather's idealizing picture of the hand-in-glove cooperation of the Catholic Church with the process of American colonizing of the Southwest went unquestioned by most of her contemporaries. Mary Austin, however, voiced a strong objection. In 1932, in both her autobiography, *Earth Horizon*, and an article in the *English Journal* ("Regionalism 97–106), she berated Cather for having endorsed French religious colonialism in what she called a Spanish town. It had been, she said, "a calamity to the local culture" (*Earth* 359). Furious, Cather told Mabel Dodge Luhan that it was not her fault the priests were French. But such a riposte lacks candor. What she *could* help was her choice of whom to believe and how to place her emphasis. She believed the report of parties identified with the side that gained the upper hand, and she emphasized their rightness. Those who came to possess America did so, it seems, for reasons of divine plan. But the numerous troubling details of the countertext that invite our questioning of the historic record of American westering indicate that she was not comfortable with that simple endorsement.

The novel is not, then, "without distancing or irony" (Weidman 54–55).[39] It may be impossible to say how conscious her ironies were, but dissonances systematically introduced in the text, together with dissonances we perceive that Cather may not have intended, prepare us as readers for a great irony invoked at the ostensibly serene end. Latour, dying the good Christian death, as secure in his reconciliation to all that has happened as he is in his personal redemption, as happy in his construction of a vision of the Navajos' return to an Edenic garden as if their pain were erased, is nevertheless troubled by a subtle awareness that must have come to many of the world's successful imperialists: he liked the place better before the changes that he himself has helped to bring.

10

ART IN A DEMOCRATIC SOCIETY

> When I came piping through the land,
>   One morning in the spring,
> With cockle-burrs upon my coat
>   'Twas then I was a king . . .
>   —"The Encore"

> The goblet
> Stood in a dusty window full of charcoal,
> The only bright, the only gracious object.
>
>   —"A Silver Cup"

IN MARCH 1928 an event occurred that would have profound effects on Willa Cather's work for years to come—in a sense, to the end of her career. Her father, for whom she had always felt a special love, died suddenly of a heart attack. Only a week before, she had returned to New York from a prolonged Christmas visit with her parents that had begun with the celebration of their fifty-fifth wedding anniversary on December 5. (Figure 26 shows Cather's parents a few years before her father's death.) She had lingered almost to the end of February, enjoying her nieces and nephews, skating on the frozen river, and fantasizing that she might leave New York for good. When the telegram came, she caught a train back to Red Cloud. Arriving before dawn on the day of the funeral while other members of the family were sleeping, she kept a solitary vigil beside the body. Her father looked comfortably asleep. He had died still rosy-cheeked and youthful and sweet-tempered.[1]

After the funeral and her mother's departure to California for what was expected to be a few months' visit with Douglass, Cather stayed on at the house getting some repairs done and pondering the importance

Fig. 26. Cather's parents in their later years, possibly summer 1924.
(Nebraska State Historical Society)

of family roots. It was a time, O'Brien writes, when she experienced both grief and a "renewed sense of connection to her family and past." Later that same year Marjorie, the retarded woman who had come with the Cathers from Virginia and lived with them ever since as a household servant, after whom Cather had modeled Mandy in "Old Mrs. Harris" and Mahailey in *One of Ours*, also died (O'Brien in *SPO* 997).[2] In December, still in California, Mary Virginia Cather suffered a stroke that left her essentially helpless.

After these blows Cather entered a long period of recurring depression. She told Mary Austin that life's trials sometimes seemed to be just too much and intimated to Dorothy Canfield Fisher that she felt "crushed" by her mother's illness and had lost her bearings. Her father's death, she said, had knocked a prop out from under her, and in the wake of the fall she had been swamped by disasters. According to Sergeant, she wondered whether she could be helped by psychoanalysis (248). For the rest of her life she would tell friends that she had mostly spent this period in California caring for her mother or crisscrossing the continent on trains, going to see about her. Only three months before her mother's death, for example, she told an old acquaintance that during these years she had lived mainly at the sanitarium.[3] To be sure, she was much involved in decisions about her mother's care and did go to California to help or relieve other family members in their attendance. But she was not there nearly so much as she claimed or perhaps tried to believe. In Romines's words, the fact that she exaggerated the amount of time spent with her mother is "a telling clue" that she "felt uncomfortable with her own behavior during these stressful years" ("Coming" 395). She seems to have found the sight of her mother's condition so distressing that it provoked avoidance more than attendance on her.

The deepening gloom of Cather's later years contributed to her frequently noted withdrawal from social contacts and, I believe, to the pronounced turning again to the past that characterizes much of her later fiction.[4] The experience of losing her parents and Marjorie, whose presence in the kitchen or on the back porch at home had meant so much to her for most of her life (to the point that she had once quarreled with her mother about how Marjorie was treated), manifested itself in her work in another way as well. She turned, or returned, in her fiction to subjects relating to home ties and dailiness and to characters of relatively humble circumstance.[5]

We see something of this turn in *Shadows on the Rock* (1931), which she began in the fall of 1928 and struggled to write during the years of her mother's long invalidism, but we see it even more clearly in the three stories that make up *Obscure Destinies* (1932), written during the same period and published in magazines beginning in 1930. Both books enjoyed a strong popular reception probably traceable to their celebration of everyday, seemingly commonplace life. (Cather, for example, found comfort in the simplicity of her grandmother's room in their Nebraska house, shown in figure 27.) In *Shadows*, dailiness was combined with spatial and temporal distance. In a sense, she was again taking up material similar to that in her most popular early novels, *O Pioneers!* and *My Ántonia*, but with an emphasis on continuity, reconciliation, and understanding rather than escape.[6] She had said in 1921 that she did not believe the life of the average person was "so commonplace that a faithful delineation of him alone would not make interesting reading" (*WCIP* 27). *Obscure Destinies* demonstrates that confidence.

At the same time, much of Cather's attention during this period in her life (she was fifty-four when her father died) was given to consideration of art itself. As a journalist years before, she had devoted most of her reviews and columns to art. Her third novel, *The Song of the Lark*, had been a study of the growth of an artist based in part on close observation of singers for articles in *McClure's*. Many of her short stories—"A Death in the Desert" (1903), "A Wagner Matinée" (1904), "The Sculptor's Funeral" (1905), "A Gold Slipper" (1917), "Uncle Valentine" (1925), to mention only a handful—had dealt with artist figures or the art experience. The figure of the artist has been called the "organizing principle" for *The Troll Garden*, as the female artist was for *Youth and the Bright Medusa* (Hallgraph 169). Artists are, in a word, pervasive in her fiction. What we see in the 1930s is a resurgence of writing about art, much of it the revision or expansion of various occasional pieces, including "The Novel Démeublé," first published in April 1922, and "148 Charles Street," from the same year, for *Not under Forty* (1936).

That the title *Not under Forty* emphasizes life stages is scarcely incidental. It was here, in the preface, that she famously stated the world had broken in two "in 1922 or thereabouts." Both in the essays collected in that volume and in her fiction of the same period we see the effects of her loss of parents and her reflections on her connectedness with family. Fiction and nonfiction come together as components of a highly unified

Fig. 27. Grandmother Boak's room in Cather's childhood home.
(Nebraska State Historical Society)

phase of Cather's career as, under the stimulus of retrospection, she pondered the mystery of the artist's emergence from commonness, from ordinary human origins—that is, the mystery of her own emergence as a writer from her family background. This dual concern, in fiction and nonfiction alike, with everyday life in a democratic society and with the place in it of art and the artist culminated in 1935 in *Lucy Gayheart*. One effect of the simultaneous emphasis on both concepts, however, and in particular on their intersection, was the sharpening of a conflict we have already seen in Cather's mind, her contrary impulses toward both the humble or everyday and the aristocratic or exceptional. At times this conflict issues in assertions of class exclusivity directly at odds with her affirmation of people of "obscure destinies."[7]

Shadows on the Rock was published the month Cather's mother died, August 1931. It was her first novel since *Death Comes for the Archbishop* in 1927, and the two are often read as companion pieces, even by those who take at face value Cather's quip about the absence of women in *Archbishop*. Both novels are occupied with the presence in the New World of two great cultural and social entities of Europe, the Catholic Church and France, or French traditions.

After the publication of these two works, Cather was widely believed to have become Catholic. It was an understandable inference. Clearly, she was deeply drawn toward the contemplation of spiritual values and ultimate certainties, and her statement in a letter that she did not *think* she would become Catholic indicates she may have been considering such a step. Indeed, she had long ago imagined herself as a birthright Catholic, writing in an unpublished poem called "Sunday on the Siene" [sic] about the Catholic Church back in the wheatlands of Nebraska where her brother served as acolyte.[8] Such effusions can be regarded as expressions of momentary inclinations or perhaps as additional manifestations of her ability to imagine herself in a variety of roles. Her correspondence during the difficult period following her father's death and her mother's stroke does not invoke religion or spirituality as a consolation, as one might expect of someone devout. In later years, particularly during World War II, she would make sporadic assertions of the consummate truth of Christianity and the nothingness awaiting the world if its light was put out, but her reach toward the church in *Archbishop* and *Shadows* was essentially a reach toward its outward manifestations, both aesthetic and as an institution providing stability, at a time when she keenly felt her own instability. It is no coincidence that both novels, even while conveying a sense of vast journeys and strenuous endeavors, show a disposition to retreat behind thick structural walls.

Both novels turn toward the past for their venues and values, *Shadows* to a more distant past than *Archbishop*, the seventeenth century as opposed to the nineteenth. This turn to the past is often cited as the chief characteristic of Cather's later fiction. She would again turn to the past in her last completed novel, *Sapphira and the Slave Girl*, and even further into the past, to medieval times, in the uncompleted manuscript on which she had apparently been working for years at the time of her death, "Hard Punishments." The past is a powerful presence in her essays and short stories of this period as well, such as "The Old Beauty," written in 1936, and "The Best Years," written in 1945 (both published posthumously). The "best years" are the lost years, the first, apparently, to flee. But her emphasis is not simply on the past as a haven from the present and its troubles, but on the question of how the values of the past might be carried forward into the present and what aspects of the past could not or perhaps should not be carried forward. As Chris Wilson has written of the midcentury surge of historic preservationism, this "search for historic integrity" can well be seen as a "symbolic expression of the desire for social order" (265).

Cather is often thought to have rejected, in her late work, "the world of the machine," or even to have done so "grumpily" (Nelson 148), but it is the Mrs. Ferguesson of "The Best Years," not Cather in her own voice, whose refusal to ride in her husband's car (*SPO* 757) has been taken to indicate such a rejection of the "modern world." Cather's use of distanced narrators should make us cautious in reading the words and actions of her characters. She herself expressed pride in her father's driving, and in a letter to Zoë Akins used the metaphor of a big, powerful automobile to define what she admired in a particular actress.[9] What she feared and recoiled from was a modern world cut loose from any anchorage in the past. Even Archbishop Latour's assertion of conservative European values is made in the service of new conditions and change, the transfer of New Mexico to the United States and the need to make its people into "good Americans." Cécile Auclair in *Shadows on the Rock* rebels against her father's time-hallowed view of Canada as merely an outpost of his true home in France by redirecting the center of her vision to the New World. She welcomes (with obvious narrative approval) the innovation of placing a beaver, Canada's national animal, in the traditional French crèche at Christmas.[10]

In many ways, then, these two novels, separated by a time of intense emotional strain for Cather, are appropriately seen as a thematic and stylistic pair. Even so, *Shadows on the Rock* is a very different kind of book —one that is at least equally well paired with *Obscure Destinies*, published only a year later. Despite its preoccupation with French culture and the drama and hardships of colonization in an inhospitable environment, *Shadows* is very much a novel of dailiness, affirming the values of the ordinary and of what Romines calls "domestic ritual." It is not a book that anyone can ever have found exciting, which is not to deny that it is luminous and significant. Its point, very much like that of *Obscure Destinies*, is precisely that the daily, the unexciting, is luminous and ultimately beautiful, the very stuff of life itself—an important point for Cather to try to hold onto at a time when she was inclined to think existence an exercise in futility.[11] In other words, it asserts that home is not only where the heart is, but where meaning is.

In making this proposition, Cather was in a sense recanting her earlier determination to leave home. In Skaggs's words (*After* 139), she was giving her parents the good daughter they never had. More than that, she was pondering her family connections and the nature of social connectedness generally. *Shadows* is the story of a father of modest means but great personal cultivation who leads his family (a wife and *one* child) to a new place where he and they become respected and the daughter assumes the task of perpetuating cultural tradition. In writing this story, Cather was (re)writing the story of her own emergence in strength and authority from her familial source, fictively cleared of the distracting and competing younger siblings with whom she had had to share parental love. Her own emergence was very different from that of Cécile, who chooses to stay at home and demonstrate her strength by perfecting her mother's domestic traditions as a foundation for a new society. Willa, that other young girl with "shingled head," rejected domesticity to build a career in a men's world. Both stories, however, relate the daughter's displacement of the mother. Cécile literally replaces as household authority the mother who dies, and Willa deposed a strong mother's dominance by asserting her will to freedom. Not that Cécile's domesticity was entirely alien to Cather. She did draw satisfaction from *occasional* domestic tasks, proudly reporting in letters her success in cooking for a family of six and mastering the art of pastry during her mother's illness. She once mentioned working alongside her French maid in defrosting the refrigerator. And like Cécile she saw her work as the perpetuation of culture in an alien world.

If *Shadows on the Rock* explores the female child's embeddedness in family and the process of her maturation, it also explores the web of connectedness linking families into a social network. The Auclairs, father and daughter, are joined with others in the small town on the rock by ties of acquaintance, memory, and mutual assistance, as well as commerce. The social and political world of the novel, seventeenth-century Quebec, is scarcely a democratic one, but rather a hierarchy well symbolized in the verticality of its setting, with the secular and religious elite living on the peak and the poor or disreputable at the bottom of Quebec's rock, along the shore. Euclide Auclair's combination pharmacy shop and dwelling is located midway on the steep street connecting top and bottom. Strictly middle class, as were the Cathers, Auclair interacts with all: the bishop, the count, his middle-class neighbors, the poor son of a prostitute; and like the Cathers, he regards those less fortunate than himself with noblesse oblige.[12] The ideal society, so the novel implies, is not one in which all are on a level plane but is a hierarchy drawn together by interdependence.

Similarly, the three stories in *Obscure Destinies* center on the nature of family ties and the larger social network in which families are embedded in rural or small-town communities. They are concerned with social relations and interdependencies, as well as their limits, in a "snappy little Western democracy" (*OD* 112) of farmers, store owners, and railroad men. Here, gradations of social class are much less marked and of less concern than in the similar worlds of *A Lost Lady* and *My Mortal Enemy*. The characters in "Old Mrs. Harris" are either plain folk or gentility in reduced circumstances. Even the Rosens, whose home contains fine books and whose frame of conversational reference includes opera, are not so much people of means as people of personal dignity who value education and literary distinction. Mr. Rosen keeps a dry-goods store, as does Mr. Dillon in "Two Friends," modeled on the father of Cather's friends the Miner sisters.[13] Mr. Templeton, father of Vickie in "Old Mrs. Harris" and son-in-law of Mrs. Harris herself, lends money on land but makes such poor investments that he can scarcely pay his bills. "Neighbour Rosicky," returning to the immigrant society Cather had painted in *My Ántonia*, centers on a midwestern Bohemian farmer of moderate means and his relation to family members as he nears the end of his life. Each of the stories deals with people of no outward distinction, in a relatively fluid social structure, and with bonds of friendship and mutual assistance.

These bonds are most striking, perhaps, in "Old Mrs. Harris," where the local railroad executive takes the Templeton boys out on a run on a service vehicle, his wife lets townspeople use her kitchen and yard for an ice cream social, a neighbor brings coffee cake, and the chore girl (the

lowest of the low) mercifully rubs old Mrs. Harris's feet. Even the seemingly thoughtless and self-centered Victoria Templeton, the mother in
the grandmother-mother-daughter sequence, gives dimes and personal
kindness to the children of a disreputable laundry woman so they can
enjoy the ice cream social, an act that goes far toward amending our
response to her characterization as a household prima donna. Social
distinctions exist but are relatively unobtrusive; genuine poverty is kept
out of sight, as is genuine wealth; and the pang of feeling excluded or
stigmatized can be relieved by the gift of a bowl of ice cream. Most dramatic of all is the help extended by the Rosens, the Templetons' child-
less neighbors, who for no reason except their interest in a bright young
person allow Vickie the run of their library and even provide money
when her somewhat feckless father is unable to send her to college.
Cather seems to have been engaged in a forgiving reassessment of her
dying mother, also a southern woman whose graciousness was mingled
with vanity and imperiousness, trapped, like the Victoria in the story,
in a seemingly endless succession of pregnancies. Their similarity is
marked by the closeness of the names, Victoria and Virginia. Cather
also seems to have been engaged in a reminiscence and hopeful reconstruction of her relation to her hometown, imagining it as a collection
of kindly adults who want the best for her and are glad to do their bit. In
reality, she sometimes believed that most of the people of Red Cloud
envied her and deprecated her achievements.

Like *Shadows on the Rock*, the three stories of *Obscure Destinies* are
domestic, quiet, and unmomentous. Dailiness, they say, the stuff of which
life is made (*SR* 198), is not to be scorned by the literary imagination
even if it is by the young person whose desire is to get away to college
and the life "unguessed at and unforeseeable" that awaits (*OD* 156).
Vickie's impatience with the life around her is shown to be a mark of im-
maturity. Death haunts all three stories—the death of farmer Rosicky,
the deaths of the two friends, the quiet death of Vickie's self-denying
grandmother in "Old Mrs. Harris." Each asks the question of how such
ordinary lives, having ended, are to be valued, how well or poorly the
social bond served their emotional needs, and how beauty was found or
created in seemingly ordinary circumstances, in the details of everyday
life. One answer is that even housekeeping, if carried out as a meaningful ritual emphasizing quality and order, can be a construction of the
beautiful—as Cather proclaimed in a 1921 speech, declaring that the

"Americanization committee worker who persuades an old Bohemian housewife that it is better for her to feed her family out of tin cans instead of cooking them a steaming goose for dinner is committing a crime against art" (*WCIP* 147). In a letter to her mother she once called her French maid's housekeeping an art in its own right.[14]

Mrs. Rosicky may have heavy work to do as a farm wife, but her windowsills are filled with geraniums and she gladly gives away blooms. She prefers to enjoy life instead of "always skimping and saving" (*OD* 24), just as her husband preferred, when he lived in New York, to spend a dollar on the opera even though money was scarce and he could never get ahead. The beauty of their life is their willingness to enjoy it and to share their enjoyment, as when old Rosicky spontaneously goes to wash dishes for his daughter-in-law so she and her husband can go to the movies. Unembarrassed by doing everyday work, even so-called woman's work, he knows the value of simple enjoyment and wants them to have it. His "gift for loving people" is "like an ear for music or an eye for colour" (57), a kind of artistic talent.

Similarly, in "Old Mrs. Harris" loving kindness is beautiful, as are the small details people can add to their everyday lives if they have the knack or take the trouble: Mrs. Harris's reading to her grandchildren, Mrs. Rosen's artful housekeeping, Victoria's spontaneous gestures at moments when she forgets herself and her social status, the Rosens' taste for amenities such as engravings, good cuisine, and good books rather than aggressive moneymaking. There is considerable irony in the statement that Mr. Rosen was "the only unsuccessful member of a large, rich Jewish family" (*OD* 88), since in human kindness and in constructing a life of quiet beauty he is very successful indeed. In these respects he and Mrs. Rosen are much like Cécile, of *Shadows*, whose housekeeping is associated with the construction of beauty and whose personal value is demonstrated by the happiness with which she performs acts of kindness for a poor child and a grotesquely afflicted outcast. Both books' pondering of gestures of kindness to the humble is continued, indeed, from *Death Comes for the Archbishop*.

The problem is, if part of Cather wanted to see beauty in the ordinary, another part of her saw beauty only in the extraordinary, the exceptional. Often this meant that she identified art with aristocracy. Although she attempted to resolve that dilemma through the concept of a natural aristocracy of innate ability rather than wealth and social status, it remained a dilemma never fully resolved. During the years following the death of her father the tension between the two concepts was painfully bound up with tensions between past and present and between the sense of belonging and the sense of separation.

CATHER'S RENEWED fixation on the idea of art and its importance in human life seems to have been stimulated in part by her introduction in 1930 (significantly, by Jan and Isabelle Hambourg) to the celebrated Menuhin family. Moshe and Marutha Menuhin were the parents not only of the child-prodigy violinist Yehudi but of two younger daughters who were also extraordinarily accomplished musicians, Hephzibah and Yaltah. Cather was soon gushing about them, especially the "beautiful" Yehudi, to her friends. A family whose life centered on music, who were multilingual and habitually international, the Menuhins epitomized for Cather an affinity for Old World high culture combined with familial closeness.

This second element is not to be forgotten in estimating what the Menuhins quickly came to mean to her. In a note to Irene Miner Weisz written on the train after a visit in March 1931, she mentions the Menuhins in a paragraph that begins by talking about her visit to her *parents* for their fifty-fifth anniversary, in December 1927. This curious elision hints that the Menuhins were serving her as idealized surrogates for the family she was losing. They would remain, so she wrote E. K. Brown near the end of her life, one of her chief interests and joys. But beyond that they would serve as her "story" or "European novel" of the artistic life.[15] The Menuhin children seem to have taken "Aunt Willa" to represent a kind of "natural" American "rooted in the earth," but her activities with them were of quite another sort. She brought them volumes of Shakespeare and German poetry to read aloud (Menuhin 128, 130). The international element in her effort to broaden their educations confirms Yehudi's impression of what they represented for her: "what she felt had not been her birthright—the old, the European, the multilayered" (129). In claiming them, she claimed all that.

Not coincidentally, perhaps, it was during the first years of this doting friendship, bringing her into direct contact with the international musical world, that Cather conceived and wrote *Lucy Gayheart*, the story of a Nebraska girl who becomes enamored of the musical life in general and as represented in the person of a singer who moves freely between

Europe and the United States. She finished the first draft in late October 1933. January 1934 found her still struggling to shape the book out of the draft, but by July she had it ready to begin serialization in *Woman's Home Companion*.[16] It appeared in book form in August 1935, after publication of the final number of the serial version. Cather was in Europe at the time, spending six weeks in Italy with Edith Lewis followed by two months in France with the Hambourgs, during Isabelle's long final illness.

During the same period in which she wrote *Lucy Gayheart*, Cather also produced or revised the essays that made up *Not under Forty*. These merit attention in their own right, more than any except "The Novel Démeublé" have received, but they also demonstrate the unity and focus of Cather's thinking during these years. Centered on art and the practice of art, they form an important context for the fiction she was then writing—or more than a context, they serve as an echo or a cross-genre reflection. She explored in the essays the same issues she was exploring in fiction. Rarely do we encounter such reflexivity between a writer's fiction and nonfiction.

As far as its influence on subsequent understanding of Cather's work, "The Novel Démeublé" is the centerpiece of the volume. Opposing "imaginative art" and its "eternal material" to "journalism" and the "teeming, gleaming stream of the present," she formulated a theory of minimalism in the very years when Hemingway was coming to ascendancy. It was not a new idea for her. Since at least 1913 she had been insisting that "art ought to simplify" (*WCIP* 8). From even earlier days she had admired and almost certainly emulated the compression of Classical Latin, which she called in 1937 a model of terseness to cling to in a time of debased language.[17] In addition, she formulated in "The Novel Démeublé" a theory of ineffability, thereby announcing her effort to demand of language more than language could ordinarily give, to press its resources to an ultimately Romantic level so that the experience of literature would derive from (in two of the most famous of her much-quoted phrases) "whatever is felt upon the page without being specifically named there" or "the inexplicable presence of the thing not named" (*SPO* 837; *OW* 41).[18] Gelfant has observed cogently that Cather may have been reckless in locating "the affect of language" so fully in "the sensitivity of a reader who must respond to what was not on the page" (*Women* 23). The riskiness of this valorization of the reader has been evident in the history of criticism of her works. But her point is not ineffability alone, but a kind of clearing of the decks for what is most important. In the now-familiar final paragraph, she stated her goal of an uncluttered fiction whose effect would not depend on physical sensation and detail with an exclamatory hyperbole reaching beyond even her own disfurnished effects: "How wonderful it would be if we could throw all the furniture out of the window" of the novel and, in the dictum of Dumas *père*, "make a drama" simply from "one passion, and four walls" (*SPO* 837; *OW* 42–43). The ideal fiction, it seems, would not only approximate drama (literally, a play) by bringing a story before the reader with fewer words and more emotional impact than narrative usually did, but would achieve a kind of classicism and a fusion of art with religion. Once we throw that furniture out the window we "leave the room as bare as the stage of a Greek theatre, or as that house into which the glory of Pentacost descended."

An equally important essay in *Not under Forty* so far as its connection with *Lucy Gayheart* and Cather's other work of the early 1930s is "A Chance Meeting." Based on an actual encounter with the niece of Gustave Flaubert in the summer of 1930 at Aix-les-Bains, this essay was first published in *Atlantic Monthly* in February 1933, the year Cather drafted *Lucy Gayheart*.[19] Considering Flaubert's importance to her as a literary model, her chance meeting with Mme. Franklin Grout, an elderly woman who proved to be the "Caro" of his *Lettres à sa nièce Caroline*, was indeed, as Woodress labels it, "a marvelous coincidence" (*Literary* 422). We may also think it a marvelous coincidence that this was the same summer she met the Menuhins.

As the essay explains, Mme. Grout impressed Cather with her personal dignity and her devotion to the arts, going out to sketch despite the August heat and attending concerts and operas. In defiance of "the limitations of old age," she walked erectly and quickly and maintained an interest in the new, that is, "the way in which Ravel was played, when in the course of nature her interest in new music should have stopped with César Franck, surely" (*SPO* 815–19). Setting up this fact, Cather slyly refers to having heard at one of the concerts attended by Mme. Grout "such a rendition of Ravel's *La Valse* as I do not expect to hear again." So much for her own supposed resistance to newness! Only after their acquaintance had progressed considerably did the old woman reveal her identity. "The room was absolutely quiet, but there was nothing to say to this disclosure. It was like being suddenly brought up against a mountain of memories" (*SPO* 821). Mme. Grout, a living linkage to a figure whom Cather endowed with near-mystic stature, embodied the living tradition of art and possessed "a capacity for pleasure such as very few people in this world ever know at all" (*SPO* 828). Cather would give Lucy Gayheart that same responsiveness to aesthetic experience.

In 1936, three years after the first publication of "A Chance Meeting" and in the same year as its appearance in *Not under Forty*, Cather drew on the encounter with Flaubert's elderly niece for "The Old Beauty," a story that remained unpublished at her death. She retained the setting at Aix-les-Bains, with the Grand-Hôtel d'Aix where she had met Mme. Grout becoming the "Hôtel Splendide," but changed the time frame from 1930 to 1922, moving the story closer to the end of World War I, to the year in which "the world broke in two."[20] The sense of beauty in ruin glimpsed in the old lady Cather encountered in 1930 is accentuated in the story's Gabrielle Longstreet, now known as Mme. de Couçy, and there is an added odor of scandal about her. The "old beauty" has been an object of gossip because of her succession of relationships with protective males. A male narrator, Seabury, is added who had once saved her in a perilous situation. Now, many years after that event, he fortuitously encounters Mme. de Couçy through having stopped at Aix because it was a "spot that was still more or less as it used to be" (*SPO* 697). The setting is a vestige of the past, as is the "old beauty" herself. In addition, and importantly, the story accentuates the essay's emphasis on the rarity of beautiful experiences in a sea of the ordinary. But they are a rarity that must be paid for: Seabury thinks gloomily about the "extortionate price for any exceptional gift whatever" (*SPO* 700). Or as Harry Gordon says in *Lucy Gayheart*, "the day of counting costs comes along in the end, Lucy mio" (*LG* 89).

The yearning toward the past that pervades "The Old Beauty" also pervades "148 Charles Street," an essay revised and considerably lengthened for *Not under Forty* from its original 1922 version. Here the beauty of the past is represented in the literary and artistic salon held for over half a century by Annie Adams Fields, widow of publisher James T. Fields, at her home in Boston, ending with her death in 1915. Once again aesthetic loss is identified with the Great War as, with a curious evasiveness, Cather asks, "When and where were the Arnolds overthrown and the Brownings devalued? Was it at the Marne? At Versailles, when a

new geography was being made on paper?" (*SPO* 848). The war has often been seen, of course, as a catalyst for the great change in sensibility
that we call modernism, diminishing in "stature and pertinence" the
"'masters' of the last century" and leaving them "remote and shadowy,"
the old faith in their cultural sway "shaken." Even in the prewar days
when Cather visited at 148 Charles Street, where she met Sarah Orne
Jewett, the "aristocracy of letters and art" that prevailed within stood in
marked contrast to the "noisy street" of a more democratic or at least
more common everyday life (*SPO* 838–39). Once again, then, she juxta-
poses the everyday and the world of art. As a kind of spatial equivalence
of the change wrought by the war, a garage now stands on the site.

This kind of contrast between the fine and the common and a willingness to identify the beautiful with the aristocratic runs throughout
Not under Forty. So, too, does the idea of the female artist or appreciator
of beauty. Two of the six essays, both revised from original publication in
1925, are about women writers: Jewett, the beauty of whose work always
blossoms in the ordinary, and Katherine Mansfield, whose method,
Cather says, was "to approach the major forces of life through compar-
atively trivial incidents" (*SPO* 877; *OW* 108).[21] All of these ideas come
together in *Lucy Gayheart.*

Lucy Gayheart is a powerfully valedictory novel—perhaps, as Skaggs
reads it, a "novel of forgiveness" of Isabelle McClung Hambourg (*After*
164), but even more, forgiveness of Red Cloud and Cather's family, or
even of herself. The autobiographical significance of the retrospective,
pardoning view is evident in her unusually specific dating of the story.
The opening sequence is placed at the end of the Christmas 1901 holiday, thus January 1902. From that we can date the rest of the novel. The
following Christmas finds Lucy at home grieving the death of Clement
Sebastian, the great singer for whom she served as practice accompanist
during part of that year; on Christmas Day 1902 she writes to her piano
teacher in Chicago saying she wants to come back. She dies, then, in
January 1903. Book Three is placed twenty-five years later. If that is
"winter" 1927, as the text indicates, the death of Lucy's sister Pauline
five years before must have occurred in 1922. Once again Cather's imagination reached for that enigmatic year when the world broke in two.

In December 1927 (and one would assume into or through January
1928) Cather had enjoyed good skating during her long visit in Red

Cloud; hence the opening ice skating scene. But hence, too, the association of skating with death, because soon afterward her father died. The long meditation that comprises most of Book Three, as Harry Gordon looks back on what Lucy had meant to him, is in a sense the meditation on her own departure in pursuit of art that she can imagine that her father would have engaged in if she had died in his place. It is especially important, then, that the tone of Harry's meditation is forgiving. Part of what Cather needed to forgive herself, in the wake of her parents' death and her subsequent refusal to revisit Red Cloud, was the entire set of life choices that had taken her away.[22] She had enacted the struggle she identifies in "Katherine Mansfield" as the "tragic necessity" of "escaping, running away, trying to break the net which circumstances and [her] own affections" wove about her (*SPO* 878, *OW* 109). Like Lucy with Clement Sebastian, she could claim to have gone "all the way" with art whereas she had not quite, since she still regretted the loss of home and homeliness, commonness.

Looking back on her life choices, Cather also looks back on her work. The most obvious of the novel's numerous retrospective echoes are of *The Song of the Lark*, but others are of "The Joy of Nelly Deane," a 1911 story of another vivacious young woman who dies because of a "rigid" male (Meyering 126), and her short stories about singers in general. The orchard scene in Book Two recalls the orchard scene in *O Pioneers!*, and Lucy's anxiety about the felling of the apple trees recalls the felling of the cherry tree in *One of Ours*. Other resonances of *One of Ours* are Harry's quixotic service in an ambulance unit during the Great War and his wife's satisfaction in being independent. The Gayhearts' attendance of a performance of *The Bohemian Girl* recalls Cather's story of the same title, while opera scenes in Chicago recall the excursion to the opera in *The Professor's House*. The resurgence of Lucy's will to live when she falls through the ice and realizes she is in mortal danger recalls the near-suicide scene in *The Professor's House*, but this time there is no rescue. References to the creation of beauty and order through domestic ritual—the neat maintenance of a bedroom, the creation of a household of "colour and warmth" (*LG* 138)—importantly reprise *Shadows on the Rock*. Importantly, that is, because of the connection with the larger theme of the place of beauty and art within common dailiness.

Looking back, Cather also summoned from the past two figures who served as models for her heroine. One was a girl named Sadie Becker, who had been an accompanist in New York before her family moved to Red Cloud. It must have seemed to Cather, when this personage suddenly turned up in her hometown, as though the world of art had dropped down into the midst of the ordinary. Known for her ice skating, the Becker girl subsequently became an object of gossip (Rosowski, *Voyage* 220). The other was a Miss Gayhardt whom Cather met at a dance a few months before she left Nebraska for her first job, and whom she found appealing and rather sad.[23]

Lucy Gayheart herself is a rather common girl. Her name, perhaps a pointer to the popular romance genre from which Cather departs, suggests vapidness, a quality Cather highlights by spelling it in this hearts-and-flowers way, Gayheart, rather than in the German of the Miss Gayhardt from whom she borrowed it. The text cues us to the change when Sebastian guesses that Lucy's family is German. In German, too, the name Gayhardt slightly echoes *gehör*, which means "hearing" or "a musical ear." That is Lucy's one real distinction at the outset: she *hears;* she absorbs, apprehends, and intensely responds to experience. Like her father, she has a disposition that takes "satisfaction out of good health and simple pleasures" (*LG* 5), and she regards the study of music as "a natural form of pleasure" (4). That disposition is not unimportant; the first requirement of the artist is the ability to invest oneself in experience. Her assumption that she will gain a "means of earning money" and then go back to Haverford to live by giving piano lessons is not presented as an unworthy one, unless one is a serious artist.

Lucy, initially, is not. This is her great difference from Thea Kronborg, to whom she is regularly and negatively compared. Both come from ordinary little towns and families of ordinary means. Skaggs is severe but not inaccurate in writing that they "start from the same kind of impecunious family background set in the same kind of culturally impoverished midwestern small-town place" (*After* 151). Thea's ability and drive are evident from the beginning, while Lucy's do not emerge until very near the end. Initially, she is simply one of those "sensitive protagonists" of Cather's who "yearn for escape from an uncongenial family" (Gelfant, "What" 91). The rhythm of the train she takes to Chicago makes her think of "escape, change, chance . . . life hurrying forward" (*LG* 20). The motion that characterizes Lucy has been seen as all "movement that goes nowhere" and "the primary moral she conveys" as the need for a sense of direction and the will power to pursue it.

I have come to see her characterization instead as a calculated risk and the point of the book (perhaps not so well realized as it might be; Cather conceded the book was not among her best) as the way the artist flowers out of the silly girl, or in Susan Hallgarth's words, the fact that "the most stereotypically feminine of women can learn to take herself seriously and choose to pursue the 'fugitive gleam'" (170).[24]

In both novel and heroine, the common and the transcendent are curiously juxtaposed, even intermingled. The bright star of the beautiful shines out at the end of a day of fun in the opening scene, just as art grows miraculously out of ordinary beginnings. The artist manqué herself blossoms as an image of beauty in the memories of ordinary people such as Lucy's would-have-been lover, Harry Gordon. Gelfant sees in these juxtapositions Cather's attempt to turn the sentimental love story into "an allegory of Romantic desire" (*Women* 120). Cather admitted (to a reader who had noticed her alteration of the text of the *Elijah* oratorio sung by Sebastian) that the story came dangerously close to the sentimental but ascribed its sentimentality to a young person's hero worship rather than erotic love. The distinction is important. The novel may verge on but does not fall into sentimentality for two reasons: its purposes are not trite, and it deals with the growing-up process of a very young girl, in whom sentimentality seems natural. Drawing on her memories of two young women, Cather sought to examine the dissonances, or surprising modulations, generated when a fairly ordinary person conceives a serious love for beauty and the rigor of art. Lucy has the first, an instinctual love for beauty, when we meet her in the opening ice skating scene. She gains the second, the love for the rigor of art, just in time to die in the closing ice skating scene. She begins as an appreciator or absorber of beauty and ends at a point of readiness to be a producer of it, a serious artist.[25]

Cather's structural sense in this late work is extraordinary. Even the brief introductory chapter establishing a community memory of Lucy initiates important patterns and anticipates the retrospective view at the end.[26] It establishes in the first half-dozen words the presence of the treacherous Platte River; it posits Lucy's characteristic motion (notably, "with intense direction"); it locates the Gayheart house on the west edge of town, where Harry Gordon walks at the end; it tells us that Lucy and her father are people who delight in daily life and that Lucy is not, at this point, a girl who thinks of a career: all that in a brief introduction.

Then in the second chapter comes the ice skating, with its energy and freshness, its physical joy and incipient sexual charge, and the perhaps tarnishing but purposeful detail of Lucy and Harry's slipping away to drink a little Scotch, setting up the idea of false warming in the ice skating scene at the end of the book, when Lucy's hot anger keeps her from noticing that the river has shifted its course.

More important, the opening ice skating scene leads to a moment as crucial to Lucy's character as Thea's salute to the eagle in Panther Canyon is to hers. The everyday abruptly shifts to the transcendent:

> Suddenly Lucy started and struggled under the tight blankets. In the darkening sky she had seen the first star come out; it brought her heart into her throat. That point of silver light spoke to her like a signal, released another kind of life and feeling which did not belong here. It overpowered her. With a mere thought she had reached that star and it had answered, recognition had flashed between. Something knew, then, in the unknowing waste: something had always known, forever! That joy of saluting what is far above one was an eternal thing, not merely something that had happened to her ignorance and her foolish heart. (9–10)

Her extraordinary responsiveness to beauty is established at a stroke, and with it the motifs of stars and of heights and depths that will play throughout the book.

This flashing out of the star points us to an elaborate Keatsean parallel that has its origins in Keats's "Bright Star" sonnet. Gelfant, in reading the novel as an allegory of Romantic desire, emphasizes the pervasive presence of Keats, mentioning echoes of the great odes and "The Eve of St. Agnes," but despite observing that "the stars remain steadfast" (*Women* 140), she does not identify the allusion. The first line of the sonnet— "Bright star, would I were steadfast as thou art"—asserts a relationship between self and star, precisely as Lucy claims, and identifies her need for steadfastness, the quality to which she works her way at the end, just before her fatal skating. Playing through the novel along with the image of the star is the sonnet's wish to remain

> Pillow'd upon my fair love's ripening breast,
> To feel for ever its soft fall and swell,
> Awake for ever in a sweet unrest,
> Still, still to hear her tender-taken breath . . .

Lucy's head lies against Sebastian's shoulder (75, 105) and, she "drift[s] into" his "soft, deep breathing" (73, 75). The sonnet's concluding "And so live ever—or else swoon to death" anticipates the stark alternatives before Lucy at the end of the novel. Unable to live ever at the pitch of bright transcendence epitomized by the star, she falls into restlessness and anger and so sinks to death.

Cather buried Keats in this text almost as deeply as she buried *Parsifal* in *One of Ours*. Still, however profoundly she participated in the Romantic aspiration toward the star of supernal beauty, she was also a modernist whose vision of the artist's tragic death was not of an ecstatic swooning but an ironic entrapment by the branches of a submerged tree. Lucy hopes to rise above the pettiness of hometown life just as she was "lifted up above the sweating city" in the elevator to Sebastian's studio, where "the trivial and disturbing" were "shut out" (*LG* 110), but she will be dropped into ordinary life again just as she "got into the elevator" at the end of a half-day practice session and "dropped down into Chicago" (63). The trivial and the supernal, low and high, are intertwined; she cannot simply turn her back on the one and have the other.

If Lucy's purpose in escaping Haverford is unclear, it becomes even less clear after she becomes enthralled by Clement Sebastian. As his practice (not performance) accompanist, she focuses her desire on him, as both a sexual and an aesthetic object. During this period her gay heart becomes a submissive heart; she gains happiness only from serving (accompanying) him, while he feeds on her youthful vitality to counteract his own lassitude. Devotion to beauty becomes devotion to a person, an ego. Sebastian provides lessons for her as an artist, such as the lesson that words in a song convey meaning beyond their literal reference ("the thing not named"), but she cannot absorb them until she transfers her ardor from the singer to the song. During their first work session he sang "If with all your heart you truly seek Him"; she must come to understand "Him" in a nonliteral way.

Lucy will not regain her intensity and engage in true seeking until she stops trailing after this male to whom she looks for meaning and then, after his death, stops trailing after Harry Gordon for emotional succor (Gelfant, *Women* 137). When she stops fixating on the star performer, Sebastian, and returns her vision to the distant star of art— significantly, after watching a performance by a woman artist—she gains the will to leave Haverford for good. The thought "flashe[s] into her mind," as the distant star had brought her a "flash of understanding" in the opening skating scene, that perhaps "Life itself," not Clement Sebastian, was the lover toward which she had yearned (*LG* 155). The next day, Christmas Day (the day of divine beginning; again, religion and art are one), she writes to her teacher Auerbach that the only answer for her is "to do the things I used to do and to do them harder" (156). Having at last gained a sense of direction, she sets her face toward art and its rigor. But in this ironic novel, setting her face toward life turns out to be setting her face toward death. Her discovery of her purpose comes too late. If she has not gone "all the way," as she tells Harry she did with Sebastian, knowing full well that he would misunderstand, she has at any rate gone too far and down too many wrong roads.

Frustrated by the delay Auerbach proposes and irritated by her sister's small-mindedness, she rushes out into a day colder than she realized and is driven to fury by Harry Gordon's refusal to give her a ride. In her anger she fails to notice signs that the river has shifted its channel and skates out onto thin ice. Failing to notice is a fatal deficiency in an artist.

As in *The Song of the Lark*, art entails considerable ruthlessness, and part of Cather's valedictory impulse here, to the extent that she is writing displaced autobiography, may be the urge to say she is sorry for that. Lucy has spent a lifetime simply assuming the help and subordination of her father and sister, without ever thinking of the cost to them. The novel extends understanding and perhaps regret to even such a person as Pauline, who is almost always disagreeable and small-minded, never beautiful. Pauline's claim that she and her father had "made a great sacrifice" so that Lucy could study music rings true, even if she does say it gracelessly, having hoarded the receipts. We cannot suppose she really enjoys raising an onion crop to counteract their father's not being "a good manager" (*LG* 5). Certainly we believe it when the narrator intimates that Lucy was sometimes "a hard person to live with" (161). Cather, too, could be hard to live with. She once wrote a letter of apology to her mother promising to be calm and pleasant next time.[27] The artist is a drain on those around her, and her escape wish entails guilt toward those she climbs over in leaving.

One way in which Cather tries to expiate that guilt is by making a plea for sympathy, by showing the sufferings and hardships of the artist. A more important way is by proposing that art and the artist serve as means of beautifying everyday life for those who are not artists themselves. Contemplating her own mortality in the wake of her parents' death, she sought by making that proposal to claim a value for her life beyond the personal. She had celebrated the beauty *of* the everyday in *Shadows on the Rock* and now reasserted the idea, in part by showing that taking pleasure in simple things for their own sake allows quotidian life to become an experience of beauty, but also by showing the potential for common life to be redeemed by unexpected irruptions of beauty. At a number of points in the text, beauty blossoms naturally in the midst of the everyday. The appearance of the star at the end of the opening ice skating scene is a particularly significant instance from its association with Lucy's first name (meaning light) and with Christmas, when she will move toward a redeemed selfhood. Another is the "pink glow" that comes into the eastern sky shortly before sunset, for those who have the eyes to look (158).[28] The artist serves society by facilitating moments of humanly created beauty that redeem experience from the commonplace just as natural beauty does. We see such a moment when Sebastian's valet, coming through the studio with a bag of dirty laundry, pauses to listen and feels so moved that he exclaims "in a husky voice," "*Ecco una cosa molto bella!*" (40). Ordinary working people, "plumbers and brewers and bank clerks and dressmakers," who sing in a choral society with which Sebastian appears in concert find in the experience "something to help them through their lives" (57).

The culminating example of art's appearance within the commonplace is the road production of *The Bohemian Girl* that Lucy and her father and Pauline attend shortly before Christmas. An aging soprano with "worn" voice sings "humdrum music to humdrum people" so well that she gives "freshness to the foolish old words," allowing the "old songs, even the most hackneyed," to reach their "full value" (*LG* 152). An audience of small-town people, many of whom have shown themselves to be mean-spirited enough, have a moment of fineness dropped into their lives. This tired singer, past her prime, invests her full art in a performance that could have been routine, simply a way to make a living. Why, Lucy asks, was it "worth while" to her to give more? (153). No answer is given, yet one knows the answer. It is worthwhile because art is worthwhile; it is its own reason. Lucy's self-definition as an artist is rekindled in response. She feels a "wild kind of excitement" and wants to claim the singer's experience as her own, to "run away tonight, by any train, back to a world that strove after excellence" (153). From that evening on, she forms "something that was like a purpose," precisely what she had lacked during her previous years of escape and study.

The time setting of Lucy's transformation is significant: Christmas, the time when, in the theological system to which Cather gave at least nominal allegiance, the divine enters human life. The day before Christmas she is filled with energy. "Wad[ing] through deep snowdrifts" to take treats to friends and neighbors, she is possessed by something like "the feeling children have about Christmas, that it is a time of miracles, when the angels are near the earth, and any wayside weed may suddenly become a rose bush or a Christmas tree" (154). Because of her renewed —or actually new—sense of being caught up into artistic purpose, the "fugitive gleam" of beauty she used to intuit has become "an actual possession" (155). Like an incarnation, it is a sacramental event. Sebastian, the man, becomes "the door and the way" (echoing the biblical "the way and the life") to the knowledge of artistic discipline (155). She knows now that if she knocks at that door, it will be opened to her. Throwing open her window (a particularly meaningful act for Cather), Lucy reaches out, not toward her romantic memories of Clement Sebastian personally, but toward the sources of his art, and recalls the line he had sung, now with the full statement completing the conditional clause: "*If with all your heart you truly seek Him, you shall ever surely find Him.*" The completion of the line, supported by the concentrated allusion to both Matthew 7:7 and John 14:6 in "the door and the way," transforms into an idea about art a religious idea that Cather had used earlier in *My Mortal Enemy*, where "in religion seeking is finding" (77). Once again, as she had in her first days in Pittsburgh in 1896, she conflates the two. Religion is art; art is religion.

Lucy does not, of course, achieve her goal of going back and working harder. Anger and resentment drag her down as inexorably as the river drags her under when her skate catches an underwater tangle of branches, after the ice gives way under her. Death, it seems, wins. Clement Sebastian's death at the end of Book One comes when he is pulled down into the cold water of Lake Como by the grasp of his performance accompanist, who does not swim. Lucy's death at the end of Book Two occurs when she is pulled down into the freezing water of the Platte River by an equally unrelenting underwater grasp. Book Three, set twenty-five years later, begins with death: the funeral of Lucy's father, attended by Harry Gordon. Little happens. Yet Cather said not only that Book Three was the best part of the novel and the one most in her own voice (by which she may have been referring simply to her practice of ending with a retrospective view) but that Book One would not make sense without Book Three.[29]

It is interesting that she did not say the *novel* would not make sense without Book Three, but that Book One would not. The story in Book One of Lucy's abject hero worship and her failure to be an artist in her own right, the story in which her character is "handled roughly by the narrator" (Urgo, *Myth* 114), would make perfect sense by itself if the book ended there. The point would be to show how silly a girl with notions about Capital-B-Beauty can be. What would not make sense about Book One without Book Three would be why the novel continued past that point, why the story was worth any more attention. In a sense, the transformation in the artistic consciousness that occurs near the end of Book Two answers that question, but only for Lucy herself and only if the irony of her death is the last word. But Cather did not usually favor ironic endings. The real story is what happens after Lucy's death, what she means to her hometown.[30]

Cather said of *The Song of the Lark* that her point from first to last was Moonstone. For most readers, the main interest from first to last is Thea. In *Lucy Gayheart* Cather rewrote *Lark* as the story of a girl more ordinary than exceptional and the story of apparent failure rather than conspicuous success. The point of *this* story is how rare it is for a woman to have enough self-knowledge, honesty, energy, and courage to escape from culturally defined roles and emotional ties, to break free of deadening ordinariness and deliver herself into art" (Hallgarth 170). Or to turn that around, how hard society makes it for a woman to do so. In *Shadows on the Rock*, Cécile resolved the problem by not conceiving of it as a problem; she embraced the destiny that society imposed and found beauty in it. But the female center of the shadow story, Jeanne Le Ber, finds society's pressure so intolerable that she escapes by embracing an even harder destiny, that of the cloister and mortification of the flesh. In *Death Comes for the Archbishop* the theme of society's pressure on women to conform is yet more covert. After introducing it in glimpses of women's straitened lives, Cather refused even to see that it was there, choosing to describe the novel as a book altogether without women. In *Lucy Gayheart* she was more nearly direct in dealing with the idea of resistance to gender conformity that she had embedded among the things not named in her previous two novels.

Even more emphatically, she rewrote *Lark*—this time convincingly —as the story of what society can make of the woman who breaks free of ordinary patterns of living to embrace the life of art. In Book Three she asks how society constructs the meaning of its experience of such a woman.

Society in the person of Harry does not succeed in doing much with the gender implications of the story. In Lucy's mind, freedom from gender constraints is crucial to the slow liberation that Chicago brings her. There she can "come and go like a boy" (*LG* 22). She is "rather boyish" in Sebastian's mind as well; he urges her to dream they are both twenty and "taking a walking trip in the French Alps" as he and a male friend had once done in his youth (*LG* 67, 72). In part, he thinks this way because it is convenient to evade the fact that she is thinking of him sexually, or more precisely, romantically. Harry, too, thinks of Lucy as, in a sense, a boy, a fourteen-year-old "slip of a girl in boy's overalls, barefoot" (190), but does not pursue the issue of what happened to the irrepressible spirit she then represented. What happened was the pressure of assumptions and expectations brought to bear on a female of marriageable age. In a sense, gender killed Lucy. But that meaning is in the text for the reader, not for Harry.

Instead, what Harry makes of Lucy is a glimpse of beauty, or devotion to beauty, that helps him reconceive the rest of his rather humdrum life among people "more or less like himself." The ordinary prevails, and the ordinary person never experiences that flash of identification with the star that Lucy felt. Yet such people know that *she* has it, and such knowledge makes them aware of the possibility of something more. Remembering her, Harry goes to the window and stands "looking up at the bright winter stars" (*LG* 185). No flash is recorded for him, but we have to suppose it is better to look at the stars than not to look at them. Harry knows that Lucy was "sustained by something that never let her drop into the common world" (181), even though her body certainly "dropped" and he had once insisted that biological facts were all. The biological fact is that she died. But the "feeling," as she had once defined the importance of an Impressionist painting (85), continues. What she has meant to the town is a demonstration that commonness is not the whole story, that there can also be spots of beauty—and in choosing this phrase I am thinking very specifically of Wordsworth's "spots of time." For Harry, Lucy exists as a kind of mental star. No longer "despairing" and "beseeching" (not after her yell of anger!), she is a distant image near the "far horizon line" (like the evening star) that he associates with "the fine things of youth, which do not change" (189). Yet he also thinks of her *as* change, as motion. Her essence, in his memory, is recorded in her running footprints. Nowhere does Cather reveal more clearly her affiliation with the philosophy of Henri Bergson, who defined reality as change.[31] Permanence, Bergson taught and Cather teaches here, is process, an endless escaping from rigid categories.

The pursuit of art, then, as personified by Lucy, is redemptive for the non-artist, the nonpursuer. Indeed, Cather presses the idea of redemption very far toward a religious sense. Harry's anger at himself and at Lucy has been taken away by her suffering. The artist is a suffering servant. She has also been redemptive in his life by loosening up his thinking, opening him to alternative possibilities, and thus helping him become a different sort of banker than he might have been. Certainly the novel is not explicit on this point; we would not expect a Cather novel to be. Harry went away to the war, and people felt "a change in him when he came back." For one thing, he became more friendly with Mr. Gayheart, and for the past eight years—that is, since 1919; once again Cather's chronology is important—played chess with him several times a week (*LG* 176–77). Nothing directly links Lucy's creativity with these changes. Yet the one example given of Harry's "strange" behavior (as his chief clerk sees it) is an instance when he was merciful in a foreclosure after having paid tribute to her memory (179–80).

Harry's world, too, it seems, broke in two ("kingdoms had gone down and the old beliefs of men had been shattered"), and part of what was left behind in the old time was "that day when he refused Lucy Gayheart a courtesy" (185). Now all that remains is her piano and the knowledge that she was "the best thing he had to remember" (187). Going into the Gayheart house one last time, he takes a single souvenir: a silver-framed picture of Clement Sebastian. His reminders of her, as if he needed any, will be the imprint of her bare running foot and an image of the kind of artist she wanted to be or to serve.

How such an artist arises from the lineage and society of ordinary people remains a mystery, even a kind of miracle, like the flashing out of Lucy's star. But if one artist can come out of a place like Haverford, there is no reason why another cannot. The townspeople think of Lucy, not with resentment of her desire to escape and not as a scandal (despite gossip), but simply in terms of movement and intensity, the building blocks of her art. The place of art in a democratic society is both to provide redemptive glimpses of beauty and, by showing that not everyone sees the world alike, to create the possibility of change. The artist's function in a democracy, then, is ultimately a political as well as a religious one.

11

RECRIMINATION AND RECONCILIATION

Grandmither, gie me your still, white hands, that lie upon your breast,
For mine do beat the dark all night and never find me rest
—"'Grandmither, think not I forget'"

Mothers soft lullabies sighing,
And the dead, under all!
—"In Media Vita"

IN *Shadows on the Rock* Cather crossed the Canadian border to imagine
the past and its ideals of female development. In *Sapphira and the Slave
Girl* (1940) she crossed a border of a different kind, the Mason-Dixon
Line, to reencounter the South and reconstrue a more personal past as
well as a social and political one. In doing so, she once again examined
issues of female development. It is hard to imagine two novels more
dissimilar in setting and tone and in the complexity with which they
engage issues that are yet so similar.

With *Shadows* she initiated a series of major works centering on issues
of family relationships, especially between mother and daughter, and on
the problem of the daughter's emergence from such relationships. She
again took up the idea of the girl lacking a mother in *Lucy Gayheart* but
complicated the situation by giving Lucy a sister who is in some ways
like a mother. Pauline is also a blocking figure much like the envious sister in *The Song of the Lark*—at once devoted and cold, sacrificing and
resentful of sacrifices. The theme of motherhood and mothering, or
their lack, is both carried forward and (as in "Old Mrs. Harris") problematized (see Zitter 288). Recognizing the mixed nature of her relationship with a sister who is at once motherly and nonmotherly, Lucy

realizes what Cather had tried to avoid recognizing in her own family: "Personal hatred and family affection are not incompatible" (*LG* 141).

The same sharp ambivalence pervades *Sapphira*. As Cather turned increasingly toward issues of family relationships in the wake of her father's death and then her mother's, and especially toward the complex female inheritance from which young women emerged (or not) into independent selfhood and work, the conflicted nature of her relationship to her family, and in particular her mother, continued to occupy her. In what proved to be her last novel, she addressed that issue by returning to her southern origins with a directness unparalleled in any of her preceding work, a directness that led her to write herself into the novel in her own person in a way that deconstructs the boundary between fiction and nonfiction. Writing herself and her family into the text in multiple roles, she split their troublingly inconsistent personas into separate characters, apparently in the hope of defining them at last. But even though the novel ends with restoration and reunion, its ambiguities remain unresolved. We are left with more of a statement of "the mixed nature of all human beings" and the "ultimately impenetrable" nature of meaning than a clarification or a laying to rest of tensions (Gwin 137, 149).[1]

Much the same can be said of the novel's meditation on history, the South, and the problems of the American *polis*. *Sapphira* has sometimes been read as a book as much about "American historical identity" as it is about family identity and reconciliation (Urgo, *Myth* 86; Reynolds 46). And appropriately so. It displays a compelling sense of the oppressive weight of history and the social injustices deeply embedded within the American myth of economic and social advancement. However keen her desire to convey delight in customs remembered from childhood and a society she could think of as representing stability, however much she wanted to see within the hierarchies of that society a pervasive good will expressing itself through noblesse oblige, she could not evade the undercurrents that ran through a situation of such inequality. Characteristically, both her affirmations and her misgivings are buried deep in the text as inferences to be drawn from hints and juxtapositions. The fullness of her novelistic intentions (and tensions) relies, as always, on things not named. That they *were* intentions, not solely unintended meanings emerging from unconscious or unacknowledged levels of awareness, is established by a letter in which she defined her purpose in the novel as the suggestion of an elusive sense of evil, which she called "the Terrible," lurking within everyday domestic life.[2] One of the un-named terrible presences positioned behind the surface trappings of the novel is the oppressive set of public concerns and fears from which she was taking refuge by turning toward the past. *Sapphira* is a text both of the Great Depression and of the threat of war.

IN CROSSING the border between North and South and between fiction and nonfiction, Cather also transgressed, and thereby called into ques-tion, the border between the private and the public, a boundary that has historically been of particular significance for women's lives. Seeking reconciliation with her mother through an act of the imagination set in the mother state, Virginia, she also envisioned a reconnection of past and present and a reconciliation of issues of gender and of race, the latter an issue traditionally identified with north-south sectionalism. But the mother state is the site of slavery, emotional as well as institutional, and thus of guilt and the need to escape. It is as if, in returning to her place of origins, Cather returned to her youthful sense of home as a place of imprisonment and to her own family's participation in one of the nation's great evils and its heritage. When Langston Hughes wrote her a letter of congratulation, she replied that she had known personally all the "colored people" in the book and had been very fond of some of them.[3]

Cather made this multidimensional return at a time when her own life had broken in two and seemed to go on breaking up. During the 1930s she had lapsed into deepening depression and withdrawal. After her father's death and her mother's protracted dying, she was struck another hard blow when reviewers of *Shadows on the Rock* accused her of escapism. The influential Granville Hicks spoke scathingly of her work as "supine romanticism." Paradoxically, the book was a great success commercially. The public, it seems, wanted goodness, domestic compe-tence, and especially escape from the troubles of the Great Depression. Romines has argued cogently that like the "Little House" books by Laura Ingalls Wilder, which began appearing in 1932, *Shadows* responded to the Depression-era emphasis on caution and ingenuity in stretching household resources (*Constructing* 113–14). In that sense, it is not escap-ist at all. But its address of the issues of its day was indirect, to say the least, and Marxist or Marxist-influenced critics such as Hicks accused her of turning her back on social ills. She replied, after a judicious interval, in a letter to *The Commonweal* that appears in *On Writing* as "Escapism."

With its references to "the Radical editor" and "loyalty to a party" (*OW* 20), it all but names the camp of the enemy. Despite her appearance of self-assurance, however, she was once again, as with *One of Ours*, acutely distressed by adverse critical reception.

In 1935 Cather's life was further darkened as Isabelle fell seriously ill with nephritis. Jan Hambourg brought her to New York for medical attention while he attempted to bolster their sagging finances by concertizing, after having been inactive for many years, and Cather tired herself with daily attendance at the hospital. When the concert schedule took them to Chicago, she went along and took a room in a hotel across the street from theirs to continue her caregiving. Toward the end of the summer the Hambourgs went back to France. A week later Cather sailed for Europe with Edith Lewis to restore herself and, she said, regain her soul. She seems to have enjoyed a good rest. But after nearly three months, part of it spent with Isabelle while Edith visited other friends, she felt she must go home, even though she found it very hard to leave, knowing the gravity of Isabelle's condition. In accordance with Isabelle's wishes, she and Edith slipped away without saying goodbye.[4]

Although Cather had wanted badly to get back to work, she found herself unable to do so, citing as cause the year's prolonged strain on her nerves. She spoke of wishing to go to Red Cloud but, as she would year after year, said she did not feel up to it and had better wait. She made transparent excuses to avoid a visit from her old friend George Seibel. During the summer of 1936 she was cheered by having her brother Roscoe's twin daughters with her at Grand Manan but then complained to Fanny Butcher that she had missed her solitude.[5] She was distressed by illnesses of friends and of the husband of her favorite niece, Mary Virginia. In December a quarrel erupted with Zoë Akins, who had brought to her attention a stranger's stage version of *A Lost Lady*. Cornelia Otis Skinner, with whom she had enjoyed an acquaintance that began with a letter in praise of "Two Friends," died. Filmmakers (whom she referred to with profanity) were after *My Ántonia*, and Ferris Greenslet pestered her for permission to put out an edition of *Ántonia* with illustrations by Grant Wood. Irritating reports of her long-ago visit with A. E. Housman appeared. Her letters became, for the most part, growls and laments.

The year 1938 brought disasters. In May, as if in fulfillment of long-standing anxieties, someone smashed her right hand in the door of a drug store. On June 13 the brother who had been nearest and dearest to her, Douglass, died of a sudden heart attack. On October 10 Isabelle died. She had lost, she said, the two people she loved most in the world—a statement that curiously sets aside Edith Lewis, always a puzzling shadow figure in Cather's life. She told Irene Miner Weisz, with grim brevity, that she scarcely knew how to go on. Several months later she wrote somberly to Dorothy Canfield Fisher that it had been the hardest year of her life and she would never be the same again.[6] She wished people would leave her alone and not try to comfort her with letters and visits. She did not *want* comfort, she complained, but only peace and quiet and time to think—about a lot of things.

Besides her personal devastation, Cather was distressed by the gloom and hardship of the Great Depression. With another curious omission, this time of her mother, she wrote Mary Miner that she was glad her father had not lived to see such hard times, and lamented to Mary Austin that it was a dreadful time to have to live through. Emotionally, the Depression hit her hard. How hard it hit her financially, as book sales declined along with the rest of the economy, is hard to say. Unlike many Americans, she at any rate continued to have an income. But she felt the financial strain of the Depression through increased charitable giving as she attempted to stave off ruin for families she cared about in Nebraska, whose troubles she regarded as an inherited duty—a belief in which we can see the continuing traces of her southern origins. She made it a practice to send boxes of foodstuffs and clothing to various families on the Divide, sent checks to Annie Pavelka, and saved the Pavelka farm from foreclosure. Resisting appeals in behalf of organized charities (by Mary Austin and Mabel Dodge Luhan, among others), she directed her contributions instead to the maintenance of individual families. Her emphasis on Sapphira's strength and on the restoration and persistence of familial unity in the novel reflects in part her wish to affirm the ability of family units to survive the pressures of these troubled times. Indeed, her frequently noted tendency during these years to withdraw from wide social contact and her resistance to mass solutions such as those undertaken by the federal government under the presidency of Franklin D. Roosevelt are part and parcel of this effort to keep believing in individual and familial adequacy.[7]

It is entirely in keeping with Cather's lifelong emphasis on the individual, often the exceptional individual, that she would prefer personal charity to general programs of relief. Her ingrained dislike of collective behavior was expressed in an exclamatory note to Ferris Greenslet in which, responding to an advertising department request for a list of her clubs, she thanked God that she did not belong to any club in the world except the Episcopal Church Guild in Red Cloud. That was not strictly true, but close enough. She distrusted mass movements and organized activities, telling Henry Seidel Canby, for example, that people ought to stay at home and work instead of attending an international meeting planned by PEN, the writers' organization. As she continued to provide financial help, apparently of modest amounts, to various acquaintances and relatives in Nebraska even long after the war, she remarked to Carrie, surely gratuitously, that she always preferred to help individuals rather than institutions.[8]

In addition to her worries over the Depression, she realized that the world was once again heading into the calamity of war. While Europe braced itself, political leaders and ordinary citizens in America carried on a debate over neutrality. At a time when Cather's personal world had been broken by the deaths of those she loved best, it appeared that the world was about to break in two again, if not be smashed altogether. She implored Yaltah Menuhin to see Venice before bombs destroyed it. Ferris Greenslet, almost as much her friend by now as her editor, agreed that amid "wars and rumors of war" it was indeed "a bad world."[9]

Clearly, Cather had ample reason to wish she could retreat to a more congenial time, free of the griefs under which she was sinking. For years during the middle and late 1930s she worked on her book about the Virginia society in which she had been born and had spent her early years, repeatedly dropping the project as both emotional and physical blows (her damaged hand, repeated bouts of influenza, eye fatigue) rained down on her, but repeatedly resuming it. Work on the novel offered an escape from present troubles to a day when those troubles could not have been foreseen. Though its evocation of a time when war was brewing reflects the years when it was written, the book often seems old-fashioned. Its way of life belonged not only on the far side of that rift Cather often invoked, before World War I broke the world in two, but on the far side of the Civil War, which broke the *South's* world in two. Escaping to the past, she confronted there a world riven by jealousies and resentments, racial and sexual injustice, and (though the characters in the novel do not seem to realize it) the imminence of war.

In writing of this world, Cather continued her practice of formal experimentation, once again, and even more emphatically than before, unsettling the reality base of her fiction by unsettling the distinction between fiction and fact. In both its indirectness and its formal experimentation, for all that it is disguised by a seemingly old-fashioned surface, *Sapphira* seals Cather's place not only within modernism but as an anticipator of postmodernism.[10]

OUT OF THE troubled brew of *Sapphira*'s origins there emerged a novel peculiarly "unpleasant" (Skaggs, *After* 167) in both its general atmosphere and its central character. Surprisingly, critics have sometimes spoken of it as a tribute to a gracious society. Elements of tribute are there, to be sure: a certain quaintness of custom seen in niceties of table service and other household practices, a closeness of personal acquaintance, the mutual dependence of at least some neighbors on one another (people left a candle lighted and the front door open if they needed help at night), and the beauty of hills and woods that so delighted Cather during her springtime visit in 1938. Edith Lewis's recollections of Cather's attention to the blossoming woods along the road up Timber Ridge (183) are confirmed in her *Field Book of American Wild Flowers*, where she wrote "Virginia 1938" beside listings of flowering dogwood (318) and calamus or sweet fig (16) and "Timber Ridge, Virginia, 1938" beside the entry for pinxter flower or wild honeysuckle (336). An extended celebration of the dogwood, the wild honeysuckle, and the flowering locust enters the novel when Sapphira's daughter, Mrs. Blake, climbs Timber Ridge to see a family of hill folk (*SSG* 115–17). The passage is interesting in the way it switches between the past tense for narration and the present for direct tributes to Virginia. Assertions that the dogwood "never loses its wonder" and locust trunks "make the toughest fence posts a farmer can find" convey the enduring value of the South's beauties, notwithstanding the uglier traditions we see elsewhere.

If Cather was trying to establish a contrast between permanent beauty and transient social problems, such a distinction is undermined by the novel's demonstration of an ongoing heritage of racism and class distinction. Whatever its elements of tribute, they exist in tension with darker, more disturbing elements. She could not confront either the South or her own charming, intense, severe mother without ambivalence. Both evoked guilt and claustrophobic anxiety, even as they evoked her tribute and her wish to evade the problems of the present.

Once again, as in *Lucy Gayheart*, the time setting is defined with great explicitness: 1856, with an epilogue twenty-five years later. The epilogue, then, occurs in 1881, the next-to-last full year Cather lived in Virginia. The physical setting is equally specific: Back Creek, an area in the hill country of northern Virginia west of the Blue Ridge, near what became West Virginia—the area where Cather lived her first nine years. The Mill Farm, where Sapphira Colbert reigns supreme while her husband, Henry, operates the mill and sleeps in a room in the mill house, is clearly the home of Cather's maternal great-grandparents, Jacob and Ruhamah Seibert, whose daughter Rachel Seibert Boak was such an important presence in Cather's childhood (Woodress, *Literary* 482).[11]

Grandmother Boak is transparently fictionalized as Rachel Blake, Sapphira and Henry's abolitionist daughter. Her daughter Mary Virginia, Cather's mother, becomes Mrs. Blake's daughter Mary, seen first as a little girl and then in the epilogue (though not identified there by name) as a grown woman, an idealized mother and the central figure of a circle of women who constitute both cultural memory and a renewed postwar society. And there in the epilogue the author herself steps into the book with what has been called "startling suddenness" to speak in her own voice recalling a scene from her actual childhood. In a flash the story is relocated from the world of fiction to the world of factual memory. Novel becomes memoir, although its retrospective narrator, now implicitly and problematically defined as a real-world person named Willa Cather, would have had no way of knowing, in the person of her child self, all of the foregoing events, let alone the inner workings of characters' minds, knowable only to omniscience. It is one of the most "disconcerting" (Gwin 134) endings in American literature.

The easily recognizable translation of family history that I have described is not, however, quite so neat after all. Cather's mother may be identifiable as the daughter of Mrs. Blake and the ideal mother of the epilogue, but traces of her character—her imperiousness, her devotion to grooming and appearances, her peculiar combination of charm with hardness—are also represented in Sapphira. This dual identification of Mary Virginia Cather has been attributed to critics' "confusion about names and relationships" (Hamner 348) but is in fact an accurate reading of the multiply conflicted text. The duality of, on the one hand, the manipulative, powerful woman (in these respects, much like Cather's depiction of Mary Baker Eddy) whose ego drives her to oppress others and, on the other, the nurturing woman who is the source of the child's delights seems to have been an accurate enough rendering of Jennie (as in "carry me back to old Virginny") Cather. But the complication goes further. In attributing characteristics of her mother to Sapphira and thus (by making her the mother rather than the daughter of Rachel Boak) distancing her to the position of great-grandmother, Cather in effect moved Grandmother Boak closer—as, in some ways, she was.[12] Such a repositioning would have greatly reduced the emotional complications of the memories she was invoking, since the grandmother could more easily serve as the object of unconflicted love. At the same time, projecting her experience of the "bad mother" and the "good mother" onto two different fictional figures eased the process of reconciliation with the mother that Cather needed, allowing her to be reconciled to the one without altogether accepting the other.

If Cather's mother is split into two separate representations in the text, Cather herself is split into three or four. Clearly, she is the child witness of the final scene. She is also the adult who remembers that child and remembers Virginia; as such she is clearly present to us at the end in the voice of the italicized terminal note that announces herself unable to determine how to spell the name Pertleball. In the person of Rachel Blake, the plain-faced, forthright power for good, she is alienated from her mother, Sapphira, and then more or less reconciled after the experience of disaster, the death of one of Mrs. Blake's two daughters from diphtheria (*SSG* 293). And certainly Cather is Nancy, the slave girl who escapes the oppressive power of the evil mother (the mistress, Sapphira) and makes good, returning with elevated language and a sumptuous wardrobe, as did Cather herself. In becoming Nancy, she has fulfilled her childhood claim of being a "dang'ous nigger." She has become black but remained white, thus participating in both Nancy's transformation itself and the avid viewing of the transformation, in a scene in which, as Toni Morrison writes in *Playing in the Dark*, black return is staged-managed for a white child's pleasure (27–28).[13]

In multiple ways, then, Cather calls subjecthood into question: in her assignment of biographical models to different fictional representations; in the shifting nature of characterizations (Sapphira is both a sinister plotter and courageous Christian, both an abusive and a companionable mistress; Jezebel is both a loving, beloved companion and a "gorilla" who reverts or pretends to revert to a would-be cannibal at the end); in

Nancy's transformation; and especially in the problematic nature of the connection between child self and adult self, let alone between real-world self and narrating voice. In all these ways she problematizes identity itself.

Sapphira and the Slave Girl is a text torn by oppositions of race and class, yet troublingly affirming of the very social systems it exposes as evil. Despite sympathizing with and applauding the slave girl's liberation, despite affirming the idea of liberation by showing the suffering caused by various figurative kinds of slavery, Cather nevertheless preserves vestiges of the hierarchical class system built on an economy of black slavery, and she leaves the novel's position on race far from clear. Nancy's deliverance to Canada and freedom via the Underground Railroad, for example, is engineered by benevolent whites, while Nancy herself is overcome by fear and begs Rachel Blake to take her back home, which would mean taking her back to slavery. It is an understandable enough reaction, since the Mill Farm is the only home Nancy has ever known; indeed, it is a reaction that conveys rather precisely Cather's own ambivalence toward home and mother.[14] Even so, it can be read as an indication that blacks do not know what is good for them and have to be directed by white liberals.

Whether Cather actually believed that is not clear. Given the racial attitudes expressed in her depiction of Blind d'Arnault in *My Ántonia* and her labeling of Nancy as having an innate "foolish, dreamy, nigger side" (*SSG* 178), we may well believe she did. Even the fact of Nancy's transformation—returning after twenty-five years in Canada as a dignified, gracious, competent person speaking refined English rather than her previous dialect—can be taken in either of two ways: as showing the wrongness of racial prejudice or as showing that she could emerge in this way only by being separated from other blacks. That is, it may show simply that she was (to invoke a concept that consistently shaped Cather's vision) an exception.

To be sure, the system of slavery is confronted and shown, in a variety of ways, to be evil. The fact that a civilized, otherwise gracious man and woman could sit at breakfast and debate whether to sell another person —as Henry and Sapphira do in the opening scene, leading up to Henry's declaration, "We don't sell our people" (*SSG* 6)—is label enough. But the novel goes on to display a cross woman's striking a young girl with a hairbrush for petty reasons, a black mother's being so co-opted by the slave mentality that she counsels that same girl to be sweet to her abuser and wheedle her into better temper, and a deliberate plotting of rape (though it would surely not have been called that) when Sapphira knowingly tries to exploit the corrupt tradition of white masters' compelling black slave girls. Even Henry, a good man who has grave misgivings about the institution of slavery, has been so corrupted by it that when his most trusted slave, Sampson, with whom he has worked side by side and to whom he has offered freedom, comes asking him to protect Nancy, he sends him away with an empty promise to "look after her." He in fact does nothing, but subsequently scapegoats the girl because he has himself begun to think of her sexually (190–92). Another incident shows the descent into madness of a young slave who fell in love with the personal servant of a visitor to the Mill Farm and was unable to marry her because of their chattel status. An interpolated tale of the capturing and transport from Africa of Jezebel, Nancy's great-grandmother, shows unflinchingly the cruelty of the slave trade.

Cather offers these powerful indictments, yet she equivocates. Spectacularly venturing into a means-end problem, she asserts—not directly but in the indirect discourse of Henry's muddled thoughts—that despite the cruelty illustrated in Jezebel's story "certainly, her capture had been a deliverance" (*SSG* 108), because being captured and carried off into slavery had given her the opportunity to become a Christian. Later in the novel she equivocates again, offering the equally hackneyed picture of emancipated slaves who do not wish to leave their masters. The specious notion that slaves and masters were bound by love and its corollary that masters were ultimately the losers in the system, since they had to support and protect their incompetent chattel, were favorite arguments of southern apologists. Cather's invocation of such a line of defensive special pleading shows that she was at least as involved in apologetics as in criticism of her time and place of origin.

As an heiress from mid-Virginia, Sapphira participates in the cruelty of slavery and is tainted with its guilt. She owns not only an inherited cohort of slaves—less those she sold back to the county from which she moved, Henry's statement that they don't sell their people notwithstanding—but their descendants as well. But her guilt, in the text, is personal as well as collective. Scarcely a figure for whom a reader can feel any fondness, more antagonist than protagonist, Sapphira dissimulates, hatches devious plots, and oppresses Nancy to the point that the girl entertains thoughts of suicide. Her husband, the miller, defers to her wishes in almost everything, partly from an awareness of his lower social origins and partly in recognition of her preeminent personal force, but balks at her wish to sell Nancy. Henry is set up, then, as the more sympathetic of the two, reflecting Cather's own feeling for her father. Although Henry's refusal to agree to Sapphira's plan to separate Nancy from her family forever is soundly principled, it is compromised by the fact that he is dotingly fond of the pretty young girl, who may be, in fact, his own niece (we are never sure). Cather's point seems clear: that an evil system taints all who are caught up in it. Corruption spreads from the central evil of southern society, slavery, to permeate the whole, very much as diphtheria spreads among Back Creek schoolchildren, carrying off one of Rachel Blake's two daughters.

The reason for Sapphira's bitter and certainly unworthy dislike of Nancy is her awareness of Henry's fondness for the girl, which is to say, her reading of the situation in terms of the well-established social pattern of white masters' lust for slave women. Thwarted in her wish to sell Nancy, Sapphira invites a notoriously profligate Colbert nephew for a visit, firmly expecting that he will take the girl sexually and thus ruin her. Why sexual experience in this context would be regarded as ruin is not clear. Presumably she believes Henry would not be so attracted to a pregnant or at any rate sexually used Nancy as to a virginal one, or else that Nancy's cheerful spirit would then be broken, reducing her appeal. It is at this point that Rachel Blake intervenes, arranging for the girl to be spirited away to freedom via the Underground Railroad. Distressed by the predicament of having to choose between loyalty to wife and loyalty to daughter, Henry takes at best a passive role. Refusing to give Rachel the money she needs in order to make necessary arrangements, he tells her that there will be money in his coat, which will be left hanging beside an open window during the night. That is, he puts his daughter in the position of having to steal.

Henry's cowardice at this juncture has been roundly condemned. On this point, however, Cather was better informed, historically, than her readers. We know from her correspondence with the director of the New York Public Library that during the 1920s she worked there so regularly that he customarily set aside a small private room for her use.[15] We know from other sources that she did considerable historical research in preparation for *One of Ours, Death Comes for the Archbishop*, and *Shadows on the Rock.* It would appear that in preparation for *Sapphira*, too, she supplemented her recollections of what she had heard with a rather careful study of events leading up to the Civil War. In specifying 1856 as the time setting at the opening and working back and forth in time in traceable increments, she made the novel coincide with a series of events that steadily increased tensions between the South and the North.

Readings of *Sapphira* have been surprisingly little historicized, considering the overtness of its turn to the past and historically significant events. Gestures are made toward the Civil War and slavery, and the secession of the western section of Virginia and creation of the state of West Virginia are mentioned, but for the most part critics seem to have assumed that Cather's view of history was entirely personal and romantic, even superficial. If we take a different approach and assume that her evocation of public events from the years leading up to the Civil War (especially the years 1850 and 1856) was an informed one rather than a self-indulgent kind of antiquarianism, certain details, including Henry Colbert's seemingly pusillanimous role in Nancy's escape, become more explicable.

The historical resonance of the story is established largely through a summary narrative of Rachel Blake's marriage and widowing. In developing the sequence of these events, which become rather confusing but can be worked out with perseverance, Cather was revising and compressing the corresponding period in the life of her grandmother, Rachel Boak, who was married in 1830 and widowed in 1854 (Woodress, *Literary* 18). Calculating on the basis of what is given, we can determine that the novel's Rachel Blake was married in 1837, making her years in Washington with her husband extend to mid-1850. In March 1850 Daniel Webster made a speech in the Senate in which he attempted to tread an ethically narrow line regarding slavery. Later in the spring Henry reads an old issue of the *Baltimore Sun* and learns about Rachel's husband's death. Since the *Sun* made it a practice to print Congressional speeches in their entirety, the possibility is constructed that he might have seen Webster's speech. Thus his own troubled attitude on the issue may reflect a reading of that speech. The connection is tenuous, to be sure. But another event of 1850 bears more directly on the action and makes Henry's avoidance of an active role in Nancy's escape understandable, if not likable. In that same year, 1850, the Fugitive Slave Law was passed. Under its provisions, any active participation on his part would have put his family at risk not only of public humiliation but of stiff and potentially impoverishing fines.[16]

Knowledge of the editorial policies of a second newspaper becomes pertinent as well. The postmistress, Mrs. Bywaters (an actual name in the Back Creek neighborhood, as Charles Cather's diary for 1865 tells us), subscribes to the *New York Tribune*, sent to her in plain wrappers.[17] That fact and her comment that the copy she lends Rachel Boak might be "handy to start a fire with" (*SSG* 145) gain significance when we know that Horace Greeley's *Tribune* had turned passionately anti-slavery by the 1850s and by 1856 was arguing for abolition. No wonder Mrs. Bywaters's father thinks it is imprudent for her to receive the paper. When the novel is read in historical context in an informed way, without the assumption that Cather was evading or ameliorating it, her characterizations of Mrs. Bywaters and Rachel Blake, as well as Henry Colbert, become bolder, her facing of the harshness of the times becomes squarer, and the general tenor of the book becomes more unsettling of social pieties.

Read in this historicized way, the novel's embeddedness in the realities of its own time, the time of its writing—the late 1930s—also becomes less evasive, more confrontational, and in a sense more troubling. Taking as her subject the South and slavery, and announcing it in the title, she focused on the social problem of race. We cannot suppose she was entirely uninformed about the struggles that had gone on during her thirty-plus years as a New Yorker. Such events as the Great Migration from the South, the burgeoning of black population and culture in Harlem, the debate over whether African Americans might serve in World War I and if so whether they might be armed, the highly publicized parade of the "Harlem Hellfighters" returning from France in 1919, and the postwar betrayal of African American veterans and surge of lynchings throughout the South—all these had been played out in her daily newspaper, if not virtually on her doorstep. To be sure, Cather betrays the stain of racism herself. Few Americans of her day would not have. But her attitudes toward race had proved amenable to change as time went on. Commenting retrospectively in 1944 on the experience of having met African American actor and singer Paul Robeson at the Menuhins' a decade or so earlier, she associated racial prejudice with her southern origins in a way that suggests critical detachment. She recalled that as she approached the Menuhins' apartment through Central Park she found herself wondering whether she was going to feel somewhat "southern" but found, once in his presence, that the greatness of the man himself laid all that to rest.[18]

In choosing to write about slavery in the South, then, Cather was critiquing her own roots but also addressing the roots of a collective guilt that continued to hang over her country and divide it. At the time she was writing, a racist power was threatening war in Europe. Her fictional subject, a society evading issues of social justice at a time of approaching war, was indirect, but nonetheless timely. She may have felt impelled by the troubles of her day, personal as well as public, to retreat to a beloved past, but she found there many of the same troubles. Her preoccupation with those historic troubles reflects her disquietude about the contemporary ones.[19]

Another of the problems in American society that Cather locates in *Sapphira* is that of social class in a democratic society. The world of the novel is riven by class divisions. Sapphira, the imperious and notably devious mistress of the household and farm, has married beneath her, apparently to avoid the humiliation and inconvenience of being a spinster, and has chosen to move to Back Creek in order to remove her hardworking husband from the notice of aristocratic friends. Even her co-opted slave Till, Nancy's mother, values "position" and looks down on the mountain people around them as "white trash," preferring people of "quality" (*SSG* 72–74). How Cather regards these class distinctions is not reduced, or reducible, to clear formulation. She delineates clearly enough the differences in speech patterns and behavior that prevail among the various groups who populate her novel, white as well as black. Her white hill folk speak as heavily marked a dialect as do the slaves, and their lives seem given to thievery, assault, and unseemly pregnancies. Yet the strongly affirmed Rachel Blake socializes with people she likes regardless of class and happily attends the Baptist Church that her mother despises, rather than the more aristocratic Episcopalian. The illiterate Mrs. Ringer whom Rachel visits is shown as a personable, intelligent woman who takes a lively interest in the world around her, and her son displays "true courtesy" despite his mean circumstances (121).

Cather recognizes, too, the tie between social class and racism and the complexity of their intersections. One of the most positive of her minor characters points out that being white is the only thing poor whites have to "feel important about" (*SSG* 81), and Henry Colbert knows that even the poorest of the white hill people would not change places with the most highly ranked slave in a prosperous household (229). Yet at the end Cather reinforces distinctions of class and race in a number of ways: in the "deference" paid to "her" mother, in the pointedly racial separation of dinner service, with the white family eating first and their black guests waiting for the "second table," and in Till's stubbornly maintained distinction between the "quality" families she had observed in lowland Virginia and the people of the hills who are not "anybody much" (295). The words "anybody much" are the last words of the novel except for the italicized note appended to the last page with Willa Cather's own name attached, as if in signature. The novel proper ends, then, in an assertion of class distinction. The more things change, it seems, the more they remain the same. Despite emancipation, the Civil War, and the economic decline of the South, and despite Nancy's own rise to prosperity and correct grammar, she still has a "mistress" and a "master" (285). We might infer that the class system in which some are mistresses and masters and others are domestic servants is a kind of perpetuation of slavery, but we cannot say whether Cather *intends* to imply such an idea.

Intentionality is always elusive in Cather's fiction, partly because of its indirect, compressed style but partly, too, because her texts are so multivalent, so deeply pervaded by repressed tensions. Seeming to write simply, she in fact writes ambiguously, both in the sense that her texts reflect her own deep uncertainties and in the sense that they respond to, and in quiet ways illustrate, the ambiguities of human experience. *Sapphira* is a nexus of dark motifs and social conflicts: slavery and mastery, social class, race, the interaction of sex and cruelty, deviousness, incest, the frightening coexistence of good and evil. Anatomizing the society she knew in northwestern Virginia (or the precursor of the society she knew —an important distinction to which we will return), Cather also anatomizes the hidden impulses lurking beneath the surface of things. The novel of manners turns out to be the gothic novel in disguise.[20] Indeed, it is impossible to distinguish between the two. The picture of Henry and Sapphira at breakfast, with their slave standing by to bring more bacon, dissolves into a revelation of irrational jealousy, malevolence, and skilled deception. Neither is less real than the other. If Sapphira lurks spider-like at the center of her household, plotting against those of greater virtue but less power than herself, she is also the immobilized victim, confined to her chair by dropsy (presumably, swelling from heart disease). If she enslaves, she is also enslaved.[21] Toward the end, her sinister evil seemingly forgotten, she becomes the forgiven and forgiving (though never precisely warm) mother and the courageous facer of death. Again, neither aspect is less real than the other. More disconcertingly, perhaps, one can never be sure which Sapphira one is going to encounter. For all her effort to separate the good mother from the bad mother, Cather returned herself and her readers to the plight of the child whose mother's temperament is unpredictable.

Just as the novel of manners becomes the gothic, the novel of escape from the historic moment becomes the historicized facing of recurrent social facts. Cather had increasingly yearned (as her 1936 preface to *Not under Forty* tells us) to return to a time she could idealize, before the changes wrought by the Great War. Now, facing the devastation of another war and the personal devastations of Douglass's and Isabelle's deaths, she turned toward a yet more distant past. In March 1939, over a year before she completed *Sapphira*, she told Dorothy Canfield Fisher that having suffered the hardest year of her life, she found consolation in the one activity that could carry her through. She had abandoned the book, she said, but had taken it up again in response to the unspeakableness of another war because the routine of writing provided respite from bad news.[22]

Retreating from the masculine world of military confrontation, she turned to a world centered in female power and female community. There she identified her heritage: in a moment of mother-daughter reconciliation, observed by another mother-daughter pair who are also, in her imagination's forgiving compensation, reconciled. But the actual historical and biographical material from which she constructed this whole (in one sense a world not yet broken, in another sense a world broken but restored) is marred by problems of personal and social injustice too intransigent for her to ignore. Hence the ambivalence with which she regards it, her "divided attitude toward the land of her earliest memories" (Zettsu 101). This ambivalence is evident in the awkwardnesses and ambiguities of the text.

In part, these ambiguities are there by design. Such details as the quiet references to historically significant facts and the political stance of specific newspapers cannot be supposed accidental. They evince the care with which she worked and also, in their subtlety, her continuing devotion to novelistic indirection, the construction of a fictional rhetoric of the thing not said. They are also, I believe, the evidence of a stubborn integrity that finally would not allow her to retreat to the comfort of the past without acknowledging its elements of discomfort. But the ambiguities of the text are also reflections of her own unacknowledged conflicts and human blind spots. At certain moments—her easy reference to a "little nigger boy" (*SSG* 186) or to Nancy's "foolish, dreamy, nigger side" (178), her matter-of-fact recording that the celebration of reunion entails a second table for blacks/servants—*Sapphira* becomes not only a novel about the ways in which the troubles and evils of the past proliferate in the present, but also a demonstration of the fact that they do. The joy of the final scene, seemingly an effort to sweep aside the cruelties, oppressions, and estrangements of the past and replace them with an idyllic "female community," is marred by the clear evidence that these elements of the past continue into the present.[23] Nancy, no longer a slave but a polished and gracious woman, still has a master and mistress; Till, still suppressing her recognition of the significance of her own past by devoting herself to the idealization of her oppressor, remains a "black voice for the white . . . slavocracy" (Gwin 143); the gloom of earlier sections of the novel persists despite the joy of the ending. The real gloom, however, is not the gothic darkness of Sapphira's plotting but the fact that the social evils chronicled in the novel outlast even the breaking of the world.

IN THIS AMBIVALENCE toward the past, for all her appearance of romantic escapism, we see one of the clearest traces of Cather's affinity with American modernism. Stylistically, her work may appear to be a far cry from the experimental fiction and poetry by which we have customarily defined modernism. Even stylistically, however, when we go beyond superficialities to observe the breaks and discontinuities and the reliance on silences that call the seemingly straightforward assertions of her textual surfaces into question, we have to revise our estimate of her writing as a belated survival of a more naive time. Contrary to the stodgy Victorian taste attributed to her by so exemplary a modernist as Katherine Anne Porter, Cather expressed enthusiasm for a work that was in every way startling and modernist, Gertrude Stein's collaboration with composer Virgil Thomson *Four Saints in Three Acts*, which she saw in New York on February 20, 1934.[24] When we examine with informed care, rather than easy generalizing, her persistent "inventive experiments" in novelistic structure (Skaggs, *After* 177), we have to recognize in them the experimentalism of a modernist.

Modernism is far more than merely style and structure, however, and when we look beyond technique we see in Cather's work a fundamental multiplicity of vision, including a pull toward the past even in the midst of a commitment to the new. In its sense of time, modernism is a state of mind broken in two. Miles Orvell writes that in American modernism "the search for the new was accompanied by a backward look, a retrospective yearning to identify with the romanticized past." Such a dual gaze, he continues, is found "in Cather, Eliot, Faulkner, Williams, Fitzgerald" (7).[25] This is not a group in which we are accustomed to seeing Cather's name. Yet she shares the compulsive turn to the past that we see in Faulkner's narratives of the South and Eliot's or Pound's incorporation of archaisms. She shares, as well, Fitzgerald's or Faulkner's or Eliot's sense of modern deterioration. Most emphatically she shares their sense of fragmentation or brokenness, if not to the point of composing her works in cryptic language and radically discontinuous segments, at any rate in her insistence on the world's having broken in two, reflected in the gaps in linear time that break the surface of her fiction. Such a gap precedes the reconciliation scene in *Sapphira*, and similar gaps open in *A Lost Lady*, *My Mortal Enemy*, and virtually all the rest of her full-length works. The impulse driving these gaps and the taking up of the narrative thread at points years later might seem to be the desire to gain a retrospective view that could pull everything together and make sense of it all. But in fact the retrospective view at the end of her novels is at least as likely to raise questions as to tie up neat fictional packages.

The inconclusiveness of Cather's novels is not merely structural or evasive, a refusal to clarify her intentions. It manifests an underlying conception of the indeterminacy of being. Like other modernists who conceived themselves as being cut off from or denied access to truth or reality and who therefore posited a "world elsewhere," she conveys an epistemology not only of inability to know but of ultimate unknowability.[26] Yet I would argue that Cather does not so much attempt to create in fiction an alternative to the "reality" to which, as an alienated and broken would-be knower, she is denied access, as she creates fictions that undermine the distinction between the real and the fantasized, between fact and fiction. An insistent deconstruction of that opposition becomes finally her truest claim to be not only *not* a throwback to romantic realism, but an anticipator of the reality play that we associate with literary postmodernism.

Here I want to return to the scene at the end of *Sapphira and the Slave Girl* when Cather intrudes herself into the text. She later decided the experiment was ill-advised, and wrote to Henry Seidel Canby that she shared his discomfort with the ending and regretted the shift from third-person to first-person point of view. Yet she immediately offered an implicit defense of the ending, insisting that the events described in the final section really happened and Nancy's reunion with her mother provided the reminiscences that enabled her to write the book at all.[27] It is as if the switch from fictional narrative to nonfictional first person had been made in spite of herself. Yet that switch was not only a gesture consistent with less conspicuous intrusions of the author's self throughout the novel but, in its implications for the reality claims of the text, a gesture such as she had made on other occasions. As Skaggs writes, "The author intrudes directly into this novel *as author,* from the beginning" and "refused to maintain the distinctions between fact and fiction" (*After* 180).

Cather is in fact writing metafiction. In the opening scene with Sapphira and Henry at the breakfast table, the example offered by Skaggs as a site of authorial intrusion, she undermines the fictive illusion by speaking of the novel qua novel: "How these two came to be living at the Mill Farm is a long story—too long for a breakfast table story" (*SSG* 5). Compounding her act of telling with the scene being told, she implies that if she were to give us that "long story," she would be doing it at the breakfast table herself or at any rate within the time Sapphira and Henry spend breakfasting—as if they really were doing so or as if the act of narration occurred, not outside the story being narrated, but within its framework of time and space. The various pointers to actual historic precedent also function to blur the boundary between fact and fiction *precisely because* Cather does not maintain the fictive illusion, or verisimilitude, usually sought after in historical fiction.

Still, it is the abrupt arrival in the text of a real-world person from outside the text that is the most blatant instance of such intermingling.

At that point, addressing the reader in an insistent first person ("I was something over five years old, and was kept in bed on that memorable day because I had a cold"), Cather interrupts the flow of third-person narrative convention to redefine the story as a factual account—a claim that, as we have seen, cannot be strictly true, since her child self knew only the reconciliation, and the family members from whom she heard the story of Nancy's escape would not, in a real as opposed to imagined world, have had access to various of the thoughts and incidents that make up the preceding text. Moreover, in the course of that text "Cather" has spoken in the present tense to vouch for the beauty of the (fictional?) setting. The final words of text per se, Till's direct-discourse assertion that Sapphira should not have migrated to Back Creek "'where nobody was anybody much'" (*SSG* 295), not only demonstrate Till's continuing allegiance to white aristocracy but are assertions contrary to, and thus invalidated by, what has gone before. Not only Nancy and Mrs. Blake but also Mrs. Bywaters, Jezebel, and several others have patently been established as persons of consequence, at least in terms of courage and moral character.

Beneath these final words of narrative appear the words "THE END," centered on the page, and then, in italics, a kind of explanatory note. First comes a conventional disavowal that one can imagine to have been Alfred Knopf's idea for legal reasons, the kind of disavowal that appears in the front matter of many novels: "In this story I have called several of the characters by Frederick County surnames, but in no case have I used the name of a person whom I ever knew or saw." Here, though, the placement of the formulaic statement on the last page, where several lines of novelistic text also appear, and with only slightly more separation by white space than that preceding the words "THE END," draws it into proximity to the book itself, almost as if it were quasi-text.[28] But Cather goes beyond the formula of disavowal to add, in a chatty conversational tone: "My father and mother, when they came home from Winchester or Capon Springs, often talked about acquaintances whom they had met. The names of those unknown persons sometimes had a lively fascination for me, merely as names: Mr. Haymaker, Mr. Bywaters, Mr. Householder, Mr. Tidball, Miss Snap. For some reason I found the name of Mr. Pertleball especially delightful, though I never saw the man who bore it, and to this day I don't know how to spell it." Some of the people she mentions have appeared in the text, some not.[29] In any event, by introducing them "merely as names" she calls attention to the verbal signs themselves and drains them of *either* fictive *or* nonfictive reality. Moreover, she again makes an assertion contrary to fact, having just spelled *Pertleball* even though she claims not to be able to do so. She then appends, again in all capitals, her own name, "WILLA CATHER," in the position of a signature to a letter. The appended note, if not the entire preceding text, becomes a letter to the reader, thus a text belonging to yet another genre, not fiction and not memoir or history but personal address.

Footnotes and similar documentation or asides are scarcely conventional parts of novels, but of factual or analytic writing such as the kind you, reader, are now reading. They belong to the "real" world, the world of fact. By appending her note to the text of the novel, Cather deconstructs the reality status of both, note and novel. Certainly she was not the only modernist to call attention to the textuality of text, but her confidential tone and her apology for her own inadequacy as orthographer (unable to spell out the text she wishes to write) forego the more usual modernist gesture of claiming a superior reality status for fiction. Rather, she empties the text of its imaginative density even as she vacates the subjects whose names she calls attention to *as* names.

As I have pointed out with respect to the opening scene, Cather calls attention at other points in *Sapphira*, as well, to her own act of fiction writing, with explanatory asides, shifts of tense or tone, and direct addresses out of the fictive space to the reader in factual space: "Even today, if you should be motoring through Winchester on the sixth of June," she begins. She points out that "motorists" find the beautiful "Double S" section of the steep road "now denuded and ugly," in contrast to the way it was "in the old times" (*SSG* 171). These moments in the text are not signs of naive writing, as readers may suppose who are unaccustomed to thinking of Cather as a modern or an experimental writer; they are metafictional devices that cast "a shadow of hyper-self-awareness over the events depicted" and "stave off readings of the novel as a naïve act of historical fiction" (Urgo, *Myth* 91).

Such gestures are not peculiar to *Sapphira*, but in Cather's earlier novels they are rarely so blatant or startling as the shifts of reality status here. On at least two other occasions she employed footnotes that act in much the same way as the epilogue and appended note to *Sapphira*. In *My Ántonia* she provides instructions as to how to pronounce the main character's name, as if we were going to need to speak to or about her and Cather were serving as teacher or introducer, rather than a creative imagination subsumed in the narrative voice and severed from us by the gulf between fact and fiction; or as if (and this is, in fact, true) she as author realized that as we read we will want to hear the name in our minds, and so she must step out from behind the fabric of narration to provide that helpful information. The assumption seems to be that Ántonia is a real person, with a real name that has a correct pronunciation, rather than an imagined subject whose name is arbitrary.[30]

An even more pronounced instance of the appended informational note that shatters the fictive illusion occurs in *Death Comes for the Archbishop*, where Cather acknowledges having misrepresented a historical fact. After reporting the rumor that the Indians of Pecos Pueblo, home of Bishop Lamy's guide Jacinto, "sacrificed young babies to the great snake, and thus diminished their numbers," she undercuts this report by asserting, on her own narrative authority, that it seems "much more likely that the contagious diseases brought by white men were the real cause of the shrinkage of the tribe." Exploring this likelihood and its effects, she claims that the "population of the living streets" of Jacinto's pueblo was "less than one hundred adults," but at once denies that claim in an explanatory note keyed to the text by asterisk: "In actual fact the dying pueblo of Pecos was abandoned some years before the American occupation of New Mexico" (*DCA* 123).[31]

We have already discussed Cather's motivation for invoking Pecos Pueblo. Since it had actually died or been abandoned within postcolonial times, it lent itself to use as demonstration of the vanishing of the Native American, a "fact" both desirable, if one were committed to the imperial conception of the United States, and readily lamentable. But even if she was determined to incorporate Pecos rather than some fictional pueblo for which she could make up a name, there were other ways to do so. Jacinto could be identified as a member or a son of the group that left Pecos and took refuge at Jemez. Or Latour could pass near Pecos on one of his journeys and be told about the abandonment of the pueblo. One can imagine any number of alternatives. Instead, she chose to incorporate the historic fact, keep the actual name, revise the fact to suit the time setting of her novel, and then tell her reader that she had done so. Pointedly insisting on the fictive nature of the text, she deconstructs historic as well as fictional reality, much as she does by including historic

personages with their actual names (Kit Carson, Padre Martínez) as
fictional characters to whom she gives invented words and actions. This
is a far cry from mere allusion to actual people and events, which has
always been found in fiction. It is more like the indubitably postmod-
ernist short stories of Max Apple, where baseball becomes a metaphor
for political debate, with Fidel Castro on the mound, or the author's
anxiety about literary reputation becomes a boxing match between
himself and Norman Mailer, with old-time boxer Archie Moore as ref-
eree. We have a sense of having one foot planted firmly in each of two
dimensions, reality and fantasy, or perhaps in neither.

AN IMPULSE of play with the reality status of fiction and fact was in various ways characteristic of Cather's writerly mind throughout her long
career, gathering strength in her later work and culminating in *Sapphira
and the Slave Girl*. It is an impulse that appears, for example, in her repeated pseudo-documentary explanations of how "she," or, more precisely,
the narrator, came to know whatever story it is that she is telling. She
takes up and uses as a structuring principle the device of the explanatory
frame story. "Willa Cather" recalls a train ride on which she encountered
Jim Burden, who recalls, in terms that approximate Cather's real life, an
earlier train ride across half a continent when he first saw Ántonia. As he
does so, this fictional narrator shows how fiction, a book about Jesse
James, shaped his perception of "fact." Or again, the opening of "Two
Friends" walks the reader from such real-world events as "the invention
of the motor-car" and "the War . . . that happened a hundred years after
Waterloo" (that is, World War I) to a fictional time "long ago, before"
and to two fictional characters who were men she actually knew in that
long-ago time of her youth. *My Mortal Enemy* begins with Nelly Birdseye's seemingly factual explanation of how she came to know what she is
about to tell us. *Death Comes for the Archbishop* begins with an imagined
scene in which fictional prelates discuss the appointment of the fictional
Latour as vicar apostolic in response to the very real circumstance of the
Treaty of Guadalupe Hidalgo, ending the Mexican War. Fact enters
fiction and becomes its occasion.

    Play with the reality status of fact and fiction also characterizes several
of Cather's essays, particularly from the 1930s and later, such as "Escapism," "On *Shadows on the Rock*," and "Light on Adobe Walls," which bears
the imprint of her preoccupation with aging and ending. If her short

stories and novels approach or even inhabit the boundary between fiction and nonfiction from one side, her essays often do so from the other. In the case of "A Chance Meeting" and the overtly fictional treatment of the same idea, "The Old Beauty," they approach it in mirroring fashion. The story could almost be considered a revision of the essay, which itself adopts a largely narrative rather than reflective rhetoric, opening very much as a short story might: "It happened at Aix-les-Bains, one of the pleasantest places in the world. I was staying . . ." (*SPO* 815). The opening of the essay "148 Charles Street" also establishes time and place very much in the manner of a story: "Late in the winter of 1908 Mrs. Louis Brandeis conducted me along a noisy street in Boston and rang at a door hitherto unknown to me" (838). Much like Cather's customary beginning of stories and novels by explaining the narrator's "knowledge" base, "Katherine Mansfield" opens in a narrative mode establishing the stimulus for the essay: "Late in the autumn of 1920, on my way home from Naples, I had a glimpse of Katherine Mansfield through the eyes of a fellow passenger. As I have quite forgotten his real name, I shall call him Mr. J—. He was a New Englander, about sixty-five years of age, I conjectured; long, lean, bronzed, clear blue eyes, not very talkative. His face, however . . ." (872). Mr. J— is, if not a fictional character, at least a fictional-seeming one, and his story of another voyage (much like Jim Burden's other train ride) during which he was companioned by the child who would become the great writer leads back to the first "frame" with a question about Mansfield's short stories, which then triggers analytic commentary on them. The opening situation becomes an introductory frame for a story-within-a-story, both of which introduce Cather's own "story" of Mansfield. Once again, fact and storytelling interpenetrate.

In her prefatory note to *Not under Forty*, Cather, in fact, called the six pieces collected there "sketches" rather than essays. Her inscription in the copy she sent Elsie Sergeant speaks of them as stories: "These are true stories, told just as they happened" (Sergeant 268). Sergeant adds that Cather's use of the word "story" here is "interesting." Indeed it is. As Hermione Lee comments, the inscription is "a characteristically deceptive simple statement" (349). Linking this "simple statement" with *Sapphira* and with two of the narrative essays or sketches mentioned above, Lee continues in what is perhaps the most incisive and thought-provoking statement of Cather's deconstructive fiction/nonfiction yet

made in the critical literature: "*Sapphira and the Slave Girl* is also presented by Cather as a true story, based on her family's history just as it
happened . . . But its fictiveness creates, by analogy, uncertainty about
the 'chance meeting' between life and fiction in the other 'true stories'
of her old age. How much did Cather idealize her memories of 148
Charles Street? And how much did she 'make up' about Flaubert's niece?
How much, in turn, had Flaubert's niece 'made up' her Flaubert?"

Cather wrote in "Light on Adobe Walls" that in *The Tempest* Shakespeare seems to have "outgrown" his artistic "toys" (*OW* 125). As she
neared the end of her creative life, she seems to have "outgrown" the
"toys" of genre, with their sometimes useful but sometimes artificial
distinctions, and to have contemplated putting them away. If she was
engaged, in *Sapphira and the Slave Girl*, in a dual autobiographical move
of recrimination and reconciliation (and clearly she was), she was also
engaged in the culminating stages of a long-term effort both to estrange
and to reconcile the modes of writing identified with fact and with
fiction, and the qualities of imagination they represented. Her conception of the presence of the one in the other is strikingly conveyed in the
postscript to a letter she wrote Yaltah Menuhin during the time when
she was completing this last novel. Calling Yaltah's attention to J. M.
Barrie's "enchanting" re-creation of the biblical shepherd boy David,
she said that she had been rereading First and Second Samuel because it
was necessary to have the plain facts in one's mind in order to appreciate
what the creative artist was doing in his fiction.[32] The work of which she
was speaking was a play, but one could say much the same of her novels
and stories: that one must have the facts in mind in order to appreciate
the fiction. One also needs to have the fiction in mind in order to appreciate the nonfiction.

12

ENDING / CONCLUDING

Hath the love that lit the stars,
    Fills the sea and moulds the flowers,
Whose completeness nothing mars,
    Made forgot what once was ours?
        —"The Poor Minstrel"

Hardships and perils, prophecy and vision,
The leadership of kin, and happy ending
        —"Macon Prairie"

IN THE LAST years of her life Willa Cather continued to write sporadically while struggling against depression, concern about the state of world events, and a deepening proclivity toward withdrawal. None of these traits was new to her, but as she aged and as a second world war threatened what had seemed to her the very structure of worthwhile human existence, they increasingly controlled her state of mind and her behavior.[1] Edith Lewis believed that "her friendships came to mean more and more to her" after their 1932 move to the apartment on Park Avenue (177), but even Cather's oldest and dearest friends were held at arm's length, and she admitted that when meeting new people she was rather like a porcupine. Her letters of the late 1930s and the 1940s are dominated by gloom and ill health. Whether her depression resulted in large part from the deterioration of her physical well-being or both sprang from a common origin is not clear. As her grieving for the deaths of Douglass and Isabelle prolonged itself, she complained to various old friends about influenza, eye strain, hand problems, and general dullness. When Mabel Dodge Luhan sent her a copy of *The Laughing Horse*, a satiric literary magazine published in Taos by Witter Bynner's secretary and friend Spud Johnson, she replied that it had prompted her first laugh in a long time.[2]

One of the things weighing on her mind as the troubled decade of the thirties drew to a close with the grim prospect of an emptier personal life and a massive war was America's role as a world power. Like many others, Cather was already sorely stressed by the spectacle of Depression-era misery as she watched the world's plunge into yet another war, and she bewailed the loss of the old time before Europe was flooded by hatred and economic distress overtook America. The heritage of all history, she felt, was in peril, leaving humankind without a refuge. Her references to such a refuge as a Safe Kingdom imply that her "Kingdom of Art" was in danger of failing. Yet it was all she had to counterpose to the dangers all around. Her donation of a set of the Autographed Edition for a fundraiser for Finland was emblematic: What she thrust into the breach was art.[3]

Writing was her consolation, a means not of ignoring problems but of countering them. As the German Wehrmacht overran Europe and threatened England, her disheartenment took on an increasingly public dimension. She confided to Greenslet that "none of the personal sorrows she had recently lived through had shaken her" so severely as had "the doom that had been gathering for the last few months over almost everything that had made the world worth living in or for"—that is, over Europe and its treasures. Worrying about friends in England and France, she managed to be pleased with the 1940 re-election of Franklin Roosevelt despite her disdain for the New Deal, because she thought he would do more for Great Britain than Wendell Willkie, the Republican candidate.[4] Lewis recalled that, far from being uninterested in the war, she "felt it too much to make it the subject of casual conversation" and wrote in her notebook, on the fall of France, "'There seems to be no future at all for people of my generation'" (184).

In 1941 Cather met a person whose books she had been reading for at least a decade who would be important in her life for several years, the Norwegian writer of historical fiction and Nobel Prize winner Sigrid Undset. Knopf had published Undset's book about the invasion of her home country, and Cather recommended it to friends with enthusiasm, extolling Undset's truthfulness and her explosion of American illusions about Communism in Russia—this while the U.S. and Russia were allies. Undset served as a hero to whom she could cling for renewal of spirit.[5]

As the '40s wore on and Cather continued to be buffeted by worry about the state of the world, ill health, family troubles, and gloom, she became so withdrawn from social contact that close family members did not even have her telephone number and, in early 1942 when Roscoe lay ill, had to reach her by telegram in care of the Knopf offices. In July of that year she underwent an appendectomy and removal of her gall bladder, with resulting loss of appetite and weight loss. The number of pounds she reported having lost during her summer ordeal gradually increased as letter succeeded letter: twelve pounds in a letter to Greenslet on September 7, fourteen in a letter to Carrie Miner two days later, eighteen in letters to Julian Street on September 21 and to Elsie Sergeant on December 18. She blamed the operation, together with the increasing discouragements of the war, for her prolonged lapses in correspondence with old friends.[6]

Her spirits rose or fell depending on the fortunes of war. By November 1942, though life still seemed grim and difficult, she felt that she could hold up if only Rommel were driven out of Egypt. Liberation of the Mediterranean, she thought, would open the door for good things to come. In December she exulted that Churchill was simply splendid. But by March 1943 her spirits had again sunk and she was certain that most of what she and others had loved in the world was being wiped out, centuries of human striving smashed to bits. She could not foresee a world in which she would care to live, but preferred to think about the heritage of old England and to read its great books such as *Wuthering Heights* and *Silas Marner*. As the year ended, she adopted for the closing of her letters a phrase she had picked up from a friend's Christmas greeting: Happy New Year anyway.[7]

During these years of strain and grief, Cather increasingly turned to religion, or at any rate to a fixation on western tradition, which she invested with religious authority. Her Christmas greetings in 1943 took on an explicit Christian rhetoric not in evidence before. Perhaps the most overt statement of such a turn in her sensibility appeared in the card she sent George Beecher, the bishop who had confirmed her and her parents in the Episcopal Church. The front picture, Canterbury Cathedral, she labeled the stronghold of civilization, and inside the card she wrote that humanity seemed to be nearing a world without Christianity and when that light went out there would be nothing but ultimate darkness and the gnashing of teeth. She added that she had once

again been reading the Venerable Bede.[8] Her tone of certitude here
about eternal things rings of very much the kind of pious assurance she
had mocked in her youth.

Taking refuge in religion did not avail, however, to bolster her spirits.
She continued to isolate herself and to write what she herself described
as gloomy letters. To her old friend Irene she reported how relieved she
was that Mary Virginia, her favorite niece, stayed at a hotel during a visit
to New York and restricted herself to brief drop-ins. The emotional
strain of longer visits, she said, would have been exhausting; it was better
for her to stay away. In the spring of 1945, in a long letter to Carrie
Miner Sherwood in which she said that she was also writing to Mariel
Gere to make excuses for not coming to their class reunion, she admitted being so emotionally debilitated that if she became agitated in any
way she couldn't sleep, felt weak, and began to cry uncontrollably. Her
doctors, she said, called it a case of nervous exhaustion.[9]

Yet she could not avoid emotional strain as she thought about the
devastation in Europe and the misery of Nebraska boys who had been
sent off to islands in the Pacific where they had to lie in the mire and be
bitten by insects, as if in punishment for some unknown crime. Her language carries an overtone of fist-shaking at the eternal. We can hear in
it, indeed, an echo of the title of her unfinished last project, "Hard Punishments." She confessed to bitterness and, as if wishing she could have
shunted off her despair onto another generation, lamented that so
much destruction had to come within a single lifetime. It didn't seem
fair. She and her contemporaries had been through one war, which was
bad enough, and now they had to witness another. Why, out of all of
human history, did her generation have to see everything wiped out?
Seeking an explanation but falling into suspicion of gossips at home, she
assured Bishop Beecher that when neighbor no longer envied neighbor
or took pleasure in another's bad luck, wars would cease. The decay of
her personal relationships and the evil abroad in the world had come
together in her mind in a way that saw political forces as expressions of
personal malice. Her vision of the world remained rooted in the individual, even as it darkened. Trying to find security in memories of an
idealized Red Cloud, she asked plaintively, as if it were an emblem,
whether the old Amboy mill was still operating.[10]

As the war dragged on, she kept trying to reply to at least a few of the
servicemen who wrote to her about her books, but admitted that her

awareness of homesick soldiers in foxholes had become a nervous strain. Always a person to whom good food was important, she complained of the difficulty of finding acceptable restaurant fare or adequate household help who might cook an evening meal. The simple daily needs of life were becoming burdensome. Yet by mid-1945 she seemed to summon up a trace of her old strength. Though she still lamented the dreariness of the war, she began occasionally to think of it in ways other than the obvious fear and worry. She observed to Fanny Butcher (mistakenly) that wars were not conducive to art in any form and began to let herself believe that the world might one day regain its health. She insisted to Stephen Tennant that when that happened, outmoded views about the role of writers as artists would come back into fashion. Positioning herself as a mentor to writers of the future, she scolded Tennant for talking about writing rather than actually doing it and urged him to emulate her long-admired master Flaubert by taking a healthy interest in the world around him.[11]

In September of that year, however, her brother Roscoe died. This last bereavement plunged her back into gloom. She spoke of it as the hardest trial she would ever endure. As if forgetting what she had previously said about Douglass and the intensity of her grief for him, she lamented to Irene Miner that Roscoe had been the closest of her brothers and with his death a spring had broken inside her.[12] As usual after an emotional trauma, she fell ill. In her Christmas card to Irene that year, she expressed a yearning for small country churches, but said the only one like that she ever went to now was in Maine, where she had begun spending her summers. The wistfulness of the inscription seems to indicate a realization that her yearning for religious consolation was a kind of daydream, not a serious pursuit. Rather than her usual holiday greetings to Fanny Butcher and Zoë Akins, she wrote formal declarations that the loss of Roscoe had wrought a fundamental change in her and she wanted a few of her closest friends to know it.[13]

When the war in Europe ended, her spirits rose. In the early spring of 1946 she received a long letter from Sigrid Undset, now back in Norway, which despite its revelations of destruction, losses of loved ones, and material hardships expressed a sturdy confidence that her fellow Norwegians could rebuild their country. Having long considered Undset remarkable, Cather must have felt her own hopes shored up by the tone of the letter. Indeed, she was soon engaged in lively book talk in letters to Greenslet, baiting him in very much the old way about the evils of anthologies and radio adaptations (two of her particular cranks) and continuing to promise she would consider giving permission for such adaptations, only to refuse. She scolded Elsie Sergeant for even thinking of editing a Viking Portable of her work and professed herself amazed that any self-respecting writer would agree to such a thing. In short, much of her old liveliness reappeared as she reflected on old times, often in a mellowed mood, and achieved perspective on the overall shape of her life. We see these processes at work in the posthumous story "Before Breakfast," either the last or the next to last work she wrote.[14]

While complaining of snideness on the part of many family members and Red Cloud acquaintances, Cather nevertheless strove to reconcile herself to her family by strengthening her ties with two of her nieces, Mary Virginia Cather Mellen and Helen Louise Cather Southwick. A continuing process of posthumous reconciliation with her mother is also evident in a letter to Helen Southwick in which she praised her mother's willingness to keep "hands off" her soul and let her be herself (Woodress, *Literary* 20). Though still holding old friends such as the Miner sisters and Mariel Gere at arm's length, in letters reminiscing about experiences long past she repeatedly sought to reassure them, and perhaps herself, of her love for them. She signed her 1946 Christmas card to Irene "With love and happy memories," and in a note to Carrie written near the end of the year she exclaimed, apparently in response to a newspaper clipping Carrie had sent her, that she simply loved stories of the first Thanksgiving Day (seemingly transferred to the Great Plains) with its old-fashioned pastries made with marrow from buffalo bones. (Carrie Miner Sherwood appears in figure 28.) A tone of exclamatory happiness continues in a note to Dorothy Canfield Fisher that, while undated as to year, seems to have been written shortly after January 1, 1947, Cather's last New Year's Day. How glad she had been, she said, to hear from Dorothy on Christmas morning, and how she did love December, when the world could sometimes seem as fresh and sparkly as it had when she was twenty. Less than a month before her death she wrote an affectionate letter to Bishop Beecher extending condolences for the death of his wife and saying that she herself took comfort in remembering her parents' kindness to various of the country people who lived near Red Cloud and came into town on personal business. Such kindnesses lived on, she said, beyond the short span of human lives.[15]

Fig. 28. Carrie Miner Sherwood at age 100, holding photograph of Cather.
(Nebraska State Historical Society)

IN 1946, for the first time, Cather responded favorably to an overture
from a scholar who wished to write a biographical study of her. She
wrote at least four letters to Professor E. K. Brown, unprecedented in
their warmth and candor. The first opens by saying how much she appreciated his attentive and sympathetic reading of her books. She went on
to reveal misgivings about *O Pioneers!* (saying it misrepresented relations
between certain ethnic groups on the Divide) and to state that *Death
Comes for the Archbishop* was "of course" her best work. She told Brown
the circumstances of her initial conception for the novel, confirmed her
affection for the Southwest, and refuted Mary Austin's supposed claim
that the book had been written in her house, as well as similar claims
rumored to have been made by "a madwoman" named Wheelwright
(Mary Cabot Wheelwright, founder of the Wheelwright Museum in
Santa Fe). Perhaps most revealing, in this first letter to Brown, is an
admission that the reason she had not been writing recently was loss of
enthusiasm.[16]

Three months later, in January 1947, Cather wrote a brief second letter to Brown holding out the hope that she might grant him an interview when he came to New York in the spring to give a lecture. At that time, she said, they might talk over their personal values.[17] We can only wish such an interview had taken place. Her values are evident, however, in the thankful tone of her reminiscences about various impressive or, as she called them, "great" people she had known. Mentioning as examples Annie Fields, Louis Brandeis and his wife, and critic William Archer, she said that she felt blessed by having been able to learn from such people. She recalled going with Archer to see an early production of John Millington Synge's *Playboy of the Western World* and his admonition to her to keep her mind open to newness in art. Now, she said, she did not feel put off by innovators, even those she did not enjoy, such as John Dos Passos. What she did feel put off by was people who sought to expurgate artistic expression by editing out, for example, parts of Shakespeare. Coming from an aging writer who had often seemed hostile to newness, it is a remarkable statement of confidence in free artistic expression and the ultimate value of art, even experimental art.

A third and fourth letter to Brown complete the sequence, at any rate as it survives. In the third, dictated on March 23, she expressed an almost spiritual sense of the beatitude of human relationships, this time with respect to Yehudi Menuhin and his family. She would rather have missed almost any other chapter of her life, she said, than the Menuhin chapter, which had given her so much happiness for many years. They had come to visit the day before, and the very rooms of her apartment retained a sense of their presence and of their goodness to her.[18] After her many expressions of bitterness and gloom, such luminous statements can only seem restorative. They are not to be forgotten as we strive to achieve a sense of Cather's mind in its totality.

By this time in her life she could scarcely sign her name. Due to continuing problems with her right thumb, her handwriting, which was never very legible, had deteriorated to an oversized scrawl. Yet she continued to dictate letters. The last letter she wrote (or the last that I have found) was written on April 17, 1947, to Dorothy Canfield Fisher. She never received Dorothy's reply, dated April 24. On that day she suffered a fatal cerebral hemorrhage. The subject of this final correspondence was her hope to set the record straight about their meeting with A. E. Housman almost half a century before. In a sense, it is a valedictory statement of her affiliation with one of the voices of poetry that heralded, if it did not genuinely participate in, the great surge of new writing that we know as modernism.

CATHER WAS not entirely accurate in telling Brown, in her letter of October 1946, that loss of enthusiasm had kept her from writing much lately. True, she had not been writing *much*, nor had even that been done really recently, but the little writing that she had done in these last years was not without enthusiasm. In 1944 and '45 she worked sporadically on "Before Breakfast," a peculiar and seemingly inconclusive story that is little discussed, but one that she herself spoke of warmly, in part because she enjoyed the process of creating a story once again but at least in part, it would seem, because of the substance of the story itself. In a series of letters written the first week of January 1945—her New Year's letter to Irene Miner Weisz on the 4th, notes to Zoë Akins on the 5th and 6th, and another to Irene on the 6th—she mentioned the collapse of her right hand and the fact that it had happened when she was working on a story she greatly enjoyed. It had been an interruption, but she was removing the brace two hours a day to work because she found the story so absorbing. Three months later she confided to Carrie, too, that she had truly been enjoying her work until her hand flared up the previous summer.[19] This is the last reference I have found to the interrupted story. Its completion seems to have gone unrecorded, and she seems to have made no effort to have it published.

Quite aside from how one estimates its artistic merits, "Before Breakfast" holds special interest from being Cather's last or perhaps next-to-last story. Simply from its position in the sequence of her work, it becomes a summing up, a final statement. But it is also a summing up in its pondering of the vast sweep of history, geological as well as human. At the same time, it is a very personal story, a final statement that is self-reflective in two senses: in reflecting or expressing the self and in being a reflection *about* the self, an act of reflection on herself as a person.

The autobiographical resonance is clear in the April 1945 letter to Carrie Miner Sherwood, but even without such confirmation it is clear enough in many of the details of the story. The island location off the coast of Canada, the cabin with no plumbing, and the cliffs overlooking the ocean mark the setting as Cather's retreat at Grand Manan where, as in the story, the business mail was not forwarded. The central character,

Henry Grenfell, is "delicate," sleeps poorly, and has weak eyes (*SPO* 765). According to her own statement, Cather had been weak, or delicate, ever since her gall bladder operation in 1942, could not sleep if she experienced the slightest emotional upset, and was having trouble with her eyes to the point that the only books she could read were those with extra large type.[20]

The title "Before Breakfast" places the story at the beginning of a new day. Perhaps we can read that as a new day dawning after the war. The reference to beginnings, combined with the reflective third-person consciousness of being old and pondering last (ultimate) things, implies a kind of totality, as if this is a story of life from beginning to end. And indeed it is. It is a reflection on *a* life, but that one life serves to represent existence itself. Moving back and forth between his early memories, the present moment, and the discomfiture that has caused him to sleep poorly, Henry Grenfell's mind moves, too, between his own life and the panorama of geologic time that had been opened to him the previous evening by his conversation with a scientist who shared the ferry ride to the island. He begins to think of the one in terms of the other. Recalling himself as a thirteen-year-old trying to support a mother and two younger sisters, with no assets except necessity and "the ginger to care hard and work hard," he thinks that he was like "a throw-back to the Year One," that is, the origin of things, "when in the stomach was the only constant, never sleeping, never quite satisfied desire" (*SPO* 765). From that beginning, Grenfell—like humankind from its beginnings— has advanced to a successful but morose maturity.

For most of the years of his adulthood, nature has been nothing to Grenfell but a retreat from his urban life as principal of a legal firm and an arena for proving himself not a weakling by killing things on annual hunting trips. Now, driven to reflect on the meaning of human life within the alarming spectacle of vast time opened to him by the geologist, he begins to see himself not so much reduced by its vastness as gathered up into a great whole. Standing at his window, he spies a hare, "silly" and "ill at ease," "puzzled and furtive." He sees the animal, not as game, but as a "kind of greeting" from the natural world. For the reader, parallel details link Grenfell and hare: their eyes (the hare's protrude, Henry's need drops; "poor hare and his clover, poor Grenfell and his eye-drops!"), the similarity of their hurrying "up the grassy hillside" and plunging into the woods (*SPO* 758–59, 766). Once there, Henry lightly, but significantly, greets a fallen spruce as "Grandfather"—his surroundings are becoming a kind of family, he is a part of them and like them. Vegetal adaptations to the harsh climate are seen in terms that humanize them. "Hugg[ing]" the earth and "cre[eping] up the hillside through the underbrush, persistent, nearly naked" (767), they are like humanity, seeking shelter, evading the torments of an "unkind climate," and persisting, going on through adversity.

Reaching the headland, Grenfell looks down at the surf (as Cather so often enjoyed doing) and witnesses a small allegory of human history, or perhaps, since the person he observes is explicitly compared to an elemental life form associated with the sea (a clam), of existence itself. This representative of humanity and the human spirit, or the spirit of all life, is appropriately enough, emerging as it does from Cather's female creative imagination, female. It is the scientist's "lovely" daughter, whom Grenfell had seen the night before. The Venus-like offspring of intellect or theory, she is herself seen in terms of stubborn physical strength and self-definition. Coming to the water of life's origins, she strips to naked flesh (the story says a pink bathing suit, but clearly she looks naked) and plunges into the rough surf, which Henry knows must be paralyzingly cold at this northern latitude. Beginning to strip down himself, so that he can at least make an effort to save her when she founders, as he is convinced she will, he sees her instead swim out to the rock that seems to have been her goal and swim safely back again. "She hadn't dodged. She had gone out, and she had come back." Such determination and such achievement in spite of adversity, even in something so small and arbitrary as reaching a particular rock in one's morning swim, endows life with meaning and satisfaction: "She would have a happy day" (*SPO* 769). Henry, too, it seems, will have a happy day. He returns to his cabin reassured and delighted, confident that "plucky youth" will continue to give the dare to the seas of existence.

How are the two—the allegory of the swimmer and Henry's crisis of confidence in reaction to the scientist's revelation of vast impersonal forces—related? Like Cather herself, he has become more familiar than he wished with the discoveries of modern science, which in 1944 seemed to her to have produced little more than the means of destroying everything that mattered. Like Cather, he has come through a crisis of despair, a dark night of the soul, literally a very dark "bad night" in which he was tormented by "revelation, revaluation, when everything seem[ed] to come clear" (*SPO* 761). Like Cather, he has contemplated the loneliness of the universe and has wondered if its vast history has been worth it. Like Cather, he is still not sure but is inclined to feel more hopeful. The simple existence of loveliness, as seen in the girl, is a reassurance. After all, she did not literally spring from her father's gloom-inspiring theories but from his physical passion. Sex, it seems, is involved in the reawakening of hope; perhaps the next time Henry sees the planet Venus in the dawn, he will think of it somewhat differently than as an uncaring "ageless sovereignty" (759).

Even more, the girl is a demonstration of ongoing energy, ongoing willingness to try things. What she and the (implicitly feminized) humanity she represents will try, where they will go other than out to a rock and back, remains unclear. Still, however much she may resemble "a little pink clam in her white shell" of a coat (*SPO* 769), she is far more beautiful than that clam. The process of evolution has produced a beautiful life form indeed. At the end, still uncertain, with nothing resolved, Henry Grenfell returns to his cabin (in Lee's words) "pleased with what he has seen" and with the competence displayed by the geologist's daughter, "his appetite sharpened, to eat his breakfast" (374–75). That detail is an affirmation of the life process wonderfully characteristic of Cather, who for most of her life did enjoy her food. Grenfell is now inclined to chuckle over the evolutionary spectacle rather than bemoan it: "'Anyhow, when that first amphibious frog-toad found his water-hole dried up behind him, and jumped out to hop along till he could find another—well, he started on a long hop.'"

It is an ending of bemused reconciliation. Like a detached spectator in a theater or a circus, Grenfell, or Cather, regards the show with amusement, with a modicum of optimism, and above all with interest. Even at the advanced age of seventy-plus, she regarded attentively a humanity that had come a long way, hopped a long hop. She herself had hopped a long hop. She seems to have felt good, on the whole, about having been a part of the evolutionary pageant. Whether someone or something was steering the "frog-toad" in its quest—that is, whether there was a divine principle in charge—was a question that she simply, at this late point in her life, left alone.[21] A mind of the twentieth century, she accepted the discoveries of science, realized that they left a lot unexplained, and took the show for what it was worth.

WILLA CATHER died the afternoon of April 24, 1947, after a day when she had awakened "a little tired" and stayed in bed (Lewis 197). She was buried at Jaffrey, New Hampshire. The epitaph on her headstone is a line from *My Ántonia:* "That is happiness; to be dissolved into something complete and great." The words are beautiful and fitting. But an even better epitaph might have been taken from her letter to E. K. Brown precisely three months before her death. There she pondered the enrichment of life that comes from knowing, or even knowing about, truly great people. What they do for us, she wrote, is to free our minds from the shallow cant we have been conditioned to revere. They free us to live more honestly and more authentically—as well as more lovingly.[22]

Such a willingness to relinquish commonplaces of false wisdom and to live out the life that seemed to her most authentic, without regard for received pieties and preconceptions, was the essence of the free-spirited Willa Cather. To be sure, that Willa Cather, torn by the conflicts of her inheritance and her own time but struggling to address those conflicts adequately and honestly, was often concealed inside an outer shell of stodgy propriety. It was a shell, like the shell of the clam in "Before Breakfast," that protected the vulnerable naked self inside and afforded her the privacy she needed to go on living and writing as she chose. She prepared a face to meet the faces that she met, and the face she prepared has unfortunately been taken at times as the real one. What the real self of Willa Cather was we cannot say with certainty. Like the peculiarly dual "frog-toad" in mid hop, it was a self still evolving and a far more complex, far more interesting self than the safe and sanitized figure she has sometimes been made out to be.

NOTES

ALL OF the chapter epigraphs are from Cather's poetry as reprinted in the Library of America volume *Stories, Poems, and Other Writings* (1992), which follows the 1933 edition of *April Twilights and Other Poems*. The original (1903) *April Twilights* consisted of thirty-seven poems. Thirteen were deleted and twelve added for the 1923 *April Twilights and Other Poems* published by Knopf. In 1933 one more poem, "Poor Marty," was added.

The following abbreviations are used to identify the sources of documents cited in the notes:

Allegheny	Allegheny College, Pelletier Library, Meadville, Pa.
Amherst	Amherst College, Amherst, Mass.
Arkansas	University of Arkansas, Fayetteville
Beinecke	Yale University, New Haven
BPL	Boston Public Library
Buffalo	Buffalo and Erie County Public Library, Buffalo, N.Y.
Church	First Church of Christ, Scientist, Boston
Colby	Colby College, Miller Library, Waterville, Maine
Columbia	Columbia University, New York City
Dartmouth	Dartmouth College, Hanover, N.H.
Duke	Duke University, Durham, N.C.
EPFL	Enoch Pratt Free Library, Baltimore, Md.
Exeter	Phillips Exeter Academy, Exeter, N.H.
Georgetown	Georgetown University, Washington, D.C.
Harvard	Harvard University, Houghton Library, Cambridge
HRC	University of Texas, Harry Ransom Humanities Research Center, Austin
Huntington	Huntington Library, San Marino, Calif.
Indiana	Indiana University, Lilly Library, Bloomington
JPML	J. Pierpont Morgan Library, New York City
Kentucky	University of Kentucky, Margaret I. King Library, Lexington
LC	Library of Congress, Washington, D.C.
Loyola	Loyola University, New Orleans
Michigan	University of Michigan, Bentley Historical Library, Ann Arbor
Middlebury	Middlebury College, Middlebury, Vt.
ND	University of Notre Dame, Notre Dame, Ind.
Nebraska	University of Nebraska, Love Library, Lincoln
Newberry	Newberry Library, Chicago

NHHS	New Hampshire Historical Society, Concord
NPL	Newark Public Library, Newark, N.J.
NSHS	Nebraska State Historical Society, Lincoln
NYPL	New York Public Library
Penn	University of Pennsylvania, Van Pelt-Dietrich Library, Philadelphia
PLY	Patricia Lee Yongue, Private Collection
Princeton	Princeton University, Firestone Library, Princeton, N.J.
PSU	Pennsylvania State University, University Park
Richmond	University of Richmond, Boatwright Memorial Library, Richmond, Va.
Stanford	Stanford University, Stanford, Calif.
TWU	Texas Woman's University, Blagg-Huey Library, Denton
UNC	University of North Carolina, Chapel Hill
UNH	University of New Hampshire, Durham
USC	University of Southern California, Los Angeles
Vermont	University of Vermont, Bailey/Howe Library, Burlington
Virginia	University of Virginia, Alderman Library, Charlottesville
WCPM	Willa Cather Pioneer Memorial, Red Cloud, Neb.
Wellesley	Wellesley College, Margaret Clapp Library, Wellesley, Mass.
WSHS	Wisconsin State Historical Society, Madison
Yale	Yale University, University Library, New Haven

PREFACE

1. In this, though not in many other important respects, I agree with Patrick W. Shaw, who begins his psychoanalytic study of Cather by stating, "Like many artists, Willa Cather knew personal conflict" (1).

1. East / West, Home's Best

1. Throughout this study, I rely heavily on James Woodress's *Willa Cather: A Literary Life* for factual information.

2. See Sharon O'Brien's explanation that she wished to link herself to a hero who, because he was dead, could not interfere with her distinct goals (*Emerging* 107–9). Equally, she could have linked the "William" she affected during her adolescence to her grandfather Cather, still alive and respected in the community, but linked it instead to this uncle.

3. Woodress (*Literary* 17) says concisely that William Cather "profited by his Union allegiance."

4. WC to Dorothy Canfield Fisher, April 3 [1928], Vermont; to Zoë Akins, Dec. 22 [1932], Huntington; to Ferris Greenslet, n.d. [about Nov. 25, 1940], Harvard bMS Am 1925 (341). Cather was in need of comfort at the time, following the deaths of her brother Douglass and close friend Isabelle McClung Hambourg, in June and October of 1938.

5. Woodress (*Literary* 28), quoting with slight changes (for instance, in capitalization) WC to Irene Miner Weisz, Feb. 27, 1942, Newberry.

6. See the family tree in Hermione Lee (25), showing two tuberculosis deaths in Cather's father's generation alone.

7. Charles Cather to Mr. and Mrs. George P. Cather, Jan. 22, 1874, Beinecke.

8. When George and Frances Cather left Virginia, they apparently knew only that they were going to the Midwest. On Dec. 12, 1873, Mrs. G. M. Cather wrote to Jennie Cather Ayre from Iowa that they had "talked about Nebraska & Kansas both" (NSHS). William Cather to Charles Cather, Feb. 21, 1883, Nebraska.

9. Caroline Cather to Jennie Cather Ayre, April 17, 1873, NSHS. WC to Mrs. Ackroyd, May 16, 1941, Virginia. Margie Anderson's brother Enoch also accompanied the Cathers, as a farm hand, but he drifted on when they moved to town, like the hired men in *My Ántonia*.

10. The Little Blue River was traced by John C. Fremont's party in 1842, only thirty-one years before the first Cathers came to the Divide. See Donald Jackson and Mary Lee Spence (1:173, 178–79) and Charles Preuss (12).

11. Cather, interview reported in the *Philadelphia Record*, Aug. 10, 1913; rpt., *KA* 448 and also *WCIP* 10. Woodress (*Literary* 42–43), quoting WC to Witter Bynner, June 7, 1905, Harvard bMS Am 1629 (21). Cather, "On the Divide," *Overland Monthly*, 1896; rpt., *CSF* 495–96.

12. O'Brien points out that Cather's language in the 1913 interview, in describing her adjustment to life on the prairie, "first equates mother and daughter: both are homesick and ignored," but later "differentiates herself from her homesick mother and surpasses her, mastering the land that left her mother incapacitated" (*Emerging* 68). Woodress (*Literary* 44), approximately quoting WC to Witter Bynner, June 7, 1905, Harvard bMS Am 1629 (21). It is not clear why Woodress regards this letter and the 1913 interview as exaggerations.

13. WC to Carrie Miner, April 21, 1930, WCPM.

14. A more comprehensive survey of Cather's attention to Germans is given by Peter Sullivan (10–11). The importance of early dislocation and the oppositional pull between movement and enclosure is well recognized among Cather's biographers and critics.

15. WC to E. J. Overing Jr., president of the Board of Education in Red Cloud, April 30, 1909, read at commencement in 1909 and published in the *Red Cloud Chief* May 27, 1909, WCPM; rpt., *WCIP*, 174–76. Katherine Anne Porter's "Reflections on Willa Cather" gives an appealing picture of Cather's home education (*Essays* 30–31).

16. WC to Mariel Gere, June 1 [1893?], written on letterhead imprinted Office of C. F. Cather / Real Estate and Loan Brokers / Red Cloud, Neb.; to Mariel Gere, June 16, 1894; to Carrie Miner Sherwood, March 13, 1919; all WCPM. Regarding the growing anti-Semitism of America in the 1920s and the eruption of nativism in general, see Walter Benn Michaels (127).

17. My thanks to Cynthia Griffin Wolff for calling attention to this point at the 1997 Willa Cather Seminar in Winchester, Va. Sarah Bernhardt, for example, had a "predilection for male rôles" (Horville 59).

18. As I argue in chapter 2, Cather's experiences in the theater also contributed to her negotiation between and among gender roles. See Judith Butler's discussion of "the variable construction of identity" (5).

19. At the Willa Cather Seminar in June 1997 Wolff likened Cather's adolescent self-presentation to adolescent behaviors such as dyeing one's hair pink or green. Wolff also speculated, on the basis of research into prairie conditions, that the cropping of the young Cather's hair may have been occasioned by a case of head lice. If so, her flamboyantly boyish dress may have been an effort to outface the embarrassment of the situation by using it in a quasi-theatrical way, to create a persona. For relations with her mother, see Woodress ("Dutiful" 23, 21, 30), conceding that the two "often clashed in her youth." Something of the severity of that clash is conveyed in an undated letter from Cather to Dorothy Canfield apparently following an exchange of letters between Canfield and Cather's mother in May 1903; see the Dorothy Canfield Fisher papers, Vermont; see also an undated letter from Cather to Jennie Cather revealing conflicts over her mother's sensitivity about the retarded hired girl, Marjorie (TWU).

20. Frances Cather to Jennie Cather Ayre, Dec. 28, 1873, NSHS. Carroll Smith-Rosenberg states that crushes among female students of the New Woman generation were common (250–52).

21. Like Wolff, Helen Buss wonders at "the wisdom of the parents who tolerated and permitted" her experiments in self-image (141).

22. See, however, Buss's critique of Woodress's determined reading of Cather in terms of purposefulness (126–27).

23. Regarding Cather's tie to her mother, see Buss (139–41), who argues that she "remained her mother's child all her life." Cather's letters do not always bear out Buss's insistence that even in old age she "yearned to be with her extended family as often as possible." Woodress (*Literary* 20) closely paraphrases and partly quotes WC to Helen Louise Cather Southwick, Oct. 24, 1946, extracts made by E. K. Brown, Beinecke.

24. See, however, Bernice Slote's argument that Cather "had a rather glittering life of it, both professionally and socially," during this year ("Writer" 22–23). Woodress gives a balanced summary of the frustrations of this period (*Literary* 89–111). His incisive comment that Red Cloud "both attracted and repelled her" (60) puts its finger on her dual impulse with a nice precision.

25. Henrik Ibsen, *The Lady from the Sea and Other Plays*, trans. Clara Bell et al. (1890), with flyleaf inscribed and dated in Cather's hand, HRC. WC to Mariel Gere, May 2, 1896, WCPM.

26. WC to Mary Hunter Austin, Nov. 9, 1927, Huntington, MS folder AU 1939; to Mabel Dodge Luhan, Nov. 22 [1932?], Beinecke.

2. "AVID OF THE WORLD, ALWAYS WONDERING"

1. Much has been made of Cather's signing herself William. Her signature on a childhood composition on dogs, however, makes it clear that she did not first take up the name in adolescence. See "Dogs," NSHS. WC to Mrs. Helen Louise

Stevens Stowell, Aug. 31, 1888, WCPM. Five years later Cather was still using a language of kingly power to describe her status in her father's office, telling the Gere sisters that she reigned there alone; WC to Mariel, Ned, and Frances Gere, June 30, 1893, WCPM.

2. WC to Mrs. Helen Stowell, May 31, 1889, WCPM.

3. Ready availability of national magazines and a high degree of family interest are indicated by the presence in the Cather family library of "home-bound volumes of the *Century* and ladies' magazines of the eighties" (Slote, *KA* 39).

4. Mary Suzanne Schriber states that in the later nineteenth century "the female traveler who ventured into international spaces was often a type of the New Woman" (41); Cather so ventured in 1902. See also Lynn D. Gordon (213–15, 223).

5. What Walter Ong says of Learned Latin is equally true of Classical Greek: "Because of its base in academia, which was totally male—with exceptions so utterly rare as to be quite negligible—Learned Latin . . . was sex-linked, a language written and spoken only by males" (113). The visual separation of head from body in Woodress's account was pointed out to me by Susan Stabile, Texas A&M Univ., personal communication.

6. However, an account written many years later by a woman who grew up in Red Cloud somewhat over a decade after Cather emphasizes the rationality of her "simple, easily-donned" attire; see Elsie Goth, "Story by Willa Cather's Neighbors," *WCIP* 131.

7. Sally Sims reports that some doctors, however, cautioned that "certain anatomical and physiological peculiarities" made it dangerous for women to "undergo excessive physical strain." According to Sims, physicians also, oddly enough, made pronouncements about appropriate fashions for bicycling (130). Severa regards the bicycle as "the most influential element in the reform dress movement in the decade of the nineties" and goes on to quote the report of a midwestern weekly newspaper in 1894 that "today women in trousers riding a bicycle cause little or no comment" (466). We can guess that if these trousered "wheel" women had been perceived as male impersonators, they would have stirred considerably more reaction.

8. WC to Ellen and Frances [Gere], July 30, 1895, WCPM.

9. WC to Mariel Gere, July 16, 1891, WCPM.

10. Susan Rosowski points out, however, that under the influence of botanist Charles E. Bessey, a noted faculty member and textbook author at the University of Nebraska, Cather would retain a lifelong ecological sense and an interest in direct observation ("Ecology" 37–51).

11. WC to Will Owen Jones, June 2, 1927, *Nebraska State Journal*; rpt., *WCIP*, 180.

12. It is this publication that Edith Lewis is referring to when she mistakenly credits Cather with "help[ing] to found" the *Hesperian* (32), which according to Woodress (*Literary* 75) was "the oldest campus literary publication" at the University of Nebraska.

13. The letters in question include four to Louise Pound located at Duke Univ. and two to Mariel Gere at WCPM. Cather seems to have been referring to the ending of her ardent relationship with Pound when, in a letter to Mariel dated June 16,

1894, she speaks of a scar that would never heal and thanks Mariel for her patience in listening when she ranted about the beauty, grace, and artistic talents of some feminine person and went into raptures over touching her hand by accident. The amorous nature of the relationship, sometimes explained away by critics who do not wish to see Cather as a lesbian, seems evident in these letters. Marilee Lindemann, who examines the letters "as literary documents and rhetorical performances," notes that Cather "used the word 'queer' six times in writing to or about Louise" (17–18).

14. Dorothy Canfield to WC, Jan. 1, 1905, Vermont.

15. WC to Ferris Greenslet, Oct. 23, [1916], Harvard bMS Am 1925 (341), folder 3.

16. WC to Mariel Gere, May 2, 1896, WCPM. Mildred Bennett, noting Cather's latter-day "hold[ing] forth about her poverty-stricken college career," insists that she "did not have to make her own way" and points out very sensibly that her graduation ball gown, her elaborate outfit for attending the opera in Chicago, and equally elaborate photographs of Cather in both seem to indicate "no undue hardship" (215–16 and unnumbered photograph pages following 222).

17. An interviewer reported in *Century Magazine* in 1925 that for Cather writing had been "purely a source of pleasure" distinct from the matter of "earning a living," for which she "employed other methods" (*WCIP* 75).

18. Regarding the evolving meaning of the word *lady*, which Cather used in her attack on clubs, see Karen J. Blair (1–2, 59–60, and passim). Sandra M. Gilbert and Susan Gubar observe that some of Cather's "critical statements raise interesting questions about the concept of female misogyny" (174).

19. Joan Shelley Rubin (108) labels women's study clubs "groups dedicated to perpetuating genteel formulations of culture." On Cather's bohemianism, see, for example, WC to Mariel Gere, Aug. 4, 1896, and Sept. 19, [1897?], WCPM. Lucius Sherman's *Analytics of Literature* may have elevated a system of word counting to ludicrous heights (Woodress, *Literary* 80), but it also argued that art arose from the sharing of emotion through suggestiveness, or "things not said," extolled "the ability to produce most effects by fewest means," and spoke explicitly of "the kingdom of art" (122, 313, 130, 252). These parallels with Cather's noted essay "The Novel Démeublé" were pointed out by Evelyn I. Funda in a 1997 paper.

20. See Yongue (43–56 and 111–25) and also Sergeant (58), who notes Cather's "respectful[ness] of wealth and swagger."

21. WC to Ellen and Frances [Gere], 30 July 1895; to Grace [?], Aug. 29, 1894; WCPM. In summarizing the importance of journalism in creating a "space in which women could imagine themselves in a variety of [professional] writing roles," Schriber observes that "if a woman chose to seek entrée to genteel publications addressed to an elite or highbrow audience, she could adopt the persona of art critic" (135). Quite obviously, Cather did so choose. WC to the Gere sisters, Jan. 2, 1896, WCPM.

22. WC to Mariel Gere, April 24, 1912, Nebraska.

23. In a review published Feb. 4, 1899, in the *Lincoln Courier,* Cather praised the comedienne and male impersonator Johnstone Bennett as "the trimmest tailor-made New Woman of them all" (*W&P* 543–44).

24. Gilbert and Gubar comment, in *Sexchanges*, on her boyish attire in adolescence and reprint the Steichen photo, but they do not mention the graduation ball gown or her later femininely marked flamboyance in dress.

25. WC to Mrs. Helen Stowell, May 31, 1889, WCPM. WC to Louise Pound, n.d. (dated by Olivia Pound June 15, 1892) and June 29, 1893, Duke Univ.; to Mariel Gere, June 16, 1894, WCPM.

26. Cather's copy of the *Poetics* is not inscribed but bears characteristic markings, many of which have the ring of lecture notes. Her copy of Shakespeare's *Songs, Poems, and Sonnets*, ed. William Sharp, is inscribed and heavily marked. Her copies of Hugo's *Hernani* and *Ruy Blas* are inscribed, and the latter bears the notation "State University, Lincoln, Nebraska." Volumes 1 and 2 of the *Poetic and Dramatic Works* of Browning, in 6 vols. (1890), are inscribed, the second showing "1891," and both volumes bear annotations of a definite classroom nature. She seems especially to have studied "Sordello." All at HRC.

27. Cather told a correspondent in 1929 that she had begun to read French when she was fifteen or sixteen and for many years preferred French writers from Victor Hugo to Maupassant to their English contemporaries; WC to Mr. Feuillerat, Nov. 6, 1929, Yale.

28. Cf. the meaning of "metropolis" in Mary Louise Pratt's *Imperial Eyes: Travel Writing and Transculturation* and Edward Said's *Culture and Imperialism*. Cather's identification with the metropolis, in the sense of a center of economic power that would express itself in imperialistic enterprises, would bear fruit in *Death Comes for the Archbishop*, where the two priests at the center of the narrative are engaged in an explicitly imperialistic endeavor whose value she questions in only the most indirect and disguised, perhaps unconscious, ways, while overtly giving it her endorsement.

29. I am explicitly contesting the view of Gilbert and Gubar (175) that Cather "distrust[ed]" and distinguished herself from New Women. Their treatment of the late story "The Old Beauty" as a "critique of 'liberated' womanhood by contrasting the elegance of an aging socialite with the vulgarity of two New Women" illustrates the danger of generalizing about Cather by conflating her early views with her late ones or by ignoring the contrarieties in her work.

30. Jeanette Barbour, "A Woman Editor," *Pittsburg Press*, March 28, 1897; rpt., *WCIP*, 2 and xxxii. The name of the city was then usually spelled without an *h*. On the rational dress movement, see Patricia Marks's study of satiric rhetoric in magazines and newspapers both in England and in the United States (2–3, 159–61, and passim); see also Sally Sims (125–45).

3. ESTABLISHING A CAREER / ESTABLISHING GENDER

1. WC to Will Owen Jones, March 22 [1927], Virginia; copy also at NSHS.

2. WC to Mariel Gere, March 12 [1896]; to Mariel, Ellen, Frances, Allie, and Maysie Gere, Jan. 2, 1896; to Mariel Gere, May 2, 1896; WCPM.

3. WC to Charles Gere, March 14, 1896, WCPM.

4. Woodress's conjecture that Cather got her magazine job on Gere's recommendation is at least a "reasonable guess," as he labels it (*Literary* 111). The *Home*

Monthly, a five-cent quarto-size magazine, had been taken over by T. E. Orr that very year, 1896, after having begun publication in 1894 as the *Ladies' Journal*; see Frank Luther Mott (*History* 89). Slote's two introductory essays in *The Kingdom of Art* are the most authoritative source of information about Cather's university and apprentice years.

5. Lois Rudnick (79n.). Cf. June Sochen (ix), who points out that by 1910 the Census Report recorded that "more American women were working than ever before." The definition of "work force," however, never included women who kept boarding houses or took in laundry.

6. WC to Mariel Gere, n.d., except Friday [July 1896]; to Mrs. Gere, July 13 [1896]; to Mariel Gere, Aug. 4, 1896; to Mariel Gere, Oct. 4, 1896; to Mariel Gere, April 25, 1897; to Mariel Gere, n.d., except Friday [July 3?, 1896]; to "Ned" Gere, n.d. [July 27, 1896]; all WCPM.

7. O'Brien's assertion that Axtell was unknowingly admitting into his devout household a "self-proclaimed atheist" (*Emerging* 225) is a considerable overstatement, though Cather had indeed expressed freethinking views and displayed not a little impatience with organized religion. Shaw (1) enumerates among her conflicts being "a free thinker reared amidst Calvinist dogma." WC to Mariel Gere, Aug. 4 [1896], WCPM.

8. Woodress (*Literary* 118), quoting with two minor changes WC to Mariel Gere, Jan. 10, 1897 (apparently an error for 1898), WCPM.

9. WC to Mrs. Charles Gere, July 13 [1896]; to Mariel Gere, Aug. 4, 1896; WCPM.

10. WC to Mrs. George Seibel, July 23, 1897, WCPM.

11. WC to Will Jones, prob. Sept. 7, 1897, WCPM. Slote, in her transcription located at Univ. of Nebraska, dates the letter Aug. 31, but comparison with other letters indicates the later date is more likely. For a similar use of the word *white* see WC to Will Owen Jones, Jan. 15, 1896 (in error for 1897), WCPM.

12. Porter to Donald Elder, Jan. 30, 1941, Papers of Katherine Anne Porter, Univ. of Maryland–College Park Libraries. WC to Frances Gere, June 23, 1898, WCPM.

13. See Christopher Sten (25–29). Sten surmises that a third visit to Washington in May 1917, a month after Congress had declared war, contributed material for *One of Ours.*

14. Woodress avoids giving a date for their meeting. Lee (57) states positively 1899. Byrne and Snyder (39) place the meeting as spring 1899. Edith Lewis's assertion of March 1901 is disproven by Cather's letter to Dorothy Canfield dated Oct. 10, 1899, written from the McClung house.

15. Byrne and Snyder (39) agree that Isabelle had "a reputation for the same Bohemianism which James Axtell had suspected of Cather."

16. For a sampling of the comments of Cather's former students, see Byrne and Snyder (54–64).

17. WC to Dorothy Canfield Fisher, prob. April 9, 1921, Vermont.

18. WC to Louise Pound, June 15, 1892, Duke Univ.

19. WC to Mariel Gere, Aug. 1, 1893; to Edith Lewis, Oct. 5, 1936; both WCPM. Lionel Menuhin Rolfe, a nephew of Yehudi Menuhin, clearly assumed

that "Aunt Willa's" "life-long relationship" with Lewis, which he calls "scandalous in those days," was lesbian (50). Will Owen Jones to Mrs. Charles Gere, Aug. 25 [possibly either 1905 or 1911], Nebraska.

20. In her complex and sometimes troubled relationship with her mother, Cather was typical of New Women, who, "by rejecting marriage and insisting on careers, had repudiated their mothers' world" (Smith-Rosenberg 257).

21. Lee (70) calls McClung the "beautiful romantic 'lost lady' of Cather's life."

22. WC to Mariel Gere, April 25, 1897, WCPM. Slote, partial transcription of Frances Gere to Mariel Gere, April 11, 1900, Nebraska. On the basis of interviews with people who knew both Cather and Nevin in Pittsburgh, Byrne and Snyder (33–35) conclude that she may have "felt a romantic affection" for Nevin but nothing more serious, and they blame the demonstrable hostility of his wife, Anne Nevin, on other factors. WC to Elizabeth Shepley Sergeant, May 21 [1912], JPML. Unless otherwise noted, photocopies of Cather's letters to Sergeant are located at Virginia.

23. Cather's departure from her teaching job to an associate editor position at *McClure's* in 1906 is usually seen as the result of McClure's suddenly having "carried her off" (Woodress, *Literary* 152). She may, however, have done "occasional jobs for McClure" as early as May 1903 (Southwick 94).

24. According to Curtin's listing in *The World and the Parish*, the columns are distributed as follows: during her student years, over 150 in the *Nebraska State Journal* and the *Hesperian* plus a few in the *Lincoln Evening News*; between her graduation and her move to Pittsburgh, 80 in the *Journal* and the *Lincoln Courier*; and during her period of greatest activity as a journalist in Pittsburgh (through 1902) almost 300, including the accounts of her 1902 trip to Europe. A few are duplicates or near duplicates; however, since she sometimes used pseudonyms there may be others that have not been identified.

25. Cf. open letter to Harvey E. Newbranch, editor, *Omaha World-Herald*, published Oct. 27, 1929, as "Willa Cather Mourns Old Opera House," *WCIP*, 184–87.

26. This fact is emphasized by Demaree Peck (esp. 25–33).

27. WC to Will Owen Jones, May 20, 1919, Virginia.

28. Stokes, Booth, and Bassnett (1–2, 11). Actresses, they argue, also served emblematic roles in relation to nationalism, with Ellen Terry, for example, providing "visions of youth and health" that "proved that all was still well with the world" in a time when the British Empire was becoming "over-ripe," and Eleanora Duse, in Italy, offering "an image of the neurotic, troubled soul of an emergent nation" (11).

29. Throughout this section I am drawing on the headnotes provided by Curtin in *The World and the Parish* for factual information such as dates of birth and death. Bennett's assertion that Cather ghostwrote the autobiography of the phenomenally popular British actress Ellen Terry (188) is not confirmed by Woodress, Lee, or O'Brien.

30. She must have been delighted when her name appeared on the cover of *The Golden Book* in May 1927 in a list that included Thackeray (Mott, *History* 120).

31. Rosowski (*Voyage* 8 and passim.); cf. O'Brien (*Emerging*). For the contrary view, that Cather conceived of the true artist as an "imperial self" taking "visionary

possession" of the Other and egoistically absorbing the world into herself, see Peck (e.g., 17 and 30–36). Such either/or definitions of Cather's artistic vision are, I believe, inherently inaccurate.

32. In her introduction to *Willa Cather: 24 Stories*, Sharon O'Brien states that Cather "believed" her youthful statement about women's having only love (ix).

33. Susan Bassnett, "Eleanora Duse," in Stokes, Booth, and Bassnett (143–45). When used in connection with acting styles of the late nineteenth and early twentieth century, terms such as *containment*, *control*, and *realism* need to be taken in a qualified sense. See J. C. Trewin (112, 118) on Bernhardt's rivalry with Duse.

34. Said (124) quotes a press release for a 1986 production listing in the processional scene "1 aardvark, 1 donkey, 1 elephant, 1 boa constrictor, 1 peacock, 1 toucan, 1 red-tail hawk, 1 white tiger, 1 Siberian lynx, 1 cockatoo, and 1 cheetah."

35. Bernhardt is only one in a series of female Hamlets summarized dismissively by Trewin (121). Horville (59) simply states that she "played a great number" of trouser roles. On the *travesti*, see Marguerite Coe (79).

36. William Winter (239–40), quoted in John March (508).

37. Modjeska's exclusion from Russian Poland resulted from a speech she had made before the World's Fair Auxiliary Woman's Congress in Chicago in 1893 (*W&P* 37).

4. FINDING A VOICE / MAKING A LIVING

1. Published resources available for studying Cather as journalist consist of two collections: *The Kingdom of Art*, edited by Slote, and the two-volume *The World and the Parish*, edited by Curtin, published four years after *Kingdom* and based partly on Slote's compilation. The bulk of these two well-annotated compilations and their wide citation in scholarship create an illusion of accessibility. But in fact Cather's early nonfiction is only fragmentarily accessible and in extremely confusing form. The parameters of the two collections overlap, but only partially, Slote's including material published 1893–96 in both commercial and student newspapers (with appendixes reaching back to 1891 and forward to 1913 and 1915), Curtin's covering 1893–1902 but excluding material in student publications while extending Slote's bibliography for the earlier period. Even for columns identified in common, the material does not always overlap, since both volumes print excerpts, not complete columns. The excerpts are arranged according to topical rubrics, not necessarily in chronological order. Only by actually cutting and pasting can one gain a sense of sequential pattern or development, and it then becomes evident that some columns are represented by only a few lines.

Slote's principle of selection was to assemble what she could regard as expressions of the author's "first principles and critical statements," omitting early writings that did not fit that rubric. Curtin attempted to represent the "articles and reviews" generally. For statements of aesthetic principle or critical evaluation, then, there is considerable overlap *for the years 1893–96*. Some pieces of columns whose topics exclude them from Slote appear in Curtin. The abundant writings of the Pittsburgh years whose topics *would* suit them for Slote are to be found only in Curtin. Uncollected resources are available on microfilm at the Nebraska State Historical Society in Lincoln and at the Newberry Library in Chicago.

2. Despite the bluntness with which race was observed and labeled in the latter years of the nineteenth century, American racial consciousness was not so markedly a matter of black and white as it would become in the first decade of the new century, nor had it yet modulated into the overtly racist nativism of the 1920s. Walter Benn Michaels traces these modulations in *Our America*.

3. See *Willa Cather's Collected Short Fiction* (*CSF* 343, 351, 548). There is no complete collection of Cather's stories. I have used this edition wherever possible except for the *Troll Garden* stories, for which I refer to Woodress's scholarly edition (*TG*). Stereotyping of Chinese appears in two early short stories, "A Son of the Celestial," *Hesperian*, Jan. 15, 1893, and "The Conversion of Sum Loo," *Library*, Aug. 11, 1900.

4. Loretta Wasserman argues that her stereotyping characterizations "may be subverting the very stereotype presented" (3). I do not believe that is true, at any rate, of this early sketch.

5. Slote, "Writer in Nebraska," 17, and "The Kingdom of Art," 33. The terms "meatax" and "biting frankness" were used by Cather's mentor at the *Nebraska State Journal*, Will Owen Jones.

6. Robert W. Cherny points out that the *Nebraska State Journal* was "one of the two leading Republican newspapers in Nebraska" and "stood adamantly against the Populist movement ("Populists" 208).

7. WC to Sara Teasdale, May 10 [1931], Wellesley; transcription in Macmillan Company Records, NYPL.

8. Louise H. Westling comments that Kipling "depicted with gusto the late-nineteenth-century imperial version of the classical heroic spirit Cather had absorbed from her studies of Homer and Virgil" (62).

9. O'Brien reminds us that George Sand was "an important model for many nineteenth-century literary women," including George Eliot (*Emerging* 186).

10. Implicitly rejecting the condemnation heaped on Cather for the "manly battle yarn" column, Shi (8–9) argues that it should be seen as comparable to Margaret Fuller's advice to women to "nurture the 'masculine' side of their nature and produce a more vigorous literature" and Mary Cassatt's determination to be a "'masculine and assertive' painter."

11. Elaine Showalter argues that sensationalist women writers of the nineteenth century subverted the ideals and conventions of the domestic novel and gave voice to those women of their audience who may also have wanted to rebel against their domestic roles (159).

12. A similar note of class consciousness is struck in Cather's "The Count of Crow's Nest." A frowsy singer praising the value of scandal explains that if it were not for the *Confessions*, no one would "know anything about Rousseau. . . . That keeps him popular; even my hairdresser reads it." The protagonist comments sarcastically, "Of course it is something to have immortality among hairdressers" (*CSF* 465).

13. WC to Ellen and Frances [Gere], July 30, 1895; to Mariel Gere, Dec. 27, 1895; to the Gere sisters, Jan. 2, 1896; WCPM.

14. Woodress (*Literary* 142) seems to have seen only part of the dilemma when he commented that the review "shows no sympathy at all for nineteenth-century women trapped in matrimony."

15. Lynn Gordon points out that academic and professional women who were "college women of the first generation," the 1880s and '90s, "frequently lived in close lifelong partnerships" (223). Interestingly, in an article about the famous contralto Ernestine Schumann-Heink and several other female performers, Cather mentioned their marriages and domestic lives (Mme. Schumann-Heink was the mother of nine children) without acknowledging that they constituted exceptions to the rule that a woman artist could not give proper attention to her work if she was married, let alone had children; *W&P* 755–60.

16. E. K. Brown, handwritten extract from WC to Helen Louise Cather Southwick, Sept. 17, 1946, Beinecke. She added that she hoped her niece had not seen the volume, because much of it was not very good.

17. Cather reflects on the concept of authenticity in a late letter to E. K. Brown relating an anecdote from not long after the publication of *O Pioneers!* When she downgraded the book in a chance conversation with Louis Brandeis, he praised it as "sincere." Her account to Brown seems to endorse that label; WC to E. K. Brown, Oct. 7, 1946, Beinecke.

18. Paul Fussell identifies "lads" as a favorite usage of the Georgian poets and those of early, but not post-Somme, World War I. Definitively employed by Housman in *A Shropshire Lad,* the word conveyed "a whole set of tender emotions about young soldiers," all of which would become obsolete or be expressed in a different language after the change in sensibility associated with awakening to the full brutality of the war (Fussell 293).

19. Bennett (200–201). A photograph of the inscription appears in Bennett's book.

20. See also Sheryl L. Meyering (237).

21. Garvey (92–94), who emphasizes the story's contrast of effete East and vigorous West, comments that Tommy's feat would have been very nearly the record for distance and speed on paved and level roads, let alone rough and hilly ones.

22. The punctuation of the quoted passage was correct in the February 1904 original publication in *Everybody's:* "tall, unpainted house, with weather-curled boards, naked as a tower; the crook-backed ash seedlings" (*TG* 169). Ann Romines's reading of the story (*Home* 128–34) contests the conventional reading, which assumes the narrator's view is accurate and takes no notice of the fact that Georgiana's own interpretation of her feelings is never given. A letter to Will Owen Jones in response to his published outrage at her disparagement of Nebraska, however, seems to indicate that the narrator's view accurately conveys Cather's intention; she attempts to beg off from Jones's charge on grounds that Nebraska has changed since the period depicted in the story. WC to Dorothy Canfield, n.d. [March 1904?], Vermont; to Will Owen Jones, March 6, 1904, Virginia.

23. See Rosowski (*Voyage,* 20–22) and Marilyn Arnold (*Short* 43–44).

24. Brown (114) observes that "Paul's Case" is a "sort of coda" for the collection, the thematic unity of which may indicate that Cather was "struck by the manner in which [James] always arranged his short-story collections thematically."

25. WC to James Canfield, May 21, 1903, and to Dorothy Canfield, Nov. 6, 1903, Vermont.

26. Slote (*KA* 95) challenges Brown's reading on grounds that "the greedy and insensitive are everywhere, and even in art there are both Trolls and Forest Children." The Forest Children appear in Kingsley's allegory.

27. Elizabeth Moorhead Vermorcken, who met Cather in 1905 at the McClung home, described her as "a fine healthy specimen of young womanhood" who seemed to possess "absolute frankness and honesty" (Moorhead 48). The "real me" phrase is from an interview in the *Omaha World Herald*, Nov. 27, 1921 (*WCIP* 37). Cather later labeled "The Willing Muse" dull and bristled at an editor's proposal to represent her by such banal work; WC to Fred Louis Pattee, Dec. 2 [1926], PSU.

28. WC to Sarah Orne Jewett, Dec. 19 [1908], Harvard bMS Am 1743.1 (15).

29. The articles ran in *McClure's* from January 1907 through June 1908, and the resulting *Life of Mary Baker G. Eddy and the History of Christian Science* was published by Doubleday in 1909 with Milmine, who apparently "didn't write a word," shown as author. The extent of Cather's authorship is discussed by David Stouck in his introduction to the 1993 reprint. See also L. Brent Bohlke ("Eddy" 288–94). Despite denials elsewhere, Cather stated in a letter to E. H. Anderson, head of the New York Public Library, Nov. 24, 1922 (Library Archives, NYPL), that she wrote the entire book except the first chapter. Letters to William E. Chandler, attorney for Eddy's son in a lawsuit filed in 1907, show that Cather was aggressive in her research and was sole author; NHSHS.

30. Brown (ix), copy located in the Papers of Katherine Anne Porter, University of Maryland–College Park Libraries. Quoted by permission.

31. WC to Sarah Orne Jewett, May 10, 1908, Harvard bMS Am 1743, referring to a copy of *A White Heron and Other Stories* (1886) that Jewett had given her on March 29 of that year, now found at the HRC. It is inscribed by Jewett.

32. Slote and Rosowski judge *Alexander's Bridge* to be anything but Jamesian, on grounds that it "put[s] together pre-established meanings to build an external story" rather than forming itself "organically" (Rosowski, *Voyage* 34, citing Slote, introduction to *AB*, viii). However, in emulated techniques as well as its drawing-room world, it is certainly Jamesian.

33. The name Bartley Alexander, often and plausibly read as an allusion to Alexander the Great, was taken from Hartley Alexander, who graduated from the University of Nebraska in 1897, two years after Cather, and became a professor of philosophy there in 1908 (Rosowski, *Voyage* 253; also March, *Companion* 8).

34. Elsa Nettels also makes this linkage (146).

5. Indoor / Outdoor

1. My indebtedness to Joseph Urgo's *Willa Cather and the Myth of American Migration* is evident throughout this chapter. Even so, I sharply disagree with Urgo's belief that Cather "writes . . . against" a narrative of settlement, in favor of a "metaphysics of homelessness" (53, 41). Rather, I see her as writing from a conflicted sense of yearning toward *both* settlement and movement. Woodress (*Literary* 255)

summarizes and partly quotes WC to Elizabeth Shepley Sergeant, April 25 [1913], JPML.

2. In her essay "Miss Jewett," Cather cited Jewett: "The thing that teases the mind over and over for years, and at last gets itself put down rightly on paper—whether little or great, it belongs to Literature" (*SPO* 849).

3. WC to H. G. Dwight, Aug. 24, 1911, Amherst; to S. S. McClure, Oct. 21, 1911 and Nov. 17, 1911, Indiana. Surprisingly, she later told H. L. Mencken that she wrote "The Bohemian Girl" and the first draft of *O Pioneers!* before, rather than after, *Alexander's Bridge;* WC to Mencken, Feb. 6 [1922], NYPL.

4. For example, letters to Mariel Gere, Aug. 4, 1896, Aug. 10, 1896, Sept. 19, 1897, WCPM.

5. For her show of surprise at the story's reception, see WC to Elizabeth Shepley Sergeant, n.d., but postmarked March 1, 1912, JPML. For her visit to "the Bohemian country" in 1912, WC to Louise Pound, June 28 [1912], Virginia; to Sergeant, April 29, 1912, JPML, and July 5 [1912], Virginia; to Annie Adams Fields, July 24, 1912, Huntington. For Isabelle's intervention in a "misunderstanding" at *McClure's,* WC to Cameron Mackenzie, Nov. 3, 1911, Indiana. Sergeant's and Akins's assurances about the story are indicated in letters to Sergeant, March 1, 1912, and to Akins, Oct. 31 [1912], Virginia.

6. WC to Mr. Winter, Nov. 5 [prob. 1913], WCPM.

7. To be sure, Pound and Eliot turned toward Classical models less canonical than Virgil. On Cather's stylistic modernism, see Middleton.

8. See Cather, "Nebraska" (236–38). The Sioux controlled much of Nebraska until close to the time the Cathers began to settle there, but Cather in effect erases them in writing of "the feeble scratches on stone left by prehistoric races, so indeterminate that they may, after all, be only the markings of glaciers, and not a record of human strivings" (*OP* 25; Fischer 32–34). Cf. Westling (67). Cather's awareness of the presence of the Sioux is demonstrated by her reference to the naming of the town of Red Cloud in an interview in 1913 (*WCIP* 9).

9. Woodress (*Literary* 237), quoting WC to Sergeant, n.d., JPML.

10. Woodress (*Literary* 237), quoting WC to Sergeant, n.d. but probably early 1913, JPML. Cather scoffs at the standard notion that Dvořák built his symphony out of Negro melodies.

11. It is not clear why Stouck believes it is "particularly" likely that the characters of this book are composites.

12. WC to Sergeant, April 14 [1913], JPML.

13. Alexandra's trip is by no means taken to learn about "more-popular farming techniques," as Peck asserts (81). The farming techniques she learns in the river valley and applies to high-land farming are new ones just being developed on the basis of university research that prove so distinctly *un*popular that her brothers fear they will be ridiculed.

14. I am grateful to my student Jean Carol Griffith for her paper surveying totalizing masculine theories of American literature and the West. Her rereading of Alexandra's dream has strongly influenced my own.

15. WC to Sinclair Lewis, Jan. 14, 1938, Yale. Lee (332) uses the word "gullible"

from this letter but without the point regarding immigration. Even Cather's early novels imply anxiety that America faced "'barbarian' incursions as waves of immigrants from the poorer fringes of Europe poured into Ellis Island" (Reynolds 48).

16. Woodress (*Literary* 250–51), closely paraphrasing and partly quoting WC to Elizabeth Shepley Sergeant, Sept. 12 [1913], JPML. WC to Sergeant, Sept. 22 [1913], JPML.

17. WC to Ferris Greenslet, March 28, 1915, Harvard bMS Am 1925(341).

18. See WC to Elizabeth Shepley Sergeant, July 4 [1913], JPML, where she refers to Thea Kronborg as Kronstall (the name not yet finalized) and speaks about how she plans to construct her wardrobe. She may have pulled the name out of a telephone directory; WC to Sergeant, Oct. 11, 1913, mentions reading directories in various cities, including the letters *L, K,* and *O* in Minneapolis, where there would have been many residents of Scandinavian extraction. O'Brien notes that Alexandra draws on imagination and inspiration, has a "muse" (the Divide itself), and displays an artist's concern with technique in pursuing her "artistic project" (*Emerging* 434–38). WC to Will Owen Jones, May 29 [1914], Virginia.

19. WC to Elizabeth Shepley Sergeant, Nov. 19 [1913], JPML; Woodress (*Literary* 135, closely paraphrasing WC to Frances Gere, June 23, 1898, WCPM). On Fremstad's vigor, see WC to Will Owen Jones, May 29 [1914], Virginia (quoted with slight variations by Woodress, *Literary* 258). WC to Sergeant, April 25 [1913], Pierpont Morgan.

6. EMERGENCE / NOSTALGIA

1. Woodress (*Literary* 225, quoting WC to Mariel Gere, April 12, 1912, WCPM). If the operation was gynecological, a possibility suggested both by her reticence as to its nature and by her age, thirty-eight, the gendered quality of the landscape in which she recovered her vitality (seen by Moers, O'Brien, and others) becomes doubly significant, as does the fact that she enjoyed what was apparently her first heterosexual flirtation in years. Once again, she was experimenting in the performance of gender.

2. O'Brien's reference (414) to the "'unguarded sexuality' Cather attributed to Panther Canyon" elides the fact that it was not Cather but Ellen Moers who attributed "unguarded sexuality" to the topography there.

3. Philip Hoare attributes to Lee a view of Cather as "asexual" (212). Woodress (*Literary* 6, quoting WC to Elizabeth Shepley Sergeant, May 21 [1912], JPML, which bears a note by Sergeant stating that Lewis asked her to "reserve" the letter). On the serenade, see WC to Sergeant, June 15 [1912], JPML.

4. Woodress (*Literary* 8, quoting WC to Elizabeth Shepley Sergeant, May 21 [1912], JPML. Probably Cather's clearest conception of artists' models had been established by George DuMaurier's 1894 novel *Trilby,* in which Trilby poses in the nude.

5. WC to Louise Pound, June 28 [1912], Virginia. The date of her arrival in Red Cloud is specified in a letter to S. S. McClure, June 12 [1912], Indiana. Woodress (*Literary* 237, quoting WC to Elizabeth Shepley Sergeant, n.d., noted by Sergeant as early 1913, JPML).

6. WC to Will Owen Jones, May 20, 1919, Virginia; to S. S. McClure, June 12 [1912], Indiana. This same letter to McClure gives irrefutable evidence that despite later denials Cather did write the biography of Mary Baker Eddy. There were articles in the Christian Science series, she said, that she simply "could not write the way he wanted them" (Woodress, *Literary* 230, closely paraphrasing the letter).

7. David Stouck ("Austin" n.p.) argues that Cather borrowed from Austin's "The Conversion of Ah Lew Sing" (*Overland Monthly* 1897) in "The Conversion of Sum Loo" (1900). Three poems by Austin were published in *McClure's* in late 1911 and 1912, while Cather was managing editor. See Stout ("Austin" 39–60).

8. Nancy Porter asserts that *The Song of the Lark* was "directly influenced" by Austin's work (296). Blanche Gelfant compares the two novels (246), and Sally Allen McNall ("American" 43–52) examines parallels of both to Mary Wilkins Freeman's *The Butterfly House* (1912) and Elizabeth Stuart Phelps's *The Story of Avis* (1879). Cather's awareness of both writers is evidenced by passing comments in her journalism (on Phelps, *W&P* 731; on Freeman, *W&P* 482, 582, 865). See also Grace Stewart. Since the life experiences of Austin and Cather were similar in many respects and their novels are strongly autobiographical, the textual parallels might seem coincidental, but when we consider how numerous and how close they are, it seems more likely that Cather had read the book and it remained in her mind when, in late 1913, the year after its publication, she began work on material with similar themes.

9. She described to her Aunt Franc the apartment, the process of fixing it up, and four beautiful Persian rugs she was proud to own, but omitted any reference to Lewis's role or even her existence; WC to Mrs. George P. Cather, Feb. 23, 1913, Nebraska.

10. WC to Sarah Orne Jewett, Oct. 24 [1908], Harvard bMS Am 1743.1 (15).

11. Floyd Dell favorably reviewed *O Pioneers!* shortly before he left Chicago for New York in 1913. He and Cather were friends in the '20s. For a sense of spatial and social relationships in Greenwich Village, see Steven Watson; I have particularly used the map on 124–25.

12. WC to Mrs. George P. Cather, Feb. 23, 1913, Nebraska; to Elizabeth Shepley Sergeant, April 22 [1913], JPML. Woodress (*Literary* 253), largely quoting WC to Sergeant, April 22 [1913].

13. See also Gilbert and Gubar (271–78).

14. H. L. Mencken rejected the story for *Smart Set* because he felt it might be libelous. The main character was modeled on the deceased singer Lillian Nordica, and her last husband, George Young, was portrayed unflatteringly in the story. Young threatened a lawsuit after it appeared in *McClure's* (Meyering 67).

15. Mrs. C. F. Cather to Dorothy Canfield, May 18, 1903; WC to Dorothy Canfield, n.d. [prob. about May 20, 1903]; Vermont.

16. The tension between these two urges is a central issue in my reading of Cather (see Stout, *Through*). See also Sally Peltier Harvey (50–51).

17. WC to Elizabeth Shepley Sergeant, Dec. 7 [1915], JPML. WC to Ferris Greenslet, June 30 [1915], reveals that the first mock-up of the book jacket had Thea born in Moonstone, Arizona, rather than Colorado, and her escapade with Fred to *New* Mexico rather than to Mexico (Harvard bMS Am 1925 [341], folder 2).

Though her correction of the errors was phrased jocularly, the incident must have taken its place among her reasons to think Houghton Mifflin was not giving her books due attention.

18. Greenslet pointed out that the first two parts of the total six were "longer than all of the rest of the book put together," raising fears that readers would think the latter sections perfunctory. Cather's reply defending the steady diminishment in scale suggested he let her explain more fully in person. He seems to have had no further qualms, or at least not to have thought they were worth pressing. Greenslet to WC, April 5 and 7, 1915, and WC to Greenslet [April 6, 1915], Harvard bMS Am 1925 (341), folder 26.

19. Romines ("Coming" 408) points out the parallel of the refusals to come to the mother's deathbed—Thea's in *The Song of the Lark* and Jeanne Le Ber's in *Shadows on the Rock*.

20. WC to Elizabeth Shepley Sergeant, April 29 [1912], JPML.

21. Regarding the influence of Puvis de Chavannes, see also Robert Hughes (116), cited in Phyllis Rose (143).

22. See Clinton Keele. An undated letter to Annie Fields, prob. April 1908 (Huntington), confirms that Cather frequented the Boston Public Library.

23. When men are shown at leisure in American painting of the period, they are involved in vigorous activities (Van Hook 147–48).

24. Cather's awareness that a chaperone was expected is clear in a letter written in the summer of 1915, when she was supposedly working on proofs of *Lark* for Houghton Mifflin. Discussing an aborted plan to travel to Germany for *McClure's*, she adds that since McClure would be along there had to be a third party. WC to Ferris Greenslet, n.d. [except "Saturday," prob. July 24, 1915], Harvard bMS Am 1925 (341), folder 2.

25. As Judith Fetterley points out, Thea's exceptionalism consists in part in the fact that she "grows up to get what she wants" (222). What this entails, in addition to her artistic achievement and career satisfaction, is a world that includes a Fred Ottenburg: someone who can be both erotically satisfying and supportive. The main character in Austin's *A Woman of Genius* also travels with the man she loves without benefit of marriage, but there the relationship is explicitly, rather than implicitly, sexual.

26. WC to Dorothy Canfield Fisher, Sept. 2 [1916], Vermont.

27. WC to Dorothy Canfield Fisher, Sept. 2 [1916], Vermont.

28. WC to Dorothy Canfield Fisher, March 15 [1916], Vermont. Cather's use of the word *genius* here may be a marker of her lingering awareness of Austin's *A Woman of Genius*.

29. WC to Ferris Greenslet, n.d., but replying to his of April 5, 1915; Harvard bMS Am 1925 (341).

30. Ferris Greenslet, a uniquely knowledgeable source on such a point, reported in 1943 that Cather had come to think *Ántonia* "an 'old-fashioned, romantic, and badly-constructed tale'" (119). It is a tantalizing statement. One wonders if the weakness she had come to see in the book was its liability to being read in Jim's nostalgic terms.

31. Deborah Lambert's constructively resistant reading is flawed by her failure to distinguish between Jim's perspective and Cather's. She thus sees the book as a betrayal of the vision Cather enunciated in Alexandra and Thea. Although Lambert seems to heed Blanche Gelfant's decade-earlier injunction to read *Ántonia* for its negations and evasions, she disregards Gelfant's reading of Jim as a disingenuous and self-deluded narrator ("Forgotten"). The ironic reading of Jim Burden has been influential in Cather studies but is by no means universal. As recently as 1990 Susie Thomas judged that Cather wrote convincingly as Jim Burden (100).

32. Cather's impulse to locate her new heroine in traditionally female spaces such as the kitchen—to make, Romines writes, "a housekeeping woman the *center* of a fiction for the first time" (*Home* 149)—may have emerged from her satisfaction in successfully taking over the family kitchen in Red Cloud in the late summer of 1916. She wrote to Sergeant that there had been "eight in the family all the time" and it had kept her hustling, but "on the whole" she had "enjoyed it." Having attained "the secret of good pastry at last," she believed she would "never be intimidated by a kitchen range again" (Woodress, *Literary* 284, quoting WC to Elizabeth Shepley Sergeant, Nov. 13 [1916], JPML).

33. I place considerable weight on the designation Cuzak's rather than Ántonia's and the fact that Jim refers to them as boys though there are several girls. It should be noted, however, that when he first encounters the children he asks if they are Mrs. Cuzak's boys (*MA* 319).

34. Thurin (211) finds Lena, on the contrary, "almost a caricature of a certain kind of 'new woman.'"

35. Woodress proposes as model Belinda Mulrooney, "a single woman in her twenties who crossed the Chilkoot Pass in early 1897, . . . established restaurants and hotels, invested in real estate, and bought the claims of discouraged miners" (*MA*, explanatory notes 471).

36. William J. Stuckey writes that Jim is too preoccupied with his ideal of Ántonia to question his demands on her (477).

37. On the blurry line between autobiography and fiction, see Leah Hewitt.

7. COMING TO AMERICA / ESCAPING TO EUROPE

1. WC to R. L. Scaife, 8 March 1917, Harvard bMS Am 1925 (341).

2. On Irish immigration and assimilation, see Noel Ignatiev. It is significant that the biography of McClure written by his son-in-law, Peter Lyon, is entitled *Success Story*.

3. The Chinese Exclusion Act of 1882 was "the first law that prohibited the entry of immigrants on the basis of nationality"; see Ronald Takaki (7–8).

4. "The Daughters of the Poor" is not so totalizing as Freedman would seem to indicate. So far is Turner from branding Jews as the sole perpetrators that he names other ethnic groups as co-offenders and insists that the "Jewish church" has "fought" the prostitution ring "with all its power." But this semblance of evenhandedness is in fact specious; the series as a whole is virulently anti-Semitic. Its hostility to Jewish immigrants may reflect public reaction to a huge labor strike in the New York gar-

ment industry in 1909 by predominantly Jewish female shirtwaist workers; see Takaki (293–97). In the same year, 1909, the *Survey* published an article on Slavic immigrants that similarly reinforced prejudices against immigrants by referring to the Slavs' "widely recognized vices" and calling them "as dumb as horses" (Miles Orvell 48–50). The fact that such nativist articles were appearing in one of the country's leading magazines in 1909–10 gives reason to question Guy Reynolds's claim (73) that the years 1916–18 saw the issue of Americanization "usurped by nativism."

5. Conflicted feelings toward the editorial policy in which she participated may have contributed to the strain that drove Cather to take a long leave of absence in 1912. She referred to it as irritability on the job; WC to S. S. McClure, June 12 [1912], Indiana. In 1911 she complained to Elsie Sergeant that she was tired of another reformer's (i.e., other than Turner) obsession with white slavery; WC to Elizabeth Shepley Sergeant, prob. June 4, 1911, JPML.

6. WC to Hugo Munsterberg, May 13, 1911, BPL.

7. Joseph Urgo's preference for "locating larger patterns of significance" rather than "differentiat[ing]" among the experiences of distinct immigrant groups (*Myth* 64) produces admirable conceptual synthesis, but there were real differences in the ways in which different groups were received.

8. WC to Elizabeth Shepley Sergeant, July 5 [1912], Virginia; and WC to Annie Adams Fields, June 27, 1912, Huntington.

9. Reynolds (73–78) usefully places *My Ántonia* in the context of the popular debate over immigration and assimilation.

10. Robert W. Cherny reports that in 1890 Germans comprised 37.6% of all immigrant Nebraskans, Swedes 12.1%, Irish 10.8%, Czechs (Bohemians) 7.8%, English 6.6%, Danes 5.7%. In Webster County, out of a population of 11,210 there were 550 Germans, 191 English, 184 Canadians (some French, some English), 105 Bohemians, and 84 Swedes ("Nebraska" 32–33).

11. WC to Carrie Miner, March 13, 1918, WCPM. See also Sullivan.

12. The "abominable" quality Jim Burden senses in Blind d'Arnault's playing may have to do with Jim's inability to deal with his own sexual feelings; the pianist's approach to his instrument is described in sexually laden terms as a kind of coupling. I am indebted for this insight to my student Erin Frazier (see March, *Companion* 198–200). A similar performer called "Blind Boone" who played in Red Cloud several times may also have been a model for d'Arnault.

13. Takaki (27–35) demonstrates the continuity of colonialist aggression by showing how English settlement of Ireland was justified not only by the claimed savagery of the Irish people but by the vacancy of the land. The "void" left by the English slaughter of Irish people "meant vacant lands for English resettlement." Even Sir Thomas More used as a rationale for English colonization of Ireland the "fact" that "the natives did not 'use' the soil but left it 'idle and waste.'" A similar rationale was used after World War II for the takeover of land occupied by the Palestinians in the creation of the modern state of Israel.

14. George P. Cather to Jennie Cather Ayre, March 17, 1876, NHSN. Jennie Cather Ayre, a younger sister of Charles Cather and thus an aunt of the infant Willa, died of tuberculosis shortly after moving to Nebraska.

15. Fischer (35) suggests that Cather was probably acquainted with the "mythological" Black Hawk through his Anglo-written "autobiography" and summarizes Richard Slotkin's argument that "as the Indian threat decreased . . . the nostalgic impulse toward the Indians increased" (Slotkin 356–60).

16. See Chris Wilson (89–92) on boosterism by the Santa Fe Railway.

17. Cather contests conventions of the popular Western by redefining it in terms of domesticity and female authority, much as Mary Austin had in precedents of which she was keenly aware.

18. WC to Mr. Glick, Jan. 21, 1925; transcription by E. K. Brown, Beinecke.

19. WC to Carrie Miner Sherwood, Jan. 27, 1934, WCPM. Woodress (*Literary* 473), quoting WC to Ferris Greenslet, March 8, 1936, Harvard bMS Am 1925 (341), folder 19. WC to Zoë Akins, Oct. 28, 1937, Huntington. Cather shared the alarm of "elite universities" in the 1920s about "the increasing numbers of Jewish students," toward whom they directed "new admissions criteria . . . to curb their enrollment" (Takaki 11).

20. WC to Sinclair Lewis, Jan. 14, 1938, Beinecke. Among critics who have contested simplistic readings of the novel, see Sally Allen McNall on regarding it as a site for considering social and cultural complexities ("Immigrant" 22–30).

21. Skaggs (*After* 27) makes the point that "normally, any one of Cather's novels can be linked with another that it reverses," but she links *One of Ours* primarily with *Alexander's Bridge* rather than *My Ántonia*, as I am proposing.

22. Inscription dated April 1928 in Carrie Miner Sherwood's copy of *One of Ours*, NSHS.

23. WC to Dorothy Canfield Fisher, prob. March 8, 1922, Vermont. On Canfield Fisher's role in the completion of *One of Ours* see Madigan ("Canfield 115–29); Madigan ("Introduction" 1–11); and Stout ("Making of One of Ours" 48–56).

24. Cherny ("Populists" 214) points out that the supposed serenity of the novel is also disrupted by Ántonia's or her family's victimization by a land speculator, an owner of grain elevators (Mr. Harling, who attempts to control her social life), a money lender, and a railroad man—a foursome representing "each of the major Populist complaints." This does not mean that Cather was adopting a Populist perspective; exceptionalist and individualist as ever, she resisted constructing this series in class terms.

25. WC to Elizabeth Shepley Sergeant, n.d., postmarked Sept. 28, 1914, and Nov. 13, 1914, JPML. Woodress (*Literary* 260), partially quoting WC to Frances Cather, Nov. 17 [1914], WCPM.

26. Ferris Greenslet to WC, Dec. 15, 1914; WC to Greenslet, Dec. 21 [1914]; Harvard bMS Am 1925 (341). WC to Hugo Munsterberg, July 17, 1911, BPL; to Greenslet, prob. July 24, 1915, Harvard bMS Am 1925 (341), folder 2. Greenslet to WC, Sept. 9, 1915, Harvard bMS Am 1925 (341), folder 27. Greenslet to WC, Jan. 22, 1917, Dec. 18, 1916, and April 26, 1917; Harvard bMS Am 1925 (341), folder 28.

27. WC to Dorothy Canfield Fisher, March 15 [1916], Vermont; to Greenslet,

Dec. 16 [1916], Harvard bMS Am 1925 (341), folder 5; to Mary Rice Jewett, Dec. 29 [1916], Harvard bMS Am 1743.1 (234). On McClure's voyage on the Peace Ship and travels through Axis countries, see Peter Lyon (360–75).

28. WC to Ferris Greenslet, n.d., Harvard bMS Am 1925 (341), folder 24. Another old friend, George Seibel, was outspokenly pro-German. Seibel was the editor of the Pittsburgh *Volksblatt and Freiheits Freund* and authored two pamphlets: *Made in America* and *The Hyphen in American History.* I have found no indication that Cather saw these, but Seibel usually made her aware of his writings.

29. WC to Ferris Greenslet, June 25 [1917] and July 2 [1918], Harvard bMS Am 1925 (341).

30. WC to Fanny Butcher, Jan. 9 [1941?], Newberry. Frederick T. Griffiths astutely observes that Cather "practices the Tolstoyan art of seeing war and peace as describable within the same reality" and that her "technique of using books of peace to set up the terms of the books of war derives from *War and Peace*" (268–69).

31. Deborah Williams has aptly and succinctly called *One of Ours* a novel that "unravels itself as fast as it knits"; personal communication with the author, February 1998.

32. WC to Ferris Greenslet, Jan. 12, 1921, Harvard bMS Am 1925 (341), folder 13.

33. WC to Brother Emil Mohr, May 7, 1937, ND.

34. Both Georgiana of "A Wagner Matinée" and Mrs. Wheeler of *One of Ours* were based on Cather's Aunt Franc, mother of Grosvenor Cather, the cousin killed at Cantigny and the original for Claude. Skaggs writes (*After* 8) that the name Georgiana is "a giveaway" for Mrs. George Cather.

35. Woodress (*Literary* 304), partly quoting WC to Dorothy Canfield Fisher (March 8 and 13, 1922); again (March 8, 1922); Vermont.

36. WC to Dorothy Canfield Fisher, prob. April 7, 1922, Vermont.

37. Reynolds (113–17) surprisingly labels Claude's vanity "feminising," as if only women could be vain, but goes on to argue that Cather was working to define a feminized masculinity that would not be unacceptably effeminate.

38. Blanche Gelfant likens Claude to other "sensitive protagonists" of Cather's in his "yearning for escape from an uncongenial family ("What" 91). Dix McComas writes that the war gives Claude an acceptable way of striking back at his abusive father (93).

39. Griffiths (263) points out that the "literary models" Cather "cites and employs" in the novel "notably lack that firsthand experience which in 1922 was being proclaimed as necessary: the *Iliad,* the *Aeneid, Paradise Lost, War and Peace, The Red Badge of Courage.*" Assuming that she could not write effectively about something outside her direct experience and therefore should not have tried to write a war novel, Woodress claimed in his earlier biography that the further Cather gets from what she had experienced deeply, the less reality the book has (*Life* 192–93).

40. WC to Lorna Birtwell, Nov. 27 [1922?], Columbia.

41. For a survey of American women writers about the war, see Dorothy Goldman (188–208).

42. Maureen Ryan calls Enid's story "the untold story of *One of Ours*" (70).

43. Among Cather's books now at HRC is an inscribed copy of *The New Poetry: An Anthology*, edited by Harriet Monroe and Alice Corbin Henderson (1917), which included Brooke's sonnet, as well as two of Cather's own poems.

44. The hand that keeps reaching out of the side of the trench may be a version of a newspaper photograph of a hand protruding upward from the ground that appears in the video version of Robert Hughes's *The Shock of the New*. I have been unable to locate the original. On Owen, see Jon Stallworthy (184 and 222).

45. WC to Mr. Johns, Nov. 17, 1922, Virginia.

46. Woodress writes (*Literary* 102) that despite Cather's acquaintance with Bryan during her years in Lincoon, "he never made a Democrat out of her."

47. Romines calls William Jennings Bryan's "Cross of Gold" speech, the central point of issue in "Two Friends," a "male event," but when Cather wrote an article about Mary Baird Bryan and Ida Saxton McKinley in 1896 she emphasized Mrs. Bryan's active part in the preparation and successful delivery of the speech (*W&P* 313; Cherny, "Populists" 209). Cather's return to explicit notice of the Populist movement in "Two Friends" and "The Best Years," after having satirized them in fiction only once before (in *O Pioneers!*), may have been impelled by her prolonged grieving for her father. Another of the older men she most admired, Charles Gere, the editor-in-chief of the *Nebraska State Journal*, was also staunchly Republican and anti-Populist.

48. WC to Zoë Akins, Oct. 8 [1919], Huntington; to Ferris Greenslet, May 2 [1919], Harvard bMS Am 1925 (341), folder 10; to Frances Cather, July 4 [1920], Nebraska. Lee (183), quoting with slight variation WC to Dorothy Canfield Fisher, June 17 [1922], Vermont. Lee's footnote mistakenly says 1927.

49. Seven months before *One of Ours* was published Cather asked Mencken to read an advance copy when they became available and insisted that whatever had happened to the state of mind in the country since the war, Claude's feelings had a certain fineness. She urged him to be severe on her if he thought she had been old-maidish, which was very much what he, in fact, thought. WC to H. L. Mencken, Feb. 6 [1922], EPFL, Baltimore. For Hemingway's letter, see Carlos Baker (105). Baker comments that Hemingway "would hardly have been pleased" with Sinclair Lewis's speech awarding him the Gold Medal of the Limited Editions Club on November 26, 1941, but naming him as one of a list of greatest living novelists that included Cather (531). Schwind raises the possibility that Hemingway was unwittingly correct (55, 58–59). D. W. Griffith had "professional military assistance" with the battlefield scenes of *The Birth of a Nation*, but since those scenes were filmed between July 4 and the end of October, 1914, it is unlikely that these professionals had much notion of Great War battlefield landscape (Robert M. Henderson 150, 152).

50. Kirk B——— [?] to WC, Dec. 24, 1922, WCPM. A letter signed "Caroline H. Walker, mother of John Denton Walker, whose body lies in France," Oct. 10, 1922, says, "The last ten pages of your book were written especially for the mothers, and as one of them I thank you. *We know:*—but I cannot understand how you do." One from Charles Bayley Jr., owner of a book shop in Minneapolis, Sept. 30, 1922, declares the last pages of the novel "the most perfect picture of the war that I have read." Not all readers agreed with the arbiters of literary culture.

51. It was estimated that 90 percent of the American troops at the front had lice. The delousing procedures preparatory for return to the States were especially elaborate; see Benedict Crowell and Robert Forrest Wilson (18–24).

52. WC to Dorothy Canfield Fisher, prob. May 8, 1922, Vermont; to Viola Roseboro', June 5 [1920], Virginia; to Helen McNeny, June 15 [1920], WCPM; WC to Mary Rice Jewett, July 26, 1920, Harvard bMS Am 1743 (335). The reference to getting away to France is in WC to Dorothy Canfield Fisher, prob. March 9, 1923, Vermont.

8. FACING A BROKEN WORLD

1. WC to Dorothy Canfield Fisher, prob. April 7, 1922, Vermont.

2. WC to Dorothy Canfield Fisher, March ?, 1923, Vermont; to Ferris Greenslet, Jan. 21 [1921], Harvard bMS Am 1925 (341), folder 13.

3. Mencken, Bourne, and Boynton are quoted by Woodress in his "Historical Essay" in the Scholarly Edition of *My Ántonia* (393, 397), which also summarizes sales figures.

4. Alfred A. Knopf to WC, Sept. 21 [1921], copy, Newberry. Barry Gross states flatly that *One of Ours* is Cather's "worst book" (68).

5. WC to Dorothy Canfield Fisher, prob. March 21, 1922, Vermont.

6. Sinclair Lewis to WC, Nov. 21, 1930, JPML.

7. Examples of the sense of a break in time, including Woolf and Cather, are given by Sandra D'Emilio and Sharyn Udall (153).

8. Read quoted by Joyce Medina (11). Lee (173) writes that the book's "broken-backed" structure (David Daiches's term) is explained by her desire to "give the feeling of a broken world."

9. WC to Ida Tarbell, n.d., Allegheny.

10. Lee, for example, believes that "a sense of unease" pervades The *Professor's House* and *My Mortal Enemy* but the "mood of anxiety" lifted when Cather turned to the "apolitical" *Archbishop* (184, 267). Woodress writes (*Literary* 380) that *My Mortal Enemy* "drained the last bit of gall from her system," allowing her to turn to "the rich affirmations of *Death Comes for the Archbishop*" and find "happiness in historical recreations."

11. WC to Dorothy Canfield Fisher, prob. April 9, 1921, Vermont.

12. WC to Irene Miner Weisz, Jan. 6, 1945, Newberry; to Ferris Greenslet, Feb. 15, 1926, Harvard bMS Am 1925 (341), folder 16.

13. WC to Mary Virginia Cather, March 2, n.y., TWU.

14. Billington relates the Ogdens to the "moral and spiritual degeneration" of Marian Forrester "as she came in contact with the corrupt railroad builders and corruptible politicians who controlled the state." His assertion that Perkins's daughter took umbrage at Cather's portrait of the family is confirmed by a letter to historian Frederick Jackson Turner, March 31, 1931, in which she stated, "I've always resented Willa Cather's Lost Lady. She drew upon her imagination and our family in Burlington and gave an absolutely false and arrogant impression of my mother and of me tho' she would probably say she had never heard of us" (448).

The readiness with which Cather linked the railroad with pioneer heroism derived from the fact that the Burlington came to Red Cloud during the years between her aunt and uncle's arrival and her own, the years she associated with true frontiering. In 1927 she regretted having to miss a dinner of the American Society of Civil Engineers due to illness, having expected to attend as the guest of the president of the Great Northern Railroad; WC to Mary Virginia Auld, n.d., but with envelope postmarked Jan. [date unclear], 1927, copy, Nebraska. Westling (59) argues that Cather's "finest novels" create "a public myth that grants literary validation to the process of exploitation that the railroads set in motion."

15. Cather also declared in "The Novel Démeublé" that Blazac's attention to the minutiae of Paris life, including "the game of finance," was "unworthy of an artist" (*OW* 38). Balzac has been seen as one of the most preoccupied with economic forces of all novelists; e.g., see Edward J. Ahearn (127). Yet Cather also praised his "unity of great art with great emotions" (1896, *W&P* 553), and her copies of Balzac at HRC show careful reading.

16. From the fact that Cather wrote Ferris Greenslet on Oct. 10 1921 (Harvard bMS Am 1925 [341], folder 14) that the house in Toronto had been closed, I am inferring that plans for the move had been made or were being made by the time of her visit.

17. Lee (183), quoting with slight variation WC to Dorothy Canfield Fisher, prob. June 17, 1922, Vermont.

18. Martha Banta associates a move toward simplification or minimalism in fashion and interior decorating in the first decade of the twentieth century with the "aesthetic of absent things" that Henry James cultivated late in his career and calls "elegance as refusal" an "elitist position . . . quite in keeping with the modernist spirit in art" (256–57). Her argument is strikingly applicable to Cather's aesthetic of reduced ornamentation.

19. C. Barry Chabot writes that the narrative in *A Lost Lady* is "most often from the vantage of Niel Herbert" (54). I would say it is most often from a double vantage.

20. Tomoyuki Zettsu observes that Cather's "ambivalent representation of female sexuality . . . is a mark of the novel's modernity" (99).

21. Lee rather surprisingly speaks of the "refusal in her fiction of experimentalism and fragmentation" but then refers to her "preoccupation" with "fractures" from the past as evidence of her affinity with "great modernist works" (189–90).

22. Dalma Brunauer, in one of the earliest essays to cast Niel as a discredited narrator, argues that "while Niel's response is occasionally the same as the author's, taken as a whole, it is not" (47). In contrast, Peck (168) writes that "Niel's response to Marian and her story is the author's own." Sergeant records Cather as having said, in a 1928 conversation, that "every play that amounted to anything" (and we can confidently assume she would have said every novel as well) "contained secret reactions, inner feelings that diverged from what was actually being said" (249).

23. Orvell (407), citing Nathan Rosenberg, *Technology and American Economic Growth* (1972).

24. Patrick Shaw (95–111) recognizes the evocation of a house of prostitution but does not note that the text insistently labels the house Captain Forrester's.

25. Lee believes that Cather saw the same actions as being qualitatively different because "when the nineteenth-century settlers staked their claims and homesteaded, mastering and domesticating the terrain . . . the force of the ideal gave them inalienable rights of property," whereas "with the replacement of ideal by commercial values in the next generation, property rights became questionable" (176). The similarity between Forrester's land acquisition and Peters's calls this comfortable distinction into question. As Urgo writes, "the Captain's relations with Indians were not qualitatively different from Ivy Peters" ("Context" 185).

26. Shaw complains that Marian "fails to uphold the biological imperative to produce children" (101). Quite aside from the assumptions that underlie this charge, it does not accord with the text.

27. In 1939 Cather conducted a sybaritic correspondence with Julian Street including a lengthy disquisition prompted by his reference to a particular wine, Château Cantenac-Brown 1926. Perhaps, she suggested, he meant Château Brane Cantenac, which she herself preferred to Mouton-Rothschild, the wine he had named as his favorite. She agreed with Street as to Montrachet and Richebourg but not with regard to champagnes, finding Perrier-Jouët slightly too dry and preferring a good year of Louis Roederer; WC to Julian Street, Dec. 19, 1939, Princeton.

28. Robert K. Miller, who directed my attention to this point, also remarked, with I believe notable insight, "Maybe Niel is one of her failures"; private conversation, April 17, 1998.

29. Walter Benn Michaels (45–47) discusses the racial sleight-of-hand in *A Lost Lady* as evidence of a new "valorization of the . . . essentially *pre* national" and thus a means of distinguishing between those who might be American citizens (i.e., immigrants) and those who were really Americans (the native born).

30. This recurrent and significant imagery can be linked to the war; photographs and paintings of its devastation were widely circulated, as well as seen in person by many writers and artists. An interesting variant and one closer to Cather appears near the end of Dorothy Canfield Fisher's novel *The Deepening Stream* (1930), when an American couple returning from wartime France notice garbage floating on the water as they come into port.

31. WC to Will Owen Jones and to Zoë Akins, both prob. Dec. 6, 1922, Virginia; to Ida Tarbell, about Dec. 10, 1922, Allegheny.

32. WC to Bishop George Beecher, Feb. 13 [1934] and Sept. 28, 1940, Nebraska. Following Woodress, Skaggs states that Cather wrote *A Lost Lady* "during the winter and spring of 1922," prior to "her one teaching stint at Bread Loaf," and adds that "the dates are important" (*After* 46). If so, it is worthwhile to be as precise as possible. She was at Bread Loaf from July 12 until July 31 or August 1. In a letter to Wilbur Cross, Oct. 11, 1922 (Beinecke), she stated that she hoped to finish a new novelette before going abroad. Notes to Blanche Knopf indicate she finished last-minute changes on the typescript in January 1923 and anticipated correcting proofs before she left for Europe in the spring. We can say, then, that it was completed no sooner than October 1922, but more precisely in January 1923. WC to Blanche Knopf, Dec. 29 [1922] and Jan. 18, 1923, HRC.

33. WC to Bishop George Beecher, Dec. 25, 1943, written on a printed card, Nebraska.

34. WC to Irene Miner Weisz, Aug. 11 [postmarked 1923], Newberry.

35. Cf. Ann Fisher-Wirth, "Cather's writing always betrayed a keen sense of loss" ("Dispossession" 1:37).

36. WC to Miss McAfee at *Yale Review*, Feb. 7, 1924, Beinecke.

37. WC to Dorothy Canfield Fisher, Oct. 22 [1925], Vermont.

38. WC to Mr. and Mrs. Partington [?], June 23 [prob. 1921], Newberry. Frances Gere speculated that Cather "ha[d] it pretty bad" for Nevin; Gere to Mariel Gere, April 11, 1900, transcription by Bernice Slote, Nebraska. Woodress states that the "provenance" of the story is unknown but places its writing as "before going to Red Cloud for Christmas" of 1924 (*Literary* 359). A linkage Cather made in a letter that fall between music and a type of story characterized by emotion may reflect the linkage of the two in the story; WC to Mr. Miller, Oct. 24, 1924, Newberry. A reference to a story in progress, in WC to Miss Lathrop, prob. Nov. 22, 1924, Colby, may refer to either "Uncle Valentine" or *The Professor's House*.

39. WC to Irene Miner Weisz, prob. Feb. 17, 1925, Newberry; to F. Scott Fitzgerald, April 28, 1925, Princeton.

40. The idea of a piece of fiction structured by a pair of houses had been with Cather for some time. On Dec. 20, 1896, she gave a rave review to Henry James's *The Other House* (*W&P* 552–53). WC to Zoë Akins, Sept. 7 [prob. 1924], Huntington.

41. Maxfield (75) challenges the identification of St. Peter with Cather herself proposed by Leon Edel in a 1954 essay expanded in his *The Stuff of Sleep and Dreams*. WC to Dorothy Canfield Fisher, Feb. 27 [1924], Vermont.

42. Robert K. Miller ("Room") has suggested that Cather may have written *The Professor's House* in part as a response to H. L. Mencken's essay "The National Letters," which had much to say about professors, profiteering, and Eurocentric international awareness.

43. Similarly, Lindemann (103) sees Tom's reading of Latin poets as a possible contribution to his "self-destructive desire to participate in the war." Eric Gary Anderson reads *The Professor's House* as "Cather's better war novel" (134). Gay Barton finds that Cather "makes certain issues of cultural appropriation overt in 'Tom Outland's Story' that are merely hinted at in 'The Ancient People,'" from *The Song of the Lark*.

44. A picture postcard Cather sent to Elsie Sergeant in 1912 included a printed text about Acoma noting, but in muted terms, its fall to the Spanish and the labor required for building a church on the massive mesa; WC to Sergeant, May 30 [1912], Virginia.

45. WC to Ferris Greenslet, April 15 [1924], Harvard bMS Am 1925 (341).

46. Blanche Knopf to WC, Oct. 30, 1926, HRC. Fanny Butcher's noting of "the fundamental hatred of the sexes one for the other and their irresistible attraction one for the other" prompted Cather's reply that she had been writing about exactly that basic attraction and repulsion; WC to Fanny Butcher, Oct. 27 [1926], Newberry.

47. WC to Yaltah Menuhin, Sept. 3 [1937?], Princeton.

48. WC to Fanny Butcher, Oct. 27 [1926], Newberry; to Mrs. Charlotte Stanfield, Oct. 16 [postmarked 1926], Virginia; to Will Owen Jones, May 7, 1903, Virginia; to Mary Austin, Feb. 10, 1927, Huntington; to Mary Virginia Auld, prob. Feb. 19, 1927, copy, Nebraska.

49. A time setting of 1900–1901 is also confirmed by the reference to Jean de Reszke's return to the Metropolitan Opera, which occurred at that time, after a long illness in London (*MME* 38).

50. There has been a stubborn debate over the years about the meaning of the phrase "my mortal enemy," with some readers identifying Nellie Birdseye and some indicating more abstract forces. After Fanny Butcher wrote in her review that Myra's husband, "who is the apotheosis of devotion, has always been, fundamentally, her mortal enemy," Cather responded that she had gotten the point perfectly; Oct. 27 [1926], Newberry.

9. WHOSE AMERICA IS THIS?

1. Takaki's invocation of Caliban emerges from an abundance of revisionist readings of *The Tempest* since about 1980 and a use of such readings as a basis for anti-colonialist discourse. For a survey of "the School of Caliban," see José David Saldívar (123–35).

2. For Cather's attraction to a southern "aristocratic heritage," see McDonald (11–13).

3. Reynolds (149) similarly regards Cather as a writer who "chooses *not* to reinscribe the dominant ideology."

4. Zettsu (96) argues persuasively that the name Tom "along with its bearer's 'faithful' behavior as a servant kept by a man from Kentucky" resonates "a world of racial conflicts."

5. Reynolds's description of the "broken-backed" structure of *The Professor's House*, upon which critic after critic has attempted to impose coherence, as a "meditated experiment in form" (146–47) similarly brings Cather within the scope of modernism. Cf. Robert J. Nelson (2, 17): Cather's works characteristically incorporate "a countertext if not an antitext . . . at odds with the major or main text."

6. Notes in Cather's copy of Honoré de Balzac, *Comedie humaine*, vol. 13, trans. Ellen Marriage (1895–1900), HRC.

7. Wasserman calls the belief that Cather resented Hambourg "conjectural" and reads Marsellus as "the true inheritor of the Outland legend" (14–15).

8. WC to Blanche Knopf, July 10 [1931], HRC.

9. Woodress, in the index to *Willa Cather: A Literary Life*, labels the strain of anti-Semitism in Cather's mind "imputed" and seems surprised that Marsellus has been seen as reflecting "bias" (283).

10. WC to Elizabeth Shepley Sergeant, Oct. 4 [1922], JPML.

11. Reynolds uses "the incorporation of America" in connection with *The Professor's House* (124–49). His discussion proposes striking parallels between Cather's novel and Thorstein Veblen's *The Theory of the Leisure Class* (1899).

12. *Rif* is a more recent term meaning "reduction in force." Cather describes

the process without acronyms or euphemism: "the office staff was cut in two" (*MME* 51).

13. See also Marta Weigle and Kyle Fiore (6, 11, and passim). I am indebted to Susan Rosowski for pointing out that Cather apparently read a 1917 book by Paula Gunn Allen's uncle, John M. Gunn, *Schat-Chen: History and Traditions of the Queres Indians of Laguna and Acoma*.

14. WC to Mabel Dodge Luhan, June 12 [1925?], Beinecke.

15. Edith Lewis to Mabel Dodge Luhan, July 20 [1925]; WC to Mabel Dodge Luhan, prob. July 13, 1925; Beinecke. Cather's sources in *Archbishop* have been much studied. See, for example, Edward and Lillian Bloom (209, 221–28).

16. *Archbishop* is indeed "eirenic" on the surface and in many ways also in substance, but its peaceful affirmations conceal problematic undercurrents. WC to Blanche Knopf, Oct. 27 [1925], HRC; to Irene Miner Weisz, Jan. 11, 1926, Newberry.

17. WC to Ferris Greenslet, Feb. 15, 1926, and n.d., prob. May 1926, Harvard bMS Am 1925 (341), folder 16; to Paul Reynolds, about April 26, 1926, Columbia.

18. Woodress (*Literary* 394), quoting WC to Mabel Dodge Luhan, May 26 [1926], Beinecke; to Mary Virginia Auld, n.d. [postmarked Feb. 19, 1927, copy, Nebraska. As Woodress reports (550), she refers to the movie dog as her "crush." WC to Blanche Knopf, May 28 [1926], HRC; to Mabel Dodge Luhan, prob. June 5, 1926, Beinecke. Fred Harvey Indian Detours was organized in 1925, and in 1926 the company began offering "outing[s]-by-motor through the Spanish and Indian Southwest" as a "pleasant break in the [transcontinental] all-rail journey." Weigle and Fiore (28), quoting an Atchison, Topeka & Santa Fe Railway publicity publication.

19. WC to Alfred A. Knopf, June 3, 1926, HRC; to Mr. Bridges, June 10 [1926], Princeton. Cf. WC to Blanche Knopf, n.d., but stamped into the Knopf office on Jan. 11, 1928, HRC. WC to Mary Austin, June 26, 1926, Huntington; to Mabel Dodge Luhan, Nov. 22, 1933, Beinecke. The inscription is quoted by Woodress (*Literary* 395) and by T. M. Pearce (205).

20. WC to Blanche Knopf, Sept. 22 [1926] and n.d., but received Oct. 7, 1926, HRC.

21. "Intimate immensity" is Gaston Bachelard's term, used by Judith Fryer in her study of Wharton's and Cather's spatial sense. WC to Zoë Akins, Sept. 7 [1924?], Huntington.

22. Cather's copy of F. Schuyler Mathews's *Field Book of American Wild Flowers* (1902) at HRC. It is a particular delight to the researcher to find inserted at page 288 a two-headed clover, its thread-like stem and tiny root ball still intact, apparently picked and placed there by Cather herself. On a back flyleaf is written in pencil a variant, perhaps a draft, of her poem "Recognition." Curiously, a front flyleaf (pp. iii–iv) has been neatly cut out, leaving a half-inch stub.

23. WC to unnamed sister, Oct. 27 [1925], TWU. Woodress (*Literary* 396), quoting WC to Ida Tarbell, prob. Oct. 7 or 14, 1927, Allegheny. WC to Fanny Butcher, Oct. 27 [1926], Newberry; to Mary Virginia Auld, n.d. [postmarked Feb. 19 [1927], copy, Nebraska; to Elizabeth Shepley Sergeant, Nov. 19, 1913, JPML; to Dorothy Canfield Fisher, March 8, 1922, Vermont.

24. Cornelia Otis Skinner to WC, prob. fall 1927, WCPM.

25. WC to Paul Reynolds, typed copy of handwritten original made at Reynolds's office, dated as having been received April 26, 1926, Columbia.

26. Patricia Clark Smith sees in Cather's commitment to the model of the *Odyssey* the key to a rhetoric of empire in *Archbishop* ("Achaeans" 107). Cather's heroizing of Latour may have sprung in part from her esteem for a Father Haltermann she had met in New Mexico, who returned to his native Belgium as a chaplain to Belgian fighters in World War I and died. If so, this is yet another way in which the war entered her work. See WC to unnamed religious sister, Nov. 23, 1940, Loyola.

27. The continuance of Native culture and the desire of Native peoples to have their own ways and their own religion are a separate matter. One aspect of the romanticizing of the Southwest in which Cather took a latter-day part was an emphasis on Spanish-ness both of tradition and, among the descendants of the landholding upper class, of bloodline. This urge to claim Spanish as opposed to Mexican identity was most evident in California, but it colored the development of the folklore society in New Mexico as well as other aspects of the state's culture and history. A useful discussion can be found in Wilson.

28. Bette S. Weidman points out that two other "glancing hints of a Mexican point of view not fully exposed in the novel" are provided by Magdalena and Mrs. Kit Carson (67). Lynn Bridgers links Lamy's and Machebeuf's disputes with the New Mexican clergy to "a legacy of mutual distrust between the Spanish and the French" in Europe (128). Ray John de Aragon sees the explanation in Lamy's desire for "priests that would be totally obedient to him" and his fear that "some of the New Mexican priests might harbor an inner allegiance to the old bishop of Durango" (140). WC to E. K. Brown, April 9, 1937, Beinecke.

29. Fray Angelico Chavez quotes an extract from the Pastoral Letter on the subject circulated by Bishop Zubiría on July 21, 1833. Bridgers points out (128) that Martínez's birthplace, Abiquiu, was a "penitente stronghold."

30. Reviewers regularly pondered the question of whether Cather's books were novels in any precise sense.

31. Thomas J. Steele and Ronald S. Brockway, in an editorial comment added to the reprinting of Howlett's biography of Machebeuf, call Cather's portrait of Fathers Gallegos and Lucero as well as Martínez "unfair" and "savagely libelous" and bemoan the fact that her book has "continually given the illusion of history"; see "Willa Cather's Use of History and Especially of Howlett's *Machebeuf* in *Death Comes for the Archbishop*," in W. J. Howlett (450). Edith Lewis to Mabel Dodge Luhan, July 20 [1925], Beinecke. Howlett also blackens Martínez with respect to the Bent assassination. E. A. Mares asserts that there is not a "shred of historical evidence" that Martínez "organized the Taos uprising." Instead, there is considerable written evidence of his pity for both the victims and the (perhaps equally victimized) perpetrators as well as evidence of an "undying hatred" of Martínez on the part of Bent (27–30). Mares judges the novel "badly flawed by cultural parochialism and narrow and ugly ethnic perspectives" (42).

32. For sources of the snake legend and other details of the "Snake Root" chapter, see notes in the Scholarly Edition of *DCA* (441–44).

33. Robert J. Nelson (38) unaccountably reads the rumbling sound as "the voice of the devil" and demonizes the colonized Indian by explaining that Jacinto, who listens intently to the sound from the depth, is naturally attuned to the "voice of evil." Clearly, he conceives of Latour's mission in terms of power relations.

34. In its mildness, Cather's account of the atrocity of Acoma and the building of the church on top of the mesa resembles the printed text on a postcard she sent Elizabeth Shepley Sergeant on May 30 [1912], Virginia:

> The Pueblo of Acoma was conquered several times by the soldiers of Spain. The Conquest for the Cross was made in 1629 by Fray Juan Romirez, who remained among the Acomas for twenty years and built the first church that the Southwest had ever known. This church was destroyed in 1680 during a Pueblo revolt. In 1689 the huge church now at Acoma, which has walls 60 feet high and 10 feet thick, was commenced. The church must have cost the labor of many generations for every particle of the material used in its construction was carried up from the plains below.

35. Cf. Wilson (153). Lummis was one of the primary writers in the vein of southwestern romanticizing, editor of the magazine of the Los Angeles Chamber of Commerce, and coiner of the phrase "See America First." Cather drew on his writings for details in *Archbishop*.

36. At least one such supporter of Martínez, Ray John de Aragon, presents a picture of the padre that would seem to be equally distorted toward the other extreme. Chavez, whom Bridgers accuses of "an intensity that borders on the paranoid" (107), is considerably more moderate. On at least two occasions (characterizations in "A Diamond Mine" and *A Lost Lady*) Cather had been threatened with lawsuits. Her adaptations of actual events and people in *Death Comes for the Archbishop* might be seen within this context as another instance of her willingness to circulate unfavorable characterizations of actual persons when they served her novelistic purpose.

37. WC to Paul Reynolds, about April 26, 1926, Columbia.

38. A different view of Kit Carson is presented in the diaries of Charles Preuss, the cartographer who accompanied John C. Frémont on three of his expeditions, including one when Carson was guide. Preuss saw him as crude and unprincipled.

39. WC to Mabel Dodge Luhan, Nov. 22 [1932], Beinecke. Patricia Clark Smith (120–21) argues with considerable plausibility that even though Cather seems "throughout most of the novel mainly to admire Latour" and to write "an astonishing document of colonialism," she becomes more "deliberately" ironic toward the end, and the book is finally, "at least in part, a conscious critique of colonialism."

10. ART IN A DEMOCRATIC SOCIETY

1. See, for example her happy letter to Blanche Knopf from Red Cloud on Dec. 31 [1927], stamped into the Knopf office on Jan. 3, 1928, HRC. WC to Dorothy Canfield Fisher, April 3 [1928], Vermont; to Mrs. Stowell, April 11 [1928], WCPM. Lee cites E. K. Brown in asserting that Cather "promised her father on his deathbed" that she would write a novel set in Virginia (357). Yet Cather was not with her

father on his deathbed. Lee is correct, however, in judging that "everything Cather wrote in her late fifties and sixties was affected by the close conjunction of her father's death and her mother's stroke" (290–91).

2. Cather commemorated Marjorie's passing with the poem "Poor Marty," which was added to *April Twilights* in the 1933 edition.

3. WC to Mary Austin, May 9, 1928, Huntington MS folder AU 1940; to Dorothy Canfield Fisher, n.d. (from Long Beach, Calif.), prob. June 1 or 2, 1929, Vermont; to Carrie Miner Sherwood, July 25 [1929?], WCPM; to Eleanor Austerman, Jan. 16, 1947, Virginia.

4. Skaggs writes that in the years leading up to 1935 and the publication of *Lucy Gayheart* Cather grew "steadily more inaccessible to the public, whom she clearly distrusted" (*After* 150).

5. A quarrel occurred between Cather and her mother when the local newspaper wrote about Marjorie as a mysterious figure. Cather blamed her mother for the unpleasant publicity, saying she should not have tried to keep Marjorie out of the public eye, because gossip was the inevitable result. Mrs. Cather seems to have felt that Cather's reaction to the incident generated discord between herself and her husband. WC to Mary Virginia Cather, March 3, [1925], TWU.

6. Cf. Rosowski: although Cather returned to the materials of her early work, "her emotions about those materials were different" in that here her characters do not prove themselves and achieve significance by "escaping the ordinary" but by "accepting life as it is" (*Voyage*, 189–90).

7. Note Cather's ingratiating attentions to the British aristocrat Stephen Tennant as well as a letter to George Austerman, owner of the Shattuck Inn, expressing concern that land around Jaffrey be sold only to the "right" kind of people; March 31, 1938, Virginia. The terms in which she designates the questionable or undesirable people she hopes will *not* buy there do not necessarily refer to social or economic class but do carry such an implication and are clearly exclusive in intent.

8. WC to Read Bain, Oct. 22, 1931, Michigan. The poem is found in holograph in the Rare Books Room, Pattee Lib., Penn. State Univ., erroneously labeled as having been written about 1902. Such a dating is plausible, since that was the year of Cather's first trip to Europe, and the lack of polish and the naive tone of the draft would seem to place it early in her writing career. But references to the patriotic tone of services in the little church at home and to the first Battle of the Marne clearly identify the poem as a product of the World War I years or after, perhaps the summer of 1920, when she viewed wartime devastation in France and located the grave of her cousin Grosvenor.

9. WC to Blanche Knopf, Dec. 4 [1922], HRC. Although written in the year in which Cather said the world "broke in two," this letter expresses notable enthusiasm for new ways. WC to Zoë Akins, prob. Nov. 21, 1922, Huntington (datable by the opening of Akins's play *The Texas Nightingale*, starring Jobyna Howland, whose "big power" Cather compared to a fine car).

10. Skaggs reads the incident of the beaver in the crèche as a "lewd pun" on the slang term for female genitals, arguing that the beaver is incorporated into the sacred scene "just as medieval actors deliberately incorporated the bawdy into their

Nativity plays" (*After* 142). But standard dictionaries of slang indicate that the use of *beaver* in this sense became common only decades later. The Random House *Historical Dictionary of American Slang* (1994) records only one such usage before 1965.

11. See Romines (*Home* esp. 152–63). WC to Dorothy Canfield Fisher, March 10 [prob. 1930], Vermont.

12. McDonald argues (15) that a "tradition of noblesse oblige was very much a part of Cather's Southern upbringing."

13. Cather seems to have worried how the Miner sisters would receive "Two Friends." When it appeared in the July 1932 *Woman's Home Companion* she wrote Carrie that Dillon was not intended as a direct portrait of their father; July 4 [1932], WCPM.

14. WC to Mary Virginia Cather, Nov. 26 [prob. 1921], TWU.

15. WC to Irene Miner Weisz, n.d. (postmarked March 12, 1931), Newberry; to E. K. Brown, March 23, 1947, Yale. The Menuhins as a "story" or perhaps fairy tale of the artistic life is from Sergeant (263). The idea is revised to "European novel" by Yehudi Menuhin in *Unfinished Journey*, 130. Yaltah Menuhin's son Lionel Menuhin Rolfe wrote that Cather was "fascinated by the Menuhin children" (174).

16. Skaggs also notes that meeting the Menuhins in 1930 may have had an impact on *Lucy Gayheart*. Referring to Jan Hambourg, she writes, "Music, fleeting youth, lost love, and musicians who steal away one's loveliest image of youth, may therefore have blended in her associations before she began writing Lucy's story—or Harry's" (*After* 205 n. 7). WC to Blanche Knopf, Oct. 26 [1933], HRC; to Zoë Akins, Jan. 2 [1934], Huntington; to Carrie Miner Sherwood, July 3 [1934], WCPM.

17. WC to Brother Emil Mohr, May 7, 1937, Notre Dame.

18. The "thing not named" has often been identified with Cather's impulse to conceal her sexuality. See, for example, O'Brien (*Emerging* 205) and Stout (*Strategies* 68, 95).

19. WC to Dorothy Canfield Fisher, Dec. 1 [1930], Vermont.

20. Woodress (*Literary* 474) points out the resonance of the story's being set in 1922. Ammons reads "The Old Beauty" as a story that "mourns the passing of European global empire" ("Canon" 259). Although I agree with Ammons that Cather was "invested in master narratives of Western cultural dominance and white superiority" (265) and find her notice of the story's time setting and villainous immigrant particularly provocative, minor errors detract from the persuasiveness of her essay. Ammons implies that Aix is so profoundly an island of the past that *all* the women at Seabury's hotel dress conservatively and wear no makeup (258). But in the story these phrases apply only to Mme. de Couçy and her companion (*SPO* 697 and again 705, where it is emphatically "only" she who "used no make-up"). If she represents "empire's ravage" (Ammons 263), it is peculiar that she controls space, rather than being invaded or controlled, when she dances. That is, she remains imperious.

21. Gelfant points out (*Women* 265) that another point of connection between the "Katherine Mansfield" essay and *Lucy Gayheart* is that the essay's "discussion of the 'double life' in families . . . seems immediately relevant to the Gayhearts."

22. In Skaggs's reading, which places Cather in the cast of characters both as Lucy and as Harry, this meditation is also her meditation in the person of Harry on

Isabelle's choice of another man and another life. By early 1930, if not before, Cather began to say that she was not up to the emotions that would be aroused by going home; WC to Irene Miner Weisz, Feb. 6, 1930, Newberry. She returned for a family reunion in her parents' home during the Christmas season of 1931, a few months after her mother's death, but never again, despite repeatedly telling Carrie Miner Sherwood that she was coming.

23. See WC to Mariel Gere, May 2, 1896, WCPM. She did not react to the original Miss Gayhardt in the satiric or belittling way that critics have seen her as reacting to her own character.

24. Skaggs (*After* 157). See Stout (*Window* 76), summarizing readings of Lucy as weak and an object of authorial satire. Other such references are provided by Gelfant (*Women* 261). WC to Carrie Miner Sherwood, Dec. 9 [prob. 1935], WCPM.

25. The idea of the artist manqué would have had powerful resonance for Cather, both for obvious reasons, as she looked back over her career at a time when she felt generally disheartened, and because the phrase literally means the artist with a crippled hand. Crippling, particularly of the hand, was a haunting preoccupation made all the more agonizing by a series of injuries and ailments of the hand late in her life. WC to Carlton F. Wells, Jan. 7, 1936, Newberry. Wells had inquired about her rendering of the words of the oratorio as "*If with all your heart you truly seek Him*" (*LG* 34) rather than "truly seek Me." Her explanation of the change illustrates the care with which she constructed texts. Hallgarth (169) astutely links the movement from appreciation to commitment in *Lucy Gayheart* with the satiric presentation of the male artist's dictum in "Flavia and Her Artists" that women "are simply not meant to be great artists" because they only "appreciate and absorb—they do not produce."

26. I do not agree with Brown (294) and Rosowski (*Voyage* 219) that the opening sections of the novel are heavy or "wooden." Book Two, which seems to wander from one thing to another, is diffuse to effect: Lucy, during this period, is figuratively wandering.

27. WC to Mary Virginia Cather, Nov. 26 [prob. 1921], TWU. The letter is unusually fulsome, apparently from a desire to make up for her cross or agitated behavior during her summer visit.

28. The reason for Lucy's thinking Harry is one of those who have the eyes to look, despite his demeanor or disguise of ordinariness, supports the idea that Harry as well as Lucy is a self-representation by Cather. She recalls that he used to know "every tree and shrub and plant"—as Cather did herself, as demonstrated by annotation of the field guide she carried for more than twenty years.

29. WC to Carrie Miner Sherwood, July 3 [1935], WCPM. Near the end of her life Cather would tell E. K. Brown that she did not esteem *Lucy Gayheart* very highly but still found the last section interesting; WC to E. K. Brown, Oct. 7, 1946, Beinecke.

30. Here I am explicitly endorsing Urgo's argument in *Myth* (115 ff.).

31. Bergson was an enthusiasm Cather shared with such New Bohemians of Greenwich Village as Hutchins Hapgood, who numbered Bergson along with "Post-

Impressionism, the I.W.W., anarchism, the radical woman movement, [and] the thrill of the socially and politically new" among things that made up "the sum and substance" of his existence; quoted by Watson (135).

11. RECRIMINATION AND RECONCILIATION

1. In Romines's words (*Home* 174), "the mix is more complex than in any other Cather novel: autobiography, history, and fiction are inextricably interwoven." Although Lee sees in *Sapphira* "a violent last resistance to a coercive maternal figure" (370), it is not so univocal as that statement implies.

2. Arnold (325), closely paraphrasing WC to Viola Roseboro, Nov. 9, 1940, Virginia 6494-b.

3. WC to Langston Hughes, April 15, 1941, Beinecke.

4. WC to Carrie Miner Sherwood, July 26 [1935], WCPM; to Yaltah Menuhin, Oct. 23 [1935], Princeton.

5. WC to Carrie Miner Sherwood, Dec. 9 [1935], WCPM. Letters putting off going to Red Cloud include, for example, WC to her sister Elsie, her brother Roscoe, and Carrie Miner Sherwood, Dec. 6, 1940, WCPM; to Carrie, Nov. 3, 1941, WCPM; to Irene Miner Weisz, April 18, 1942, Newberry; to Josephine Frisbie, April 6, 1944, WCPM. On the twins' visit, WC to Fanny Butcher, Dec. 18, 1936, Newberry.

6. WC to Miss McKinder [about July 31, 1938], HRC; to Ferris Greenslet, Oct. 12 [1938], Harvard bMS Am 1925 (341), folder 20; to Irene Miner Weisz, Oct. 14 [1938], Newberry; to Dorothy Canfield Fisher, March 5 [1939], Vermont; to Carrie Miner Sherwood, June 28, 1939, WCPM.

7. WC to Mary Miner Creighton, Dec. 6, n.y. [prob. 1936], Newberry; to Mary Austin, Oct. 22, 1931, Huntington. McDonald points out (15) that Cather's sense of responsibility for Nebraska families in danger of losing their farms was part of an inherited southern tradition rooted in social class. WC to Mary Austin, Oct. 22, 1931, Huntington; to Mabel Dodge Luhan, Dec. 18, 1936, Beinecke. Her statement to Mabel that she was sending families in Nebraska every bit of money she could spare seems to have been an exaggeration, but it is true that she was sending gifts of money as well as clothes (usually castoffs) and food. She told Carrie Miner Sherwood that the Red Cross was the only charity she knew of that did what it claimed to do; June 5 [prob. 1940], WCPM. She complained to Mabel Dodge Luhan that the New Deal seemed to work in the best interests of only the loafers, while cutting her income by three-fourths; WC to Mabel Dodge Luhan, Dec. 18, 1936, Beinecke.

8. WC to Ferris Greenslet [about Jan. 10, 1938], Harvard bMS Am 1925 (341), folder 24; to Henry Seidel Canby, March 2, 1938, Beinecke; to Carrie Miner Sherwood, Sept. 25, 1946, WCPM.

9. WC to Yaltah Menuhin, Sept. 3 [prob. 1938], Princeton; Ferris Greenslet to WC, Oct. 2, 1939, Harvard bMS Am 1925 (341).

10. Once again Romines succinctly anticipates my point: "With her epilogue, she blurs and extends the boundaries of postmodern fiction to come" (*Constructing* 191).

11. Given the darkness of this gothic tale, the extent of its familial reference is surprising. It is consistent, however, with the thematic pattern of the irruption of strangeness and threat into the familiar that Rosowski describes as an omnipresence of the irrational (*Voyage* 238).

12. Elizabeth Jane Harrison points out the ambivalence and irony of Cather's invocation of family precedents (66). Cf. Stout (*Window* 99).

13. As Zettsu suggests (87), it was entirely possible that the Virginia girl who spent her early childhood in the Reconstruction period and its aftermath was in-stinctively aware of the extent to which the idea of a "nigger"—when adopted by a well-bred white young lady—could be dangerous to the ordered and genteel South-ern community in which she lived.

14. By naming the farm where they were slaves in Virginia "Sweet Home," Toni Morrison conveys a similar attitude toward the home in the slaveholding South on the part of former slaves in *Beloved*.

15. E. N. Anderson to WC, Jan. 28, 1926, NYPL.

16. Tomas Pollard, in his groundbreaking study of the novel's submerged poli-tics, points out that Rachel Blake is in Washington "during a time of intense politi-cal debate on slavery while living with a member of the House of Representatives." Punishment for aiding a fugitive under the Fugitive Slave Law of 1850 was impris-onment for up to six months and a fine of up to $2,000. "Imagine Henry's dilemma. He can remain loyal to his wife, betray his daughter, and keep Nancy in a position where she might be raped by a man he despises. Or, by helping Nancy escape, he can choose to risk his marriage, his reputation, the capital accumulated in his busi-ness, and the respect of most of his friends and neighbors" (Pollard 42, 44).

17. Charles Cather, Willa's father, noted in his diary when he was seventeen that on Monday, Jan. 30, 1865, he "rode home in Mr. Bywater's [sic] sleigh," and on Sunday, Feb. 26, he "took Dr. Hayton's daughters over to Mr. Bywaters." The diary, found in the Woman's Collection at Texas Woman's University, gives a keen sense of daily life in an area regularly traversed by both Union and Confederate troops.

18. E. K. Brown transcription of WC to Helen Louise Cather Southwick, Feb. 12, 1944, Beinecke.

19. Minrose Gwin errs by a year in stating that *Sapphira* was released the day Pearl Harbor was bombed (137). Edith Lewis (184) lists the war as one of the "catastrophe[s]" out of which *Sapphira and the Slave Girl* emerged.

20. Comments by both Lewis and Sergeant indicate they believed she meant to write a novel of manners recording and celebrating the customs of southern society. Lewis recalled of their trip in 1938 that though the area was "very much changed," she "looked . . . through it, as if it were transparent, to what she knew as its reality" (183). Sergeant saw *Sapphira* as "a sort of document, a kind of 'historical' novel" (279).

21. Marilyn Arnold sees both Sapphira and the society of which she is a part as being immobilized by their own rigidity ("Human" 325).

22. Lewis states that Cather finished *Sapphira* at Grand Manan in Sept. 1940 (184). It was published on Dec. 1 of that year. Lewis's recollection is confirmed by a letter to Ferris Greenslet dated Sept. 21, 1940 (Harvard bMS Am 1925 [341], folder

21) in which Cather says that she finished the home stretch of the new book at her island retreat. In a letter to Zoë Akins (Huntington) apparently written in late August or early September while she was still at Grand Manan, she says that she had finished the book there, the first proofs were now coming in, and she would return to New York in a few days. WC to Dorothy Canfield Fisher, March 5, 1939, Vermont; to Ferris Greenslet, March 2, 1938, and Oct. 27 [1938], Harvard bMS Am 1925 (341), folder 20; to Dorothy Canfield Fisher, Oct. 14, 1940, Vermont.

23. For example, she wrote to H. L. Mencken (Feb. 21, 1940, NYPL) to verify one of these references, asking whether the *Baltimore Sun* was in publication in 1850 to confirm her belief that it was. Harrison argues an idyllic reading of the ending (66).

24. WC to Mabel Dodge Luhan, May 1 [1934], Beinecke. For Porter's judgment of Cather's retrograde tastes, see "Reflections on Willa Cather" in her *Collected Essays and Occasional Writings*.

25. Gwin also links Cather and Faulkner in arguing that *Sapphira and the Slave Girl* is ultimately impenetrable (149).

26. Cf. Richard Poirier.

27. WC to Henry Seidel Canby, Feb. 4, 1941, Beinecke.

28. My description of the last page refers to the first edition, which is followed in the Vintage paperback. The placement of the explanatory note was a problem for Greenslet as *Sapphira* was being prepared for Houghton Mifflin's Autograph Edition. He wrote Cather on Dec. 5, 1940 (Harvard bMS Am 1925 [341], folder 41) proposing that it be moved to the customary place at the front of the volume in order to avoid the slight infelicity of having the two things [i.e., note and text of novel] under the eye together. What struck Greenslet as an infelicity is precisely what I read as a source of interest and energy. Cather responded on Dec. 13 (Harvard bMS Am 1925 [341], folder 21) that the press could use its own judgment. This uncharacteristically passive attitude toward a design question reflected both her uncertainty about breaking the fictive illusion with the autobiographical statement at the end (expressed in her letter to Canby) and her general enervation at the time.

29. Both the name Bywaters and the name Snapp—spelled with two *p*'s—appear in Charles Cather's 1865 diary.

30. A fictional character's name cannot be entirely arbitrary, of course, since to be believable it needs to accord with the asserted ethnicity—in this case, Bohemian.

31. Later in *Archbishop* Cather again breaks the fictive illusion by inserting a parenthetical explanation that "Mexicans are very fond of sparkling wines" and recounting an incident that occurred "only a few years before this" (193), that is, before the time being spoken of in the novelistic action. Again the reader is switched from one dimension to the other, from fiction to "fact," but a fact of a questionable nature.

32. WC to Mrs. William Stix (Yaltah Menuhin), [prob. Jan. 25, 1939], Princeton.

12. ENDING / CONCLUDING

1. WC to Zoë Akins, June 4, 1938, Huntington. Cather confessed that during the period leading up to her gall bladder operation she was cross and easily provoked;

she hoped the correction of her physical disorder would allow her to be more patient with irritations; WC to Zoë Akins, Dec. 4, 1943, Huntington. A diatribe against moviemakers (one of the great bêtes noires of her late years) follows, indicating that the surgery had not yet done so.

2. WC to Mabel Dodge Luhan, June 30, 1938, Beinecke.

3. WC to Carrie Miner Sherwood, Sept. 4 [1937?], WCPM; to Dorothy Canfield Fisher, Oct. 14, 1940, Vermont; to Zoë Akins, Feb. 15, 1940, Huntington; to Ferris Greenslet, Feb. 24 [1940], Harvard bMS Am 1925 (341), folder 21.

4. WC to Ferris Greenslet, March 2, 1938, Harvard bMS Am 1925 (341), folder 20. Similarly, she spoke of Yehudi Menuhin's music as a consolation to people for their lost faith; WC to Yaltah Menuhin, Dec. 19 [1939], Princeton. Woodress (*Literary* 480), largely quoting WC to Ferris Greenslet, June 10, 1940, Harvard bMS Am 1925 (341), folder 21; to Carrie Miner Sherwood, 15 July [1940], WCPM; to Greenslet, Sept. 21 and Nov. 9, 1940, Harvard bMS Am 1925 (341), folder 21.

5. WC to Mary Miner, Feb. 19, 1942, WCPM. For Cather's friendship with Undset, see Sherrill Harbison (53–59). Cather was not alone in her veneration of the Norwegian resistance. John Steinbeck's *The Moon Is Down*, which located among Norwegians "the courage to resist evil against long odds," was a best-seller in 1942 and 1943, the same years in which Cather was most interested in Undset (see John Morton Blum 48).

6. Jack Cather to WC, March 16, 1942, WCPM. On July 22, 1943, Cather expressed distrust of her remaining brothers and sisters, asking her niece Helen Cather Southwick not to share any of her letters with them; Beinecke, extracts made by Brown. WC to Julian Street, Sept. 21, 1942, Princeton.

7. WC to Carrie Miner Sherwood, Nov. 15, 1942, WCPM; to Zoë Akins, Dec. 6 [1942?], Virginia. Similarly, on Oct. 14, 1940 (Penn.), in a letter to Van Wyck Brooks, she praised Churchill's inspirational messages and deplored the aloof sophistication of the day's young college men, who regarded devotion to a righteous cause as naive. WC to Dorothy Canfield Fisher, March 31 [1943], Vermont. On great English (and also Russian) books, see WC to Zoë Akins, Dec. 4, 1943, Huntington, and WC to Mr. Phillipson, 23 Dec. 1943, WCPM. For the New Year's greeting, see the same letter to Akins and WC to Sergeant, Dec. 31, 1943, JPML.

8. WC to Bishop George Beecher, Dec. 25, 1943, NSHS.

9. WC to Irene Miner Weisz, Dec. 31, 1943, Newberry; to Carrie Miner Sherwood, April 29 [about 1945], WCPM.

10. LC to Viola Roseboro', Feb. 12, 1944, Virginia; to Bishop George Beecher, March 28, 1944, Nebraska. Some confusion of impulse, reflecting confusion in the public rhetoric that urged citizens to support the war effort even as it condemned war as an evil, is evident in her praise of Beecher, less than two months later, by allusion to the old song "Old Soldiers Never Die": no, she wrote, they just went on fighting for God; WC to Bishop George Beecher, June 10, 1944, Nebraska. Earlier, when a friend had sent her a picture of the mill, she had taken comfort in knowing that there were still green trees and running water in Nebraska. Now she sought reassurance that it was still there; WC to Josephine Frisbie, April 6, 1944, and Sept. 27, 1940, WCPM.

11. WC to Ferris Greenslet, Jan. 24, 1945, Harvard bMS Am 1925 (341), folder 23. Cf. her lament about the burden of letters to homesick soldiers in WC to Stephen Tennant, Feb. 16, 1945, PLY. WC to Fanny Butcher, April 19, 1945, Newberry; to Lizzie, June 13, 1945, WCPM; to Stephen Tennant, Feb. 16, 1945, PLY.

12. WC to Mariel Gere, [prob. Oct. 19, 1945], WCPM; to Irene Miner Weisz, Oct. 22 [1945], Newberry. The image of the broken spring must have struck her as conveying her feelings precisely; she used it again a week later in a letter to Ferris Greenslet, Oct. 30, 1945, Beinecke. An attached note states that Greenslet gave it to E. K. Brown, "leaving it to him to decide whether it should be destroyed," but Brown had not done so at the time of his death. As if clinging to the last of the siblings with whom she had felt close, she transferred her previously asserted preference for Douglass to Roscoe. She and Douglass had had a couple of little quarrels, she said, but never she and Roscoe. She told Sergeant that Roscoe had been the brother with whom she traveled about the West and Southwest when she and Sergeant first knew each other (WC to Sergeant, Nov. 21, 1945, JPML), although in fact it was Douglass with whom she visited and rambled about in 1912.

13. WC to Irene Miner Weisz, [Dec. 17, 1945], Newberry. Identical wording in WC to Fanny Butcher, Jan. 3, 1946, Newberry, and WC to Zoë Akins, Jan. 3, 1946, Huntington.

14. Sigrid Undset to WC, March 17, 1946, Newberry; WC to Ferris Greenslet, March 29 [1946] and June 1, 1946, Harvard bMS Am 1925(341), folder 24; to Sergeant, Aug. 16, 1946, JPML; to Greenslet, Aug. 28, 1946, Harvard bMS Am 1925 (341), folder 24. Lewis states that Cather wrote "Before Breakfast" at Northeast Harbour, Maine, in the summer of 1944 and "The Best Years" some time the following year (196). Cather's letters, however, seem to indicate that although she began "Before Breakfast" in the summer of 1944, she was unable to complete it then. The question of when she finished the story is not clarified in the letters. "The Best Years" is also valedictory in tone, though not in the same way.

15. WC to Mr. and Mrs. Weisz, [Dec. 18, 1946], Newberry; to Carrie Miner Sherwood, Dec. 18 [1946], WCPM; to Dorothy Canfield Fisher, Jan. 3 [1947?], Vermont; to Bishop George Beecher, March 12, 1947, Nebraska, transcription by Bernice Slote.

16. WC to E. K. Brown, Oct. 7, 1946, Beinecke.

17. WC to E. K. Brown, Jan. 24, 1947, Beinecke.

18. WC to E. K. Brown, March 23, 1947, Beinecke.

19. WC to Irene Miner Weisz, Jan. 4, 1945, Newberry; to Zoë Akins, Jan. 5 and 6, 1945, Huntington; to Irene Miner Weisz, Jan. 6, 1945, Newberry; to Carrie Miner Sherwood, April 29 [1945], WCPM.

20. WC to Ferris Greenslet, Oct. 30, 1945, Beinecke.

21. Mary Ruth Ryder sees in Grenfell's "resurrected spirit" an element that "lends itself readily to the Christian myth," even though the imagery of the story is primarily of Venus and Aphrodite (280). Thurin (362) argues, I believe correctly, that the story simply ignores Christianity, finally accepting both a scientific account of life and the uncertainty of imperfect scientific knowledge.

22. WC to E. K. Brown, Jan. 24, 1947, Beinecke.

BIBLIOGRAPHY

WORKS BY CATHER

Alexander's Bridge. 1912. Rev. ed., Boston: Houghton Mifflin, 1922.

The Autobiography of S. S. McClure. Intro. Robert Thacker. Lincoln: Univ. of Nebraska Press, 1997. Reprint of S. S. McClure, *My Autobiography* (New York: Frederick A. Stokes, 1914).

Death Comes for the Archbishop. 1927. Willa Cather Scholarly Edition. Ed. Charles W. Mignon, with Frederick M. Link and Kari A. Ronning. Historical Essay by John J. Murphy. Lincoln: Univ. of Nebraska Press, 1999.

Early Stories of Willa Cather. Ed. Mildred R. Bennett. New York: Dodd, Mead, 1957.

The Life of Mary Baker G. Eddy and the History of Christian Science. Intro. David Stouck. 1909, showing Georgine Milmine as author. Reprint, Lincoln: Univ. of Nebraska Press, 1993.

A Lost Lady. 1923. Willa Cather Scholarly Edition. Ed. Charles W. Mignon and Frederick M. Link, with Kari A. Ronning. Historical Essay by Susan J. Rosowski; Explanatory Notes by Kari A. Ronning. Lincoln: Univ. of Nebraska Press, 1997.

Lucy Gayheart. 1935. Vintage Classics Edition. New York: Random House, 1995.

My Ántonia. 1918. Willa Cather Scholarly Edition. Ed. Charles Mignon with Kari Ronning. Historical Essay by James Woodress; Explanatory Notes by James Woodress with Kari Ronning, Kathleen Danker, and Emily Levine. Lincoln: Univ. of Nebraska Press, 1994.

My Mortal Enemy. 1926. Vintage Classics Edition. Introduction by Marcus Klein. New York: Random House, 1990.

"Nebraska: The End of the First Cycle." *The Nation* 117 (1923): 236–38.

Not under Forty. 1936. In *Stories, Poems, and Other Writings*, ed. Sharon O'Brien. New York: Library of America, 1992.

Obscure Destinies. 1932. Scholarly Edition. Ed. Kari A. Ronning. Historical Essay and Explanatory Notes by Kari A. Ronning. Textual Essay by Frederick M. Link with Kari A. Ronning and Mark Kamrath. Lincoln: Univ. of Nebraska Press, 1998.

One of Ours. 1922. Vintage Classics Edition. New York: Random House, 1991.

O Pioneers! 1913. Willa Cather Scholarly Edition. Ed. Susan J. Rosowski and Charles W. Mignon, with Kathleen Danker. Historical Essay and Explanatory Notes by David Stouck. Lincoln: Univ. of Nebraska Press, 1992.

The Professor's House. 1925. Vintage Classics Edition. New York: Random House, 1973.

Sapphira and the Slave Girl. 1940. Vintage Classics Edition. New York: Random House, 1975.

Shadows on the Rock. 1931. Vintage Classics Edition. New York: Random House, 1971.

The Song of the Lark. 1915. Bantam Classics. New York: Bantam Books, 1991.

Stories, Poems, and Other Writings. Ed. Sharon O'Brien. New York: Library of America, 1992.

The Troll Garden. 1905. Reprint, ed. James Woodress. Lincoln: Univ. of Nebraska Press, 1983.

Willa Cather: 24 Stories. Ed. Sharon O'Brien. New York: Penguin Meridian, 1988.

Willa Cather in Europe. Ed. George N. Kates. New York: Knopf, 1956.

Willa Cather on Writing. Intro. Stephen Tennant. 1949. Lincoln: Univ. of Nebraska Press, 1988.

Willa Cather's Collected Short Fiction, 1892–1912. Ed. Virginia Faulkner. Intro. Mildred R. Bennett. Lincoln: Univ. of Nebraska Press, 1965.

DOCUMENTARY SOURCES

Allegheny College, Pelletier Library, Meadville, Pa.

Amherst College, Amherst, Mass.

University of Arkansas, Fayetteville

Boston Public Library

Buffalo and Erie County Public Library, Buffalo, N.Y.

Willa Cather Pioneer Memorial, Red Cloud, Neb.

Colby College, Miller Library, Waterville, Maine

Columbia University, New York City

Dartmouth College, Hanover, N.H.

Duke University, Durham, N.C.

First Church of Christ, Scientist, Boston

Georgetown University, Washington, D.C.

Harvard University, Houghton Library, Cambridge

Huntington Library, San Marino, Calif.

Indiana University, Lilly Library, Bloomington

University of Kentucky, Margaret I. King Library, Lexington

Library of Congress, Washington, D.C.

Loyola University, New Orleans

University of Michigan, Bentley Historical Library, Ann Arbor

Middlebury College, Middlebury, Vt.

J. Pierpont Morgan Library, New York City

Nebraska State Historical Society, Lincoln

University of Nebraska, Love Library, Lincoln

New Hampshire Historical Society, Concord

University of New Hampshire, Durham

Newark Public Library, Newark, N.J.

Newberry Library, Chicago

New York Public Library

University of North Carolina, Chapel Hill
University of Notre Dame, Notre Dame, Ind.
Pennsylvania State University, University Park
University of Pennsylvania, Van Pelt-Dietrich Library, Philadelphia
Phillips Exeter Academy, Exeter, N.H.
Enoch Pratt Free Library, Baltimore, Md.
Princeton University, Firestone Library, Princeton, N.J.
University of Richmond, Boatwright Memorial Library, Richmond, Va.
University of Southern California, Los Angeles
Stanford University, Stanford, Calif.
University of Texas, Harry Ransom Humanities Research Center, Austin
Texas Woman's University, Blagg-Huey Library, Denton
University of Vermont, Bailey/Howe Library, Burlington
Wellesley College, Margaret Clapp Library, Wellesley, Mass.
Wisconsin State Historical Society, Madison
Yale University, Beinecke Library and University Library, New Haven, Conn.
Patricia Lee Yongue, Private Collection

SECONDARY

Abel, Elizabeth. "Narrative Structure(s) and Female Development: The Case of *Mrs. Dalloway.*" In *The Voyage In: Fictions of Female Development*, ed. Elizabeth Abel, Marianne Hirsch, and Elizabeth Langland, 161–85. Hanover, N.H.: Univ. Press of New England, 1983.

Ahearn, Edward J. *Marx and Modern Fiction*. New Haven: Yale Univ. Press, 1989.

Ammons, Elizabeth. "Cather and the New Canon: 'The Old Beauty' and the Issue of Empire." In *Cather Studies III*, ed. Susan J. Rosowski, 256–66. Lincoln: Univ. of Nebraska Press, 1996.

———. *Conflicting Stories: American Women Writers at the Turn into the Twentieth Century*. New York: Oxford Univ. Press, 1991.

Anderson, Eric Gary. *American Indian Literature and the Southwest*. Austin: Univ. of Texas Press, 1999.

Apple, Max. *The Oranging of America*. New York: Grossman, 1976.

Arnold, Marilyn. "'Of Human Bondage': Cather's Subnarrative in *Sapphira and the Slave Girl.*" *Mississippi Quarterly* 40 (1987): 323–38.

———. *Willa Cather's Short Fiction*. Athens: Ohio Univ. Press, 1984.

Austin, Mary. *Beyond Borders: The Selected Essays of Mary Austin*. Ed. Reuben J. Ellis. Carbondale: Southern Illinois Univ. Press, 1996.

———. *Earth Horizon*. 1932. Reprint, Albuquerque: Univ. of New Mexico Press, 1991.

———. "Regionalism in American Fiction." *English Journal* 21 (1932): 97–106.

Baker, Carlos, ed. *Ernest Hemingway's Selected Letters, 1917–1961*. New York: Scribner's, 1981.

Banta, Martha. "The Excluded Seven: Practice of Omission, Aesthetics of Refusal." In *Henry James's New York Edition: The Construction of Authorship*, ed. David McWhirter, 249–60. Stanford: Stanford Univ. Press, 1995.

Barton, Gay. "'He Was Thoughtful, Critical, and Respectful'—A Reading of Willa Cather's Appropriation of Native American Culture." Paper presented at the Willa Cather Pioneer Memorial Spring Conference, Red Cloud, Neb., 1998.

Bassnett, Susan. "Eleanor Duse." In *Bernhardt, Terry, Duse: The Actress in Her Time*, by John Stokes, Michael R. Booth, and Susan Bassnett. Cambridge: Cambridge Univ. Press, 1988.

Bennett, Mildred R. *The World of Willa Cather.* Lincoln: Univ. of Nebraska Press, 1951.

Bersani, Leo, and Ulysse Dutoit. *Caravaggio's Secrets.* Cambridge: MIT Press, 1998.

Billington, Ray Allen, ed. *"Dear Lady": The Letters of Frederick Jackson Turner and Alice Forbes Perkins Hooper, 1910–1932.* San Marino, Calif.: Huntington Library, 1970.

Blair, Karen J. *The Clubwoman as Feminist: True Womanhood Redefined, 1868–1914.* New York: Holmes & Meier, 1980.

Bloom, Edward A., and Lillian D. Bloom. *Willa Cather's Gift of Sympathy.* Carbondale: Southern Illinois Univ. Press, 1962.

Blum, John Morton. *V Was for Victory: Politics and American Culture during World War II.* New York: Harcourt Brace, 1976.

Bohlke, L. Brent. "Willa Cather and *The Life of Mary Baker G. Eddy.*" *American Literature* 54 (1982): 288–94.

———. *Willa Cather in Person: Interviews, Speeches, and Letters.* Lincoln: Univ. of Nebraska Press, 1986.

Brandon, Ruth. *Being Divine: A Biography of Sarah Bernhardt.* London: Martin Secker and Warburg, 1991.

Bridgers, Lynn. *Death's Deceiver: The Life of Joseph P. Machebeuf.* Albuquerque: Univ. of New Mexico Press, 1997.

Brittain, Vera. *Testament of Youth.* 1933. Reprint, New York: Wideview Books, 1980.

Brown, E. K., with Leon Edel. *Willa Cather: A Critical Biography.* Lincoln: Univ. of Nebraska Press, 1953.

Brunauer, Dalma H. "The Problem of Point of View in *A Lost Lady.*" *Renascence* 28 (1975): 47–52.

Buss, Helen M. "Willa Cather: Reading the Writer through Biographies and Memoirs." In *Cather Studies IV,* ed. Susan J. Rosowski, 118–43. Lincoln: Univ. of Nebraska Press, 1999.

Butcher, Fanny. *Many Lives—One Love.* New York: Harper, 1972.

———. Review of *My Mortal Enemy,* by Willa Cather. *Chicago Tribune,* 23 Oct. 1926.

Butler, Judith. *Gender Trouble: Feminism and the Subversion of Identity.* New York: Routledge, 1990.

Byrne, Kathleen D., and Richard C. Snyder. *Chrysalis: Willa Cather in Pittsburgh, 1896–1906.* Pittsburgh: Historical Society of Western Pennsylvania, 1980.

Chabot, C. Barry. *Writers for the Nation: American Literary Modernism.* Tuscaloosa: Univ. of Alabama Press, 1997.

Chavez, Fray Angelico. *But Time and Chance: The Story of Padre Martinez of Taos, 1793–1867.* Santa Fe: Sunstone Press, 1981.

Cherny, Robert W. "Willa Cather and the Populists." *Great Plains Quarterly* 3.4 (fall 1983): 206–18.

———. "Willa Cather's Nebraska." In *Approaches to Teaching Cather's* My Ántonia, ed. Susan J. Rosowski, 31–36. New York: Modern Language Association, 1989.

Chodorow, Nancy. *The Reproduction of Mothering: Psychoanalysis and the Psychology of Gender.* Berkeley: Univ. of California Press, 1978.

Coe, Marguerite. "Sarah and Coq: Contrast in Acting Styles." In *Bernhardt and the Theatre of Her Time*, ed. Eric Salmon, 67–89. Westport, Conn.: Greenwood Press, 1984.

Crow, Charles L. "The Patrimony of Blue Mesa: *The Professor's House* and Museum Theory." *Willa Cather Pioneer Memorial Newsletter and Review* 41 (1998): 53–57.

Crowell, Benedict, and Robert Forrest Wilson. *Demobilization: Our Industrial and Military Demobilization after the Armistice, 1918–1920.* New Haven: Yale Univ. Press, 1921.

Curtin, William M., ed. *The World and the Parish: Willa Cather's Articles and Reviews, 1893–1902.* 2 vols. Lincoln: Univ. of Nebraska Press, 1970.

de Aragon, Ray John. "Padre Antonio José Martínez: The Man and the Myth." In *Padre Martinez: New Perspectives from Taos*, ed. E. A. Mares, 125–51. Taos, N.M.: Millicent Rogers Museum, 1988.

———. *Padre Martinez and Bishop Lamy.* Las Vegas, N.M.: Pan-American, 1978.

D'Emilio, Sandra, and Sharyn Udall. "Inner Voices, Outward Forms: Women Painters in New Mexico." In *Independent Spirits: Women Painters of the American West, 1890–1945*, ed. Patricia Trenton, 153–80. Berkeley: Univ. of California Press, 1995.

Doyle, James. *The Fin de Siecle Spirit: Walter Blackburn Harte and the American / Canadian Literary Milieu of the 1890s.* Toronto: ECW Press, 1995.

DuMaurier, George. *Trilby.* New York: Harper, 1894.

DuPlessis, Rachel Blau. *Writing beyond the Ending: Narrative Strategies of Twentieth-Century Women Writers.* Bloomington: Indiana Univ. Press, 1985.

Edel, Leon. *The Stuff of Sleep and Dreams: Experiments in Literary Psychology.* New York: Harper and Row, 1982.

Fetterley, Judith. "Willa Cather and the Fiction of Female Development." In *Anxious Power: Reading, Writing, and Ambivalence in Narrative by Women*, ed. Carol J. Singley and Susan Elizabeth Sweeney, 221–34. Albany: State Univ. of New York Press, 1993.

Fischer, Mike. "Pastoralism and Its Discontents: Willa Cather and the Burden of Imperialism." *Mosaic* 23 (1990): 31–44.

Fisher, Dorothy Canfield. "Daughter of the Frontier." *New York Herald Tribune*, May 28, 1933, 7, 9.

Fisher-Wirth, Ann W. "Dispossession and Redemption in the Novels of Willa Cather." In *Cather Studies I*, ed. Susan Rosowski, 36–54. Lincoln: Univ. of Nebraska Press, 1990.

———. "Queening It: Excess in *My Mortal Enemy*," *Willa Cather Pioneer Memorial Newsletter* 40 (1996): 36–41.

Freedman, Jonathan. "Angels, Monsters, and Jews: Intersections of Queer and Jewish Identity in Kushner's *Angels in America*." *PMLA* 113 (1998): 90–102.

Frost, Robert. *Complete Poems.* New York: Holt, Rinehart and Winston, 1964.

Fryer, Judith. *Felicitous Space: The Imaginative Structures of Edith Wharton and Willa Cather.* Chapel Hill: Univ. of North Carolina Press, 1986.

Funda, Evelyn I. "Willa Cather and Lucius Sherman: A Dialogue." Paper presented at the annual meeting of the Western Literature Association, Albuquerque, Oct. 1997.

Fussell, Paul. *The Great War and Modern Memory.* London: Oxford Univ. Press, 1975.

Garvey, Ellen Gruber. "Reframing the Bicycle: Advertising-Supported Magazines and Scorching Women." *American Quarterly* 47.1 (1995): 66–101.

Gelfant, Blanche H. "The Forgotten Reaping-Hook: Sex in *My Ántonia.*" *American Literature* 43 (1971): 60–82.

———. "'What Was It . . .?' The Secret of Family Accord in *One of Ours.*" In *Willa Cather: Family, Community, and History,* ed. John J. Murphy, 85–102. Provo, Utah: Brigham Young Univ. Humanities Publications Center, 1990.

———. *Women Writing in America: Voices in Collage.* Hanover, N.H.: Univ. Press of New England, 1984.

Giannone, Richard. *Music in Willa Cather's Fiction.* Lincoln: Univ. of Nebraska Press, 1968.

Gilbert, Sandra M., and Susan Gubar. *Sexchanges.* Vol. 2 of *No Man's Land: The Place of the Woman Writer in the Twentieth Century.* New Haven: Yale Univ. Press, 1989.

Gilmore, Leigh. *Autobiographics: A Feminist Theory of Women's Self-Representation.* Ithaca: Cornell Univ. Press, 1994.

Goldman, Dorothy. "'Eagles of the West?' American Women Writers and World War I." In *Women and World War I: The Written Response,* ed. Dorothy Goldman, 188–208. New York: St. Martin's, 1993.

Gordon, Lynn D. "The Gibson Girl Goes to College: Popular Culture and Women's Higher Education in the Progressive Era, 1890–1920." *American Quarterly* 39.2 (1987): 211–30.

Greenslet, Ferris. *Under the Bridge: An Autobiography.* Boston: Houghton Mifflin, 1943.

Griffith, Jean Carol. "Masculine Dreams, Feminine Reality: Willa Cather's *O Pioneers!* and the Making of a Female Agrarian Hero." Paper presented at the annual meeting of the Western Literature Association, Albuquerque, Oct. 1997.

Griffiths, Frederick T. "The Woman Warrior: Willa Cather and *One of Ours,*" *Women's Studies* 11 (1984): 261–85.

Gross, Barry. "Willa Cather and the 'American Metaphysic.'" *Midamerica* 8 (1981): 68–77.

Gwin, Minrose C. *Black and White Women of the Old South: The Peculiar Sisterhood in American Literature.* Knoxville: Univ. of Tennessee Press, 1985.

Hall, Joan Wylie. "Treacherous Texts: The Perils of Allusion in Cather's Early Stories." *Colby Library Quarterly* 24 (1988): 142–50.

Hallgarth, Susan A. "The Woman Who Would Be Artist in *The Song of the Lark* and *Lucy Gayheart.*" In *Willa Cather: Family, Community, and History,* ed. John J.

Murphy, 169–73. Provo, Utah: Brigham Young Univ. Humanities Publications Center, 1990.

Hamner, Eugénie Lambert. "The Unknown, Well-Known Child in Cather's Last Novel." *Women's Studies* 11 (1984): 347–57.

Harbison, Sherrill. "Sigrid Undset and Willa Cather: A Friendship." *Willa Cather Pioneer Memorial Newsletter and Review* 42 (1999): 53–59.

Harrison, Elizabeth Jane. *Female Pastoral: Women Writers Re-Visioning the American South.* Knoxville: Univ. of Tennessee Press, 1991.

Harvey, Sally Peltier. *Redefining the American Dream: The Novels of Willa Cather.* Rutherford, N.J.: Fairleigh Dickinson Univ. Press, 1995.

Heilbrun, Carolyn. *Writing a Woman's Life.* New York: Norton, 1988.

Henderson, Robert M. *D. W. Griffith: His Life and Work.* New York: Oxford Univ. Press, 1972.

Hendrick, Burton J. "The Skulls of Our Immigrants." *McClure's* 35.1 (May 1910): 36–50.

Hewitt, Leah. *Autobiographical Tightropes.* Lincoln: Univ. of Nebraska Press, 1990.

Hicks, Granville. "The Case against Willa Cather." *English Journal,* Nov. 1933. Reprinted in *Willa Cather and Her Critics,* ed. James Schroeter, 139–47. Ithaca: Cornell Univ. Press, 1967.

Hilgart, John. "Death Comes for the Aesthete: Commodity Culture and the Artifact in Cather's *The Professor's House.*" *Studies in the Novel* 30 (1998): 377–404.

Hitchcock, Mary E. *Two Women in the Klondike: The Story of a Journey to the Gold-Fields of Alaska.* New York: Putnam's, 1899.

Hoare, Philip. *Serious Pleasures: The Life of Stephen Tennant.* London: Hamish Hamilton, 1990.

Horville, Robert. "The Stage Techniques of Sarah Bernhardt." Trans. Eric Salmon. In *Bernhardt and the Theatre of Her Time,* ed. Eric Salmon, 35–66. Westport, Conn.: Greenwood Press, 1984.

Houtchens, Alan, and Janis P. Stout. "'Scarce Heard amidst the Guns Below': Intertextuality and Meaning in Charles Ives's War Songs." *Journal of Musicology* 15 (1997): 66–97.

Howlett, W. J. *Life of Bishop Machebeuf.* 1908. Ed. Thomas J. Steele and Ronald S. Brockway. Reprint, Denver: Regis College, 1987.

Hughes, Robert. *The Shock of the New.* New York: Knopf, 1981.

Ignatiev, Noel. *How the Irish Became White.* New York: Routledge, 1995.

Jackson, Donald, and Mary Lee Spence, eds. *The Expeditions of John Charles Frémont.* Vol. 1, *Travels from 1838 to 1844.* Urbana: Univ. of Illinois Press, 1970.

Jewett, Sarah Orne. *The Letters of Sarah Orne Jewett.* Ed. Annie Fields. Boston: Houghton Mifflin, 1911.

Keeler, Clinton. "Narrative without Accent: Willa Cather and Puvis de Chavannes." *American Quarterly* 17 (1965): 119–26.

Klein, Marcus. Introduction to *My Mortal Enemy,* by Willa Cather. Vintage Classics Edition. New York: Random House, 1990.

Lambert, Deborah. "The Defeat of a Hero: Autonomy and Sexuality in *My Ántonia.*" *American Literature* 53 (1982): 676–90.

Lee, Hermione. *Willa Cather: Double Lives.* New York: Pantheon Books, 1989.

Lewis, Edith. *Willa Cather Living: A Personal Record.* New York: Knopf, 1953.

Lindemann, Marilee. *Willa Cather: Queering America.* New York: Columbia Univ. Press, 1999.

Lindsay, Vachel. "Bryan, Bryan, Bryan, Bryan." *Collected Poems.* New York: Macmillan, 1925.

Lyon, Peter. *Success Story: The Life and Times of S. S. McClure.* Deland, Fla.: Everett/ Edwards, 1967.

Madigan, Mark. "Introduction: The Short Stories of Dorothy Canfield Fisher." In Dorothy Canfield Fisher, *The Bedquilt and Other Stories,* 1–11. Columbia: Univ. of Missouri Press, 1996.

———. "Willa Cather and Dorothy Canfield Fisher: Rift, Reconciliation, and *One of Ours.*" In *Cather Studies I,* ed. Susan J. Rosowski, 115–29. Lincoln: Univ. of Nebraska Press, 1990.

March, John. *A Reader's Companion to the Fiction of Willa Cather.* Ed. Marilyn Arnold. Westport, Conn.: Greenwood, 1993.

Mares, E. A. "The Many Faces of Padre Antonio José Martínez: A Historiographic Essay." In *Padre Martinez: New Perspectives from Taos,* ed. E. A. Mares, 18–47. Taos, N.M.: Millicent Rogers Museum, 1988.

Marks, Patricia. *Bicycles, Bangs, and Bloomers: The New Woman in the Popular Press.* Lexington: Univ. Press of Kentucky, 1990.

Maxfield, James F. "Strategies of Self-Deception in Willa Cather's *Professor's House.*" *Studies in the Novel* 16 (1984): 72–86.

McClure, S. S. *Obstacles to Peace.* Boston: Houghton Mifflin, 1917.

———. "The Tammanyizing of a Civilization." *McClure's* 34.1 (Nov. 1909): 117–18.

McComas, Dix. "Willa Cather's *One of Ours:* In Distant Effigy." *Legacy* 14 (1997): 93–109.

McDonald, Joyce. *The Stuff of Our Forebears: Willa Cather's Southern Heritage.* Tuscaloosa: Univ. of Alabama Press, 1998.

McNall, Sally Allen. "The American Woman Writer in Transition: Freeman, Austin, and Cather." In *Seeing Female: Social Roles and Personal Lives,* ed. Sharon S. Brehm, 43–52. New York: Greenwood Press, 1988.

———. "Immigrant Backgrounds to *My Ántonia:* 'A Curious Social Situation in Black Hawk.'" In *Approaches to Teaching Cather's* My Ántonia, ed. Susan J. Rosowski, 22–30. New York: Modern Language Association, 1989.

Medina, Joyce. *Cézanne and Modernism: The Poetics of Painting.* Albany: State Univ. of New York Press, 1995.

Menuhin, Yehudi. *Unfinished Journey.* New York: Knopf, 1977.

Meyering, Sheryl L. *A Reader's Guide to the Short Stories of Willa Cather.* New York: G. K. Hall, 1994.

Michaels, Walter Benn. *Our America: Nativism, Modernism, and Pluralism.* Durham, N.C.: Duke Univ. Press, 1995.

Middleton, Jo Ann. *Willa Cather's Modernism: A Study of Style and Technique.* Cranbury, N.J.: Associated Univ. Presses, 1990.

Miller, Robert K. "Room to Think: Mencken, Cather, and the American Professo-

riate." Paper presented at the annual meeting of the American Literature Association, Baltimore, 1997.

———. "What Margie Knew." In *Willa Cather: Family, Community, and History*, ed.
John J. Murphy, 133–37. Provo, Utah: Brigham Young Univ. Humanities Publications Center, 1990.

Moers, Ellen. *Literary Women*. Garden City, N.Y.: Doubleday, 1976.

Moorhead, Elizabeth. *These Too Were Here: Louise Homer and Willa Cather*. Pittsburgh: Univ. of Pittsburgh Press, 1950.

Morrison, Toni. *Playing in the Dark*. Cambridge: Harvard Univ. Press, 1992.

Mott, Frank Luther. *Golden Multitudes*. New York: Macmillan, 1947.

———. *A History of American Magazines*. Vol. 4: *1885–1905*. Cambridge: Harvard
Univ. Press, 1957.

Murphy, John J. "Biblical and Religious Dimensions of *My Ántonia*." In *Approaches
to Teaching Cather's* My Ántonia, ed. Susan J. Rosowski, 77–82. New York: Modern Language Association, 1989.

———. "Historical Essay." In Willa Cather, *Death Comes for the Archbishop*. Scholarly Edition. Lincoln: Univ. of Nebraska Press, 1999.

———. "*One of Ours* as American Naturalism." *Great Plains Quarterly* 2 (1982):
232–38.

———. ed. *Willa Cather: Family, Community, and History*. Provo, Utah: Brigham
Young Univ. Humanities Publications Center, 1990.

Nelson, Robert J. *Willa Cather and France: In Search of the Lost Language*. Urbana:
Univ. of Illinois Press, 1988.

Nettels, Elsa. *Language and Gender in American Fiction: Howells, James, Wharton and
Cather*. Charlottesville: Univ. Press of Virginia, 1997.

O'Brien, Sharon. Introduction to *Willa Cather: 24 Stories*, ed. Sharon O'Brien. New
York: Penguin, 1987.

———. *Willa Cather: The Emerging Voice*. New York: Oxford Univ. Press, 1987.

Ong, Walter J. *Orality and Literacy: The Technologizing of the Word*. London:
Methuen, 1982.

Orvell, Miles. *After the Machine: Visual Arts and the Erasing of Cultural Boundaries*.
Jackson: Univ. Press of Mississippi, 1995.

Pearce, T. M., ed. *Literary America, 1903–1934: The Mary Austin Letters*. Westport,
Conn.: Greenwood Press, 1979.

Peck, Demaree. *The Imaginative Claims of the Artist in Willa Cather's Fiction: "Possession
Granted by a Different Lease."* Selinsgrove, Pa.: Susquehanna Univ. Press, 1996.

Poirier, Richard. *A World Elsewhere: The Place of Style in American Literature*. New
York: Oxford Univ. Press, 1966.

Pollard, Tomas. "Political Silences and Hist'ry in *Sapphira and the Slave Girl*." In
Willa Cather's Southern Connections: New Essays on Cather and the South, ed. Ann
Romines, 38–53. Charlottesville: Univ. Press of Virginia, 2000.

Porter, Katherine Anne. *Collected Essays and Occasional Writings*. Boston: Houghton
Mifflin/Seymour Lawrence, 1970.

Porter, Nancy. Afterword to Mary Austin, *A Woman of Genius*. Old Westbury, N.Y.:
Feminist Press, 1985.

Pratt, Mary Louise. *Imperial Eyes: Travel Writing and Transculturation.* London: Routledge, 1992.

Preuss, Charles. *Exploring with Frémont: The Private Diaries of Charles Preuss. . . .* Trans. and ed. Erwin G. and Elisabeth K. Gudde. Norman: Univ. of Oklahoma Press, 1958.

Quirk, Tom. *Bergson and American Culture: The Worlds of Willa Cather and Wallace Stevens.* Chapel Hill: Univ. of North Carolina Press, 1990.

Reynolds, Guy. *Willa Cather in Context: Progress, Race, Empire.* New York: St. Martin's, 1996.

Rich, Adrienne. *Of Woman Born: Motherhood as Experience and Institution.* New York: Norton, 1976.

Rienäcker, Gerd. "Discursions into the Dramaturgy of Parsifal." In *Parcifal, by Richard Wagner,* ed. Nicholas John, 59–70. New York: Riverrun Press, 1986.

Rolfe, Lionel Menuhin. *The Menuhins: A Family Odyssey.* San Francisco: Panjandrum/Aris Books, 1978.

Romines, Ann. *Constructing the Little House: Gender, Culture, and Laura Ingalls Wilder.* Amherst: Univ. of Massachusetts Press, 1997.

———. *The Home Plot: Women, Writing, and Domestic Ritual.* Amherst: Univ. of Massachusetts Press, 1992.

———. "Willa Cather and the Coming of Old Age." *Texas Studies in Literature and Language* 37 (1995): 394–413.

Rose, Phyllis. "Modernism: The Case of Willa Cather." In *Modernism Reconsidered,* ed. Robert Kiely, 123–45. Cambridge: Harvard Univ. Press, 1983.

Rosowski, Susan J. "Historical Essay." In Willa Cather, *The Lost Lady.* Scholarly Edition, 177–233. Lincoln: Univ. of Nebraska Press, 1997.

———. *The Voyage Perilous: Willa Cather's Romanticism.* Lincoln: Univ. of Nebraska Press, 1986.

———. "Willa Cather's Ecology of Place." *Western American Literature* 30 (1995): 37–51.

Rubin, Joan Shelley. *The Making of Middle-Brow Culture.* Chapel Hill: Univ. of North Carolina Press, 1992.

Rudnick, Lois. "The New Woman." In *1915, the Cultural Moment: The New Politics, the New Woman, the New Psychology, the New Art and the New Theatre in America,* ed. Adele Heller and Lois Rudnick, 69–81. New Brunswick, N.J.: Rutgers Univ. Press, 1991.

Ryan, Maureen. "No Woman's Land: Gender in Willa Cather's *One of Ours.*" *Studies in American Fiction* 18 (1990–91): 65–75.

Ryder, Mary Ruth. *Willa Cather and Classical Myth.* Lewiston, N.Y.: Edwin Mellen, 1990.

Said, Edward W. *Culture and Imperialism.* New York: Random House, 1993.

Saldívar, José David. *The Dialectics of Our America: Genealogy, Cultural Critique, and Literary History.* Durham, N.C.: Duke Univ. Press, 1991.

Salmon, Eric, ed. *Bernhardt and the Theatre of Her Time.* Westport, Conn.: Greenwood Press, 1984.

Schriber, Mary Suzanne. *Writing Home: American Women Abroad, 1830–1920.* Charlottesville: Univ. Press of Virginia, 1997.

Schroeter, James, ed. *Willa Cather and Her Critics*. Ithaca: Cornell Univ. Press, 1967.

Schwind, Jean. "The Beautiful War in *One of Ours*." *Modern Fiction Studies* 30 (1984): 53–71.

Seibel, George. *The Hyphen in American History: An Address Delivered at Johnstown, Pa., August 21, 1916, on German Day*. Pittsburgh: Neeb-Hirsch, 1916.

———. *Made in America: A Consideration of the Question Whether the United States, as a Neutral Nation, Should Export Armaments and Ammunition to Nations at War*. Pittsburgh: F. C. Herget, 1915.

———. "Miss Willa Cather, from Nebraska." *New Colophon* 2.7 (Sept. 1949): 195–208.

Sergeant, Elizabeth Shepley. *Willa Cather: A Memoir*. Lincoln: Univ. of Nebraska Press, 1963.

Severa, Joan L. *Dressed for the Photographer: Ordinary Americans and Fashion, 1840–1900*. Kent, Ohio: Kent State Univ. Press, 1995.

Shaw, Patrick W. *Willa Cather and the Art of Conflict: Re-Visioning Her Creative Imagination*. Troy, N.Y.: Whitston, 1992.

Sherman, Lucius. *Analytics of Literature*. Boston: Ginn, 1893.

Shi, David E. *Facing Facts: Realism in American Thought and Culture, 1850–1920*. New York: Oxford Univ. Press, 1995.

Showalter, Elaine. *A Literature of Their Own: British Women Novelists from Brontë to Lessing*. Princeton, N.J.: Princeton Univ. Press, 1977.

Sims, Sally. "The Bicycle, the Bloomer and Dress Reform in the 1890s." In *Dress and Popular Culture*, ed. Patricia A. Cunningham and Susan Voso Lals, 125–45. Bowling Green, Ohio: Bowling Green State Univ. Popular Press, 1991.

Skaggs, Merrill. *After the World Broke in Two: The Later Novels of Willa Cather*. Charlottesville: Univ. Press of Virginia, 1990.

———. "A Good Girl in Her Place: Cather's *Shadows on the Rock*," *Religion and Literature* 17 (1985): 27–36.

Slote, Bernice. "First Principles: The Kingdom of Art" and "First Principles: Writer in Nebraska." In *The Kingdom of Art: Willa Cather's First Principles and Critical Statements, 1893–1896*, ed. Bernice Slote. Lincoln: Univ. of Nebraska Press, 1966.

———. Introduction to Willa Cather, *Alexander's Bridge*. Lincoln: Univ. of Nebraska Press, 1977.

———. ed. *The Kingdom of Art: Willa Cather's First Principles and Critical Statements, 1893–1896*. Lincoln: Univ. of Nebraska Press, 1966.

Slotkin, Richard. *Regeneration through Violence: The Mythology of the American Frontier: 1600–1860*. Middletown, Conn.: Wesleyan Univ. Press, 1973.

Smith, Page. *America Enters the World*. New York: McGraw-Hill, 1985.

Smith, Patricia Clark. "Achaeans, Americanos, Prelates and Monsters: Willa Cather's *Death Comes for the Archbishop* as New World Odyssey." In *Padre Martinez: New Perspectives from Taos*, ed. E. A. Mares, 101–24. Taos, N.M.: Millicent Rogers Museum, 1988.

Smith-Rosenberg, Carroll. *Disorderly Conduct: Visions of Gender in Victorian America*. New York: Oxford Univ. Press, 1985.

Sochen, June. *The New Woman: Feminism in Greenwich Village, 1910–1920*. New York: Quadrangle Books, 1972.

Southwick, Helen Cather. "Willa Cather's Early Career: Origins of a Legend." *Western Pennsylvania Historical Magazine* 65.2 (April 1982): 85–98.

Spicer, Edward H. *Cycles of Conquest: The Impact of Spain, Mexico, and the United States on the Indians of the Southwest, 1533–1960.* Tucson: Univ. of Arizona Press, 1962.

Stallworthy, Jon. *Wilfred Owen.* Oxford: Oxford Univ. Press, 1974.

Stanton, Domna C. "Difference on Trial: A Critique of the Maternal Metaphor in Cixous, Irigaray, and Kristeva." In *The Poetics of Gender,* ed. Nancy K. Miller, 157–82. New York: Columbia Univ. Press, 1986.

Sten, Christopher. "City of Pilgrims: Willa Cather's Washington," *Willa Cather Pioneer Memorial Newsletter and Review* 42 (1998): 25–29.

Stewart, Grace. *A New Mythos: The Novel of the Artist as Heroine, 1877–1977.* St. Alban's, Vt.: Eden Press, 1979.

Stokes, John, Michael R. Booth,, and Susan Bassnett. *Bernhardt, Terry, Duse: The Actress in Her Time.* Cambridge: Cambridge Univ. Press, 1988.

Stouck, David. Introduction to Willa Cather, *The Life of Mary Baker G. Eddy and the History of Christian Science.* 1909. Reprint, Lincoln: Univ. of Nebraska Press, 1993.

———. "Historical Essay." Willa Cather, *O Pioneers!* Scholarly Edition. Lincoln: Univ. of Nebraska Press, 1992.

———. "Mary Austin and Willa Cather." *Willa Cather Pioneer Memorial Newsletter* 23.2 (1979): n.p.

———. "Willa Cather and the Indian Heritage." *Twentieth Century Literature* 22 (1976): 433–43.

———. *Willa Cather's Imagination.* Lincoln: Univ. of Nebraska Press, 1975.

Stout, Janis P. "Autobiography as Journey in *The Professor's House,*" *Studies in American Fiction* 19 (1991): 203–15.

———. "The Making of Willa Cather's *One of Ours:* The Role of Dorothy Canfield Fisher." *War Literature and the Arts* 11.2 (fall/winter 1999): 48–59.

———. "Playing in the Mother Country: Cather, Morrison, and the Return to Virginia." In *Willa Cather's Southern Connections: New Essays on Cather and the South,* ed. Ann Romines, 189–195. Charlottesville: Univ. Press of Virginia, 2000.

———. *Strategies of Reticence: Silence and Meaning in the Work of Jane Austin, Willa Cather, Katherine Anne Porter, and Joan Didion.* Charlottesville: Univ. Press of Virginia, 1990.

———. *Through the Window, Out the Door: Women's Narratives of Departure, from Austin and Cather to Tyler, Morrison, and Didion.* Tuscaloosa: Univ. of Alabama Press, 1998.

———. "Willa Cather and Mary Austin: Intersections and Influence." *Southwestern American Literature* 21 (1996): 39–60.

Stuckey, William J. *My Ántonia:* A Rose for Miss Cather. *Studies in the Novel* 4 (1972): 473–83.

Sullivan, Peter. "Willa Cather's German People and their Heritage." *The Mowers' Tree: Newsletter of the Cather Colloquium,* spring 1999, 10–11.

Takaki, Ronald. *A Different Mirror: A History of Multicultural America.* Boston: Little, Brown, 1993.

Tanner, Stephen L. "The Deeper Role of Gender Conflict in *The Professor's House.*"

In *Willa Cather: Family, Community, and History*, ed. John J. Murphy, 109–15. Provo, Utah: Brigham Young Univ. Humanities Publications Center, 1990.

Thomas, Susie. *Willa Cather.* Savage, Md.: Barnes and Noble, 1990.

Thurin, Erik Ingvar. *The Humanization of Willa Cather: Classicism in an American Classic.* Lund, Sweden: Lund Univ. Press, 1990.

Trewin, J. C. "Bernhardt on the London Stage." In *Bernhardt and the Theatre of Her Time,* ed. Eric Salmon, 111–31. Westport, Conn.: Greenwood Press, 1984.

Turner, George Kibbe. "The Daughters of the Poor." *McClure's* 34.1 (Nov. 1909): 45–61.

———. "Tammany's Control of New York by Professional Criminals." *McClure's* 33.2 (June 1909): 117–34.

Urgo, Joseph R. "How Context Determines Fact: Historicism in Willa Cather's *A Lost Lady.*" *Studies in American Fiction* 17 (1989): 183–92.

———. *Willa Cather and the Myth of American Migration.* Urbana: Univ. of Illinois Press, 1995.

Van Hook, Bailey. *Angels of Art: Women and Art in American Society, 1876–1914.* University Park: Pennsylvania State Univ. Press, 1996.

Wasserman, Loretta. "Cather's Semitism." In *Cather Studies II,* ed. Susan J. Rosowski, 1–2. Lincoln: Univ. of Nebraska Press, 1993.

Watson, Steven. *Strange Bedfellows: The First American Avant-Garde.* New York: Abbeville, 1991.

Weidman, Bette S. "Willa Cather's Art in Historical Perspective: Reconsidering *Death Comes for the Archbishop.*" In *Padre Martinez: New Perspectives from Taos,* ed. E. A. Mares, 48–70. Taos, N.M.: Millicent Rogers Museum, 1988.

Weigle, Marta, and Kyle Fiore. *Santa Fe and Taos: The Writer's Era, 1916–1941.* Santa Fe: Ancient City Press, 1994.

Westling, Louise H. *The Green Breast of the New World: Landscape, Gender, and American Fiction.* Athens: Univ. of Georgia Press, 1996.

Williams, Deborah. "Threats of Correspondence: The Letters of Edith Wharton, Zona Gale, and Willa Cather." *Studies in American Fiction* 25 (1997): 211–39.

Wilson, Chris. *The Myth of Santa Fe: Creating a Modern Regional Tradition.* Albuquerque: Univ. of New Mexico Press, 1997.

Winter, William. *Vagrant Memories.* New York: Doran, 1915.

Winterich, John T. "George DuMaurier and *Trilby.*" In *The Romance of Great Books and Their Authors.* New York: Halcyon House, 1929.

Wolff, Cynthia Griffin. "Time and Memory in *Sapphira and the Slave Girl*: Sex, Abuse, and Art." In *Cather Studies III,* ed. Susan J. Rosowski, 212–37. Lincoln: Univ. of Nebraska Press, 1996.

Woodress, James. "A Dutiful Daughter and Her Parents." In *Willa Cather: Family, Community, and History,* ed. John J. Murphy, 19–31. Provo, Utah: Brigham Young Univ. Humanities Publications Center, 1990.

———. "Historical Essay." In Willa Cather, *My Ántonia.* Scholarly Edition. Lincoln: Univ. of Nebraska Press, 1994.

———. Introduction to Willa Cather, *The Troll Garden.* Lincoln: Univ. of Nebraska Press, 1983.

——. *Willa Cather: Her Life and Art.* New York: Pegasus, 1970.

——. *Willa Cather: A Literary Life.* Lincoln: Univ. of Nebraska Press, 1987.

Yongue, Patricia Lee. "For Better and for Worse: At Home and at War in *One of Ours.*" In *Willa Cather: Family, Community, and History,* ed. John A. Murphy, 141–53. Provo, Utah: Brigham Young Univ. Humanities Publications Center, 1990.

——. "Willa Cather's Aristocrats," Parts 1 and 2. *Southern Humanities Review* 14 (1980): 43–56 and 110–25.

Zettsu, Tomoyuki. "Slavery, Song, and the South: Cather's Refiguration of Stowe and Foster in *A Lost Lady.*" *Arizona Quarterly* 52 (1996): 87–104.

Zitter, Emmy Stark. "Making Herself Born: Ghost Writing and Willa Cather's Developing Autobiography." *Biography* 19 (1996): 283–301.

Index

actresses, 104, 140; and gender, 60; social function of, 59, 60, 323 n. 28. *See also* Cather, Willa, actresses of interest to
"Affair at Grover Station, The," 73, 90
Aida (Verdi), 65
Aix-les-Bains, 203, 260–61
Akins, Zoë, 108, 180, 201, 203, 234, 253, 278, 305, 309
Alexander, Bartley (character, *Alexander's Bridge*), 102–4, 113; name of, 113, 327 n. 33
Alexander's Bridge, 89, 97, 101, 102–4, 107, 113, 117, 129, 327 n. 32; autobiographical elements in, 103, 107, 120. *See also* Alexander, Bartley; Burgoyne, Hilda; Wilson, Lucius
"Alexander's Masquerade," 104
Alexandra (character). *See* Bergson, Alexandra
"Alexandra," 107
ambivalence, in modernism, 293
American Indians. *See* Native Americans
Ammons, Elizabeth, xiii, 228, 244, 346 n. 20
Anderson, E. H., 327 n. 29
Anderson, Enoch, 317 n. 9
Anderson, Eric Gary, 340 n. 43
Anderson, Lyra Garber. *See* Garber, Lyra
Anderson, Marjorie, 8, 249, 345 nn. 2, 5
androgyny, 113, 115, 124, 148
anti-Semitism, 73, 152–53, 226, 227; American, 13, 227, 317 n. 16, 332 n. 4, 334 n. 19. *See also* Cather, Willa, and anti-Semitism
Ántonia (character, *My Ántonia*). *See* Shimerda Cuzak, Ántonia
April Twilights, 55, 87, 88
Archer, William, 308
Archie, Doctor (character, *The Song of the Lark*), 132, 133

"Ardessa," 130, 134
Aristotle, 46; *Poetics*, 321 n. 26
Arnold, Matthew, 46
art, 250; as consolation, 351 n. 4; as escape, 165, 219, 302; experimentation in, 308; and morality, 76, 77, 143; vs. reality, 86, 92–94, 219, 251; and reform, 76; and religion, 51, 66, 260, 268, 270, 273; seriousness in, 63, 75; social value of, 258, 269
artist, 91; nature of, 62, 69, 323–24 n. 31; as redeemer figure, 272–74
artistic ego, 61, 62–63, 65, 69–70
artists, as characters, 250
Atherton, Gertrude, 84, 172
Auclair, Cécile (character, *Shadows on the Rock*), 14, 253–54, 257
Auclair, Euclide (character, *Shadows on the Rock*), 14, 254–55, 257
Aunt Georgiana (character, "A Wagner Matinée"), 92, 94
Austen, Jane, 79, 80
Austin, Mary, 27, 46, 114, 127, 129, 201, 233, 244, 246, 249, 279, 307, 330 n. 7, 334 n. 17; *The Land of Little Rain*, 46, 127; *A Woman of Genius*, 120, 126–27, 330 n. 8, 331 nn. 25, 28
Awakening, The (Chopin), 84–85
Axtell, James, 51
Ayre, Jennie Cather (aunt). *See* Cather Ayre, Jennie
Ayrshire, Kitty (character, "A Gold Slipper" and "Scandal"), 130

Bachelard, Gaston, 342 n. 21
Bakst, Leon, 203
Balzac, Honoré de, 79, 338 n. 15
Bancroft, H. H., 221